THE VARIEGATED PLUMAGE
Encounters with Indian Philosophy

THE VARIEGATED PLUMAGE

Encounters with Indian Philosophy

(A Commemoration Volume in Honour of Pandit Jankinath Kaul 'Kamal')

Edited by

N.B. Patil

Mrinal Kaul 'Martand'

SANT SAMAGAM RESEARCH INSTITUTE • J&K

AND

MOTILAL BANARSIDASS PUBLISHERS

PRIVATE LIMITED • DELHI

First Edition: Delhi, 2003

Published by:
SANT SAMAGAM RESEARCH INSTITUTE
37/4, Pandoka Colony, Paloura, Jammu-181121 (Jammu and Kashmir)
In association with
MOTILAL BANARSIDASS PUBLISHERS PVT. LTD.
41 U.A. Bungalow Road, Jawahar Nagar, Delhi 110 007

ISBN: 81-208-1953-5

Distributed by
MOTILAL BANARSIDASS
41 U.A. Bungalow Road, Jawahar Nagar, Delhi 110 007
8 Mahalaxmi Chamber, 22 Bhulabhai Desai Road, Mumbai 400 026
236, 9th Main III Block, Jayanagar, Bangalore 560 011
120 Royapettah High Road, Mylapore, Chennai 600 004
Sanas Plaza, 1302 Baji Rao Road, Pune 411 002
8 Camac Street, Kolkata 700 017
Ashok Rajpath, Patna 800 004
Chowk, Varanasi 221 001

Printed in India at
ARUN & RAJIVE PVT. LTD.
10 DSIDC SCHEME-II, OKHLA INDUSTRIAL AREA PHASE-II,
NEW DELHI-110 020. TELEFAX: 26388005, 26388006, 26388007
AND PUBLISHED BY MRINAL KAUL FOR
SANT SAMAGAM RESERCH INSTITUTE
37/4, PANDOKA COLONY, PALOURA, JAMMU-181 121 (J&K)

Board of Advisors

आराधयामि मणिसन्निभमात्मलिङ्गं
मायापुरीहृदयपङ्कजसन्निविष्टम्।
श्रद्धानदीविमलचित्तजलाभिषेकै -
र्नित्यं समाधिकुसुमैर्नपुनर्भवाय॥

Pandit Jankinath Kaul 'Kamal'
(1914-1997)

Swami Lakshman Joo

Swami Nilkanthananda Saraswati

Pandit Satram Bhat

॥ नमस्कुर्महे ॥

या काचिद्द्वै क्वचिदपि दशा किञ्चिदभ्यासपूराद्
आनन्दाख्या भवभयहरा स्यात् सुभक्तस्य सद्यः।
सिद्धिः सैषा सुरपितृनृणां यस्य भक्त्या भवेन्नु
तं स्वात्मानं विभववपुषं *नीलकण्ठं* प्रपद्ये॥

अद्वैते प्रथितं समीक्ष्य रुचिरे वैज्ञानिकैरर्चितं
शिष्यैः साधुभिराश्रितं नमसितं सुज्ञैर्मुनीन्द्रैरपि॥
केसर-कुंकुमभूषितं गुणनिधिं संख्यावतां सद्गुरुं
तं वन्दे *श्रीलक्ष्मणं* नरहरिं सच्चित्सुखं देशिकम्॥

स्वच्छान्तःकरणं कृपात्तवपुषं विज्ञानमूर्तिं कथं
प्रस्तोतुं प्रभवामि तस्य गुरुता निस्सीमभूता यतः॥
आनन्दादिसुलक्षणं यतिवरञ्चानन्दकल्पद्रुमं
तं वन्दे *सद्रामं* गुरुवरं सर्वार्थसिद्धिप्रदम्॥

PHONES PBX 645-1144/1180
654-9581/9681
654-5391/8494
654-5700/5701
654-5702/5703

FAX : 654-4346

E-Mail: rkmhqbm@cal.vsnl.net.in

RAMAKRISHNA MATH
P.O. BELUR MATH, DIST. HOWRAH
WEST BENGAL : 711 202

21st January 2002

Message

My dear Mrinal Kaul,

I received your letter and am happy to learn that you are bringing out a commemorative volume to honour the memory of Pandit Janakinath Kaul and his diverse literary and cultural contributions.

Although we did not get to interact very frequently I had occasion to meet Pandit Janakinath Kaul and he had also sent me some translation works of his.

I convey to you and your colleagues my love and good wishes for success in your effort to honour Pandit Janakinath's memory.

Affectionately yours,

Ranganathananda

(Swami Ranganathananda)

महाराज कृष्ण काव
Maharaj Krishen Kaw
Tel. : 3386451
Fax : 3385807

सचिव
भारत सरकार
माध्यमिक और उच्चतर शिक्षा विभाग
नई दिल्ली-110001
SECRETARY
Government of India
Ministry of Human Resource Development
Department of Secondary & Higher Education
New Delhi-110 001

July 16, 2001

Message

It gives me great pleasure to hear that the Sant Samagam Research Institute, J&K is bringing out a commemoration volume in honour of Pandit Jankinath Kaul 'Kamal'. I have read some books of Shri Kamal and have heard about his accomplishment as a *yogi* and a *saint*. Shri Kamal was in every sense of the word an ideal man well versed in Sanskrit Grammar, Shaivism and Vedanta. His books are a testimony to the depth of his scholarship.

I wish the organizers of the institute all success in this noble endeavour.

(Maharaj Krishen Kaw)

Dr. Karan Singh
MEMBER OF PARLIAMENT
(RAJYA SABHA)

सत्यमेव जयते

3, NYAYA MARG
CHANAKYAPURI
NEW DELHI - 110 021

12.1.2002

Message

I am glad to know that the Sant Samagam Research Institute is bringing out a commemoration volume in honour of Pandit Jankinath Kaul "Kamal". He was indeed a remarkable individual with many inner and outer achievements to his credit. I send his devotees and well-wishers my warm greetings through the pages of this volume.

Karan Singh

(Karan Singh)

Kapila Vatsyayan
Phone : 6863657
Fax : 6534671
Email : vatsyayan@vsnl.net

85, SFS Flats
Gulmohar Enclave
New Delhi - 110049

October 13, 2002

Message

The illustrious and dedicated grandson of Pt. Jankinath Kaul "Kamal" has been urging me to write a message for this important commemorative volume. I have found it difficult to find adequate words to express my deep sense of awe and admiration for one who treaded the path of searching and researching a very valuable branch of Indian thought and philosophy. His life and work exemplifies the 'fire' which is ignited by sincerity and concentrated single minded dedication.

Kashmir Saivism was his calling. The towering figure of a saint and scholar, Pt. Lakshman Joo accepted Pt. Jankinath Kaul "Kamal" as disciple. The insights and scholarship of Pt. Lakshman Joo are unparallelled. He was an embodiment of experience and reflection, incisive insight and perception. Pt. Jankinath Kaul "Kamal" was a worthy and dedicated disciple. He learnt from the Guru. He went further in disseminating the knowledge through an impressive corpus of writing, translations and of course constant teaching with utmost humility and selflessness. The reminiscences of those who had known him closely make poignant reading. In an age of ego-ridden competitiveness, even in the field of intellectual scholarship, his life and work epitomize 'values' often cherished but seldom practiced.

His grandson has been inspired and infused with his spirit. This is clear from the single-minded concentration and almost single-handed effort he has put into making this volume. The contributors are well-known scholars in their respective fields. Most important is the section on Śaiva studies. This brings together the latest research on this important branch of Indian thought and philosophy.

Through these inadequate words I pay my humble tribute to a man and scholar who was great in his very humility.

Kapila Vatsyayan

JUSTICE RANGANATH MISRA
MEMBER OF PARLIAMENT
(RAJYA SABHA)

AB-89, SHAHJAHAN ROAD
NEW DELHI-110 011
TEL.: 3782204, FAX. : 3383217
Email : rmisra@sansad.nic.in

सत्यमेव जयते

Message

I am happy to gather that a commemorative volume is being brought out in the memory of Pandit Janakinath Kaul "Kamal". Janakinathji was widely known for his brilliance as a teacher, administrator and for his specialization in Yoga and Tantra. He had also specialized in Śānkara Vedānta and Kashmir Śaivism.

He had a personality which attracted people towards him and anyone around was substantially influenced by his way of living, his learning and wisdom. It is rare to find a person of Janakinathji's stature and capability and I am sure that every reader would find the volume fascinating.

I am sure the volume will provide excellent reading material to the readers of all age groups.

(Ranganath Misra)

Contents

Section-B : Cultural and Philosophical Studies

Section-C : Bhakti, Yoga and Poetics

PART-III : SPIRITUALITY AND DIVINE PATH

Preface

The Variegated Plumage: Encounters with Indian Philosophy, a commemorative volume dedicated to the memory of Pandit Jankinath Kaul "Kamal" is a collection of diverse scholarly articles and research papers contributed by the veterans who are specialists in their respective fields. Though the contents of the volume are variegated, yet they convey the same message of man's ultimate emancipation from mundane existence. According to all the schools of Indian Philosophy, attainment of liberation is the ultimate goal of human life, as has been beautifully put forth by Puṣpadanta in his hymn to Śiva;

त्रयी सांख्यं योगः पशुपतिमतं वैष्णवमिति
प्रभिन्ने प्रस्थाने परमिदमदः पथ्यमिति च।
रुचीनां वैचित्र्यादृजुकुटिलनानापथजुषां
नृणामेको गम्यस्त्वमसि पयसामर्णव इव॥

Kashmir Śaivism maintains that the attainment of freedom is possible through *Jñāna* (knowledge) and *Jñāna* consists in knowing one's own nature, which is all being (*sat*), all consciousness (*cit*) and all bliss (*ānanda*). The concept of freedom in conjunction with knowledge is the unique contribution of Kashmir Śaivism. As Abhinavagupta puts it; (*Tantrāloka - 3.1*)

प्रकाशमात्रं यत्प्रोक्तं भैरवीयं परं महः।
तत्र स्वतन्त्रतामात्रमधिकं प्रविविच्यते॥

Creation is an activity of Śiva that spontaneously emanates from His joy. The absolute Śiva in Himself is devoid of variety (all forms, differences or determination), yet all variety emanates from Him. Śiva is compared to the plasma in the egg of a peacock (*mayūrāṇḍarasavat*). Kṣemarāja has superbly put this concept in his *Parāpraveśikā:* मयूराण्डरसे सर्वशिख्यवयवानुप्रविष्टबर्होंप-

बर्हादिपूर्णरेखादिवैचित्र्यशिल्पकल्पनाकौशलवत् अवधानधनैः सूक्ष्मेक्षिकयाव-धार्यम् ॥ In the ultimate reality, the entire manifested variety is in perfect unity; it is an undifferentiated entity as the variegated plumage of the peacock with its beautiful, rich colour lying in a state of undifferentiated mass in the plasma of its egg. This is described as the analogy of the plasma of the peacock's egg in Kashmir Śaivism.

यथा न्यग्रोधबीजस्थः शक्तिरूपो महाद्रुमः ।
तथा हृदयबीजस्थं विश्वमेतच्चराचरम् ॥

The analogy of the seed (*bīja*) or that of the fluid in the egg of a peacock (*mayūrāṇḍarasa*) should not be taken to mean that duality or difference is inherently present in Śiva as potentiality, that is, necessity. What it means is that there is no duality in Śiva at all, and yet all duality comes from Śiva, just as the peacock's feathers arises from the colourless and non-differentiated plasma of the egg. In the case of the seed, manifestation of variety is not the free expression of the seed – the seed is genetically conditioned to manifest variety. But in the case of Śiva, manifestation of variety is the free expression of His pure unity. Whatever Śiva does or in whatever form He appears, it is the expression of His complete freedom. He has the power and freedom to do even the most difficult and unimaginable things and therein lies His glory. He projects the wonderous worlds of appearance, out of His free will (*Svātantrya Śakti*).

The present volume adequately covers different aspects of Indian Philosophy and Culture. The first part "In Memoriam" focuses and throws light on the life and achievements of the celebrated Sanskrit scholar and doyen of Śaiva Philosophy Pandit Jankinath Kaul "Kamal" in whose honour this work has been compiled and is being brought out.

The extensive section on Śaiva Philosophy will provide impetus to further research in the subject. The articles in this section provide a useful and befitting introduction to the fundamentals of Kashmir Śaivism and should impel the reader to delve deeper into the subject.

The second section is a collection of papers dealing with a wide range of issues in Indian Philosophy and Culture. These issues are analysed and discussed by various scholars adequately, enabling the reader to get fairly conversant with the essentials of Hindu Culture and Monistic Vedānta. The papers dealing with *Nyāya-Vaiśeṣika* will help readers to comprehend some vital topics in this logical branch of Indian thought. The paper offering a critique on the concept of mind according to Jainism deals with the topic in detail.

From time immemorial Sanskrit language and literature have fascinated the students of indology. In this volume we have learned articles contributed by reputed Sanskritists on different aspect of Sanskrit Kāvya literature.

The third section deals with a variety of topics on Bhakti, Yoga and Poetics. Faith is a very important factor in our lives. None can live without faith. Bopadeva's contribution to the Bhakti cult and the comprehensive analysis of the concept of Bhakti in the Bhagvad Gītā give a novel direction to this pregnant journey of faith. The articles on Yoga Philosophy dwell on some important aspects of this philosophy bearing, for instance, on environment as a prime factor in Yoga Sādhanā and on Yoga as a ladder to reach a state of Samādhi, which are new verdicts based on the critical analysis of the *Patañjali Yoga Sūtras.* Some papers deal with the practical significance of Yoga as expounded by Patañjali. The article on hermeneutical construction of theories of poetics conveys very pointedly how aesthetic theories took a transitional course to spiritualism and self knowledge.

The five essays in the last part spell out the spiritual culture of India.

For the convenience of readers, an opening introduction has been added to each section with critical remarks. It is hoped that this volume will serve as an encyclopaedic manual of Indian Philosophy and Culture.

St. Stephen's College, Delhi. *Mrinal Kaul*
17 October 2002

Foreword

We, the editors and the members of the Advisory Board are happy to offer this comprehensive Commemorative Volume to the academia of the East and the west. The volume is a tribute to Pandit Janakinath Kaul, who is no more with us. He had adopted a pen-name – KAMAL along with all the sublime qualities of the latter. He was indeed a full blown red lotus in the limpid waters of the Dal-Lake of the Kashmir valley. For centuries the valley is known for academic scholarship and a number of Sanskrit poeticians, rhetoricians and philosophers have contributed to the enrichment of philosophy and culture.

It was a life time commitment of Prof. Kaul to absorb the philosophical literature of this land, and he continued to do so till the last breath of his life. He lavishly gave, with great compassion, to all those who approached him, whatever he had acquired during his life time. His students and admirers are widely spread in India and abroad and a few of them have contributed to this volume. We, as editors, are extremely grateful to all of them.

With the onset of the third millennium, the world scenario is changing fast. Science and technology are taking long strides and within a few years new inventions and discoveries become obsolete and lose their significance. The frontiers of the earth, our Vasundhara, are fast expanding and the days of inter planetary traffic are not far off. Even so, we have to stand firmly on our feet and we need *terra firma* as a launching pad for our flights to infinity. We cannot afford to lose the ground on which our ancestors have built up a sound thought structure and produced philosophies of eternal values.

When we look around, we are saddened to see the state of affairs even after fifty years of Independence. Long before we gained our Independence, Swami Vivekananda had laid down a plan of action for the youth of this country. He verily wanted the youths to go to the masses and care for them in a spirit of worship. Gandhiji wanted the last man to be on his own and lead a life of contentment. All this did not happen and we are in the midst of a society where moral and spiritual values are dwindling. Consumerism is rampant and a rat-race is on to gain trivialities.

Prof. Kaul spent his life in imbuing the youth with a spirit of worshipping Śakti. He invoked Sarasvati to bless his students with supreme knowledge. His long association with Sri Ramakrishna Ashram, Srinagar, Kashmir made him a source of inspiration for the intelligent youths around him and he loved them till last.

We have therefore, arranged the responses, we have received from far and near, in the form of research papers and articles as a tribute to Pandit Janakinath Kaul. The areas covered are vital to philosophy and culture of this land. These papers will stimulate scholars for further research. All the papers are so arranged that they produce a pattern of variegated plumage of a peacock. The volume ends with essays on Spiritual and Divine Path.

We hope the reading of this volume will set the reader on the way of realising his ideal.

Mumbai *N.B. Patil*
Dipawali - 2002.

Acknowledgements

First and foremost, I would like to express my gratitude towards all the contributors for their valuable contributions. My thanks are due to all the members of the advisory board for their kind and noble suggestions to make some improvements in the volume.

The successful completion of this volume would not have been possible without the prodigious help of Prof. N.B. Patil who not only went through the whole manuscript but also revised it and added critical remarks.

Deep gratitude is expressed to Dr. Kapila Vatsyayan who received me with an open and loving heart for consultations and guidance. I thank her for her generous help in bringing out the present volume.

Special thanks are due to Mr. Arun Berry, an old stephanian and Ms. Sushma Aggarwal for taking pains in helping me to arrange finances for the publication of this Volume. Friends, devotees and students of Panditji need special mention including Sri Upinder Bhatt and Sri Vijay Dhar.

I heartily thank the St. Stephen's College Alumni for their constant support and encouragement. Mr. Arun Raj Malhotra needs special mention. Printing and publishing of the volume was impossible without his generous help. His team was helpful enough to co-operate with me at every step.

I am also thankful to Mr. N.P. Jain, Managing Director, M/s Motilal Banarsidass Pub. Pvt. Ltd. for collaborating with Sant Samagam Research Institute in publishing the Volume.

To Pratibha Kaul for designing the attractive cover page of the Volume.

I express my deep sense of gratitude to my teachers including Prof. Dinanath Yaksa, Dr. Harsh Kumar, Dr. A.D. Mathur and

Prof. A.N. Dhar.

My thanks are due to all my friends who helped me in one way or the other and made valuable suggestions. To express my gratefulness in words is inexplicable for my friend Anurag Sinha who was always there to support me morally as well as spiritually. In this regard I would also like to thank Atul Krishna, Md. Amir Sarosh, Kunal, Jogendro and Sumeer Razdan.

Finally, I express my heartfelt gratitude towards my parents Sh. Anupam Kaul and Smt. Girja Kaul for their help and encouragement.

Mrinal Kaul
Project Co-ordinator
Sant Samagam Research Institute,
J & K.

PART-I

IN MEMORIAM

शब्दाञ्जलिः

आचार्य दीनानाथ यक्ष

श्रियं दिशतु सर्वस्मै श्रीदः हि श्रीपतिस्सदा।
यत्प्रसादादमोघात्तु दीनोप्याढ्यायते यया॥

जातुचिदपि यो देवः धर्मं विपदि नाजहात्।
नमोऽस्तु गुरवे तस्मै धीराय ज्ञानमूर्तये॥

कीनाशपाशभीत्यापि न बिभेति कदापि यः।
नाशयति विमूढानां यो मोहतिमिरं सदा॥

थरत्प्रसरविक्षेपः बाधते न कदाप्ययम्।
कौतुकाल्लपितं ह्येतद् दीनानाथेन तन्मया॥

ललामभूतमुर्व्यां यं विषयीकृत्य भासुरं।
सोऽयं **श्रीजानकीनाथो** जयताज्जयताच्चिरम्॥

* * * *

भावाञ्जलिः

महामहोपाध्याय डॉ. शशिधर शर्मा

सौजन्याधारभूमिः प्रणयविनययोरास्पदं दुष्कलाव-
प्येकान्ताऽव्याजशान्तेः प्रणिहततपनं रम्यमारामधाम।
शैवानामागमानां शरणमनुरणन् मञ्जुलोदेववाण्या-
वीणाक्काणो विरेजे सुहृदनघधियां जानकीनाथकौलः॥

हिन्द्यामाङ्ग्ल्यां सुराणां गिरि च विशदयन् मर्म तन्त्राऽऽगमानाम्
श्लाघ्यस्तवं तत्र कीदृक्प्रभवतु विशयः किन्तु विद्वद्वरेण्य!
या ते सौहार्दधाराऽनुपधिरनवधिर्जीवने दृष्टसारा-
साऽद्योद्यन्ती स्मृतौ नो नयतिप्रणितरां कश्मलं किं वदामः!!

निर्मोहं लीनलोभं निभृतमविरतं विस्मृताऽऽयुः प्रबाधं
तां देवीं देवतानां गिरममृतमयीं सेवयामासिथ त्वम्।
तन्नूनं वीतबन्ध प्रमदमधुझरी-तत्पदाऽम्भोजसेवा-
हेवाकानां भवितृ त्रिभुवनविसरे निर्मलादर्शरूपम्॥

* * * *

कमलाष्टकम्

मार्तण्डेति कौलो मृणालः

नो येन नीलकण्ठेन गृहस्थेनापि योगिना।
बुद्धेरुन्मीलितं चक्षुः कमलाय तस्मै नमः॥ १॥

बिभर्ति ज्ञानराशिं यो ह्यम्बुराशिमिवाम्बुदः।
नित्यं वर्षति सर्वत्र पिपासुतर्पणाय यः॥ २॥

भूमौ लक्ष्मणरूपेण योऽवतीर्णः सदाशिवः।
जानकीनाथ! ते नमः शैवविद्याविदां वरः॥ ३॥

भ्रमरवन्निलीनोऽहं सूर्यास्ते कमलेऽमले।
प्रफुल्लकमलात् तस्मात् निर्गतो रसनिर्भरः॥ ४॥

तद्रसं रसयन्नित्यं मोदते मे सदा मनः।
अतस्तस्मै रसेशाय कमलाय नमो नमः॥ ५॥

अनाथनाथ! वन्दे त्वां शान्तिमूल! महामुने।
ज्ञानरूपस्य ते नित्यं नमामि पादपङ्कजे॥ ६॥

त्वमेव मे परिष्कर्ता त्वमेव प्रेरणास्पदम्।
त्वया विना न कोऽप्यत्र त्वमेव मेऽवलम्बनम्॥ ७॥

यस्मिन्नुदित उत्फुल्लीभवतिज्ञानपङ्कजम्।
भवेत् प्रभो! स चित्सूर्यः प्रकाशितो निरन्तरम्॥ ८॥

* * * *

A Synopsis of the Works of Pandit Jankinath Kaul 'Kamal'

Sri D.M. Sapatnekar

Published Works

1. **Ṣraddhā Pośh** (Flower of Faith) : Original poems in Kashmiri language of esoteric and spiritual nature. Pub. Trust Publishing House, Srinagar 1942.
   Revised enlarged edition. Pub. Sant Samagam Research Institute (J&K) 1998.
2. **Mukundamālā :** Hindi translation of the Sanskrit text edited with a detailed introduction. Pub. 1963.
   Second and third editions of *Mukundamālā* with selected Sanskrit hymns published respectively in 1977 and 1994. Pub. Sri Ramakrishna Ashrama, Srinagar.
3. **Gāyatrī mantra Bhāṣya :** Ādi Śankāra's sanskrit commentary translated into Hindi. Pub. 1975.
4. **Vikshipta Veena :** Original poems in Hindi of literary interest. Pub. Seemant Prakashan, New Delhi 1980.
5. **Brāhmī Vidyā :** Sanskrit text with Hindi and English translations along with introduction. Pub. Sri Ramakrishna Ashrama, Srinagar. 1981.
6. **Ādi Śankara aur unkā Advait :** A brief introduction of Ādi Śankara's philosophy in Hindi. Pub. Shiva Seva Samiti, Srinagar 1981.
7. **Śiva-Sūtra-Vimarśa :** Śiva-sūtras translated into Hindi with comprehensive commentary. Pub. Motilal Banarsidas, Delhi 1984.
8. **Pilgrimage to Amarnāth :** A brief introduction of the pilgrimage based on Bhṛiṅgīśa Saṁhitā. Pub. Sri Parmanand Research Institute, Srinagar 1985.

9. **Nāgārjuna's Two Trimśikās & Kashmir Śaivism :** Edited with English translation and an elaborate introduction. Pub. Vishveshvaranand Indological Research Institute, Hoshiarpur 1985.
10. **Amareśvara Māhātmyaṁ :** A leaf from the Bhṛiṅgīsha Saṁhitā. Sanskrit text translated with exhaustive notes in English. Pub. Sri Paramanand Research Institute, Srinagar 1986.
11. **Kṣīrbhavānī :** By Sri Samsar Chand Kaul; translated into Hindi with additions. Pub. Utpal Publications, Srinagar 1988.
12. **Vedānta Dindimaḥ :** Sanskrit text with English translation and notes. Foreword by T.M.P. Mahadevan. Pub. Utpal Publications, Srinagar 1990.
13. **Bhavānī-Nāma-Saharsa-Stutiḥ :** A Page from the Rudrayāmala Tantra; Sanskrit text with English translation & commentrary. Pub. Sri Ramakrishna Ashrama, Srinagar 1991.
14. **Bhavānī-nāma-sahasra-stutiḥ :** Sanskrit text revised and edited with *Nāmāvalī.* Pub. Sri Ramakrishna Ashrama, Srinagar 1994.
15. **Pazar Pazaravun :** Lectures of Swami Lakshman Joo in original Kashmiri. Pub. Ishvar Ashram Trust, Srinagar. 1995.
16. **Indrākṣī Stotram :** Sanskrit text with English translation and commentary. Pub. Sri Ramakrishna Asrama, Srinagar 1995.
17. **Pañcastavī** (A Pentad of Hymns to Kundalinī Śakti); Sanskrit text translated into English with explanatory notes. Pub. Sri Ramakrishna Ashrama, Srinagar 1996.
18. **Pañcastavī :** Sanskrit text revised and edited along with Roman transliteration. Pub. Sri Ramakrishna Ashrama, Srinagar 1997.
19. **The Awakening of Supreme Consciousness :** Lectures of Swami Lakshman Joo recorded, edited and translated into English. Pub. Utpal Publications, Delhi and Ishvar Ashram Trust, Srinagar 1998.

Unpublished Works

1. **Gāyarī Mantra bhāṣya of Ādi Śankarācarya :** An English translation.
2. **Vijñāna Bhairava :** Exposition in English with an introduction.
3. **Dvādaśa Mahākalī :** Exposition in Hindi with an introduction.
4. **Rūpa Bhavānī Vākya Manjarī :** Hindi translation of the Kashmiri Vaks with an introduction.
5. **Bodhapañcadaśika** of Abhinavagupta : English translation of the Sanskrit text.
6. **Śivastotravalī** of Utpaladeva : Hindi translation, commentary with copious notes.
7. **Kaivalyopaṇiṣat :** Hindi translation of the Sanskrit text.
8. **Lalleshvari Vākya Manjarī :** Hindi translation with exhaustive notes of about 175 Vaks.
9. **Prajñā Prasāda :** Original Sanskrit poems and essays.
10. **Pratibhā :** Original essays in Hindi of literary and philosophical interest.
11. **Outpourings :** Original English poems.

Published Important Research Papers and Articles

1. *Pūrṇahantā Vimarśa* : A Sanskrit paper presented at the All India Tantra Sammelanam, Varanasi. Pub. in Sarasvati Sushma, – A Research Journal of Sampurnananda Sanskrit University, Varanasi 1965.
2. *Pūrṇahantā Vimarśa :* A paper in Hindi published in Kalyana (Upasana Ank) 1968.
3. *Kashmir main Śaiva Darśana Kā Āvirbhāva :* Pub. in Malini, a research journal of Isvar Ashram Trust 1970.
4. *Utpala – A Kashmiri Mystic :* Pub. Bhavan's Journal, Bombay 1979.
5. *Utpala's Pratyabhijñā Philosophy & Saṅgrahastotra :* Pub. Vedanta Kesari, Madras 1980.
6. *Fundamental Aspects of Vedānta & Kashmir Śaivism :* Pub. Glimpses of Kashmiri Culture (V), A Research Journal of

Sri Parmanand Research Institute, Srinagar 1982.

7. *Śankara's Hymn to Gaurī :* Published in Sarada – Souvenir of Sri Ramakrishna Ashram, Srinagar 1982.
8. *Utpala :* Pub. in Samvit, New Delhi 1984.
9. *On the Parallel Development of Vedānta & Śaiva Philosophy in Kashmir :* Pub. in Indologica Taurinensia, a research journal of the IASS, Torino (Italy) 1984.
10. *Kuṇḍalinī Śakti Tadviṣayako Yogaśca :* A Research paper in Sanskrit. Published in Vishwa Sanskritam, a research journal of VVRI, Panjab University, Hoshiarpur 1987.
11. *Tripurasundarī :* Published in Sarada, Srinagar 1987.
12. *A Comparative View of Two Schools of Indian Thought with special reference to Kashmir Śaivism :* Navonmesa – a commemorative volume of MM Gopinath Kaviraj 1988.
13. *Rāmāyaṇa In Kashmiri :* Pub. in Ramayana In Indian Languages, Patna 1989. Also Kalyāna Kalpataru, 1996.
14. *Śaivism In Kashmir :* Pub. in Religions of the World, Vol I, Patna 1990.
15. *Śodaśakalāyai Śri Śārikādevyai Namaḥ :* Sanskrit Hymn in praise of Śārikā; Pub. in Vishva Sanskritam, Hoshiarpur 1991.
16. *Jñanī Bhakta Hanumāna :* Kalyana Kalpataru 1992.
17. *Tantra Śāstra Mein Amṛiteśhwar Bhairav Aur Uskā Svarūp :* Śaśigaurvāmṛitaṁ (Vol. VIII) Felicitation Volume of Shri Shashidhar Sharma 1992.
18. *Supreme Puruṣa in Stotra Literature :* Prabuddha Bharata 1992.
19. *Tripurā in Tantric Lore :* Śaśigaurvāṁṛtaṁ 1992.
20. *Śaktipāta :* A research paper in English; Prabuddha Bharata 1992.
21. *Sanātana Dharma – Two Aspects :* Kalyana Kalpataru 1993.
22. *Lalla Yogeshwarī :* Kalyan (Shiva Ank) 1993.
23. *Invocation in Lament, a pithy Sanskrit Hymn* : Prabuddha Bharat 1993.
24. *Living Free :* Prabuddha Bharata 1993.
25. *Śaktī In Kashmir Śaiva Tradition :* A Research paper presented at the seminar on Śakti and Pneuma held at

Bangalore 1993.

26. *Esoteric Appellations of Gaṇapati :* Kalyana Kalpataru 1994.
27. *Yogavāsiṣtha Aur Bhagwān Sri Rāma :* Kalyan (Ram Ank) 1994.
28. *Cultural And Spiritual Aspects of The Eighteen Armed Goddess Śārikā :* A Research paper presented at JNU, New Delhi 1994.
29. *Bhagvatkripā – Ek Vicitra Rahasya :* Vishva Jyoti, Hoshiarpur 1995.
30. *Naitiktā Aur Ātma Vikās :* Vishva Jyoti, Hoshiarpur 1995.
31. *Kuṇḍalinī Śaktyai Svarūpaṁ :* Vishva Sanskritam, Hoshiarpur 1996.
32. *Mathrā Devī – A Profile :* Malini 1996.
33. *Brahmakeli* : Vishva Sanskritam, Hoshiarpur 1997.
34. *Pratyabhijñā Expounded by Utpaladeva :* Kalyana Kalpataru 1997.
35. *Vedānta Philosophy As Expounded in Pañcadaśī :* A Research paper presented at the Bhagvan Gopinath Centenary Celebrations – 1997.
36. *Vedārtha Kā Upabṛmhan :* Kalyan (Veda Katha Ank) – 1999.
37. *Sarvaṁ Brahmamayam :* A Sanskrit Poem; Vishva Sanskritam 2000.

* * * *

Pandit Jankinath Kaul 'Kamal' being felicitated with the Certificate of Honour as a Sanskrit Scholar by the then President of India Dr. Shankar Dayal Sharma. (June-1997).

Pt. Jankinath Kaul 'Kamal' at the feet of his Śaiva Preceptor Swami Lakṣman Joo

Pt. Jankinath Kaul 'Kamal' with his wife Smt. Gunwati Kaul

Pandit Jankinath Kaul 'Kamal' – The Man and His Achievements

Professor A.N. Dhar

Born at Drabiyar, Srinagar, in 1914, Shri Jankinath Kaul 'Kamal' was well known as an accomplished scholar through his writings in the fields of Kashmir Śaivism and Vedānta, which have received countrywide recognition. He attained fame and popularity as a versatile and talented writer and earned for himself a position of special esteem because of his qualities of dedication and selfless service.

All his life, he had been a devoted teacher and scholar, content with his modest earnings, and very proficient in his work. An octagenarian who our community has reason to be proud of, he remained mostly busy in reading and writing, when he was free from domestic and social preoccupations (excluding the hours he devoted to his daily meditation). Of course, he took special delight in delivering discourses on religious and literary topics at his residence or at select places – for which he spared several hours a week in spite of his busy schedule.

His scholarly writings in English, Hindi, Sanskrit and Kashmiri, published in the form of books and articles (that have appeared in standard journals, including the *Prabuddha Bharata, Kalyan, Malini* and *Koshur Samachar*), have been favourably reviewed and commented upon by critics and scholars of note. In recognition of his valuable contribution to Hindi language and literature, he received a prestigious award from the Hindi Sansthan, U.P. Government, on Hindi Divas, on September 14, 1992, in Lucknow. On August 15, 1996, on independence day, a still more prestigious award – Certificate of Honour – was conferred on him which was presented to him by the President at Rastrapati Bhavan on June 9, 1997, in recognition of his significant contribution to Sanskrit studies.

Early Life

Jankinath ji had come up the hard way to make his mark as a man of achievements. His mother passed away when he was just 7-8 years old; his father remarried but died when his son had barely attained the age of 13. Facing hardships as an orphan, Shri Kaul lacked the means that would have facilitated his education at school. Thus he could not continue his studies beyond matriculation. After a few years of service in Women's Welfare Trust, Srinagar, he joined the teaching profession at the age of 30 and taught at the D.A.V. Institute, Srinagar, for 30 years until he retired as a senior lecturer in 1974. In view of his competence and meritorious services, the Institute re-employed him for another five years until 1979. It was during his teaching career itself that he improved his educational qualification – passed Prabhakar and got his B.A. and B.T. degrees, followed by an M.A. in Sanskrit from the University of Jammu and Kashmir. He worked as Research Officer at Sri Parmanand Research Institute, Srinagar, for 4 years (from 1981-1985). Since 1986, he held the post of Editor, Cultural Desk/Research Officer, Sri Ramakrishna Ashram, Shivalaya, Karan Nagar, Srinagar, and after his displacement from the Valley in 1989, he had been discharging these functions at Jammu.

A deep interest in spirituality, rooted in his constant quest for truth, had been the main motivation behind Shri Kaul's life-long study of Holy Scriptures. His proficiency in Sanskrit provided further impetus to his sustained study of Śaiva, Śākta and Vedāntic texts in original. Right from his boyhood days, he had the marks of a true *Jigyāsu* and *Bhakta* in one. No wonder, therefore, that he had read the works of Swami Ram Tirth in English and Urdu and also those of Swami Vivekanand with passionate zeal when he was a young man in his twenties. He had in him the makings of a poet; it was in his early youth that he started composing lyrics in Kashmiri and Hindi.

Divine Love

His intense love for the Divine brought him into contact, with a well-known scholar and saint, Shri Nilakanth. It was under his guidance that he first studied *Bhagwad Gītā* in depth along with the commentaries of Śankarācārya and Śankarānand. Shri Nilakanth, on his retirement from government service, lived in Shivanand Ashram, Rishikesh, from 1957 onwards. In 1963, he took *sanyāsa* and came to be called Swami Nilakanthanand Saraswati. He left his mortal coil in 1988. Before shifting to Rishikesh, he recommended Kamal ji to the illustrious saint-scholar, Swami Laxman joo, known in the country and abroad for his mastery of the Śaiva texts and his attainments in spirituality.

During his long association with Swami Laxman Joo, he wrote several eulogistic and devotional lyrics on him in Sanskrit, English and Kashmiri. After the Swamiji attained *mahāsamādhi*, he wrote several biographical articles on him, which appeared in various journals. In all humility, Kamal ji has acknowledged his debt to the great saint of Ishaber as to how he profited academically and spiritually from his discourses on Kashmir Śaivism and his explication of the Śaiva texts. Some of the valuable lectures of Swamiji have been recorded and rendered into English by him with great care and editorial skill. Likewise, some discourses given in Kashmiri by Swami Laxman joo on the practice of meditation and *prānāyāma* have been reproduced by him in the Nāgari script in a presentable form. During his association with the Swamiji, he also came into contact with a householder saint, Pandit Satram, who lived at Ishaber close to Swamiji's Ashram. From this saint, he learned Vidyāraṇya's *Pañcadaśī*, which he found very useful.

A study of the corpus of Shri Kamal's works reveals three things about him – his capacity for rigorous research, his wide-ranging scholarship and his writing skill as a translator, commentator and creative artist. His achievement as a writer is stupendous, considering the hardships he had to face as a man of modest means.

Poetic Sensibility

I would first like to refer to his poetic sensibility that flowered early in his life. A quick look at his book of Kashmiri lyrics *Shradha Posh*, brought out in 1998, reveals at once his devotional intensity, his deep mental involvement with the Transcendent, his spiritual aspiration as also his dispassion and his practical grasp of the technique of meditation as recommended in our *śāstras*. The very titles of some of the poems are striking and significant – *Murli nad, Sahana Panai, Viji Vav, Berang Nundabon, Samvit Pancadasi, Turya Tirth, etc.* The preacher's tone is marked in the poem *Grahasthiyas Updesh* that exhorts one to combine purity with a satisfactory performance of worldly obligations to maintain the delicate balance between *Paramārth* and our social conduct. His diction is simple and lucid and his manner straightforward. The diction is usually a mix of Kashmiri words in common use and the appropriate terms derived from the sacred texts. As an illustration, I give below my translation of the first 10 lines of the poem *Śiva Śankar Śambu*:

Settle your mind
Chanting this mantra
Śiva Śankar Śambu.
The mind cleansed,
Light will shine forth
Dispelling all darkness;
With true faith
Aided by self-introspection,
Utter the mantra
Śiva Śankar Śambu.
Get into temple
At early dawn
After a sacred bath;
Then meditate,
And ponder the mantra
Śiva Śankar Śambu.

Shri Kamal's lyrical genius as a Hindi poet blossomed forth in the volume titled, *Viksipt Vina*. This work has been specially mentioned as the author's valuable contribution to Hindi poetry in the citation that accompained the award conferred on him in 1992. The poem *Main* strikes the keynote; here is my translation of the first stanza:

> I'm the melancholy note
> From a *Vina* with broken strings;
> I am the wailing song
> That has burst forth
> From the anguished heart
> Of a helpless woman!

The various lyrics strung together in the volume reveal the depth and intensity of the author's feelings and the loftiness of his aspirations. The reader at once feels that a 'lark is singing' in the poet's breast. At the same time, the poems show how sensitive he is to pain and suffering that life brings in its train.

In sum, Shri Jankinath Kaul 'Kamal' was remarkable as a scholar and writer. Tall, slim and pleasant-looking, saintly and erudite, always neatly dressed, he exuded the culture and warmth that evoked admiration from one and all. Those who were close to him and listened to his illuminating discourses found his company invaluable. As a scholar, he was every inch professorial!

* * * *

Professor Jankinath Kaul 'Kamal''s Contribution to Kashmiri Thought and Culture

Professor S. Bhatt

Professor Jankinath Kaul 'Kamal' ranks among the leading scholars of Kashmir who made their mark as writers during the past century. Among Kashmiri Pandits, Kamal Sahib is an all time great literary and spiritual authority. He had touch of a genius as an intellectual who projected his illuminating knowledge with its broad thrust towards religious mysticism including Śaivism, Vedānta philosophy et al. During last one decade of his life, he lived in troubled times when Kashmir was overtaken by evil forces of fundamentalism. His scholarly base in Kashmir was disintegrated and Kamal Sahib became a nomad passing his time in Jammu in exile. He was basically inspired by Kashmir, its history and philosophy, its people and literature. All that was gone when he was forced to migrate in distress out of Kashmir.

Kamal Sahib in his mature old age was a wandering scholar who had to complete his mission in life – to reflect upon and write on the life and times of Kashmir.

I was in contact with Kamal Sahib during nineties when Kamal Sahib had moved to Jammu. The occasion was the book "Kashmiri Pandits : A Cultural Heritage"[1] which I was to edit and got published in 1995. I requested Kamal Sahib to include some of his writings in this consolidated volume, which has one hundred and eleven chapters from worthy and eminent scholars of our times. Kamal Sahib has eleven chapters in this book which has been circulated world-wide and looks a reference

1. See S. Bhatt Ed. *Kashmir Pandits : A Cultural Heritage,* Lancers Boo[ks] New Delhi, 1995, pages, 631.

book in Kashmiri Pandit scholarship and spiritual philosophy. In the appendices to this book I was able to add appendix two which contains published works of Kamal Sahib which he had very kindly sent to me. The book, is therefore, a tribute to Kamal Sahib's scholarship and learning. He was keen to leave his learning to posterity amidst troubled times in Kashmir. He knew Kashmiri Pandits will regroup and reorganise themselves again in future and overcome the disastrous period that they have undergone when their cultural and spiritual heritage in Kashmir has been partly obliterated by fundamental forces, when the spirit of harmony among various communities in Kashmir was being replaced by hatred and gun culture.

In this brief article I shall attempt to bring out my comments on Kamal Sahib's contribution to Kashmiri thought and culture. Let me say at the outset that Kashmiri Pandit cultural heritage of several centuries is fast travelling to various corners of the world, including the West and particularly to USA where great intellectual minds are studying Kashmiri Culture and Spiritualism, especially Śaivism, science and spiritualism. I am sure many scholars in India and the West will see fresh enlightenment from Kamal Sahib's insight into the spirit of man and the cosmic frontier.

It is often true that a man is known more after his death. This is the irony of the history of mankind. Perhaps men are busy with the present and have no time to examine the contributions to scholarship by other great minds. So, now that Kamal Sahib is no more we have time to ponder over in-depth his writings and the linkage with the progress of ideas that his writing cumulatively provide. Progress, it is said, deals with addition to knowledge about this Universe. Kamal Sahib has made everlasting impression on the history of Kashmir and of global civilization. Let us see some aspects of his insight into our life and culture.

Major Writings

Professor Kaul was essentially a spiritual philosopher. He specialized in the Hindu Scriptures. He wrote a perceptive commentary on Śaivism as practised and elaborated by revered Swami Lakhmanjoo who stayed at Ishbar in Nishat, Srinagar, Kashmir. Professor Kaul wrote for Parmanand Research Institute, Srinagar on Amarnath Yatra. He also brought into light his works on *Tantric Vidyā* in Ramakrishna Ashram, Srinagar. Besides, Professor Kamal presented papers on Hindu epics and literature at some leading academic centers in India like Banaras Hindu University, IGNCA, Jawaharlal Nehru University and Ramakrishna Mission Centers.

Prof. 'Kamal' wrote in English, Hindi and Kashmiri a number of wide-ranging books. Prof. 'Kamal' who was a senior teacher and scholar of Sanskrit prepared a critical edition of the *'Bhavānī-Nāma-Sahasra-Stutiḥ'* based on the text obtaining in the commentary titled *Devīnāmavilāsa* by the seventeenth century Kashmiri savant Sahib Kaul. He has further drawn from that treatise for his explanation of each name, as also from various scriptural works and from other qualified sources. This lends more authority to his work, even as its language ensures it a wider currency. The purpose of this book is to intelligently and gracefully reveal to aspirants of intense dovotion and love, the esoteric formulae through which the Divine qualities of Mother Goddess may be known. Prof. 'Kamal' has prepared an accurate edition of the scripture with relevant interpretations and elaborate commentary of Bhavāni's sacred names.

'*Pañcastavī*' is an ancient work of more than a thousand years of vintage, addressed to the Supreme mother of the Universe, *Mahātripurasundarī*. The hymn consist of five laudations, each with its distinct theme: *Laghustava* highlighting the dynamic power of the goddess; *Carcastava* reflective of substance; *Ghatastava* speaking of the creative *Śakti* on the threshold of manifestation; *Ambastava* invoking the goddess as the benign Mother; *Sakalajananīstava* celebrating the glory of the source of all. Prof. Kaul has collected twelve different MSS to arrive at this critical edition of Pañcastavī. Variant readings given in foot notes and explanatory notes are quite elaborate. He has recorded his original sources and has cited extracts wherever necessary. He has taken care that translation of the stanzas is lucid and enough care to record double meanings in the translation. Prof. Kaul was better placed to undertake this work. He was a blessed soul to receive the grace of his Śaiva guru Swami Lakshman Joo. His deep study of Indology and Vedānta philosophy along with that of Śākta mysticism and Kashmir Śaivism stood him in good stead in elaborating the subtle meanings of most of the mystic stanzas in these hymns. At places, he has used charts and some esoteric figures to make certain ideas clear. In sum, I can say that he displays a rare insight into the nuances of Vedānta and Śākta Tantra and expressess himself in chaste English.

'The awakening of Supreme Concionsness' is a series of seven lectures delivered by Swami Lakshman Joo to acquaint the devotees with preliminary disciplines and esoteric expressions concerning the Kashmir Śaiva mystic philosophy. Prof. Kaul recorded these lectures which were originally delivered in Kashmiri, with great faith, sincerity and love for learning. "Nothing has been left out" – had expressed Swamiji himself on seeing the MS of originally recorded material along with its English translation by Prof. Kaul himself. The book is a compedium of practical knowledge about the rise of *Kundalinī* power in man and the related discipline required for the purpose. Such hints crucial to realization of self are hardly recorded. However, when the Master like Swami Lakshman Joo and the seeker like Prof. Kaul happen to come together, these hints acquire articulation. Actually it is heart-to-heart talk. When the cup is filled outpouring falls to the lot of the souls who simply wait and watch. In this book the collections are full of sweetness and charm as these are from the mouth of a great soul of supreme devotion and high erudition.

Mother Goddess Durga is said to have emanated in sixty-four forms in the process of maintaining harmony in the universe. These forms may probably be represented by the sixty-four names sung in the stotra called *'Indrākṣī Stotram'*. Prof.Kaul has translated and ably annotated this *stotra*. This shows his accredibility as a typical exponent of the Tantric lore. He has brought his intuitive perception to bear on the whole work. His explanation of the Ahalya episode is revealing. His exposition of the number sixty-four in the enumeration of the names of the deity is brilliantly explained with rare insight. The whole translation is elevating and brings us into the vast sweep of the vision of Indra, *Indrākṣī*.

Now I throw some light on his academic and spiritual discourses that were published in the book "Kashmiri Pandits: A Cultural Heritage" : *An estimate of Śaivism in Kashmir, Śaivism and Vedānta, Utpaladeva and his Pratyabhijñā, Swami Ramji, Rupa Bhawani, Some eminent Kashmiri Pandits, Pandit Anand Kaul Bamzai, Ramayana in Kashmir, Who am I, Jivanamukhti within easy Reach, Pray Tell Me Swami Lakhmanjoo.* In chapter 30 he has written about Rupā Bhawani the saint poetess of Kashmir who was born in Srinagar in 1625 and passed away in 1721. The date of her death is now known as *Sahiba Saptami*. The commentary in this chapter speaks of the great mind of Prof. Kaul. He has unearthed the great legacy of Rupa Bhawani for the world in general and for Kashmiri Pandit community in particular. Rupa Bhawani was married at the age of seven to a man belonging to Sapru family. She was not recognized for her spiritual powers by her in-laws until the public realised her eminent spiritual qualities. Professor Kamal says that Rupa Bhavani lived in her old age in Deddamar, Safakadal Srinagar. Her place is called *Alakheswari Janmabhumi*[2]. He says that Rupa Bhawani's verses in Kashmirī language have great mystic importance.

In chapter 49, Professor Kamal has written about Anand Kaul Bamzai whom he calls 'a pioneer of modern research in Kashmir'. Bamzai is widely known for his work on the history of Kashmir, its folk-lore.[3] "His books are "The Kashmiri Pandit", "Archaeological Remains in Kashmir", "Lalla Yogeshwarī", etc. Anand Kaul Bamzai has provided a vital bridge between the

2. See Ibid., p. 157.
3. See Ibid., p. 270.

history of past and present. His son PNK Bamzai completed a three-volume work on past and the present history of Kashmir with reflection on the development of social life of the common people along with their religious beliefs and practices".[4] Kamal refers to the visit of Swami Vivekananda to Kashmir towards the end of nineteenth century when Anand Kaul Bamzai was among the important Kashmiri Pandits who received him in Kashmir.

In chapter 75, Professor Kamal provides a philosophy of life. The chapter is titled "Who Am I" and is a poem. Indeed 'Kamal' was a poet too. He writes:

> "Seeking pleasure in leisure
> Robs thee of true pleasure,
> Search then, for thy own joy
> Of incessant work and no fruit,
> Work must be owned,
> Absorption-a cheerful touch.
> Courage-carefree and love-besmeared,
> Make thee laugh away all labour......."

The above verses depict Kamal Sahib's philosophy of life and work with joy and with no attachment for fruits of labour. This is what the *Gītā* also preaches. Indeed, the world over, the idea of creative work and non-attachment is gaining ground. The people in West have come to learn the philosophical overtones of Indian minds like Professor J.N. Kaul 'Kamal', because in selfless work and sacrifice, we have a better world of harmony and joy and less pain. 'Kamal' points out the joy without longing for the fruits of action. Even absorption must carry a cheerful touch. Carry your need lightly, says the sage. And Professor 'Kamal' was a sage of high order. He advocates courage for action with love. And above all, "laugh among all labour" says 'Kamal', which speaks of the high idealism of life that he has to offer. In this age of "new spiritualism" that seems evolving in the world, these percepts of philosophy and action of life, speak volumes of Professor 'Kamal's intellect and spirits.

4. Ibid., p. 271.

He seems a true representative of the Kashmiri Pandits' thought and culture. We are proud of him indeed that he is able to rekindle the joys of renunciation, mysticism, and a new perspective of world history where great men of Kashmir have an eminent place. These outstanding men include, Utpaladeva, Lallesvari, Rupa Bhawani, Anand Kaul Bamzai, Swami Lakhmanjoo and his disciple Professor Jankinath Kaul 'Kamal' himself.

Professor 'Kamal' is much known for his works on Kashmir Śaivism - in chapters 3 and 7 of the book "Kashmiri Pandits: A cultural Heritage", he provides a historical view of this great spiritual philosophy for which Kashmir and its scholars are known in India and abroad. Among some ancient scholars of Śaivism that he points, is Abhinavagupta, who lived in the 10th century. The re-discovery of Śaiva faith was made in the eighth century by scholars like Vasugupta.[5] Professor 'Kamal' makes an assessment of Śaiva doctrine thus: "Śaivism in Kashmir was thus built and developed by those Yogis who possessed sharp intellect and efficiency in expressing clearly the mystery of the philosophy. They had direct experience of the philosophical principles of Advaita Śaiva which is analogous with Śānkara Vedānta in many respects."[6] He has given references to the works of Swami Lakshman joo "who was the most illustious living exponent of Kashmir Śaivism" in recent times.[7] He cites his important books such as Abhinavgupta's commentary on *Bhagvadgītā*, *Kramanayadīpikā*, *Sāmbapañcāśikā* and *Pañcastavī* of Dharmacarya, the Secret of Supreme Consciousness, Lectures on Practice and Discipline in Kashmir Śaivism.

The present generation of Kashmiri Pandits will benefit immensely by reading Professor Kaul in chapter 34 on "Some Eminent Kashmiri Pandits".[8] Professor Kamal has described the eminence of Swami Ramji who was a Śaiva mystic of 19th

---

5. Ibid., p. 30.
6. Ibid., p. 35.
7. Ibid., p. 36.
8. See Ibid., pp. 185-194.

century. He was born in Chinkral Mohalla in Kashmir. His disciples included Swami Mahtab Kāk, Swami Vidyādhar, Swami Govind Kaul, says Professor Kamal. He used to be in *Samādhi* for four hours daily.[9]

Other eminent sages include Pandit Śiva Kaul who was born in 1872.[10] Śiva Kaul was a writer, a poet and a sculptor.[11] Swami Mahatab Kāk was yet another sage of Kashmir. He hailed from Bijbehara in Anantnag where he lived in the latter half of the 19th century.[12] Mahtab Kāk became the disciple of Swami Ramji who was the head of Sri Rama Śaiva (Trika) Ashram. He was a saint with great dignity. Kamal says that Mahtab Kak lived later on near Harwan and Nishat Bagh.

The last great Kashmiri pandit is Pandit Narayana Dass Raina. He and his wife Arnimal served Swami Ramji. Narayana Dass used to serve great sages and being a houseboat owner, he provided one to Swami Vivekananda when the latter visited Kashmir. He died in 1945 after a long and illustrious life.

Summary

Professor Jankinath Kaul 'Kamal' was a great Kashmir Pandit who has made his mark in the history of Kashmir. In this memorial volume, we pay our humble respects to this departed soul, who continued the great tradition of Kashmiri Pandit scholarship. He had a keen insight into the history of Kashmir, in Hindu cultural Heritage, on Śaivism, on the mysteries of this universe. He was a mystic who analysed various dimensions of modern life. When a new conciousness is seen evolving in many parts of the world on global harmony and harmony with nature and universe, the philosophic views of Professor 'Kamal' will produce new enlightenment for minds keen to probe these mysteries. Many leading western scholars in United States are working on Kashmir Śaivism. Professor Paul Muller visited India and has described Abhinavagupta as the greatest genius that

9. Ibid. p. 186.
10. Ibid., p. 187.
11. Ibid., p. 189.
12. Ibid. p. 190.

India has ever produced. In the age of Information Technology, Kashmir Śaivism is bound to produce a new synthesis between science and spiritualism. The works of Professor Kamal are therefore, important for research.

To the Kashmiri Pandits in general, Professor Kamal represents a torchlight of excellence. Like Kalhana Pandit, Anand Kaul Bamzai, Professor Kaul was a many splendoured genius. We are proud of him. I am sure that scholars in India and outside India, will read more about him and about Kashmiri Pandit heritage. India is poised for progress in the 21st century. Scholars like Professor Kaul have much to contribute towards this intellectual progress.[13]

* * *

13. See S. Bhatt and V.S. Mani, India on the Threshold of the 21st Century: Shape of things to Come, JNU, Lancers Books, 1999, pages 413.

A Devotee with Determination

Sri Manohar Nath Trakru

Would you believe that there was a time, when a young fellow, who later became well known as Pt. Jankinath Kaul 'Kamal', would jokingly shout at my mother, his Mami, when passing by our house: "Radha-i, what are you cooking?" Or some such banter associated with the young! Not exactly *shout*, but he would speak out his prankish words or comments into the outlet of our kitchen *soonder*. (Only old timers would know that it was a short funnel-shaped arrangement, with a wide pipe across a wall, through which the kitchen wastewater would be carried into the outside lane). His remarks would resonate through the kitchen and our small *wout,* and regale the grown ups inside. For information of the mods, a *wout* was the ground floor main area, a sort of family room which we occupied most of the winter time, sitting generally on grass mats, eating, talking and doing other daily chores. Only one house stood in between Jankinath ji's house and ours, but the door to door distance had to be traversed along a narrow, winding lane, a distance of a couple of hundred yards. Most times when he passed by – which was a great many times every day – he would peek in, just to say the equivalent of today's "hello" to us. Any day without a prankish remark from him or without his dropping in, meant all round concern in our family and he would have to do a lot of explaining the next day, most of all to his grandmother, his maternal and mine paternal!

From the long list of his outstanding achievement, one is apt to get the feeling that Pt. Jankinath Ji was always a ponderous individual, a workaholic poring over one or the other religious tome, cogitating over subtle matters, writing or teaching all the time. But the fact is that he certainly had his ordinary, human, aspects too. For those of us who don't possess the competence to fully understand or comprehend his spiritual teachings and outpourings, even his growth through life can be as instructive as his learning and knowledge to those well versed in such matters.

Pt. Jankinath ji was a part of my childhood and early youth, a sort of non-resident elder brother to whom we would turn, not so much for help or advice, but to plan the next outing. Therefore, kindly don't expect in this short piece an analysis or assessmant of the accomplishments that made his name! I had the good fortune to be near him during my childhood and later years but none of his wonderful learning rubbed off on me. Quite early, fate took us different ways; I went to England in early fifties in persuit of a hum drum life and later settled down outside Kashmir, while he stayed on in Kashmir and flared into the beacon that he eventually became for so many.

It is natural that most people should know 'Kamal' as an outstanding scholar, a highly erudite person and one who especially excelled in spiritual matters. Undoubtedly, he was a multifaceted personality, with achievements that were truly phenomenal and the range of his knowledge so wide as to encompass a number of highly specialised disciplines. In other words, it was the 'finished product' that everyone saw, a person who was before us in flesh and blood with his accomplishments an open book, available to anybody who cared to read it. He was humble to a fault and if you saw him without knowing his identity, you would never, never suspect that you were face to face with a man of such outstanding accomplishments. One could easily be misled by his humility, simplicity and total absence of even a trace of pride in what he had achieved because he looked more ordinary than the most ordinary of us, which is saying a great deal in the present milieu of values when lesser mortals, with not even a fraction of his talent or qualities, are seen going round with garlands hanging down their necks, and pomp and show surrounding them everywhere.

Pt. Jankinath ji shunned projecting his own personality and therefore, very few know how he arrived at that pinnacle of glory. But for some of us who pride themselves at being his own "family", his life has an extra dimension – the dimension of how much simple, old-fashioned, hard work, plain *niṣkām karma*, can achieve provided one is determined and patient. His success was not something that he inherited without striving or found at his doorstep one fine morning. It was the result of only one thing: toil and incessant toil. And we were witnesses to the relentless toil, totally unconcerned about whether it would yield him results or not.

To put it bluntly, Baigash, as we used to call Pt. Jankinath ji, was not born with a silver spoon in his mouth nor brought up in the lap of luxury. His mother was my father's sister and she passed away when she was very young. A new mother came. He, along with his sister, an equally noble and affectionate soul, was brought up in circumstances that were perhaps not ideal. In course of time, his father too went away to meet his forefathers. But times then were not as bad as they are now. Life was simple, and Baigash, his sister, and new mother made it even simpler by their own innate gentleness, nobility and fortitude – and above all, a smile always on their faces.

There were many helping hands but it was primarily goddess Saraswati who smiled on Janakinath ji in a generous measure. In rapid succession, he completed one educational course after another difficult course and came out with flying colours every time. He mastered Hindi, Sanskrit, English and other subjects, garnered degree after degree and was soon in a position to take on the responsibility of marriage and after himself and his enlarged family. For a time, working in small schools first and bigger ones later, teaching and learning went hand in hand for him. Finally the stage came when his talents started to flower in various other directions and he didn't have to confine himself merely to earning a living.

In a short essay, one may sum up his long odyssey in a few sentences but actually it took him years of toil and trouble to reach anywhere. God and divine intervention might have helped him but they came only later, when he had worked himself to the bone. In his younger years, he knew neither day nor night: practicaly all his time was working time. He learnt the hard way, by self-help, without taking the help of any tutors. Of the vast knowledge and insight he gained over the years, he eventually made full use for his intellectual emancipation and also placed it at the disposal of others as well in the form of innumerable articles and discourses, besides several books. It is possible that not all of us may be able to comprehend the complexities and subtleties of all that he took in his broad sweep: his vision of Kashmir Śaiva Philosophy, the Upaniṣads, Yoga, Tantra, Vedānta and all the rest of it about which he had full and complete knowledge. Unless one is endowed with a minimum of divine spark, it can be difficult to benefit from that aspect of Jankinath ji's life. Going into that realm is no easy journey for ordinary people.

Does that then mean that if we are people of average understanding with little cognizance of matters divine, we can acquire no benefit from Pt. Jankinath's illustrious life? The answer is that if you are unable to take a complete bath in the holy Ganga, at least wash your head and face! Or atleast your face alone! The idea is to learn at least something from great souls. In this case, the graph of his work and labour is itself a very valuable lesson. If one looks only at what he achieved and how, not through somebody's *sifarish* but by sheer dedication and hard work, at the long saga of his life and struggle, we can find a lot in it to emulate. The way he pulled himself up by his bootstraps, his steadfast dedication to the god of hard work, his sheer force of will and discipline, unmindful of the hardship involved in it – all that is something worth learning at any stage of one's life.

Pt. Jankinath Ji had all along a religious bent of mind. Indeed most people of that era were religiously inclined but his interest was much more pronounced, deep and sustained. Not the ritualistic type of religion where visiting a temple is treated as the ultimate in virtue, but its much more sophisticated aspects, like the search for ultimate truth, and other such highly esoteric matters. His room at his ancestral house in Darbiyar was full of religious books, like those on Swami Ramakrishna Paramhansa, Swami Vivekananda, Swami Ramtirth and many others. Photographs of saints and savants adorned its walls. The room itself had the ambience of a *Rishi Kutia* and, at this distance of some six decades, the one clear and interesting rememberance I have is that it was extraordinarily quiet as befits a hermitage. The only audible sound was the tick tock from the pendulum of an ancient looking wall clock that he would wind once a week. On the floor of this *Kutia*-like room would Pt. Jankinath ji be sitting on a folded up mattress, the lid of a wooden box placed in front serving as a table on which he used to do his reading and wrting. That is where he went through the initial phase of his growth and embarked on a journey that brought him to the heights he eventually reached.

Almost all his friends also were of a similar religious bent of mind, young and eager on the unending quest for truth and enlightenment. Against this backdrop, it was only to be expected that he would veer towards the one master of saints of the time, Swami Lakshman Joo, to whom most people with searching minds turned for guidance. Baigash used to go to his abode at Ishaber every Sunday for an intensive study of highly venerated religious books and to listen to Swamiji's discourses. For me, the bonus out of his dedication to the Ishaber Swami was that he would take me also along to Ishaber, and also Nishat, on many an occasion. He continued to do so even after I made a *fax paus* on my first visit there! Those days I was only a child, but with the benefit of hindsight I now realize that my gaffe in a way reflected the orthodox attitudes of those days.

The incident related to the serving of Kashmiri tea at the Ishabar Ashram during the study and discourse session. It was the practice there to serve *kahwa*, and sometimes *Paranthas*, to those present in the room. Their number used to be small, may be twenty or thirty people. When the servant with the *Samāvār* came towards me to pour tea into my cup, I refused to take it. The reason? the *Samāvār* was white, the variety used by Musalmans, instead of the golden colour brass that we use. (Actually, it was the usual *Samāvār* but had been tinned over, perhaps for easier maintenance and to save the labour of scrubbing it!) In fact I also asked Biagash how was it that he was taking tea from a Musalmaan *Samāvār*? Though it was all said very quitely by a child that was I, there was a minor ripple, and it reached Swamiji also. Fortunately for me, he only had an amused smile when told what it was all about! The incident has remained clearly imprinted on my memory since then, all thanks to Baigash!

* * * *

Pandit Jankinath Kaul 'Kamal' – *A Jīvanmukta*

Professor K.L. Bhalla

It is my good luck that I came into contact with Shri Jankinath Kaul. Every time I met him I found him smiling, full of love and affection. *Jīvanmukta* is one, who is liberated while living. Living free is being in divine trance without any human effort. It is a gift of god to those who lead a righteous life.

Kaul Sahib, with the grace of the Almighty, experienced unlimited joy and enjoyed unalloyed bliss. It is something which cannot be expressed in words. For living free you need not go anywhere, it is absence of any physical or mental need when you watch beauty in its inner source, you automatically become quiet. Total attention, without any internal distraction, brings complete silence.

What is god? It is difficult to give a definite reply. The sages say – "God is silence, God is stillness." A *Jīvanmukta* keeps himself comfortably aware of supreme self. Intense mediation coupled with devotion is required to attain the stage of *Jīvanmukti*, it is constant endeavour and requires a lot of patience and dedication.

Many a time the example of *Rājā Janak* is quoted is this context. Although he was a *Rājā* yet he was free from ego and attachment. He had divine vision and experience day in and day out. Kaul Sahib, while leading the life of householder had aquired spiritual knowledge and what is remarkable, he was noble enough to share his inner insight with others. I happened to talk to him on spiritual matters and his answers were brief and apt.

Living free is the display of true wisdom and not merely that of empty breath. It is being alone, not isolated or drawn to some fanciful dream or vision. It is entering the incalculable measureless abode of the Supreme. It is Divine wonder. It is transcendence beyond any system of thought or ritual to follow. To live a free life guidance of a master is needed who has got divine knowledge.

The *Gītā* declares that the Suprme Yogi is he who regards the pleasure and pain of others like his own and does his best for them. Relief of pain is one of the aspects of Yoga where we are told that the person who alleviates pain and scatters joy is not an ordinary type of yogi but the perfect one.

According to Narsi Mehta –

> 'Blessed is he – the *Vaishnava,*
> He knows his suffering brothers' weal and woe,
> And he gives him help,
> Without a thought of return.'

I feel Kaul Sahib was a saint who was out to help and inspire devotees. In the present selfish age to become a yogi is rather difficult. There is pollution everywhere. Money is the be-all and end-all of most of the people. Even then one should try to reform oneself without bothering what others do. We should set a good example by leading a life of purity and renunciation.

It is laid down in the *Gītā* – "The yogi is superior to the ascetics, he is deemed superior even to those who perform actions without some motive. Therefore, Arjuna, you do become a yogi." In the view of Shri Murlidhar, 'Be firm and skillful in your actions. It is the will of God that you have been placed in your present position. Work with a determined will and patience. Be a person of righteous behaviour. Always remember God. Rest not till you realize the truth.'

According to Gandhiji, 'God is truth'. Kaul Sahib led a detached life in persuit of truth. It is for us to follow what he said. The best tribute to him is to live a life of *'Jīvanmukta.'* Whatever the difficulties and hurdles in our *'Sadhanā'* are, they will be removed by grace of *'guru'*. The scriptures and godly persons are there to help us. What is required is lifelong pursuit.

* * * *

Pandit Jankinath Kaul 'Kamal' – As I Saw Him

Sri B.L. Khar

I cannot claim any distinctive proximity to Pandit Jankinathji Kaul 'Kamal'. But I have been one of his nondescript admirers for the last six years and more. For the last over two years, I have been one of the pupils of his Tuesday-Evening Class. By virtue of that relationship, and, by virtue of his earlier profession, as also his cherished lifelong pursuit of teaching as non professional (that he followed assiduously almost upto his last breath), I would wish to call him 'Masterji'. (This appellation also helps me to enliven my memory of another eminent 'Masterji' of yesteryears viz. the saint-poet master Zinda Kaul, whose poetry, particularly the streak of reformist thought in it, has been a source of great inspiration to me). But the aroma of the 'KAMAL' has spread so far and wide and with such intense emotionality that no other name would now catch the imagination of the people concerned.

My twenty-eight months' tutelage under JKK should have been reasonably enough for me to set myself on an even keel. But it was not to be so. My tardiness as also my mental cobwebs stood in my way and impeded progress. Some of us in the class have been luckier. They have been able to make better use of their association with JKK. For instance, Prof. O.N. Chrungoo successfully undertook the translation of *Pañcastavī*, in lucid Kashmiri verse. Prof. A.N. Dhar was inspired to proliferate his literary writings.

When we meet somebody for the first time, the immediate things beside the countenance, that involuntarily attracts our attention, is the dress of the person. When I met JKK for the first time in 1993, he was dressed in pantaloon-coat and a fur cap. This dress at once clashed with the mental image I had formed of him two years earlier. I had drawn his image as the one in a chaste Indian or Kashmiri dress. Therefore the dress that he had donned appeared to me incompatible with the works he had till then authored. But that did not bother me for too long. I had a quick reconciliation even to the extent of my reaction getting transformed into a sort of gentle veneration for him. Dress after all is the most exterior variable standout which in no way can or should interfere with the intrinsic and the finer qualities of a person. However later on it gradually dawned on me that JKK had absolutely no proclivity for orthodoxy in the matter of dress or anything else. Talking about his dress, I am reminded of the dress he had donned on October 7, 1997 which, ominously, turned out to be the last Tuesday of the weekly evening class. He was wearing a full-sleeves imported T-Shirt with a MacDnold emblem emblazoned in bright red colour on the front side of it. He was looking ravishingly hadsome. At the conclusion of the class when I, rather nonchalantly, referred to his ultra-modern wear of the day, he, in a matter-of-fact manner, said, "My home people gave me to wear it today. It keeps my chest and my arms covered". That conclusively supported my contention that JKK had liberated himself completely from the dress-syndrome, that most of us are abjectly obsessed with.

It had never occured to me, all through my more than two years of association with him that he would be in the neighbourhood of 83 years of age. His tall, erect, graceful body-frame, his physical and mental agility, his resplendence, his charismatic appeal, his photographic memory all belied our expectations of his actual age. He appeared to have set a target of living beyond a hundred-year age. And, given his general physical and mental alertness, he would have certainly made it, (that is my hunch), but for the unfortunate fatal accident that God had to bring-in to recall him to His abode. Perhaps God wanted him for some more urgent assignment on this planet or any other life- sustaining planet in the inconceivable vastness of

His Kingdom. There appears to be no other explanation for such and similar deaths. For instance, Mahatma Gandhi had set a target of living upto 125 years of age. But God had to bring-in an assasin to recall him. Talking about Gandhiji reminds me of his physical condition even at a younger age of 78 years: among other physical infirmities, his back at the upper extremity had slightly bent, necessitating him to engage his two nieces for walking support. Contrary to that, JKK had betrayed no such symptoms at an age five years older than that of the Mahatma.

It may not be easy for me to comment on the supra-mundane faculties of JKK. Nevertheless, it would not need much of an effort for a layman like me to agree with the knowledgeable contemporaneous personages who have been acclaiming JKK as the one who has made commendable contribution to the propagation of the rich ancient Hindu ethos. The natural deduction, therefore, is that it must have involved an intensive and extensive study, at the cost of tremendously ceaseless effort, on his part to gain access to the vast treasures. John Ruskin has this to say about reading good books: "It is open to labour and to merit, but to nothing else. No wealth will bribe, no name overawe, no artifice deceive the guardians of those Elysian Gates. In the deep sense no vile or vulgar person ever enters there". When JKK was preparing a paper on *'Pañcadaśī'* in connection with the Bhagwan Gopinath Centenary Memorial Lecture, he, incidently, mentioned to me how he had to run from the piller to post to study this work on Advaita philosophy, before finally settling with Pandit Satramji for the purpose and in consequence of which he had to walk up the distance from Srinagar to Nishat and back till he had accomplished the task. This is the ordeal he had to go for studying a single work of a lighter dimension of a later period of the 14th century A.D. To what perceptively vigorous discipline he must have had to subject himself in going through the plethora of the other more serious scriptures, should leave nobody guessing. JKK's teen aged grandson, Mrinal, whom the former had been grooming to enable to take after him, has described his grandfather as a 'Living Dictionary'. Certainly,

JKK was an undisputed Walking - Talking - Deliberating Encyclopaedia of the prominent Hindu *Śāstras*.

I think a genetic transmutation also had played its role in shaping the destiny of JKK. His grandfather, Pandit Shiva Kaul was an adroit Sanskrit Scholar and a seer. In the introduction of the translation of *'Ākrandamānagiriyā Sivastuti'* (Invocation in lament to Śiva) of Pandit Shiva Kaul, JKK says: "Shiva Kaul continued with his spiritual practices and *prāṇāyāma* exercises. Finally in preparation for taking up *Sannyāsa*, he performed a *yajña* probably *Viraja homa (Puruṣa carana)* in which he distributed free, his treasure of books among the pandits who had performed the function". In the same introduction, JKK mentions how he had, at a very young age, salvaged the rat-eaten pieces of the manuscript of this compilation accidentally from his grandmother's room. That speaks volumes about JKK's perseverance and his thirst for knowledge.

The contribution made by JKK to the enrichment of the Kashmiri Hindu Cultural Ethos has quite deservedly received wide approbation. Starting with smaller compilations he, with the passage of time, had bloomed into a meaningfully matured scholar to produce *Magnum-opus* like commentaries on *Bhavānī-nāma-sahasrastuti, Pañcastavī, Śiva-Sūtra-Vimarśa, Vedānta Dindimaḥ and Indrākṣī Stotraṁ.*

JKK had an innate desire to give away all that he had acquired so painfully. He would virtually move from home to home to 'dissipate' his treasures. This he would do with all humility without a grain of the ego ever touching him. His regularity, his punctuality, his methodicity and his deftness in communicating his ideas to others, were exceptionally brilliant and would sometimes make me feel envious. Had I met JKK earlier in my youthful days, I would have certainly done much better, even at the mundane level, in my service career etc.. Prof. A.N.Dhar would often remark about JKK: "He has all the Professorial qualities".

It is certainly beyond my capacity to comment, even casually, on the spiritual attainment of JKK. Nevertheless, one can effortlessly vouch for the solid advance made by him towards the self study *(svādhyāya)*, one of the obligatory observances of the five great *Niyamas*. Gandhiji had struggled all through his life to keep up *'Ahimsa'* and *'Satya'* – the first two vows of the five great vows *(Yamas)*, the other vows (obligatory observances) having, evidently, kept pace in his life proportionately. (*Yama* and *Niyaṁa*, the Ten Commandments of Patañjali, together with *Āsana, Prāṇāyāma, Pratyāhāra, Dhāraṇā, Dhyāna* and *Samādhi* form the eight *aṅgas* of *Patañjali's* Eight-fold yoga). In my opinion, the obligatory observance of self-study *(svādhyāya)* undertaken by JKK, must have taken care of the other vows, proportionately, in his life too. JKK's book 'Pazar Pazaravun' gives a small insight into the practical aspect of his spirituality.

I may also not be able to vouch for it completely, but I have a feeling that JKK has quite appreciably reduced the gap between 'Pleasure' and 'Pain'. A state of bliss (or call it mental peace) is directly dependent upon one's ability to control excitement during the moments of pleasure and despondency during the moments of pain. In other words, accepting 'pain' as an essential complement to 'pleasure' is the key for the perennial mental peace. The paradox of duality has to be removed: A Razor's Edge'? But an attempt has to be made. JKK appears to have gone a long way on this path. Otherwise, how could it be possible for him to remain unruffled on the untimely and tragic death of a couple of his close relatives during the recent past? Or, how could it be possible for him to brush aside completely his serious heart ailment to resume his cherished pursuits as soon as he was out of the hospital bed? Or, how could it be possible for him to avoid creating a hullabaloo on his being selected for the prestigious President's award?

Two days after JKK left for his Heavenly Abode, I had an opportunity to listen to his old Kashmiri composition: *'Sannyās'* recited by his son, Anupamji Kaul, in his enchantingly sweet voice. Anyone, even with a small metaphysical perception could, after listening to this wonderful composition, comprehend the depth that JKK had attained in the field of practical spirituality.

* * * *

Saint Scholar Pandit Jankinath Kaul 'Kamal' – As I Knew Him

Sri Upender Bhat

In this world, the greatest of all *jñānas* (knowledge) is the *ādhyātmajñāna*. Having attained this *jñāna* one need not be born again on this earth. That means through *adhyātma jñāna* one is relieved from the cycle of births and deaths. Since miseries are resulted from the birth in this world, our endeavour should be for not being born again. Hence this struggle is for knowing the *adhyātma*. Therefore, the ideal life is that which is lived for the attainment of *adhyātma-jñāna* (ultimate spiritual goal) which leads further to *kaivalya* or *moksha* – the Bliss Divine.

The saint scholar *brahmalīna* Pandit Jankinath Kaul, more familiar by his pen-name 'Kamal' and also respectfully known as 'Masterji' amongst his students, was such an ideal personality ever ready to impart *adhyātma vidyā* to anyone and everyone unconditionally, whosoever approached him or came in contact with him. Very often I vividly ponder upon the following lines which the noble soul once communicated to me:

> "We mortals are flowing in the mighty stream of life like the logs of wood. While floating some join and are together for some time, then suddenly one or more get detached. They might come together again, who knows?"

again:

> "The movements of a saint are like that of a bird in the air. He comes by himself to give directions to the earnest seeker of the Truth from time to time as warranted. Therefore, one has to be earnest and not impatient."

About twenty seven years ago in March, 1975, it was the opening day of my school in Srinagar after the usual winter break. On this day, while sitting in my classroom I saw a well built, tall and graceful personality enter. It was a casual class for all in the classroom excepting myself. After an informal introduction in the classroom, the teacher directed me to see him in the school library during recess. This was the place where we first met and the ever lasting relation got set up. Later our meeting-points were: in the school or at his home, Shanti Kutir, 77-Drabiyar, Srinagar (Kashmir) and sometimes in the precincts of Sri Ramakrishna Ashrama, Kashmir which proved to be a great boon for me. It is the effect of this personal contact with this great soul of eminance that make me think and reflect upon the teachings of the great Saint Mahaprabhu Chaitanya:

"Be humbler than a blade of grass,
Be patient and forbearing like a tree;
Take no honour to yourself,
Give honour to all,
Chant unceasingly the name of God".

'Masterji' would always emphasise this and would say that the physical, intellectual, moral and spiritual progress have to go hand in hand.

It is very difficult to write about the personalities like 'Kamalji' for they do not reveal their inner self. It is only the rare fortune of those who get some glimpse into the inner self of such great souls. It is hence impossible for a person like me to write or comment on 'Kamalji's life. Therefore, I am quoting here the notable quotes about this saint scholar and a towering personality in the spiritual field, from the great personalities and saint-philosophers of India who have held him in high esteem:

His Holiness Swami Sivananda Saraswati of the Divine Life Society, Rishikesh (Himalayas) had a great regard for 'Kamalji'. Although the two never met physically yet their spiritual contacts were established through the Divine outpourings in their correspondance which was of ever lasting nature. Swamiji would instruct the aspirants visiting Kashmir to see 'Kamalji'.

A great devotee of the Mother Goddess *Mahātripurasundarī*, Pandit Raghunath Kukiloo had a profound regard for 'Kamalji'.

He once said "he does not have even a trace of ego." In his preface to the *Bhavānīnāmasahasrastutī*, Panditji writes:

> "This endeavour of Shri Jankinath Kaul is praiseworthy. He alongwith his family deserves blessings. The exhaustive explanation of the thousand names of Devi is established on the authority of scriptures. I experienced solace while going through the pages of this manuscript. This proficient commentary will surely do good even to common man especially when it is written in comprehensive English language".

The great Indian philosopher, and a sage Shri. M.P. Pandit of the Aurobindo Ashram, Pondicherry has paid glowing tributes to 'Kamalji' in his remarkable forewords to the two monumental works of 'Kamalji' on the *Bhavānīnāmasaharastutī* and the *Pañcastavī*. Shri M.P. Pandit writes in his foreword to the *Bhavānīnamasahasrastutī*:

> "We should be grateful to Pandit Jankinath Kaul for making available to the world at large the full text of the hymnal alongwith a close rendering in English and what is more important, copious explanations and notes. Pandit Jankinathji takes up each name and explains its full power. He brings out multiple significance of the name: spiritual, religious, mythological, philosophical. He explains the grammatical derivation of terms. He resolves the apparent paradoxes of contraries existing side by side. He brings out the universal character of the deity, Mother Bhāvanī, while expounding the relevance of mention of rivers, birds, animals, plants, etc. Bhavānī consciousness is present in each form on earth and beyond."
>
> "It is profound experience to read this exposition. It has, indeed, literary merits but on that account it is not a literary work. It has its historical elements, geographical pointers, aesthetic excellences, hints of yogic secrets. No effort has been spared in bringing out these riches from this treasure of perennial relevance. It is a manual of *sādhanā*, a guide to the Everest of Truth-consciousness on the ethereal heights where the homes of the Gods lie."

"Once again we thank, we bow down to the inspiration that vibrates on every page of this masterpiece of Śākta Experience."

A great scholar and spiritual monk of Sri Ramakrishna Math and Mission, Srimat Swami Jitatmanandaji Maharaj describes 'Kamalji' as an ocean of knowledge. Once while hinting to his spiritual stage, he remarked "This man has forty times knowledge as that of mine."

Swami Bodhasarananda of the Advaita Ashrama, Calcutta writes:

"............ a Sanskrit scholar of repute, 'Kamalji's whole life was devoted to the restoration of the cultural and spiritual heritage of Kashmir. His love for God was exemplary. I found his face always beaming with joy and peace. In him we have lost a great saint. Masterji's classes on the *Gītā*, *Vivekacūdāmani, Śivastotrāvalī* awakened bhakti in me. It was his greatness that he got *Bhavānaīnāmasahasrastutī* released from me.

"I remember how he shed tears like a small child while explaining a verse from the *Gītā* where Arjuna asks the question: What would be the lot of one, self controlled and striving hard through right means, who could not yet fulfil and reach the goal? Sobbing, he repeated several times, 'will our soul perish?' Quoting Shri Krishna, 'Kamalji' assured us with the words: *"None, striving on the path divine, can ever be destroyed and whatever one accomplishes will be faithfully carried over as a legacy of the individual soul in its pursuit here and hereafter"*.

From Singapore, Swami Prajnanananda of Shri Rámákrishna Mission wrote:

"In him I have lost a very close and fatherly figure. Great loss to the Kashmiri community and the nation at large".

Before concluding my write up I would like to draw the attention of the readers towards some of the facts of 'Kamalji's' life which present a picture of the person of simple living and high thinking:

Simple Living, High Thinking

Descendent of a pious family, 'Kamalji' lost his parents at a tender age. He was married while a student. He did his M.A. in Sanskrit while he was in service. His life was full of struggles. But he would face every challenge of life with a smile. He would often quote the lines heard from one of his teachers:

"उछलते रहो, गुनगुनाते रहो, मुसीबत में सीटी बजाते रहो!"

Right from his childhood 'Kamalji' never gave up pondering on various scriptures viz. the Vedas and various *śāstras*. First of all he studied these scriptures at the feet of Brahmachari Nilakanthaji who was incidentally his neighbour. Nilakanthaji was a strict master. He had recognized the qualities of his disciple in their very first meeting when 'Kamalji' was just in his teens. Having thus completed the study of various Vedic Scriptures Nilakanthaji took him to the luminary Śaivite saint Swami Lakshman joo. He was introduced to Swamiji as a poet, writer and above all an earnest seeker of the Truth. This was probably in April, 1935. On this occasion 'Kamalji' was asked to recite any of his compositions. The first two lines of the poem which he recited were:

"हस्ती को देख अपनी मस्ती में झूमता हूँ।
प्यारे को देख प्यारे मैं मस्त हो रहा हूँ"

On completing the recitation of his poem the poet saw pearl like tears trickling down the smiling brilliant face of the Sage of Ishaber. Here I remember 'Kamalji' once had explained "the union of the master and the desciple comes within fraction of a second when the pure love of the latter pierces the yogic vision and intellect of the former." This is what had perhaps transpired between the two in the very first meeting. The loving relation between the two lasted till end.

'Kamalji' also studied the scriptures with other saints and scholars of the time. Pt. Satlalji of Nishat was one of them. 'Kamalji' would travel in a *shikara* alongwith his colleagues all the way to Nishat. At times they would have a Kashmiri *'Kulcha'* soaked in the waters of Dal Lake for lunch. This reflects his earnest desire for learning. He further studied the Vedānta and Kashmir Śaivism with equal devotion and assimilation of both the systems of thought.

His life was the combination of simplicity and calmness; enthusiasm and meticulous hardwork; right understanding, pure love and wisdom. He had unshaken faith in the words of the elders and the scriptures. He would never lose his calm even in extreme situations. He would always impress upon understanding the crux of an example and not going to diversions. He would gently pull up the ear of one who would try to divert the topic. In that respect he was an excellent teacher. He had the quality of going up to the level of a student to make him understand the real meaning. He declined to read the books forbidden by his master irrespective of the fact that many of his colleagues requested hard for the same. He said "We should not do anything not advised."

He would avoid discussion on controversial topics and would advice others to do the same. In his words:

> "No amount of external advice or discourse on a spiritual topic is fruitful or virtually comprehensive unless the inner man awakes; unless the sixth sense works on it and unless the internal organs of a person get purified by observing the right sort of conduct and unless there is sincere earnestness."

The basis of progress he would stress is the discrimination (between the right and the wrong i.e. the proper understanding). Concentration and hardwork were his constant companions. Once he was at work he would get engrossed for hours together within himself and with books not getting affected by the surroundings. I saw him once working in the high temperature of 47°C as there was no electricity. He was full of sweat but he did not stop his work till it was completed. He spent nights in correcting his proofs of the *Pañcastavī* and consulting the relevant data.

'Kamalji' lived to what he believed. To give meaning to life, once while quoting Maharshi Ramana, he wrote to me:

> "To act in this world, one must die within oneself. Man is not on this earth only to be happy. He is not there to be

simply honest, he is there to realise great things for humanity to attain nobility and to surpass the vulgarity in which the existence of almost all individuals drags on."

Again 'Kamalji' once wrote:

"Life is counted by breaths and deeds not by years, do you not see lillies bloom early and fade soon, but rose that blooms in summer keeps its blossom and spreads its fragrance around it. Life is love, life is service, no matter what its span in years. Therefore serve and give love."

'Kamalji' had achieved great spiritual heights long before he was known as such by the general public especially in his own community. His monumental works on the *Bhavānīnāmasahasrastuti* and the *Pañcastavī* have now become his identity in each and every Hindu family. He equally received great honour and respect amongst the scholarly circles for his great scholarship.

'Kamalji' has immortalised himself through his higher spiritual achievements. By leaving behind the vast literature in the form of his collections of poems in Kaṣhmiri, Sanskrit, Hindi, English, Urdu and articles on various topics mainly related to Vedānta and Kashmir Śaivism which have appeared in various reputed national and international journals, besides a considerable number of published books make him omnipotent amongst his admirers. Even though his physical presence is not around us, but the memories of his radiant looks alongwith melodious voice and above all the power of his spiritual inspirations will be always bestowed upon all of us.

* * * *

PART-II

INDOLOGICAL ESSAYS

Section-A

Śaiva Studies

Śaiva Studies

In this part we present thirty papers in three sections. Section-A opens with Śaiva Studies. This is a bouque of 11 papers followed by a section on Cultural and Philosophical studies with 12 papers. The third section contains seven papers on Bhakti, Yoga and Poetics. Śaiva studies are mostly confined to Kashmir Śaivism. Pandit Janakinath Kaul was an ardent scholar of this branch of Śaivism and he was fortunate to have the blessings of Swami Lakshman Joo, an adept in this philosophy. The section opens up with Swamiji's article on Kashmir Śaivism. The five *Śaktis* and their union amongst them leading to the production of 64 *Bhairava Tantras* have been briefly narrated here in their historic perspective. The four systems viz. *Pratyabhijñā, Kula, Spanda* and *Krama* have been explained and the three *Upāyās* viz. *Āṇava, Śākta* and *Śāmbhava* have been briefly touched. Thus the reader gets himself well established in this philosophy before he proceeds to other subtle prolifications of this branch of Śaivism.

We have specially reprinted the article by late M.P. Pandit on Pratyabhijñā System, so that the readers may get a good grounding in the study of this system. Dr. Janaki had contributed her article much earlier. She is no more with us. Her studies of *Āgamās* and *Purāṇās* are helpful in understanding Śaiva rituals and symbolism therein.

Dr. Raffaele Torella of Rome University has sent for this volume his revised paper on 'The word in Abhinavagupta's *Bṛhad-Vimarśinī*'. This is a critical appreciation of the treatment of 'word' by Abhinavagupta. The study of 'word' has been engaging the attention of Grammarians and Philosophers since long and Bhartṛhari has elaborated the concept of 'word' in his Vākyapadīya. The study is central to Śaiva Siddhānta. In this article, the Professor has pointed out how Abhinavagupta has further evolved the concept of 'word' in accordance with Śaiva scriptures and also with accordance with linguistic philosophy. Raffaele Torella confines himself to the treatment of 'word' as is discernible in *Īśvarapratyabhijñā Vivṛti Vimarṣinī*. Bhartṛhari's concept of 'word' and also of Utpaladeva and Somananda are scanned in this paper. Planes of *Vaikharī, Paśyanti* and *Madhyamā* have been elucidated and various *Śaktis* which activate these planes have also been explained. He again points out how Dharmakirti, even with his different presuppositions supports Utpaladeva's and Abhinavagupta's conclusions.

Pandit Dinanath Yaksha has traced the genesis of *Tantra Śāstra* to the Vedas and *Śabdaśāstra* i.e. *Vyākaraṇa*. The *Tantra* philosophy later made its way in Buddhism and we find that Vajrayāna has in it, the elements of Tantra. Pt. Yaksha has also examined the influence of *Tantra* on *Devi Bhāgvatam* and *Nīlamata Purāṇa*. He has also presented a glimpse of later *Tantra* literature that is extant.

In a brief article Dr. Kahrs, in paying his tribute to Professor Kaul has traced the evolution of *Svacchandatantra*. This has been contrasted with other *Bhairava Tantras*. The depiction of *Bhairavas* in the sculptures of the South has also been highlighted, indicating the dualistic worship in the temples. Dr. Kahrs refers to Abhinavagupta in reestablishing the non-dualistic approach of *Svacchandatantra*.

Dr. Kapila Vatsyayan has presented Śaivism and Vaiṣṇavism in a broad perspective. She has traced the origin of Śaivism to the proto Paśupati seal of Mohenjodaro. She finds man-nature, man-animal relationship at the back of these cultish representations. She draws our attention to Śvetāśvatara Upaniṣad where Śiva is regarded as '*eka deva*', the cause of all. He is called by various names as *Hara, Īsāna, Mahāpuruṣa, īśa, Śiva* and *Maheśvara*. It also contains the philosophy of Sānkhya and Yoga. Dr. Vatsyayan cites Śiva and Skanda Purāṇas and certain canonical literature in the South, viz. Tirumurai and Meyakantaśāstra. Further, she expounds the philosophy of Vaiśṇavism. The article has gone a long way in enlightening the readers with the dynamics of both these modes of worship.

Then follows Dr. Navjivan Rastogi's paper titled 'Reaccessing Abhinavagupta'. Dr. Rastogi is involved in the study of Abhinavagupta for over decades and has discovered multiple facets of Abhinavagupta's personality and his philosophy. The more one studies Abhinavagupta, the more one finds deeper meanings in his statements and a reapprisal of one's previous studies becomes obligatory. Dr. Rastogi has been doing that and by now he has got a much larger and clearer image of the philosopher poet. Dr. Rastogi appeals to the readers to reaccess and reassess Abhinavagupta for answering our basic concerns of cultural identity, radical secular commitment, nodal centrality of Indological pursuits and divining a fresh socio-philosophical thinking with contemporary humanistic ethos.

We have two beautiful articles by Dr. Bettina Baumer – one is on Grace and the other on Anuttarāṣṭikā – a pithy octad of Abhinavagupta. Both these articles push the readers in the realm of the Self-Śiva, *Parama Śiva.* Dr. Bäumer says that Grace is always unexpected, undeserved and full of surprise. When Grace comes, it fills the whole being of the receiver with light, peace and joy. She elucidates the terms, '*anugraha*', '*prasāda*' and *Śaktipāta.* She cites examples of Grace in Christian understanding (case of Gregory Palamas) and these compare well with the expression in Anuttarāṣṭikā. By Grace, *Paśu* is transformed into *Pati.* Grace deifies the receiver. Purity and readiness of the receiver are important factors in the conferment of Grace.

Dr. Koshalya Walli has written on 'Āgamādhikāra of Ācārya Utpaladeva'. Āgamādhikāra is the third *adhikāra*, mentioned in *Īśvarapratyabhijñā Kārikā.* Dr. Walli lucidly explains here the technical terms such as *Īśvara Tattva* and *Sādākhya Tattva, Śaktis* such as *Vidyā* and *Māyā; Kalā* and *Mala* and so on. A lay reader wants to know the intricate terms in Kashmir Śaivism and such an exposition is helpful.

The section ends with a beautiful translation of Anuttarāṣṭikā followed by Dr. Bäumer's lucid commentary.

On the completion of the reading of this section, the reader will find himself well grounded in the philosophy of Kashmir Śaivism and he will feel the need to delve further and deepen his studies so as to reach the height of spiritual ecstacy.

– Editors

Kashmir Śaivism

Swāmī Lakṣman Joo

In the beginning of *Satyāyuga* Lord Śiva appeared in the form of *Svacchandanāth* with his five *Mukhas* (mouths), namely, ईशान, तत्पुरुष, सद्योजात, वामदेव and अघोर. These *Mukhas* represent His five Energies, namely. Consciousness (चित्शक्ति:), Bliss (आनन्द शक्ति:), Will (इच्छा शक्ति:), Knowledge (ज्ञान शक्ति:), and Action (क्रिया शक्ति:).

Lord Śiva wanted to enlighten the universe by manifesting the existence of the Tantras. He manifested these Tantras through His five Mouths. Some of these Tantras have separately been revealed by Śiva by each one of His Mouths while others have been recited by Him through two or more than two of His Mouths simultaneously. The Tantras that came into existence in this way are dualistic and mono-dualistic and are known as *Śiva* and *Rudra* Tantras respectively. The former are ten in number and the latter, eighteen. This makes a total of 28 dualistic and monodualistic Tantras.

When these five Energies of Lord Śiva unite with each other in such a way that each of these takes hold of the rest simultaneously, they give shape to sixtyfour *Bhairva Tantras* which are purely Monistic (अद्वैत). The thought propounded in these Tantras is called the 'Trika' Philosophy or the Kashmir Śaivism.

The Monistic thought of Tantras was re-originated in the early period of *Kaliyuga* by the sage Durvāsā who taught this philosophy to his will-born son, Tryambakanātha and to one mind born daughter Ardhatryambakā. These two schools of thought are named Tryambaka and Ardha-Tryambaka respectively.

This Philosophy, commonly known as the Trika-system, is concerned with the three-fold existence – *Śiva* (The Universal Being), *Śakti* (The Universal Energy), and *Nara* (The individual), (नरशक्ति शिवात्मकं त्रिकम्).

Kashmir Śaivism endeavours to remove the innate ignorance that separates the individual (जीव) from the Universal (शिव). This system explains that the universe is just like its creator, absolutely real. In this philosophy the Universe is the manifestation of God Himself which is brought about by His Motivating Power (स्वातंत्र्यशक्तिः). The existence of Śiva has, therefore, to be understood in the very manifestation of the Universe and not in its negation.

Kashmir Śaivism recognises no restriction of caste, creed and colour and has no place for discrimination on this basis "नात्राधिकारिभेदः कोऽप्यस्ति". In fact, this philosophy is meant for all those who have desire and yearning to attain true knowledge and liberation from the bondage of repeated births and deaths.

This philosophy has been explained in four systems, namely Pratyabhijñā, Kula, Spanda, and Krama.

Pratyabhijñā System

The Pratyabhijñā system as systematically presented by Śrī Somānanda-Nātha in the 8th century in his *Śivadṛiṣtiśāstra* and is reflected in the *Īśvara-Pratyabhijñā-Sūtras* by his disciple *Utpaladevācārya.* Pratyabhijñā means recognising one's own self. This represents an act by which one realises and re-unites with the original state (Universal consciousness). To explain, take the case of a bride who has heard all about her bride-groom, his qualities and beauty, and even has seen him many a time, but without knowing who he is. She does not recognise him unless he is shown to her and told that he is the man for whom she has been looking. Same is the case with an individual who has read and heard about his being nothing but Śiva, the Universal. But unless, he is guided by the Guru to recognise himself as one with the Lord, who is Omniscient and Omnipresent, he is unable to do so.

तैस्मैरप्युपयाचितैरुपनतस्तन्व्याः स्थितोऽप्यन्तिके,
कान्तो लोक समान एवमपरिज्ञातो न रन्तुं यथा।
लोकस्यैष तथानवेक्षितगुणः स्वात्मापि विश्वेश्वरो,
नैवालं निजवैभवाय तदियं तत्प्रत्यभिज्ञोदिता॥

(ईश्वरप्रत्यभिज्ञाकारिका 4-2)

Kula System

The Kula system was introduced by Śrīmacchandanātha in the beginning of the 5th Century A.D. Later in the 9th Century it was reintroduced by Sumatinātha. In the line of masters from Sumatinātha, Somānanda was his disciple. Śambhunātha was the disciple of Somanātha and the great Abhinavagupta was the disciple of Śambhunātha. This highest thought teaches one how one can live in totality and how can one rise from the lowest degree to the highest degree and all the while experience the nature of one's own self on the same level and state. Śiva, which is realized in Pṛithivī tattva is the same level, the same reality of Śiva which is realized in Śiva tattva. Here there is complete realization in every act of the world. As is said :

एकैकात्रापि तत्त्वेऽपि षट्त्रिंशत्तत्त्वरूपता।

(In any one element you will find all of the thirty six elements.) The essence of this system has been explained in the following verse :–

यत्रोदितमिदं चित्रं विश्वं यत्रास्तमेति च।
तत्कुलं विद्धि सर्वज्ञ शिवशक्तिविवर्जितम्॥

Thus the chief doctrine of this system explains the state of Universal Being (परमशिव) from which the entire universe arises and into which it merges.

Spanda System

The Spanda system, positively speaking, is a double edged

stir, throbbing outwardly and inwardly at one and the same moment. It is purely a spiritual stir and not any physical movement or mental restlessness. It can be explained as the extrovertive and introvertive divine volition of God. Had He not possessed such a throbbing nature He alone would have existed for ever, there would not have been any creation or any dissolution.

The teachings of the Spanda system are found embodied in the Vijñāna Bhairava Tantra, the Svacchanda Tantra and in the 6th chapter of the Tantrāloka.

This system was presented in Kashmir by Śrī Vasugupta-Nātha in the 8th Century. Kṣemarāja, the chief disciple of Śrī Abhinavaguptācārya, in his work, '*Śivasūtra-Vimarśini*', relates that Vasugupta-Nātha invoked Śiva Himself to help him in the disputations with the Buddhists who believed in the negation of the Supreme Self. To him Śiva appeared in a dream and he was ordered and guided by Him to read *Śiva-Sūtras* engraved on a rock at the foot of Mahādeva Mountain which forms a beautiful back drop to this spot. Vasugupta Nātha studied and copied the *Śiva-Sūtras* and by arguments, based on the teachings of these, defeated the Buddhist thinkers in religious discussions.

Krama System

The Krama System does not recognize either the way of the Pratyabhijñā system or of the Kula system. In the Krama system you have to rise step by step in succession. It is primarily concerned with space and time. In the Krama System it is in the end, not in its process, that you are beyond time and space.

The Krama system is attributed to *Śāktopāya* and to the twelve *Kālīs*. The twelve *Kālīs* are said to be the twelve movements of one cognition.

The rise of *Prāṇa Kuṇḍalinī* is also described in the Krama system because in it you rise from one *cakra* to another *cakra*, from one state to another state. As this is a successive process, it is found in the Krama system.

Although the Krama system existed in the beginning of

Kaliyuga having been introduced by the sage Durvāsā, it was reintroduced at the end of the 7th Century A.D. in Kashmir by the sage Erakanātha who was also known as Śivānandanātha.

For attaining the real Transcendental State of Self, Kashmir Śaivism lays down three means (उपाय) namely :– *Ānavopāya, Śāktopāya,* and *Śāmbhavopāya.*

I. *Ānavopāya* is the means concerned with (अणु) the individual soul and the mode of practice by him is to get rid of ignorance (अज्ञान) of his nature. This is the lower form of effort which consists of five ways of :– *Uccāra, Karaṇa, Dhyāna, Varaṇopāsanā* and *Sthānakalpanā.*

उच्चार करणध्यानवर्णस्थानप्रकल्पनः ।
यो भवेत्स समावेशः सम्यगाणव उच्यते ॥

(i) *Uccāra* – When a seeker develops awareness while breathing in and out by adjusting his consciousness with each and every breath.

(ii) *Karaṇa-upāsanā* which is brought into practice through organs of the senses and actions and is conducted in the actual perception of ones' field of activities in daily life. Although this practice is associated with *Śāktopāya,* it is considered to be the chief practice in this *upāya.*

(iii) *Dhyāna* is a practice based on meditation. Here the aspirant concentrates on the Lord as being in the form of a Banana-lotus, the point of concentration being in the centre of the lotus deep inside :–

कदली सम्पुटाकारं सबाह्याभ्यन्तरान्तरम् ।
ईक्षते हृदयान्तस्थं तत्पुष्पमिव तत्त्ववित् ॥

(iv) *Varṇopāsanā* is conducted on Sound (ध्वनि) which comes in hearing at the time of meditation. This *Varṇopāsanā* is chiefly a practice on *Anāhata* and leads one to the realization of the True-nature.

(v) *Sthāna Kalpanā* is a yogic practice in which one directs one's consciousness on some mediating centres in the body like the heart (हृदय), the pit of the throat (कण्ठकूप) or the space between two eyebrows (भ्रूमध्य). The Practice involves simultaneous reciting correctly mantras. It may be mentioned that all these practices of *Ānavopāya* are connected with the practice of *cakrodaya* and particular points of concentration.

II. *Śāktopāya* is a yogic practice of thought only. In this no recitation of *mantras* or breathing exercises are involved :–

उच्चाररहितं वस्तु चेतसैव विचिन्तयन्।

यं समावेशमाप्नोति शाक्तः सोऽत्राभिधीयते॥

The Sādhaka has to concentrate on any super thought like, 'सर्वमहम' = I am all, 'चिद्रूपोऽहम्' = I am all consciousness, आनन्दोऽहम् = I am Transcendental Bliss and so on. This thought must be adjusted in mind with such an awareness that no other thought comes in to break the chain of the awareness of the thought.

There is another practice on the level of *Śāktopāya* which prescribes fixing of one's mind at the time of looking at any two objects, on the points when ones eyes move from one object to another and establish the thought in the centre of these two :–

उभयोर्भावयोर्ज्ञाने ज्ञातमध्यं समाश्रयेत्।

युगपच्च द्वयं त्यक्त्वा मध्ये तत्त्वं प्रकाशते॥

The *Sādhaka* established in this awareness enters in the state of Transcendental Consciousness and passes from duality to unity. It may be borne in mind that practices of *Śāktopāya* are primarily attributed to the Krama system of Śaivism.

III. *Śāmbhavopāya* is a path in which the knowledge of the Ultimate Reality comes through the practice of making one's mind absolutely empty of all thoughts :–

अकिंचिच्चिन्तकस्यैव गुरुणा प्रतिबोधतः।

जायते य समावेशः शाम्भवोऽसावुदीरितः॥

To get well established in this course, three ways have been laid down, namely *Viśvacitpratibimbatvam* (विश्वचित्प्रतिबिम्बत्वम्), *Parāmarśodayakrama* (परामर्शोदयक्रमः), and

Mantrādyabhinnarūpatvam (मन्त्राद्यभिन्नरूपत्वम्).

(i) विश्वचित्प्रतिबिम्बत्वम् – In this the seeker lives in the awareness that the whole Universe, consisting of (वर्णाध्वा, पदाध्वा, मंत्राध्वा, कलाध्वा, तत्त्वाध्वा, भुवनाध्वा) six paths, (अध्वन्) is reflected in the mirror of one's own consciousness (संविद्दर्पण); and by the uninterrupted flow of this awareness, a seeker enters in the Universal Consciousness. He perceives the first flow of all the universal activities which result in *Śāmbhava Samādhi.*

(ii) परामर्शोदयक्रमः – The second way is to understand that the whole field of sounds, words and sentences is nothing but (अनुत्तर) the Supreme Self. To explain, break up sentences into words and let these words in turn be disintegrated into individual sounds where ultimately these merge into the Supreme Transcendental Soundless sound. In this way, by the grace of the Master (सद्गुरु), one's mind is focussed towards the *Śāmbhava* State of Samādhi.

(iii) मंत्राद्यभिन्नरूपत्वम् – The third way in the sphere of *Śāmbhavopāya* is the practice of (पूर्णाहन्ता), the Universal I-Consciousness. Here one has to develop awareness of I-Being in the world of all sounds by living in the first move of every action. By developing this awareness one enters in the Kingdom of *Śāmbhava*-State. These three ways of *Śāmbhavopāya* are associated with the Kula-system of Kashmir Śaivism.

It would not be out of place to mention that the first *Ānavopāya* is called *Kriyopāya,* because it is experienced by such methods as reciting of mantras, regulation of breath, fixation of postures and mediating on some Divine Form. *Śāktopāya* is called *Jñānopāya,* because this is adopting of methods in the cognitive field of means, such as you find in the following assertive awareness :– 'I am 'Śiva', 'I am Bliss', 'I am Transcendental God Consciousness' etc.

The third *upāya, Śāmbhavopāya,* is called *Icchopāya,* as it is attained through Will only. In this *upāya* the seeker lives in the world of first move of all actions and all cognitions. It is meant only for those great souls who have developed their awareness of (चिच्छक्ति) Cit-Consciousness through the kindness of the Master (सद्गुरुः).

There is another higher method above *Śāmbhavopāya* called *Anupāya* – effortless effort or methodless method and is with great reverence named as *Ānanadopāya.* In this state one has to reside in the awareness of Transcendental Bliss........

ततोऽपि परमं ज्ञानमुपायादिविवर्जितम्।
आनन्दशक्तिविश्रान्तमनुत्तरमिहोच्यते ॥

This is meant only for those blessed souls who have already united their individual consciousness with the Universal Consciousness. Just as the poisonous effect of a venomous cobra is transmitted to a person from a distance, in the same way a mere glance of the one who has attained the state of *Anupāya* (अनुपाय समाविष्टः) makes one enter the kingdom of Transcendental Bliss :– "भुजङ्गवद्गरलसंक्रामः"; or just as with an intentional touch of the flame of a candle another candle burns with the same splendour, in the same way the intentional touch of a great yogi residing in the *Anupāya* State sends the seeker into the same state of *Anupāya* without making the least difference between the master and the disciple.

तं ये पश्यन्ति ताद्रूप्यक्रमेणामलसंविदः।
तेऽपि तद्रूपिणस्तावत्येवास्यानुग्रहात्मता ॥
दर्शनात्स्पर्शनाद्वापि विततादभवसागरात्।
तारयिष्यन्ति वीरेन्द्राः कुलाचारप्रतिष्ठिताः ॥

Hence the methodless method of this *Upāya* no doubt bears the imprint immortality. This *Anupāya* should be adjusted in the Pratyabhijñā system of Trika through –

तीर्थे श्वपचगृहे वा नष्टस्मृतिरपि परित्यजन् देहम्।
ज्ञानसमकालमुक्तः कैवल्यं याति हतशोकः ॥

The realized soul may throw off his physical body in a sacred pure shrine or in the house of a very degraded and low caste or while leaving his body may remain in the state of unconsciousness, he is (जीवन्मुक्त) absolutely united in God-Consciousness. Hence these things do not affect him in the least :–

हिमवति गङ्गाद्वारे वाराणस्यां कुरौ प्रयागे वा।
वेश्मनि चाण्डालादेः शिवतत्त्वविदां समं मरणम्॥

* * * *

The Pratyabhijñā System

Sri M.P. Pandit

Admittedly one of the oldest of the religious systems in the Indian sub-continent, Śaivism has come to stay in three recognised forms viz. *Saṭsthala* or the *Vīra Śaiva Siddhānta,* in the Karnatak, *Śaiva Siddhānta* in the southern peninsula and the *Advaita Śaiva* or the *Trika* Doctrine in Kashmir. It is this last system that is the subject of our present study.

Śaivism in Kashmir has been called the *trika* because of the series of triads that are fundamental to that system e.g. *Śiva,* Supreme, *Śakti,* Power, *Nara,* Man; *Śiva,* Lord, *Śakti,* Power, *Aṇu* or *Jīva,* being; *Parā Śakti,* Higher Power, *Aparā,* lower, *Parāparā,* mixed; or the triad of the modes of knowledge: *Bheda,* dual, *Abheda,* non-dual, *Bhedābheda,* dual-non-dual.

The Ultimate Reality, in this Philosophy, is a Supreme, Something higher than which there is nothing, *anuttara.* It is beyond conception, beyond description. But the same Reality as related to Creation, reveals itself as the Transcendent and the Immanent. It is above the Creation, *viśvottīrṇa,* it is also immanent in the Creation, *viśvamaya.* It is a consciousness, pure and supreme, *Cit.* It is called variously as *Parā Samvit, Śiva,*[1] *Paramaśiva.* It is luminous, *prakāśa.* That is not all. The Consciousness is not only self-luminous, but it is equally self-conscious, not only *prakāśa* but also *vimarśa. Cit* is also *caitanya.* It would be like an inert[2] diamond. But it is instinct with *vimarśa,* it is aware of itself, it surveys itself. And what it so surveys as

---

1. In this system, Śiva signifies the Reality, not one of the Gods of the Hindu Trinity.
2. *Yadi nirvimarśaḥ syāt anīśvaro jaḍaśca prasajyeta;* if he had no *vimarśa* then He would be without power, inert. (*Parā Praveśikā*).

itself, it is moved, self-moved to manifest. For that is its nature. This aspect of *vimarśa,* this poise of the *Cit* aware of its existence, is the *Cit-Śakti, Cit* as *Śakti, Cidrūpiṇī śakti.* Thus we conceive the Reality turned towards manifestation as *Parama Śiva,* Consciousness and *Śakti,* Power. The two are not really two, but one in two poises. *Śakti* is *Śiva* in the creative mood. As the Consciousness is Infinite, the Power too is infinite. This Infinite *Śakti* has infinite modes, but of these five are fundamental :

Cit, the power of revelation by which the Consciousness is a glow. In the form of *Cit,* the Supreme is *Śiva.*

Ānanda, the power of the delight, bliss, in the wake of which there comes into operation a perfect freedom, *svātantrya,* to effectuate. In this form, the Supreme is *Śakti.*

Icchā, the Will to manifest. In this form, the Supreme is *Sadāśiva* or *Sādākhya.*

Jñāna, the power to know, know the ordering of the manifestation. In this form, the Supreme is *Īśvara.*

Kriyā, the power to create and assume any form. In this form, the Supreme is *Sadvidyā* or *Śuddha vidyā.*

It is through the operation of these *Śaktis,* the activity of the One *Cit-Śakti,* that the Universe comes to be as a *prasāra,* spread-out, as an *unmeṣa,* opening out of the Supreme. The universe, in this system, is not created. It is an emanation, a putting out of what is already contained in the heart of the Supreme – not indeed in the full-fledged form that we see but in seed-form, in potency, *hṛdaya bījastham viśvametat carācaram.*

This manifestation of the Universe out of the Supreme Reality proceeds through a graded deployment of stresses in this *prakāśa-vimarśamaya Cit,* Consciousness that is self-luminous and self-aware, a series of self-modifications, each modification being termed the *tattva,* Principle, of that order of creation.

In this scheme, the primal stir of the Will to manifest, *spanda,* in the Supreme, the *Parama Śiva,* is the first step. This poise of the Supreme in the creative mood is designated as *Śiva.* In this status it is the Consciousness, *Cit,* that is predominant. The unitive experience in *Parā Śiva* in which the object and the subject (of awareness-experiences) were one and indistinguishable, is now broken up by the negativing *Śakti* (*niṣedha-vyāpara-rūpā*). Due to this operation of the *Śakti* (in the form of *Jñāna śakti*), there is only the awareness of "*I*". The object so negated is again presented to the experience, no doubt, but as a demarcated "This" *vis a vis* the "I".

Once *Śiva* comes into being, i.e. the urge to manifest throbs into a stir, the other side of the *Cit,* the *vimarśa,* the kinetic aspect, comes into its own. There is an ebullitence of Delight followed by a constant affirmation of the self-awareness in the form of existence. The "I" becomes "*I am,*" *aham.* In this stage it is the *Ānanda* aspect that is predominant. This is called the *śakti tattva.*

These two states of *Cit,* it must be noted, are not so much successive as simultaneous.

The next is the stage when there is an affirmation of the Self, the "I" as all "This". "*I am This*", *ahamidam,* the emphasis falling on the "I". This is the *Sadāśiva* or *Sādākhya tattva,* (affirming the *sat,* Existence) where the Will, *Icchā* aspect of *Śakti* is dominant to affirm the *ahantā,* the I-consciousness. The "This" aspect is yet vague. This is known as *nimeṣa,* the state in which the Universe (ideal) is still enclosed within.

Further is the stage where the object or the "This" content of the experience takes fuller shape and calls for emphasis on itself. The experience here is consequently more evocative of "This" which is seen to be "I": "This am I", *idaṁ aham.* This knowledge is the result of the operation of *Jñāna Śakti* which leads at this stage – the stage of *Īśvara tattva,* known as *unmeṣa,* where the Universe is opening out.

Next is the *Sad-vidyā tattva,* where both the "I" and "This" are equally stressed – the stage of transition in which both the subject and the object are distinct and yet one in identity. Both are distinguished, yet they form part of one movement, their relation is one of *bhedābheda.* The experience here is *ahaṁ aham, idaṁ idam* and the *Śakti* dominating at this stage is the *Kriyā śakti.*

So far is the *Śuddha Adhvan,* the Pure or Ideal Way, for in spite of a progressive self-modification of the original unitive experience, the whole movement has been in an Ideal sphere, not actual so as to obscure the true nature of the Reality. There has been no real separation between the "I" and "This" *aham* and *idam,* the subject and the object.[3]

Now begins the *Aśuddha Adhvan,* the Impure Course, in which the Reality is progressively veiled and there is a growing separation between the "I" and "This". This development is brought about by the intervention of *Māyā,* a mode of *Śakti* that measures; to measure, it is indispensable to limit and divide and that is what *Māyā* does. It brings in *saṅkoca,* limitation and the manifestation – both the "I" and the "This" the subject and the object side – is subjected to this process of narrowing, of limitation and therefore of separation of the one from the other. *Māyā* operates by contracting the universal modes of Consciousness active in the Five Tattvas of the Universal Manifestation viz. *Cit, Ānanda, Icchā, Jñāna* and *Kriyā.* Thus:

1. The eternality, *nityatva,* of *Cit* is limited by *Māyā* and the *kañcuka* of Time, *kāla,* temporal determination, ensues.
2. The all-pervasiveness, *vyāpakatva,* of *Ānanda* is limited by *Māyā* and the *kañcuka* of Space, *niyati,* spatial determination, ensues. Included in this is the limitation of the *svātantrya,* freedom, into the law of Causality.
3. The all-completeness, *purṇatva,* of *Icchā,* Will, is limited by *Māyā* and the *kañcuka* of *rāga,* desire, – arising from want – ensues.
4. The all-knowledge, *sarvajñatva,* of *Īśvara* is limited by Māyā and the *kañcuka* of *vidyā,* limited knowledge, ensues.
5. The all-doership, all-powerfulness, *sarva-kartṛtva,* of *Kriyā* is limited by *Māyā* and the *kañcuka* of *kalā,* fragmentation of power and efficacy, ensues.

---

3. These Five are the Tattvas of Universal Experience. Those that follow are the Tattvas of individual experience.

Thus is the manifesting Consciousness subjected to a limitation of Its nature and clothed in the cloaks, *kañcuka,* in which the "I" and "This", the subjective and the objective statuses, the *Śiva* and *Śakti,* emerge as the *Purușha* and the *Prakṛiti. Śiva* comes forth as the *puruṣa,* the individual self-consciousness stationed in every form. His omnipotence, omniscience, amplitude, eternity, omnipresence and freedom – all suffer a diminution as a result of the operation of the *Kañcukas* and he emerges as a limited individual being. Also, what was held together as "I" and "This", two statuses or poises of the One Consciousness, are now – with the incoming of *Māyā* – effectively separated from each other.

Corresponding to the subjective *puruṣa* aspect, is the objective *prakṛti. Puruṣha* is the experiencer and Prakṛiti the experienced.

This, in the *Trika,* constitutes the scheme of creation consisting of 36 Principles or *Tattvas.*

The individual, a product of 36 *tattvas,* a culmination of the long process of increasing obscuration of Reality that is Infinite Consciousness. He has a gross body of the five *māhābhūtas,* a subtle body of eight constituents,[4] the *puryaṣṭaka,* a *prāṇa* dynamism that activates the bodies and at the centre of it all, a Consciousness that forms his self. That self is indeed no other that *Śiva.* But due to the impurities that taint his being, man is ignorant of this truth of his self. The impurity that obscures the truth is of three kinds. The first is the *āṇava mala,* the impurity of limitation which comes to be when the Supreme accepts the will to manifest. In the very act of creation, *Śiva* imposes a self-limitation on his infinity and transcendence and goes into a movement of particularisation, *aṇutva,* atomicity. This is a movement limiting the operation of the *Icchā śakti.* And the effect of *Prakṛiti*[5] is constituted of three *guṇas,* strands, *sattva, rajas* and *tamas,* which are so to say the projections of the

4. *Buddhi, ahaṅkāra, manas* and the five *tanmātraṣ*

5. *Prakṛiti,* in the *Trika,* it is to be noted, is different from the *Prakriti* in the *Sānkhya.* In the latter there is one *Prakriti* with many *Purushas* but in the *Trika,* each *Purusha* has his *Prakriti.*

Śaktis of *Jñāna, Icchā* and *Kriyā.*

Pakṛiti modifies itself, step by step, from the subtle to the less subtle, till it culminates in gross matter, as follows:

a) *Antaḥkaraṇa,* the inner instrument (or apparatus) consisting of *buddhi,* the intelligence that ascertains; *ahaṅkāra,* the egoity that appropriates to itself; *manas,* the faculty of perception and conception.
b) Five powers of sense-perception, *jñānendriyas* viz. – powers of smell, taste, sight, touch and audition.
c) Five powers of action, *karmendriyas* viz. – powers of speech, grasping, locomotion, excretion, procreation.
d) Five subtle elements of perception, the *tanmātras :* sound, touch, colour, flavour, odour.
e) These five *tanmātras* in their turn give rise, in varying combinations of themselves, to the Five Gross Elements, *Pañca Mahābhūtas* of which the Universe is constituted : Ether, Air, Fire, Water, Earth.

This contraction, *saṅkoca,* is termed in this philosophy the *āṇava mala,* impurity of limitation.

The coming of *Śiva* in the belt of *Māyā* (*aśuddha māyā*) gives rise to another type of impurity – *māyic mala;* the limitations imposed by the *kañcukas* and the subsequent adjuncts provided to the *puruṣa,* individual *jīva,* in the form of subtler and gross bodies etc. constitute the *māyā mala.*

A still further impurity that encrusts the true nature of man is the *kārma mala,* the impurity of the *Karma* he forges at every moment of his life.

To get rid of his bondage in Ignorance, man has to dissolve these three impurities. When these veiling layers of *mala* are eliminated, then alone is it possible for his Consciousness to shine in its true lustre. The *Citta* is rolled back into *Cit.* The *jīva* realises he is *Śiva.* That is not all. The realisation broadens itself into the living vision of the whole universe as *Śiva. Cidānanda,* bliss of the real "I" Consciousness is followed and completed by *jagadānanda,* bliss of experiencing the universe as *Śiva* or *Cit.* This is the full content of liberation.

The *Trika* is emphatic that it is not possible for man to achieve this liberation by his own unaided effort. He is bound by three layers of *mala* and while it may be possible to get a practical release from the *kārma mala* and even from the *māyīya mala,* by means of disciplines and austerities, physical, psychological and spiritual, it is impossible for him to get rid of the *āṇava mala.* For this inherent imperfection is not of the soul's choosing like the *kārmic* or born of association with the *upādhis,* adjuncts, like the *māyīya.* The *āṇava mala* is something taken on by Śiva on himself of his own free accord; He has for reasons of Self-manifestation, imposed on his own *Icchā śakti* a diminution, a contraction, and the *āṇava mala* is the inevitable result. Consequently he alone can remove the *mala* that he has taken on. That is why it is *Śiva,* it is his *anugraha,* Grace, that alone can effect the radical release from the *āṇava pāśa.* The flow of his Grace is called, in this *Śāstra, śaktipāta* – Descent of Grace.

Grace knows no law. It effects in a trice what appears to be impossible or involving long effort. But there are gradations in the Impact of Grace. In those in whom it descends in full measure, the liberation is instantaneous; in those who receive it moderately, the process is quickened and the progress ensured; in those who receive it least, there is effected an awakening and a start made on the journey Home of the soul.

Grace is one side of the truth. The other side consists of a certain preparation, a measure of equipment to bear the Descent and embody it. The Śāstra has four *upāyas,* means, for the purpose. We may describe them briefly under the following heads :

Ānanda upāya : A very rare but possible way in which the impact of the *śakti-pāta* is so massive and intense that there is a flood of bliss accompanied by a radical elimination of all impurities.

Āṇava upāya : A means where personal effort, *puruṣakāra,* plays a predominant part. The body, the *prāṇa* and the mind are worked upon by prescribed methods of discipline and subjected to courses of purification, and reorientation of their energies.

Sākta upāya : This proceeds on more mental and psychological lines aimed at the mergence of the individual consciousness in the Supreme Consciousness, *samāveṣa.*[6] It is also called *Jñānopāya* because here the effort is through a replacement of lower and imperfect knowledge by a progressively fuller and truer knowledge – *pratibhā jñāna.*

Sāmbhava upāya : This is meant for a smaller category of seekers, those who proceed mainly through *vicāra* and *dhyāna,* enquiry and meditation. The *Madhya* to be attained there is the Pure I-Consciousness, *akṛtrima aham.* The *sādhanā* begins with the discipline of meditation on the *Pañca Kṛtya* and proceeds through the practice of *Vikalpa Kṣaya.*

Pañca Kṛtya is the Five-fold act of Śiva which is reflected in the individual. Even as Śiva is constantly engaged in the five acts of Creation, Maintenance, Withdrawal, Concealment and Grace, the individual creature too is occupied in the fivefold act of (1) perception of an object, *sṛṣṭi,* (2) retention of what is perceived, *stithi* (3) enjoyment of its *rasa, samhāra* – during which the object is absorbed as it were in the consciousness (4) rising of the impression even after the object is removed, *vilaya,* having the effect of concealment or obscuration of pure consciousness, (5) complete absorption of the object into the original *Cit, anugraha.* By constantly observing this activity in oneself with the background of Śiva and his Fivefold Act, the consciousness is gradually processed into higher and higher forms till it is sublimated into pure *Cit.*

The other method is of *Vikalpa kṣaya.* The mind is always full of thoughts, ideas, mentations of all kinds. The practice recommended is to relax the mind, to cease to think of anything, but all the while keeping the awareness. A more positive way is

6. One of the means adopted towards this end is *śakti saṅkoca* and *śakti vikāsa.* The Consciousness that is normally turned outward and darts at objects through the senses is repeatedly drawn back and turned within towards the Self. This is *saṅkoca. Vikāsa* is when the consciousnes is firmly held within, concentrated upon the Self, though the senses are allowed their customary activity.

to concentrate within the heart and vigilantly keep out every *vikalpa,* till the mind grows into a condition of natural thought-less-ness, a condition in which the Self, the *Madhya,* the Supreme Consciousness, would emerge and come into its own. In some cases the Guru awakens, by his *dīkṣā,* the *nirvikalpa* Knowledge – the Knowledge in which there is no mental activity, the *vikalpas* are destroyed and the union takes place with the Higher Consciousness.

Whatever the method or methods, the aspirant passes through a series of statuses corresponding to the extent of the impurity eliminated and to the state of the consciousness attained. The ordinary *jīva,* for instance, is subject to the three *malas:* he is *sakala.* One who succeeds in removing from himself the *kārma mala* is called the *pralayākala;* he is still subject to *māyīya mala* and the *āṇava mala.* He who passes beyond the belt of *Māyā* and is free from the *māyīya mala* is called the *vijñānākala.* He is still tainted with the *āṇava mala;* his position is above the *aśuddha māyā* but below the *Śuddha Vidyā.* The atomicity, *āṇava mala,* is shed step by step as the *jīva* crosses from one *tattva* to another in the manifestation of the *Śuddha Māyā,* in the measure in which the distinction (ideal though it be) between the *aham* and *idam* gradually gives way to complete absorption in *pūrnāhantā,* the Full "I" ness.

He is the *Manta,* in the *Śuddha Vidyā tattva,* who experiences no doubt a distinct diversity but all in a Unity of the Self. In the *Īśvara tattva,* he is *Mantreśvara* to whom the Universe is as distinct as the Self and yet is identical with the Self. In the *Sadāśiva Tattva,* he is *Mantra Maheśvara* who experiences everywhere "I am This" with a stress on the "I" aspect of the truth. The Universe is there but only as my Being. Higher than that is the highest, the *Śiva Pramātā* – the state of Consciousness where all is not one with Śiva, but *is* Śiva. Some authorities, however, hold that after the *Mantra Maheśvara* are statuses of *Śāktya* and *Śāmbhava.*

* * * *

Pañcabhūtas in Saiva Rituals
(with Special Reference to Bhūta Śuddhi)

Dr. S.S. Janaki

The correspondence between the microcosm and the macrocosm worked out and utilised for esoteric and spiritual purposes is much prevalent in the Śaivite system, as in others. These ideas ranging from the gross to the subtle and the supreme aspects and levels are pointed out and explained in the concept of a (i) Śiva temple with its different parts like *gopura, vimāna, dhvajastambha,* and *garbhagṛha;* (ii) the *Śiva liṅga;* (iii) the rituals and (iv) the human being. There is a fund of information on the subject that can be gleaned through the Śaiva Āgamic texts, Purāṇas and Stotras. Some highlights of such correlations from the viewpoint of five elements are now presented mainly as given in the *Kriyākramadyotikā* (K.K.D.) of *Aghoraśivācārya* (also called the *Aghoraśivācārya Paddhati)* written in 12th century and commented by Nirmalamaṇi Deśika from Tiruvārūr. This is an authentic text followed by Śaivites in Tamil Nadu even now.

Before taking up the topic of the correlations from the viewpoint of five elements at different levels between human being and *Śivaliṅga,* it should be noted that some Purāṇic texts consider even the many holy *kṣetras* in different parts of India as corresponding to *cakras* like *Mūlādhāra, Svādhiṣṭhāna* and *Ājñā* or the five elements. Thus according to the *Sūta Saṃhitā (Jñānayoga khaṇḍa,* 11.50 -1) the basical *Mūlādhāra cakra* near the naval region is *Kamalālaya* or *Tiruvārūr* in Tanjore District *(ādhārah Kamalālayah), Anāhata* at the heart is Chidambaram *(Cidambaram ca hṛnmadhye),* and the *Ājñā* between the eyebrows is Vārāṇasī *(Vārāṇasī ca mahāprājña bhruvor ghrāṇasya madhyame).* The principle behind such a description is that the temples in *Kṣetras* in different parts of India symbolise and concretise certain *upāsanās* or *vidyās* mentioned in the Upaniṣads, local *sthalapurāṇas* and reiterated in the verses, songs of devotees like *Āḷwārs, Nāyanmārs, Tyāgarāja* and *Muttuswāmi Dīkshitar.*

Again, following the same principle, the five elements are traditionally considered as being geographically represented in five important temples in Tamilnadu. Thus 'earth' is associated with *Kāñcī,* 'water' with *Tiruvānaikovil,* 'fire' with *Tiruvaṇṇāmalai,* 'wind' with *Kālahasti* and 'ether' with *Chidambaram.* The *Pṛthvī liṅga* at *Kāñcī* is Lord *Ekāmreśvara* for worshipping whom Goddess *Kāmākṣhī* is said to have carved out a *liṅga* out of mud. The *Āpliṅga* is *Śrī Jambukeśvara* at *Tiruvānaikkōvil* near Trichinopoly; here the *liṅga* is found always in the water. The *Jyotirliṅga* at Tiruvannamalai in North Arcot district is well known. This place is considered so holy that even the very thought of Thiruvannamalai is supposed to lead definitely to salvation *(smaraṇād kaivalyapradam,* as said by Muthuswami Dikshita). The *Vāyuliṅga* is Lord *Kālahastīśvara* at Kālahasti, approximately 150 kms. from Chennai on the way to Tirupati. It is said that out of the two lamps in the sanctum sanctorum in this temple, the upper one seems to flicker as if under the influence of wind.

We saw above that the whole of India was thought of as a macro representation of the all-pervasive Supreme and five or six centres therein were recognised as the *cakras* in His body. In a smaller compass, five temples in Tamilnadu were seen as corresponding to the five elements. In a still narrower conceptualisation in the very precincts of the *Tyāgarājasvāmi* temple at Tiruvārūr, there are five *liṅgas* said to represent the five elements. They are respectively *Śrīvalmīkaliṅga, Hāṭhakeśvara, Sadācaleśvara, Siddhīśvara* and *Ānandeśvara.*

From these rather vague traditional ideas we can now move on to the integral association of the five elements in the matrix of Śaivite concepts of ritualistic action (*kriyā*) like the daily *pūjā,* the significance of which could be understood through the

Āgamic philosophy *(jñāna, vidyā* or *tattva)*. The Śaiva āgamas impress upon the necessity of a Śaivite to be conversant with both *kriyā* and *jñāna* aspects so that he can reach the highest goal of obtaining equality with Śiva *(śivattva)*. The fact that the individual to be liberated *(pásu)* from the worldly bondage as constituted of five elements, is seen as parallel with the lord Śiva *(pati)* as represented in the *Śivaliṅga,* in more than one way.

The rituals are performed either at home in a special pūjā room or at the temple. In either case, the entire ritual domain is to be transformed into a suitably pure condition. Of such purifications five are important. They are – the purification of the self *(ātmā),* of the place *(sthāna),* of the *mantras,* of the *liṅga* and of the substances *(dravya)* to be offered. In this paper we are concerned only with the *ātmaśuddhi,* as dealt with in *Kriyākramadyotikā*. Its procedural details in the main, are as follows –

1. Sitting in a comfortable posture the Śaivite protects the place of worship by creating a wall with *Astra (Om haḥ astrāya phaṭ)* and *Kavaca (Om haim kavacāya hum) mantras* around it.
2. He first imposes the five *brahmāṅga mantras* on the five fingers in both the hands.

   Thumb – *Om hōm Īśānamūrdhāya namaḥ*
   Pointer – *Om hem Tatpuruṣa-Vaktrāya namaḥ*
   Middle – *Om hum Aghora-hṛdayāya namaḥ*
   Ring – *Om him Vāmadeva-guhyāya namaḥ*
   Little – *Om ham sadyojāta-murtaye namaḥ*

   By the imposition of the above *mantras* related to five faces of Śiva and his five limbs, on the five fingers in both the hands, the hands are now transformed into Śiva *(Śivīkaraṇa).* They become capable of performing all subsequent rites.
3. To engender *Śivatva* in the subtle and gross bodies of the Śaivite *Bhūtaśuddhi* is to be performed. In order to do this he imagines that the *suṣumnā,* starting as two branches from the toes and continuing as such till the *mūlādhāra,* combines

as a single channel till the *Brahmarandhra.* At the regions of heart, throat, forehead etc. the *Suṣumnā* runs parallel with *Iḍā* on the left and *piṅgalā* on the right, both of them going till the nostril. From heart onwards the *Suṣumnā* is to be specially conceived as a long tubular column and with a lotus-bud turned down. Inside and outside of *Suṣumnā* is to be visualised as the supreme *Kuṇḍalinī śakti* presiding over the subtle ethereal region and spilling flows of nectar. The blazing *Śikhā bīja* of *'Hūm'* is to be imagined as located between the *Śakti* and *Suṣumnā.* Under these circumstances *Pūraka* and *Kumbhaka* are to be practised, concentrating on *'Hūm'* syllable at the level of consciousness. At this point the *prāṇa* as *Vāyu* moves upward till the *dvādaśānt* level outside. Thus the impure *vāyu* is thrown out. Incidentally by the repeated pronunciation of *"hum phaṭ"* the knots at the lotus-cakras at the heart, throat, inside the cheek, between the eye-brows and *brahmarandhra,* are said to be opened out.

Nirmalamaṇs's commentary *Prabhā* adds a critical note here that the respective lotuses at heart, throat etc. that were originally only buds turned inward, blossom fully due to *Pūraka.* They are then restrained by *Kumbhaka* and ultimately become upturned by the up-going *vāyu.*

Now the inner Supreme Being is meditated upon as located in the subtle body in the heart-lotus and dazzlingly brilliant. The *mantra 'Om hūm hām ham hām hūm ātmane namaḥ'* is recited with the necessary inhaling, collecting and exhaling of air. The *Saṃhāra mudrā* of the right hand is also shown as moving from *mūlādhāra* to the vacant space above the head, showing the free upward movement of the *ātmā* (in the form of *nāda*) along with *Kuṇḍalinī Śakti* smoothly through the respective *cakras* and uniting finally with Śiva at the *Dvādaśānta* level (K.K.D. p.57).

He meditates that his soul, now embodied in the syllable '*Ham*' and located on the crown of the syllable *Hūm* is separated from the subtle body and transmuted into *bindu,* becoming subtle, unitary and free of all defects. This sort of visualisation is to be understood from the arrangement of the *ātma mantra* as follows –

Om Hūm hām ham hām hūm ātmane namaḥ

In the above string of *mantra* – syllables, the central *'ham'* stands for *'ātman'*. It is encased *(samputita)* first by *'hām'* on either side, *hām* being the *hṛdaya* syllable; it is further emboxed between the outer two *śikhā* syllables, *hūm*.

4. In the next phase the subtle body made up of eight constituents *(puryaṣṭaka)* namely the five *tanmātras* of *śabda, sparśa, rūpa, rasa* and *gandha,* along with *buddhi, manas* and *ahaṁkāra,* is to be purified in order that the *ātmā* can be reinstated in it. This is performed by the 36 *tattvas* that constitute the body, visualised as getting back to and merging with their associate sources in the reversal order.

Accordingly, he should visualise earth reabsorbed into odour, water into taste, fire into form, wind into touch, ether into sound and these perceptible qualities *(tanmātras)* into the inert aspect of the Ego. He visualizes the active faculties known as Mouth, Foot, Hand, Anus, and Penis reabsorbed into the animate aspect of the Ego, and the faculties of knowledge called Ear, Skin, Eye, Tongue, Nose, and Mind *(manas)* into the wholesome aspect of the Ego. He visualizes the Ego reabsorbed into the Intellect *(buddhi),* that into the Qualities *(guṇas),* and the Qualities into *prakṛti. Prakṛti* along with *rāga* and *vidyā* are reabsorbed into *kalā*. Then he visualizes *puruṣa, kalā,* and *niyati,* as well as *kāla,* reabsorbed into *māyā*.

He then visualizes the *śuddhavidyā* reabsorbed into *Īśvara,* that into *Sadāśiva,* that into *Śakti,* that into *Śiva,* and finally that into the undisturbed *bindu*.

For the visualisation of this ritual it will be useful to refer to the following clarifications of the above process by *Nirmalamaṇi* in his *Prabhā* –

Firstly, the subtle body here referred to is to be identified with the 36 differentiated *tattvas* dispersed throughout the body.

Secondly, in their differentiated states these tattvas are inherently impure. Sattvas at the lower levels should ultimately be reabsorbed into the two undifferentiated sources, *māyā* and

Mahāmāyā (or *bindu*). This purity exists in final absorption.

Thus the śaivite is able to remove a large part of the impurities of the gross body, the *bhūta śarīra.* As explained in the *Prabhā* the *bhūtaśarīra,* an invariable assemblege of the five elements, is what, constitutes the individual as a human being in this world, asociated with name, form, family background etc. Their purification consists firstly in the formal recognition of their characteristics, shape, nature, presiding divinity, *kalā, maṇḍala* etc. These details are as follows :–

Element	*Pṛthvī*	*Ap*	*Tejas*	*Vāyu*	*Ākāśa*
Colour	yellow	while	red	dark	crystal white
Form	square	half-moon	triangle	hexagon	circle
Mark	vajra	lotus	svastika	six points	bindu śakti
Bīja-mantra	*hlām*	*hvīm*	*hrūm*	*hyaim*	*haum*
Kalā	*nivṛtti*	*pratiṣṭhā*	*vidyā*	*śānti*	*śāntyatīta*
Presiding deity	*sadyojāta*	*vāmadeva*	*aghora*	*tatpuruṣa*	*īśāna*
Kāraṇe-śvara	*brahmā*	*viṣṇu*	*rudra*	*īśvara*	*sadāśiva*
Svabhāva	hard	fluid	hot	mobile	void

Of the five elements Ether is all-pervasive and cannot be contained by anything else. Earth and Wind, Water and Fire are opposed to each other in many features. Therefore, the *guṇas* of Earth, for example, like hardness and smell, are considered to have been nullified by conceiving them properly in a yogic-māntric manner so that Earth is recognised as though it has got the nature of Wind.

– *Prabhā* p.69

Similarly water is conceived as having undergone changes so as to be endowed with the features of Fire. Of course, this *bhāvanā* is possible only by the yogic ways of *pūraka* and upward *recaka* through *Suṣumnā* with the necessary *mantra*-recitation. For example, in the case of *Pṛthvī* the *mantra* (ओं ह्लां ह्लां ह्लां ह्लां ह्लां निवृत्तिकलायै हः हुंफरट. K.K.D. pp. 57-8) relating it to the *Nivṛtti kalā* is uttered five times along with the Yogic process, in order to get rid of the five *guṇas* of *Pṛthvī,* namely *gandha, rasa, rūpa, sparśa* and *śabda.* Only then it is possible to imagine that the element *pṛthvī* is of the nature of *Vāyu.*

Each *udghāta* or upward *recaka* involves three *prāṇāyāmas.* Hence 15 *prāṇāyāmas* are to be performed for *Pṛthvī,* 12 for *Vāyu,* 9 for *Agni,* 6 for Water and 3 for Ether. (*Prabhā* p. 69)

Now the elements in the body having lost their full capacities, their remnant defects are burnt by the fire emanating from the toes *(Pādāṅguṣṭhotthitena agninā)* and with the recitation of *Astra mantra.*

By these varied methods, the gross and subtle bodies are converted into a māntric build, worthy of containing within their ethereal cavity, the Supreme Śiva. The *Ātmā* in the form of *Nāda,* that was taken above the head in phase I is now brought back to the heart-lotus by *Pūraka* along with the recitation of *Praṇava.* It is now reinstated in the form of a dazzling light. Its ablution is performed by the flowing nectar as a result of the vibration caused to *Niṣkala Śiva.* This is shown by the constant recitation of the *mantra* – *Om hauṁ Śaktaye vauṣaṭ.*

(K.K.D. p. 59; *Prabhā* pp. 75-6)

* * * *

The Word in Abhinavagupta's Bṛhad-Vimarśinī[1]

Prof. Raffaele Torella

The speculations on the nature of the word are indeed one of the threads that unite the diverse aspects of Abhinavagupta's vast work – aspects so diverse from each other that they have made some scholars think of a temporal division of phases (aesthetic, religious, philosophical), which seems to me hardly to correspond to the facts. All these trends coexist at the same time and nourish each other. One may only think that Abhinavaguta sees a hierarchy in them, but it is always a hierarchy projected into an all-encompassing totality, such as that of the *paramādvaita,* which makes any single highest level provisional.

Besides being one of the possible centres of Abhinavagupta's doctrine, the speculations on *vāc* also are one of the main intersection points of the religious and philosophical traditions that nourish his teaching. In the Śaiva scriptures, in the Buddhist *pramāṇa* tradition and in Bhartṛhri's work, the word, in its manifold aspects, holds a prominent position. Generally speaking, the tantras of all tendencies deal with the nature of *vāc* and its manifestations. It is probably the weight given to *mantra* by all these texts – however different they may be in tendency and

1. Earlier versions of this paper were read at the Institut für Indologie, University of Vienna; All Souls' College, University of Oxford; Section de langues et Civilisations Orientales, University of Lausanne. I thank the colleagues participating in the lectures (among them, Professors G. Oberhammer, A. Sanderson and J. Bronkhorst) for their interesting remarks. In particular, I would like to express my gratitude to the colleagues and friends Professor Ernst Steinkellner and Dr. Helmut Krasser for their valuable help in clarifying some Buddhist positions and identifying some quotations.

ideology – that firstly induces them to delve into the essence of sound and the word, in order to provide yogic and ritual practices with a theoretical framework. These speculations are connected in some way with the speculations and myths on *vāc* in the Vedas and the Brāhmaṇas and mainly concern three points: *vāc* seen as a sometimes supreme sometimes subordinate creative deity; its stages of manifestation; its relation to the mind and cognitive activity. A partly distinct trend – this too largely present in the tantras of all tendencies – is represented by the speculations on the phonemes, which are seen as the paradigmatic forms of the principles that constitute the universe. In their highest reality they form the very body of *vāc*. This trend also gives rise to reflections of a mystical-philosophical order, for the most part firmly grounded in phonetical doctrine. In this case, too, one can glimpse a yogic and ritual background; let us think of the very old practices of the imposition of phonemes or syllables (*bīja*) on the various parts of the adept's body or on maṇḍalas. In this ambit one can notice the sign of an identification of the phoneme with its grapheme which grammatical thought usually keeps rigorously separate and distinct. It is ritual that succeeds in dignifying writing in such a markedly oral cultural universe. Even though the speculations on *vāc* can be found, generally speaking, in all the scriptures that may be defined 'tantric', the tradition which Abhinavagupta more directly refers to, namely the Bhairavatantras, and in particular the Kula and Trika tantras, differs from the others as regards the greater importance and extension these speculations have in the structure of the text and, above all, as regards the diverse evaluation of the role of *vāc*.

A sign of the difference in attitude, within the Śaiva ambit, between the *advaita* tradition and the Śaivasiddhānta is furnished by the ontological level attributed to the elements that constitute the so-called six 'paths' (*adhvan*). Abhinavagupta and his followers refer to a first differentiation between signifier and signified (*vācaka, vācya; vācaka* are phonemes, mantras and *padas, vācya* are *kalās,* principles and worlds) and asign supremacy to the *vācaka,* and within it to the phonemes. This position is basically shared by the Pāñcarātra tradition[2]. On the contrary, the Siddhāntin usually assigns supremacy to the *vācya* or *artha* side, and within it to the *kalās*[3]. In some cases (Brunner 1977: XVII), the three *vācaka* or *śabda* paths are even absorbed into the path of the worlds (the lowest path for the Kāśmīrian *advaita*)[4]. In the 'realist' outlook of the Śaivasiddhānta the word is finally only an instrument having its ontological centre of gravity in meaning, in the thing expressed[5], which indirectly belittles the expressive aspect and has as a consequence that the word principle itself cannot ascend in the hierarchy of the *tattvas* beyond a certain level. It is known, indeed, that in the Śaivasiddhānta doctrine *vāc,* even in its highest form, belongs to the sphere of the *bindu,* separate from Consciousness. As Rāmakaṇṭha says in *Nādakārikā* 18 (Filliozat Ed.),

> *seyam avasthā kaiścit padavidbhir varṇyate kriyāśakteḥ /*
> *iha punar anyaivoktā puruṣāsamavāyinī ca yasmāt //*

---

2. See for example *sātvatasaṃhitā* XIX. 127-138 and *Lakṣmītantra* XXII. 10-11ab. They list the *adhvans* in the same hierachical order (*varṇa, kalā, tattva, mantra, pada* and *bhuvana*), which is different from the Kāśmīrian Advaitin's (also as regards the meaning of *kalā* and *pada*), but significantly also assignes the first and last positions to *varṇa* and *bhuvana* respectively. Cf. also the explicit statement found in *Lakṣmītantra* XVIII. 21-22ab. (see below n. 5). Cf. Dvivedi 1982:18-19.
3. Cf. e.g. *Ratnatrayaparīkṣā* 87 cd-88ab *tattvādhvā bhuvanādhvā ca varṇādhvā ca padātmakaḥ // mantrādhvā vyāpakas teṣāṃ kalādhvā bindum āśritaḥ/.*
4. The *Svacchandatantra* and its commentary by Kṣemarāja furnish an interesting example of the two doctrines facing each other. The tantra, whch is in many aspects close to the Śaivasiddhānta, presents in straightforward terms a Siddhānta-like doctrine: IV. 95cd-97ab *bhuvanavyāptitā tattveṣv anantādiśivāntake // vyāpakāni ca ṣaṭtriṃśat mantravarṇa-padātmakāḥ / tattvāntarbhāvinaḥ sarve vācyavācakayogataḥ // kalāntarbhāvinas te vai nivṛttyādyāś ca tāḥ smṛtāḥ.* Kṣemarāja, for his part, totally disregarding the unequivocal text, simply goes on to give a detailed account of the matter according to the advaitin outlook.
5. Or, at least, it belongs to a lower stratum of the cognition process. On the diametrically opposite side stand texts like the already cited *Lakṣmītantra* XVIII. 21-22ab *śabdodayapuraskāraḥ sarvatrārthodayaḥ smṛtaḥ / arthaśabdapravṛttyatmā śabdasya sthūlatā hi sā // bodhonmeṣaḥ smṛtaḥ śabdaḥ śabdonmeṣo 'rtha ucyate/.*

"Some grammarians describe this Word as a mode of being of Kriyāśakti. In our system, on the contrary, the Word is considered as being different from Kriyāśakti since it [the Word] is not inherent in the soul".

And again (20a): *puṃśakter bhinnā* "[the Word] is distinct from the power of the soul (or, in Aghoraśiva's interpretation: "distinct from each soul and its power"). A very similar statement is to be found in the *Ratnatrayaparīkṣā:* after giving an account of the four levels of the word upheld by the *śabdabrahmavādins* (so called by Aghoraśiva in the *Ullekhinī* thereon) by quoting the famous passage incorporated into the *Vākyapadīya* (VP), Śrīkaṇṭha sharply distinguishes the 'sun' of the *śabdabrahman* from the real 'sun' of the Lord (78cd-80)[6].

The position of the Śaiva *advaita* scriptures is very different. It is true that we cannot expect diffuse theoretical elaborations from them, but what can be gathered from their usually scanty indications is enough to show, first of all, a full awareness of the power of the word. The phonemes are often presented as sometimes terrific sometimes benevolent deities, able to liberate man as well as to enmesh him in the *saṃsāra.* The word permeates knowledge and, consequently, the objects of knowledge. In its highest form the word is identified with supreme consciousness itself. As Abhinavagupta says in the *Īśvarapratyabhijñāvivṛtivimarśinī* (ĪPVV) against the grammarians, to the extent that they seem to identify the totality of the word with that which is only one of its levels of manifestation: "For us, the totality of sounds is the supreme Lord himself, the goddess Mātṛkā [or the alphabet in the usual sequence] – both distinct and not distinct [from Him] – is His Power, the eight alphabetic classes are the eight Powers of the Rudras, the fifty phonemes are the fifty Powers of the Rudras"[7].

---

6. Cf. Aghoraśiva's commentary on 80cd *tām eva vāṇīṃ sūkṣmākhyām āhur ātmavido janāḥ: ātmasvarūpavidas tu śaivās tāṃ sūkṣmākhyāṃ bindukāryabhūtāṃ śabdavṛttim eva manyante, na tu puruṣasamavāyinīm.*

7. II pp. 195-196 *iha tāvat parameśvaraḥ śabdarāśiḥ, śaktir asya bhinnābhinnarūpāmātṛkādevī, vargāṣṭakaṃ rudraśaktyaṣṭakaṃ pañcāśad rudraśaktayaḥ.*

The other source from which Abhinavagupta receives the doctrine of the all-encompassing nature of *vāc,* this time profoundly and originally elaborated, is represented, as we said, by Bhartṛhari's work. Thus, Abhinavagupta's ideas on the word turn out to be the elaboration of two distinct components: the esoteric one, deriving from the Śaiva scriptures, and the linguistic-philosophical one, deriving from Bhartṛhari's teaching, which, however, also includes a scriptural and esoteric layer and, in turn, comes to be the source, many later scriptures refer to. An interesting example of the merging of these two different traditions and their terminologies may be found in a passage from the *Tantrāloka* (TĀ XI. 71ff). I can summarize it – along with Jayaratha's comments – as follows. The phonemes of ordinary language are generated by non-*māyic* phonemes, independent of conventions. The latter constitute the power of the *māyic* ones and are in turn, so-to-speak, the essence of consciousness itself. When you hear a sentence pronounced by another person, you cannot understand it if your consciousness (*pramā*) is 'covered' (*āvriyate*). You can repeat the phonemes in their order, but you cannot understand the meaning. To understand the meaning, you have to gain possession of your won *pramā,* which depends in turn on the obtainment of your own freedom, i.e. 'agency' (*svātantrya, kartṛtā*). If you experience this awakening of *pramā* (*pramāprabodha, pratibhā*), you will obtain the agency not only as regards the understanding of others' sentences but also regarding the creation of your own sentences. There is a gradation of *pratibhā* ('intuition', 'insight') depending on how much conventions are made to revert to their sources, till they attain the plane of the original (i.e. non-māyic) phonemes, which are, as we have seen, the very essence of consciousness. These various degrees range from the understanding-production of ordinary sentences to the elaboration of *śāstras,* etc. Thus, understanding and producing sentences are the two sides of a coin. He who rests in this *pratibhā* becomes proficient in poetry and eloquence; he who proceeds even farther on, reaching the height of supreme consciousness, obtains *sarvajñāna* and *sarvakriyā.*

The scriptural and Bhartṛharian components are refined, made more explicit and deepened through the scrutiny of Dharmakīrti's criticism, which is always carefully and respectfully evaluated.

This paper proposes to examine some relevant points in the ĪPVV. The first concerns the levels of the word, which is a topic of central importance in the ambit of the speculations on *vāc*. Abhinavagupta dwells on this theme – and at even a greater length – also in other works, particuularly in the *Parātriṃśikāvivaraṇa* and TĀ. But, in my opinion, the treatment in the ĪPVV has some motives of special interest. As is known, the ĪPVV, also called *Bṛhadvimarśinī,* is the commentary that Abhinavagupta devoted to the *Īśvarapratyabhijñāṭīkā* or *vivṛti,* a fundamental work by Utpaladeva, unfortunately now almost totally lost, which in turn commented on the *Īśvarapratyabhijñākārikā* (ĪPK) and *svavṛtti*. Due to its very nature, the ĪPVV allows us to glimpse, through Abhinavagupta's discourse, the original position of Utpaladeva and, in most cases, also that of Somānanda which Abhinavagupta continuously refers to (indeed, just like Utpaladeva, Abhinavagupta too wrote a commentary on the *Śivadṛṣṭi,* the *Ālocana* now lost). This puts us in the best position to grasp the different evaluation of Bhartṛhari's teaching given by Somānanda, on the one hand, and by Utpaladeva-Abhinavagupta, on the other. In saying 'Utpaladeva-Abhinavagupta' I implicitly say that a scrutiny of this section of the ĪPVV as well as of others enables us to shift the centre of gravity of the Pratyabhijñā doctrines towards Utpaladeva. Most of the times Abhinavagupta has more precisely the merit of having elaborated and made explicit what had its first formulation in the *ṭīkā*.

In verse I.5.13 of the *Īśvarapratyabhijñākārikā* Utpaladeva mentions for the first (and last) time Parā Vāc, identifying it with the very Power of the Lord: "Consciousness has as its essential nature reflective awareness; it is the supreme Word that arises freely. It is freedom in the absolute sense, the sovereignty of the supreme Self" (Torella 1994: 120). Abhinavagupta (ĪPVV II p. 187) hastens to make an obvious distinction, which however must not have seemed so obvious to Somānanda if he insisted so much on it in the *Śivadṛṣṭi*. Here it is not a question of *vāc* as the faculty of articulating sounds or as the sounds thus produced, such as the language of men, but rather of the power presiding over this activity (Utpaladeva in the *ṭīkā,* speaks of *vākśakti*) and corresponding to the very agent subjectivity of the Lord in the form of *vimarśa* 'reflective awareness'. If the body of the Lord is made of mantras – above all, the mantra par excellence AHAṂ 'I' – the word is where all the mantras arise, remain in existence and dissolve. In short, this is not *śabda* but *śabdana* 'power of verbalization, of symbolization', which makes reflective awareness possible and even constitutes its very essence. After establishing that the verse refers to the supreme plane of *vāc* (*ādyā vāc* in the *vṛtti*), the *ṭīkā* goes on to describe the phases, beginning with the last one, represented precisely by the vocal faculty, the tongue and sounds and words it produces.

On this plane there are further differentiations, first and foremost, between a word fully accomplished in its sonority (*saghoṣa*) and one pronounced in a low voice, secretly (*aghoṣa*)[8]. Both are fully articulated; what distinguishes them is the fact that the former can be heard by others and the latter cannot. The sense of hearing here plays the role of protagonist. This role progressively loses importance as the complexity of what is articulated increases: we go from the phoneme to the short word and, lastly, to the long sentence where hearing has to be integrated with other functions, such as memory, connection of distant segments, and so on, all of them being equally necessary for understanding to emerge. This is the plane of Vaikharī, the word 'which lies in the body' according to a traditional etymology. The next plane is that of the word as a mental event. Here the word is still articulated, comes about in succession and acts as the substratum of the various forms of discursive thought (*vikalpa*). We have *Madhyamā,* says Abhinavagupta ibid., when the internal faculty – that is, the mind, the intellect and the sense of the ego –

8. Cf. *Svacchandatantra* II. 146cd-147ab *ātmanā śrūyate yas tu tam upāṃśuṃ vijānate // pare śṛṇvanti yaṃ devi saśabdaḥ sa udāhṛtaḥ /* (*Uddyota* thereon; *upāṃśusaśabdau tu sūkṣmasthūlaprayatnāyāṃ vaikharyām*).

is acting and brings about discursive thought in the form of imagination, deliberation and ego-reference. It is called *Madhyamā* because the power of reflective awareness, which is its very essence, here impels the internal faculty which rests precisely in the intermediate plane (*madhyabhūmi*), that of the octuple body (*puryaṣṭaka*) and the vital energy or breath. This level of the word refers to a reality divided into subject and object (of this discursive thought), grasps it and expresses it in an internal language which is as diversified and successive as the content being expressed. It is defined by the term *cintana* 'thinking, deliberating'.

Up to this point the relation with Bhartṛhari has no problematic aspects. Abhinavagupta and Utpaladeva do follow the treatment found in the VP and the *vṛtti,* only they enrich it and adapt it to the schemes and terminology of the Pratyabhijñā. The crucial point comes with Paśyantī, not so much concerning its description as concerning the claim that it constitutes the highest level. Bhartṛhari is generally considered the upholder of the tripartition of the word, explicitly stated in verse I.159 of the VP, while the Śaiva tradition decidedly leans towards the quadripartition. As is well-known, this is the main cause of Somānanda's fierce criticism in the *Śivadṛṣṭi.* In fact, things are more complex than they may seem. In the Brahmanic tradition, which Bhartṛhari refers to, there are traces of both a quadripartite system (cf. the famous passages from the *Ṛgveda catvā́ri vā́k párimitā padā́ni* ... and *catvā́ri śṛ́ṅgā* ...[9],

9. *Ṛgveda* I.164.45 *catvā́ri vā́k párimitā padā́ni tā́ni vidur brāhmaṇā́ ye manīṣíṇaḥ / gúhātrī́ṇi níhitā néṅgayanti turī́yaṃ vācó manuṣyā̀ vadanti //.* *Ṛgveda* IV. 58.3 *catvā́ri śṛ́ṅgā tráyo asya pā́dā dvé śī́rṣé saptá hástāso asya/trídhā baddhó vṛṣabhó roravīti mahó devó mártyān ā́ viveśa //.* See also *sā vai vāk sṛṣṭā caturdhā vyabhavat* etc. (cf. *maitrāyaṇīyasaṃhitā* I.11.5), quoted in *Nirukta* (*Pariśiṣṭa*) XIII. 9.

already quoted by the *Nirukta* (*Pariśiṣṭa,* XIII.7 and 9 respectively)[10], and a tripartite one (cf. *tisró vā́cas* ... in the *Ṛgveda*[11]; *ghoṣiṇī, jātanirghoṣā, nirghoṣā/aghoṣā* in the

10. Provided that such an interpretation may be acceptale. We know that the interpretations given in the *Nirukta* and the *Mahābhāṣya* follow different lines. *Nirukta* (*Pariśiṣṭa*) XIII.9 pp. 1173-4 proposes six different interpretations of *catvā́ri vā́k párimitā...,* ascribed to *ārṣam, vaiyākaraṇāḥ, yājñikāḥ, nairuktāḥ, 'eke'* (that is, *Śatapathabrāhmaṇa* IV.1.3.15-16) and *ātmapravadāḥ* respectively; none of them refers to levels of the word. The verse is also quoted in the VP*Vṛtti,* which introduces it by explaining that "this threefold word [i.e. *paśyantī, madhyamā* and *vaikharī*] ... appears in human beings with a fourth [of itself]. In this fourth, only a certain part of it [i.e. the word] belongs to [ordinary] usage, whilst the rest trascends common usage". According to the further explanation given in Harivṛṣabha's *Paddhati* (p. 220), the word is fourfold on account of its division into noun, verb [preverb and particle]; each of these differentiated forms is manifested to the common man only for one fourth [of itself], whereas the remaining three fourths are manifested to the sages only (this is also the explanation given in Kaiyaṭa's *Pradīpa,* vol. I p. 32). Patañjali's interpretation in the *Paśpaśā* corresponds to that attributed by the *Nirukta* to the *vaiyākaraṇāḥ,* also echoed in the above passage from Harivṛṣabha's *Paddhati.* As regards *catvā́ri śṛ́ṅgā..., Nirukta (Pariśiṣṭa)* XIII.7 takes it as meaning the four Vedas (the passage as a whole is referred to the sacrifice); Patañjali, for his part, refers it again to the four parts of speech. According to Nāgeśa's *Uddyota,* Patañjali's gloss, because of the particle *ca* that is contains (*catvāri padajatāni nāmākhyātopasarganipātāś ca,* also occurring in the commentary on *catvā́ri vā́k párimitā...*), lends itself to be taken as also referring to the fourfold division of the word principle: vol. I p. 31, *bhāṣye 'padajātāni' parāpaśyantīmadhyamāvaikharī-rūpāṇi / ata evāgre 'nipātāś ca' iti cakāraḥ saṅgacchate.*
11. VII. 101.1 *tisró vā́caḥ prá vada jyótiragrā...;* see also IX.97.34 *tisró vā́ca īrayati prá váhnir...,* commented on in *Nirukta* (*Pariśiṣṭa*) XIV.14.

Mahābhārata[12]). In the VP and *vṛtti* at least a hypothesis of a fourth level seems possible, as indicated by some ambiguous passages and, furthermore, by a consideration of the overall structure of the work[13]. The Śaiva tradition itself, in addition to a quadripartion which certainly is by far prevalent, shows, besides few marginal cases of a pentapartition[14], at least an unequivocal case of tripartition in a highly respected text, such as the (*Sārdhatriśati-*) *Kālottara* (*vidyāpāda,* I.8 *sthūlaṃ śabda iti proktaṃ sūkṣmaṃ cintāmayaṃ bhavet / cintayā rahitaṃ yat tu tat paraṃ parikīrtitam //* "The gross aspect [of *nāda*] is called 'sound', the subtle aspect is made of thought, the aspect that is devoid of thought is called the supreme"). This verse must have had a widespread renown if we even find it incorporated into a work of Tantric Buddhism, such as the *Adhyātmasādhana,* ascribed to Kambala (or perhaps we should rather say 'one' Kambala), quoted in the *Caryāgīti* etc. (cf. Lindtner 1985:115)[15]. The Śaiva masters

12. 'Endowed with sound, sounding', 'become (?) soundless', 'soundless'. The verse occurs in the VP (I.164) as *ghoṣiṇī jātanirghoṣā aghoṣā ca pravartate / tayor api ca ghoṣiṇyā nirghoṣaiva garīyasī //* (according to Rau's edition); cf. *Mahābhārata* XIV.21.16, Pune Critical Edition, *ghoṣiṇī jātanirghoṣā nityam eva pravartate / tayor api ca ghoṣiṇyor nirghoṣaiva garīyasī //.* This *śloka* has been transmitted with some *variae lectiones* of which the most significant is *ghoṣiṇyor* instead of *ghoṣiṇyā[ḥ]*. The choice between the two readings has a direct bearing on the very number of the planes of *vāc*. If we read *ghoṣiṇī-jāta* [or *jāti*] *nirghoṣā* with *vaikharī,* and *aghoṣā* or *nirghoṣa* with *madhyamā-paśyantī* taken together. On the contrary, Rāmakaṇṭha unequivocally quotes this verse as an example of tripartition in his commentaries on the *vidyāpādas* of the *Sārdhatriśati-kālottara* (on I.8, p. 15) and *Kiraṇa* (on III.23cd, p. 83; *āgamāntare 'pi tisro vācaḥ proktāḥ*).
13. Cf. Torella 1994: 120-121 n. 26, with references.
14. Cf. *Mahārthamañjarīparimala* p. 124, which inserts *sūkṣmā vāc* between *paśyantī* and *parā.*
15. Evident traces of the *Kālottara* doctrine on *nāda* can be found in various later Śaiva scriptures, too, like the *Śivapurāṇa* (*Vāyusaṃhitā, pūrvakhaṇḍa,* XXIX. 4-5ab *śabdātmikā vibhūtir yā sā tridhā kathyate budhaiḥ / sthūlā sūkṣmā parā ceti sthūlā yā śrutigocarā // sūkṣmā cintāmayī proktā cintayā rahitā parā /*) or the South Indian *Pauṣkara* (*vidyāpāda* II. 27cd-28ab *āgopālāṅganābālaṃ mlecchāḥ prākṛtabhāṣiṇaḥ // antarjalagatāḥ sattvāḥ nityaṃ jalpanti tā girāḥ /,* here referring not to the threefold *nāda* of the *Kālottara* but to the fourfold *vāc;* cf. *Kālottara, vidyāpāda* I.6cd-7ab).

cannot ignore it and are obliged to embark on various dialectical acrobatics to make it compatible with the prevailing doctrine of quadripartition. The first to tackle this problem was probably Utpaladeva himself in the *ṭīkā,* as we shall see later.

But let us follow what Abhinavagupta says about *Paśyantī,* at least in outline (ĪPVV II pp. 189ff.). *Paśyanti* belongs to the plane where awareness is exempt from mental constructs (*vikalpa*), it is in itself without patial-temporal differentiations, thus making indistinct the succession which, however, persists both in the signifier and the signified pertaining to the sphere of the perceiver subject and the perceived object respectively. Paśyantī embrances them within itself veiling them with its own nature. At this level the word consists of a sort of internal discourse, like a murmuring (*abhijalpa*), where words and sentences are so-to-speak 'condensed', reduced to a compact but not altogether formless state, somewaht like the verbal expression in the sūtra style[16]. The reference point of these observations is obviously the description of *Paśyantī* in the VP and *vṛtti*; in particular, they are mostly to be seen as a long and rather intricate paraphrase of the half verse, not openly quoted, *avibhāgā tu paśyantī sarvataḥ saṃhṛtakramā* (included by Rau in the very body of the VP as I.167ab, whilst Iyer's edition puts it in the *vṛtti*)[17]. For Utpaladeva and Abhinavagupta it is *Icchāśakti* that acts in *Paśyantī,* just as *Vaikharī* has been connected with *Kriyāśakti* and *Madhyamā* with *Jñānaśakti.* But the power of Will also has the form of will to know. Therefore, Paśyantī is will but also *bodha,* knowledge. It consists of an unobstructed light belonging to *Icchāśakti.* The power of Will, supporting the senses of knowledge, which are the product of the effusion of *Vidyāśakti,* gives rise to the perception deviod of *vikalpa.* In this manner, Abhinavagupta appropriates the description by the VP and translates it here mainly into terms of gnoseology. Thus, *Paśyantī* is the moment of the perception

16. See ĪPVVI p. 16 (cf. Torella 1994: XLII).
17. Abhinavagupta literally quotes a passage from the *Vṛtti*: ĪPVV II p. 189 *yathāha tatrabhavān 'pratisaṃhṛtakramā tu saty api bhede* [to be corrected to *apy abhede*] *samāviṣṭakramaśaktiḥ paśyantī' ityādi.*

still exempt from discursive articulation (in this way, he can give a plausible explanation of its name, which is after all the present participle of *dṛś-*, and refer to *Paśyantī's* nature as *Icchāśakti* – which keeps it away from any external deployment). At the same time, *Paśyantī* is the very first 'verbalization', still enclosed but potentially about to unfold. Without some kind of subtle verbalization knowledge would be impossible. The next level, *Madhyamā,* represents conceptualization, the articulation of the content of the first perception into fully differentiated and successive concepts and words. Lastly, *Vaikharī* is the moment of communication, the plane of the word externalized and made into audible sounds.

So *Paśyantī* is the state of *nirvikalpa.* I will dwell on the way this notion – which is more problematic than it may appear – should be taken in the later part of this paper. The scrutiny of the nature of Paśyantī is accompanied by the evaluation of the Grammarians' claim[18] that it constitutes the highest plane of the word. In *Paśyantī* – say Utpaladeva and Abhinavagupta, closely following the VP and the *vṛtti* but adapting them to their own context – somehow there is still succession (according to Abhinavagupta's formulation, there is succession both in the expressive component and in the expressed component, with the difference that in the former this is not evident, '*asphuṭa*', and in the latter it is 'covered'). With this affirmation one has a twofold result: to make necessary, in the Śaiva outlook, a further plane where succession vanishes, and to create a link between Paśyantī and Madhyamā – or, in other words, critically addressing the Buddhist logicians, to fill the gap between the first moment of perception and determinate cognition. This gap would suffice to cause the whole fabric of the Śivādvaita – where all is equally penetrated by Śiva and from any plane one can have access to all the others – to collapse.

Let us examine the case of the first moment in the perception of a pond and the liquid contained in it (*saraḥ/rasaḥ;* ĪPVV II p. 191). Though this phase of perception may appear to be

18. To be more precise, Abhinavagupta speaks of the 'old grammarians' (ibid. p. 191 *jaradvaiyākaraṇāḥ*).

instantaneous and unitary, the reflective awareness that is associated with it cannot but grasp some form of succession in its object, otherwise in the subsequent moment of discursive thought (the plane of Madhyamā) we could not have the development of the distinct *vikalpas.* This is valid both in the case where *saraḥ* and *rasaḥ* are the object of an ordinary undifferentiated perception and in the case of the yogic experience named *nirvitarka-nirvicāra samādhi.* Even if one moves backwards as far as possible, that is prior to the perception itself, to the very first experience of him who wishes to see, reach and express these two objects, some diversification must be there, too, or else the wish would simply be a useless undifferentiated wish which would lead to no definite object. Of course, the example chosen by Abhinavagupta (probably following the *ṭīkā*) is not casual, being that which recurs in all the argument against the doctrine which considers the phonemes as the meaning bearers. By using this example, Abhinavagupta here means to say that *Paśyantī* contains not only the embryo of the future articulation of knowledge but also that of its verbalization, and, somehow, even of the correct sequence of the phonemes in the signifier, which, subsequently, will give rise to the manifested and audible form of the word. Therefore, there is no doubt that in *Paśyantī* there is some kind of succession, articulation of though and reflection, in a word, *cintana.*

This assertion is not without some potential unwelcome consequences. Having arisen from the need to fill the gap between *Paśyantī* and *Madhyamā,* now it risks bringing them too close to each other and even confusing the two planes (the same term *cintana* is used for both of them). Moreover, it conflicts with the famous verse of the *Kālottara,* mentioned above, which on the one hand speaks of three levels and on the other considers the last level as 'devoid of thinking' (*cintayā rahitam*). In order to show that Śiva, the author of the *Kālottara* (here called *Kālapāda-saṃhitā*), in fact intended to affirm a quadripartition – as the Śaiva philosophy deems necessary – there are only two ways: either to eliminate an element from the ideal quadripartition or to add one to the literal tripartition found in the revealed text. Utpaladeva in the *ṭīkā* chooses the former alternative, because what most matters to him is, first, to underline the presence of a germ of discursive articulation in *Paśyantī* (for the gnoseological reasons mentioned above) and, secondly, to find in this important text an explicit support for the existence of a plane beyond *Paśyantī* (higher than the others but not in terms of verticality). Very ingenuously he solves the difficulty by excluding *Vaikharī*. The first level (*sthūla*), named *śabda,* stands for *Madhyamā.* In it *śabda* is present with all evidence and succession but it is not *śabda* as 'sound' but as 'signifier' (*vācaka*). Sound, says Abhinavagupta (ibid. p. 192), being a *svalakṣaṇa,* cannot be the signifier since the soul of the signifier-signified relationship is the superimposition 'this is that' and a *svalakṣaṇa* cannot be superimposed on another *svalakṣaṇa.* The form of the jar as an object of mental construct is not different from the form of the jar as an external object. The 'manifestation' (*ābhāsa*) 'jar' is the same, it is only that in the latter case it is combined with other 'manifestations' thus forming a certain *svalakṣaṇa* (cf. Torella 1994: 89-90, n. 3) Thus, by applying his *ābhāsa* theory, Utpaladeva solves the question in these terms: the first plane (*sthūla*) has been called '*śabda*' because it contains *śabda* endowed with all its essential, structural characteristics, as 'signifier' (*vācaka*). The plane of the articulated and audible word has simply been ignored by the *Kālottara* inasmuch as what is its essential core (the *vācaka* component), that is the *śabda* proper, has already been mentioned and all the other elements that characterize the ordinary human language (like audibility and so on) are to be considered, in comparison with it, only negligible epiphenomena. Very different is the interpretation by Rāmakaṇṭha in his *Kālottaravṛtti* and *Kiraṇavṛtti,* for which a separate study (under preparation) is needed on account both of the difference in the viewpoint and the unsatisfactory state of the transmitted texts.

Then, what is in short the peculiar nature of *Madhyamā* with respect to *Paśyantī? Madhyamā* is the plane of mental construct (ĪPVV II p. 192 *madhyamaiva vikalpabhūmir ucyate*). Further developing an analogy already outlined, Abhinavagupta (ibid. p. 196) says that the māyic phonemes which form the articulated language may be compared to the external objects, like the jar. The knowledge that causes these phonemes to arise, in its *nirvikalpa* and *savikalpa* aspects, is precisely that belonging to the planes of *Paśyantī* and *Madhyamā* (homologous to it is the knowledge, differentiated into direct perception and mental construct, which causes the objects to arise, that is, to become manifest). This externalization process is achieved when the word, this time as a sense of action, makes the nature of the phonemes totally explicit placing them on the *māyā* plane, just as the other senses of action (hands and so on) do with regard to external objects.

Thus, *vāc* has been presented as object, knowledge and sense. Anyhow, each of them is only a condition, limited in itself and dependent on the two others, and in a sense, even if hierarchically ordered, they basically belong to a single dimension. It is necessary to posit another reality, totally beyond this distinction of planes and, at the same time, constituting the deepest identity of each of them. To put it in Śaiva terms, remaining within Abhinavagupta-Utpaladeva's discourse, a reality which coincides with no single plane but from where the planes derive the capacity of performing their respective functions; which cannot be measured on the basis of a greater or lesser presence of contraction (*saṃkoca,* in the sense of 'limitation, individualization') but which embodies the very will presiding over this free appearing of contraction in the various grades. It is precisely in this abscence of contraction that the essential character of the four postulated by the Śaivas lies. This is described as basically different from the three others (*tisṛbhyo'pi vilakṣaṇā iyam*) by Abhinavagupta (ibid. p. 189), who points out that Utpaladeva too had separated it from the others by the word *punaḥ*. The *Paśyantī* of the Grammarians may not aspire to such a role. In it the 'vision' is contracted by the spatial-temporal conditioning caused by its objects. Fullness, on the contrary, means being above space and time. In the sequel, Abhinavagupta puts forward a few relevant objections to his own position. The main one is this: if *Paśyantī* is the plane of experience devoid of mental constructs, the object once it has entered it should be free from its own 'heaviness' and therefore incapable of performing this limiting action with respect to consciousness[19]. Utpaladeva meant to express the same thing in the ĪPK (III.2.3ab) and *vṛtti* thereon when he said that to the subject in the condition of 'Lord' the world constituted so-to-speak his very body. However, Abhinavagupta has in mind here another definite formulation by Utpaladeva in the *ṭīkā* on verse I.1.2 which probably at this point Utpaladeva himself referred to: ĪPVV II p. 195 *tasyāṃ hi dāśāyām aiśvaro bhāvo paśor api* "In this [*māyic*] condition the state of 'Lord' can take place even for the limited subject". It is true, says Abhinavagupta later, that the codition of 'Lord' arises whenever the knowable object flows back into the knower (ibid. *vedyasya vedakabhāganimagnatvam eva tad aiśvaryam uktam*). This continuously happens in ordinary experience, where there are many small *Paśyantīs* which in turn may be absorbed into progressively greater *Paśyantīs,* like for instance the intention or the action of going out of the house with respect to the wider 'I am going to the village'. Here Utpaladeva and Abhinavagupta are evidently influenced by Bhartṛhari's hierarchy of universals (originally a *Vaiśeṣika* doctrine) and his conception of action. With respect to all these more or less limited *Paśyantīs* the plane of Sadāśiva-Iśvara represents the highest achievement, the archetype of Paśyantī, at it were. In its individual realizations this state of non-discursive knowledge comes to be limited, contracted as regards its potentially infinite expansion both by the nature of the subject (who identifies with a particular body, thinks of himself as distinct from the other subjects etc.) and by that of the object (with analogous considerations).

A full achievement of this experience is only possible when any identification of the I with limited planes ceases, the latent impregnations left by previous identifications vanish and, in the end, the body dies. But even this experience cannot claim to belong to the plane of *Parā* until it is expanded into the universal absolute. *Parā Vāc,* says Abhinavagupta, is the majesty of bliss whose

19. Ibid. p. 194 *galitasaṃcokanatvāt kathamiva tāṃ paśyantīṃ saṃkocayet ity āśaṅkhya.*

essence is freedom, disclosed by *Paśyantī* in the highest form (ibid. p. 197 *yāsau mahāpaśyantīnāṃ pratyagātmarūpāṇām avibhāgātmikā paramamahāpaśyantī tayā ca yo 'sāv ānandamahimā parasvātantryātmā ullāsanīyaḥ, sā bhagavataḥ parā vāg iti darśitam*). In this connection, one is reminded of the passage in the VP*vṛtti* where the description of *Paśyantī* is followed by an enigmatic hint at a *paraṃ paśyantīrūpam,* which one is tempted to take as a fourth level of *vāc* asserted by Bhartṛhari himself[20]. The criticism of Bhartṛhari is centred on this point alone, which is repeatedly taken up again and examined from different angles: "How is it possible to consider the plane of *Paśyantī,* where there is still succession and contraction, as the supreme plane?" Abhinavagupta and Utpaladeva make use of Somānanda's criticism only as regards this point, but they do it by totally changing the tone. Bhartṛhari is no longer fiercely attacked but, on the contrary, he even turns out to be the reference point for the whole description of the levels, including *Paśyantī.* The final considerations on p. 195, though leaving the basic criticism unchanged, may almost sound like the attempt at reconciliation: if Grammarians do not acknowledge the word as the agent of an activity that brings about reflective awareness itself, consisting in the universal mantra AHAṂ, if, in other words, they do not see it as *śbdana* but merely as *śabda,* that means that for them the word is only a poor instrument of action, even poorer than an instrument of knowledge [but, Abhinavagupta continues implicitly, those who have built all this fabric on *vāc* and call it 'supreme' cannot possibly think so, and seeing that they start from our premises they cannot but come to our conclusions][21]. It is undeniable that Bhartṛhari expressly mentions only three levels, the very fact that the second is termed Madhyamā confirms this number.

20. VP*vṛtti* I, p. 216 *paraṃ tu paśyantīrūpam anapabhraṃśam asaṃkīrṇaṃ lokavyavahārātītaṃ*

21. *Vāṅ nāma vaktīty anena vapuṣā yadi śuddhakartṛtāprāṇā aham ity asaṃkucitamahamantramayī śabdanarūpā na upagamyate vaiyākaraṇais tadā karaṇarūpā sā buddhīndriyavargād api nikṛṣṭā karmendriyasvabhāvā paśuprāṇibhis tiryagādibhiḥ sādhāraṇā dhvanijanikā ahaṃkāravṛttir eva kācit vāk pāṇyādivat, tatra ca kathaṃ paratvaṃ bhaved iti.*

Abhinavagupta and Utpaladeva, however, might have considered that just as for them only three of the four levels are homogeneous[22], the same might have been true of Bhartṛhari, who would have simply excluded from the description the one which represented the all-encompassing and absolutely undifferentiated reality of the word-principle, namely the *śabdatattva* mentioned in the opening verse of the VP. This possible interpretation must have been in the air, if at least one of the early Kāśmīrian philosophers, Rāmakaṇṭha, Utpaladeva's direct disciple, openly adopted it when in the *Spandavivṛti*[23] he identified Bhartṛhari's *śabdatattva* with the Parā Vāc of the Śaivas[24]. Others, like Kṣemarāja in the *Pratyabhijñāhṛdaya,* just as explicitly will continue to see in Bhartṛhari the upholder of the tripartition[25]. It is however, very significant that from Utpaladeva onwards the esteem in which Bhartṛhari was held by the Kāśmīrian authors was very high and even the possible disagreement about the number of the levels of *vāc* was not able to undermine it any more. The difficult issue whether Bhartṛhari did advocate a fourth level, on the basis of various indications (the mention of a *parā prakṛtiḥ,* apparently beyond *Paśyantī;* his speaking of *śabda-brahman* according to *vidyā* and *avidyā,* the fact that the verse stating the

---

22. Cf. the passage already quoted: *tisṛbhyo 'pi vilakṣaṇā iyaṃ*
23. Cf. p. 153 *tathā ca śabdādvayavāde sāmānyena śabdārthobhayarūpo 'paryantāvantarabhedo yo 'yam īśvarasya śaktiprasaraḥ, taṃ vivartavācoyuktyā vyavaharati sma / yad āha* [Cit. VP I.115 and I.1] *iti / atra brahmaparyāyaśabda-tattvatayā pārameśvaram eva rūpaṃ nirdiṣṭam /tat – iyaṃ parā śaktir eva...*
24. It is worth noting that the early Śaiva authors when arguing n favour of the quadrpartition of the word do not resort to textual authorities belonging to their own tradition but mostly confine themselves to referring to the texts quoted in the VP*vṛtti.* There is, to my knowledge, at least an early Śaiva tantra that might contain a hint to quadripartition I am referring to a passage from the *Tantrasadbhāva,* quoted by Kṣemarāja in *Śivasūtravimarśinī* p. 27, *hṛtsthā ekāṇavā proktā kaṇṭhe proktā dvirāṇavā / trirāṇavā tu jñātavyā jihvāmūle sadā śritā // jihvāgre varṇaniṣpattiḥ śabdavyāptaṃ carācaram /* (National Archives, Kathmandu, ms. A/363 f.12b).
25. *Pratyabhijñāhṛdaya* p. 18 *śabdabrahmamayaṃ paśyantirūpam ātmatattvam – iti vaiyākaraṇāḥ śrīsadāśivapadam adhyāsitaḥ.*

tripartition avowedly only regards what falls within the scope of grammar, etc.) cannot be treated on the present occasion.

I am going to conclude this paper by taking up once again a point already touched upon above, but which Abhinavagupta and Utpaladeva must have considered as crucial if they felt the need to treat it again separately in all its implications. I am referring to the presence of the word even in a cognition devoid of mental constructs. In all the long treatment in the ĪPVV (II pp. 219-240), of which I will take into account here only some of the most significant aspects, the reference point is Bhartṛhari, now definitely assumed as a master and ally, while the main opponent is Dharmakīrti. Dharmakīrti's doctrines are weighed with great attention and respect, and in spite of the different presuppositions they nourish and enrich Utpaladeva and Abhinavagupta's thought, which thanks to them progressively clarifies and deepens until it reaches its most satisfactory formulation. The commentary, more than twenty pages in length, refers to verse 1.5.19: "Even at the moment of direct perception there is a reflective awarenesṣ How otherwise could one account for such actions as running and so on, if they were thought of as being devoid of determinate awareness?" (Torella 1994: 125). Even at the first moment of direct experience, as well as in the most rapid and immediate action, there should be room for some form of intentionality, of will, and consequently of reflective awareness without which will would be directionless. Reflective awareness inevitably goes together with, and is even realized through, an inner verbalization. Abhinavagupta and certainly prior to him Utpaladeva seem to take as a critical reference point two well-known passages of the *Pramāṇavārttika* (PV), on which all the argumentation in the ĪPVV gravitates. In one (PV III. 124-125[26], belonging to the section defining the characteristics of *pratyakṣa,* which Abhinavagupta takes into consideration as a whole), Dharmakīrti proposes to

26. [PV III = *Pratyakṣapariccheda*] *saṃhṛtya sarvataś cintāṃ stimitenāntarātmanā / sthito 'pi cakṣuṣā rūpam īkṣate sākṣajā matiḥ // punar vikalpayan kiñcid āsīn me kalpanedṛśī / vetti ceti na pūrvoktāvasthāyām indriyād gatau //.*

demonstrate that *kalpanā* is absent in sensation; in the other (III. 174-191ab), of which Abhinavagupta repeatedly quotes the first *pāda* (*saṅketasmaraṇopāyam*...), he denies sensation any association with the word. On the other hand, we know that the association with the word, or, more generally, with verbal expression (*abhilāpasaṃsarga, śabdayojanā*) is precisely the chief characteristic of *kalpanā*[27]. Incidentally, on a bit closer examination, it comes out that all the PV verses cited here also occur in the *Pramāṇaviniścaya* (PVin). Furthermore, we can find scattered here and there in Abhinava's commentary some short prose passages, unnoticed by the editor, which definitely belong to the PVin, and two times the very mention '*viniścaya*'. The use of the PVin as one of the main sources for Buddhist philosophy is not a peculiarity of Abhinavagupta. In this case too, he has been preceded by Utpaladeva, as shown beyond doubt by an extant passage from his *ṭīkā* containing a prose quotation from the PVin[28]. The extensive use of the PVin made by other authors, too, such as Jayanta and, particularly, Bhāsarvajña, can tell us much about the fortune and diffusion of this text in medieval Kashmir.

Abhinavagupta says that he is mostly in agreement on the first point, but Dharmakīrti's argument holds good for denying mental construction (*kalpanā*), not *parāmarśa*[29]. Without some form of *parāmarśa*, that is, a conscious appropriation by awareness, neither the cognition of the self's state of stillness (*staimitya*), nor

27. Cf. PVin. I. 4bc ... *abhilāpinī / pratitiḥ kalpanā* (see also *Tattvasaṃgraha* 1213); *Nyāyabindu* I.5 *abhilāpasaṃsargayogyapratibhāsā pratītiḥ kalpanā*, also deriving from the above passage of the PVin (cf. Funayama 1992: 61, fn. 43).

28. The passage, not recognized as being from the *ṭīkā*, occurs in one of the footnotes of the Kashmir Series edition of Abhinava's *Īśvarapratyabhijñāvimarśinī* (vol. I p. 101, fn. 17) which presumably records the annotations found in the margins of one of the MSS used for that edition. I plan to collect and study the fragments of the *ṭīkā* found in the footnotes of the first volume of the Kashmir Series edition and in the marginal annotations of other Śāradā MSS of the Pratyabhijñā school I met with. The above quotation from the PVin has also been pointed out by Stern (1991: 158, n. 55).

29. ĪPVV II p. 229 *satyam uktam, tat tu na parāmarśābhāvasādhanāya alam.*

consequently its memory could take place, nor could we talk here about it. The essential core of Utpaladeva and Abhinavagupta's discourse lies precisely in this: to distinguish in the one case *kalpanā* from *parāmarśa* (and its synonyms) and, in the other, *abhilāpa* from *abhijalpa*. The former represent so-to-speak the dilution of the latter, their debased, entirely māyic version[30]. Buddhist criticism of the former, which seems altogether acceptable to the Kashmiri masters, indirectly guides them in a sound formulation of the latter. A basic objection by the Buddhists is this: there may not be the word in perception, since the word does not belong to the own form of the object being perceived. A cognition arising from the very force of one thing cannot illuminate another, that is, from a visual sensation a word cannot apear nor can the word arouse a visual sensation[31]. Utpaladeva and Abhinavagupta's reply moves along two lines. First, it is obvious that *śabda* as 'sound' cannot become manifest when the sensation is aroused by a jar, but the word at issue here is not a *svalakṣaṇa* 'sound' but a *sāmānya*[32] (ibid. p. 235), it is an expressive element or, to be more precise, 'a potentiality of signification' (*śabdanaśakti*); therefore, one cannot even hypothesize that its cognition may directly derive from a thing (to sum up: the responsible for the arising of the word in sensation can be neither the object nor the sensorial faculty). Secondly, the Buddhist logicians, too, do not make *śabdayojanā* 'association with words' derive from the object. Then, where do the Śaivas think this verbalization in perception arises from? Their reply is rather

30. On the opposition between *abhilāpa* (lit. 'talk' 'verbal expression') and *abhijalpa* ('murmur') see below note 37.

31. Ibid. p. 234 *indriyabalāc ca utpannaṃ vijñānam, na ca cākṣuṣeṇa jñānena śabdasya pratibhāso yuktaḥ.* The reference point is a passage from PVin I (cf. Vetter 1966: 40, n. 1), partially quoted on the same page: *indriyajñāne sā* [i.e. *kalpanā*] *nāsti arthasya sāmarthyena samudbhvāt / tab dhy arthasya sāmarthyenotpadyamānaṃ tadrūpam evānukuryāt.*

32. Ibid. p. 235 *vācako hi ayaṃ śabdo, na ca svalakṣaṇasya niyatākṣagamyasya viṣayasya sato vācakatvam* [...] *kas tarhi asau / ucyate 'sāmānya' iti.* But this is also the Buddhist position; see *Tattvasaṃgrahapañjikā* I p. 449 *abhilāpaḥ – vācakaḥ śabdaḥ, sa ca sāmānyākāraḥ* (cf. Funayama 1992: 63-64, n. 50).

complex and is nourished by Buddhist ideas. For a visual perception to occur various factors are needed: the object must be in a convenient locations, sight must be good, there must be enough light, but what may not be lacking in any kind of cognition is a so-to-speak less 'instrumental' factor: the mind's attention (*manaskāra, avadhāna*). If the form etc. is what gives sensation a content, it is *manaskāra* that causes the very arising of a cognitive light in sensation (ibid. p. 335 *saviṣayatā tāvat nīlena kṛtā, manaskāreṇa bodhatā*). Therefore, it is in the *manaskāra* that the way in which *śabdanaśakti* arises is to be sought. The potential verbal signification, made possible by the combining of reflective awareness with a word not particularized and not articulated into phonemes as yet, like a nod, is awakened by the object but only insofar as this object is supported by a particular *saṃskāra*, an impulse towards verbal signification (*śabdabhāvanā*) spontaneously deposited in the *manaskāra* from time immemorial[33]. This solution is modelled on the way the Buddhists account for pleasure or pain accompanying a sensation. The object alone does not suffice to account for pleasure[34]. This is aroused by the relation with pleasures connected with previous objects of the same kind which left their latent impression in the mind; these pleasures are awakened at the moment of perception. Thus, it is admissibile to speak, even at the first moment of perception, not indeed of an explicit *abhilāpayojanā* for which the conditions required by the Buddhists would indeed be necessary (a sequence of operations is indicated in PV III. 174-5; apprehension of the conventions, traces left by them, arousing of their recollection, application[35]), but of an inner discourse (*antaḥsaṃjalpa*)[36] only

33. Cf. ibid. p. 236 *apratiniyataśabdamelanaparighaṭitaśabdanātmakavimarśaviśeṣaprabodhe saṃketagrahaṇapaṭīyaḥsvāhitamanaskārasahitaḥ so 'rthaḥ vyāpriyate, na śuddhaḥ.*
34. Cf. PVin I, śl. 23d *nārtharūpāḥ sukhādayaḥ* (cf. Stern 1991:158).
35. Cf. ĪPVV II Pp. 223-224 *vimarśanaṃ śabdayojanayā, sā ca saṃketasmaraṇataḥ, tad api saṃskāraprabodhāt, so 'pi tādṛśadṛśaḥ ...*
36. Cf. Helarāja's comments on VP III. 3.32 (p. 145): *tathā hi buddho* [read: *buddhau*] *śabdārthayoḥ pūrvam abhedenāvasthānam / na hi vivakṣito 'rthaḥ śabdasambhedassūnyaḥ, antaḥsaṃjalparūpasya tasya pratibhāsanāt.*

acting at the 'signifier' level and appearing in the form of an indistinct verbalization – a 'murmur' (*abhijalpātmatvena*) – and not as an object (*na tu viṣayarūpatayā*)[37]. This is brought about by the *manaskāra* as 'most immediate cause' (*samanantarapratyaya*). This function, undeniable because it is established through inner awareness, consists of 'verbalization, description, indication'; it takes place in the subject at the moment of perception and is distinct from it[38]. The form of verbalization, described above as aroused by the object, is obviously only the form pertaining to the māyic world. On the contrary, it is senseless to talk of a cause as regards what is beyond māyā and consists in the permanently present and active Self.

In conclusion, a question emerges spontaneously (in our minds as well as in the Buddhist opponent's). Then, what precisely is the *nirvikalpa* state for the Śaivas; or rather, does it really exist? At this point, we already know the reply, at least in part[39]. All the

---

37. Cf. ibid. p. 238 *āntarasya vācakarūpasya abhijalpātmatvena, na tu viṣayarūpatayā, abhilāpasya yojanā yuktaiva prathamadarśanalakṣaṇe 'pi bodhe, na tu abhilāpayojanā.* However, according to the Buddhists, too, *abhilāpa* does not seem to correspond to the actual word as fully articulated but rather to its *vācaka* aspect (cf. *Nyāyabinduṭīkā* p. 47 *abhilāpyate 'neneti abhilāpo vācakaḥ śabdaḥ;* see also above note 32). Anyhow, the *abhijalpa* of the Śaivas is to be seen as a 'subtler' version of the Buddhists' *abhilāpa.* The concept of *abhijalpa* is, once again, to be traced back to Bhartṛhari. One of the possible definitions of the word meaning, given in the second chapter of the VP (vv. 119ff.), is precisely *abhijalpa* (vv. 127cd-128). In it we have the word and its meaning still forming a unity, in which however the word encloses, i.e. predominates over, the expressed object (Puṇyarāja on v. 128: *so 'yam ity abhisambandho 'dhyāsākhya ucyate / padārthasvarūpam ācchāditam ekīkṛtam iva pratyāyyate.* Still clearer on this point is Kamalaśīla, when commenting on the same verse quoted in the *Tattvasaṃgraha* (I, p. 351): *śabda evartha ity evaṃ śabde 'rthasya niveśanaṃ so 'yam ity abhisambandhaḥ, tasmāt kāraṇād yat śabdasyārthena sahaikīkṛtaṃ rūpaṃ bhavati taṃ svīkṛtārthākāraṃ śabdam abhijalpyam* [read: *abhijalpam*] *ity āhuḥ.*)
38. Ibid. *saṃskṛtaṃ yat svopādānaṃ samanantarapratyayarūpaṃ manaskārākhyaṃ tena upapāditaḥ svasaṃvedanasiddhatvād anapahnavanīyaḥ śabdanaṃ nīrūpaṇaṃ nirdeśanam iti prasiddho yaḥ pramātur draṣṭur darśanātirikto vyāparas tadāśrayā* [...].
39. See ibid. pp. 239-240.

cognitive activity of the māyic subject contracted by the so-called 'cuirasses'[40] has as its essence Impure Science (*aśuddhavidyā*), which is not independent but is a power of Parameśvara. The single congitive acts, though only partially, manifest – or, in a sense, resurrect – the light that the contracting power of māyā had dispelled, and – the core of any light/knowledge being the reflective awareness 'I' – when something suddenly becomes the object of knowledge and thus flows into the *vimarśa* 'I', it cannot be indicated as 'this' any longer. In other words, it is not the object of *vikalpa*, since this activity, which causes the separation between subject and object to arise, does not emerge. Objectivity (*idantā*), in this case, is not altogether absent but unexpressed, not full; the māyic subject, for his part, is so-to-speak 'enclosed', 'covered' (*saṃvṛta*). When the *vikalpa* arises again, the māyic subject, as a consequence, 'opens' (*apāvṛta*). The object, the 'this' (*idam*) emerges again. In comparison with the latter state, the former takes the name of *nirvikalpa*[41]. The *śabdabhāvanā,* the spontaneous impulse to verbalization, still subsists within the *nirvikalpa* state but in an enclosed and contracted form, which contrasts with the diffused and expanded *śabdabhāvanā* of the *savikalpa* state[42]. Utpaladeva and Abhinavagupta's endebtment to Bhartṛhari (with his conception of a *saṃhṛtarūpā śabdabhāvanā*[43]) is quite evident.

A last possible objection (ibid. p. 240): so, *vikalpa* means for the for the Śaivas to indicate an object as 'this', but the *vikalpa* does not grasp the real. Therefore, with respect to a perceived object we should not have the reflective awareness 'this' but only 'I'. As a consequence, there could be neither communication nor worldly transactions for they presuppose a different form of

40. On the docrine of the cuirasses (*kañcuka*) see Torella 1998.

41. Ibid. p. 240 *udite tu vikalpanavyāpāre so 'pāvṛto vartate iti tatkṛtāt dvaitārambhāt pramātṛprameyayor bhedakaḥ prameyaviśrāntaḥ idam iti nirdeśo bhavan pūrvāpekṣayā prasāritarūpaḥ svayaṃ vikalpanātmā svāpekṣayā purvatra nirvikalpakatāṃ vyavahārayati.*

42. Ibid. *saṃvṛtā hi śabdabhāvanā prasāritāṃ śabdabhāvanām vividhakalpanārūpām apekṣya tathābhūtavaividhyakalpanāvaikalyāt nirvikalpety ucyate.*

43. VP*Vṛtti* I p. 188; see Torella 1994: 125-126, n. 42.

awareness: 'I am perceiving this object which is being perceived'. Thus all everyday life would collapse. But the opponent has forgotten that, unlike the Buddhists, the Śaivas do not consider the *vikalpa* as having as its object the unreal (*avastuviṣaya*). In the universe penetrated by Śiva there is no room for absolute non-being, nor consequently for absolute error.

* * * *

Tantricism in Kashmir

Pandit Dinanath Yaksha

Nature has lavishly endowed Kashmir with certain distinctive favours which hardly find a parallel in any alpine land of the world. Set in the womb of the Himalayas and gifted with beautiful and inspiring natural scenery, it emerged as a highly advanced seat of learning from very early times, taking its place along with the famous Universities of Takṣaśilā and Nālandā. Ramparts of high mountains and seclusion of the land helped her to preserve the life and conditions of early times which it is rather difficult to resuscitate in regard to other such mountainous regions. To the poets like Bilhaṇa and others it was *Śārdādeśa,* the land of goddess Śārdā; and it was even believed that goddess Sarasvatī actually lived here and hence the *Śārdāpītha* was also known as *Śrīpītha* for conferring *sarvajña* degrees. *Śrīcakra* worship seems to have originated from this concept of the poets here regarding the characteristic learning of the land. It was only natural that the savants and *ṛṣīs* should indulge in exercises of the highest order of metaphysical speculation.

The cultural heritage of Kashmir is, therefore, very rich and derives its inspiration and strength both from her natural environs and the rich literature and literary traditions alike. Usually, the literature of a country reflects the unique and most distinctive characteristic of her people and sheds light on the varied aspects of the numerous subjects developed in the language of that area. Thus with the growth of *Tantra-śāstra,* that forms one of the important branch of the general *śāstrās* like *Kāvya, Nātya, Vyākaraṇa* and Vedānta, scholars have put forth their divergent opinions regarding the genesis and growth of this *śāstra*. All are, however, agreed on the point that the Vedas are the source of all these *śāstras* and that *śabda-śāstrà* or *Vyākarṇa* (grammar) is their expression and basic source material.

Along with the growth of a number of religious sects, numerous treatises were written to expound the basic tenets of a particular religion. The *Tantra-śāstras* also were composed to solve the knotty riddles and secret esotericism of Dharma. There are many manuals of Tantras on the diverse religious secrets still extant, though some are no doubt lost to us. The date of composition of these manuals cannot be determined with any certainity. The internal evidence, however, reveals that these are anterior to the treatises on Indian philosophy and posterior to the Vedas. Some would, however, even attribute a much earlier date to Tantras in comparison to the Vedas. It may safely be assumed that whatever was evolved in the form of religious literature seems to have been first developed in the form of *Tantra-śāstra.* A few scholars would go even to the extent of saying that in view of the complexity of the issues and problems discussed therein, these hold a place alongside the Vedas. This is so because the essence of the *mantras* of the *Tantra-śāstra* is not in any way inferior to those of the *mantras* or hymns found in the Vedas. Some of the religious principles of India are based upon the principles of *Tantra-śāstra* and in the Tāntric-base there occur glimpses of philosophic doctrines. Among the extensively ramified aspect of India's speculation the Tantras are characterised by a catholicity of outlook and are free from all personal, communal or race restrictions. They assign a very important place to women in religion and account for the growth of the Śākta cult. Justice Sir John Woodruffe (whose pen-name is Arthur Avalon) was the first to point out the philosophical and practical value of the Tantras and how the worship of *Śaktī* as World Mother gradually displaced Vedic ritualism.

Bengal, Assam, Gujrat and Kashmir were prominent centres of Tāntric cult and theories. Even in Buddhism *Vajrayāna Śākta* has its basis in *Tantra śāstra.* The Tantric cult was current in Tibet, and also in Kashmir. The Tantra is referred to in the works of acknowledged *Vaiṣṇava śāstra;* the *Devī Bhāgavata* in the ninth *skanda,* speaks of it as a Vedānta. Śaivism got ascendaney over Buddhism. The experiences gained in the Śākta cult and Śaivism find a clear exposition and manifestation in treatises on Tantras. Most of these are now lost. Nevertheless, the rituals bear a clear imprint of these Tāntric influences. This is amply justified by *Nīlamata-purāṇa* where certain rituals and sacrifices are prescribed for the people of the valley. *Khitcari amāvasī* etc. are the case, in point. In fact, certain calamities in the post-Kushana period were attributed to the giving up of these practices and accepting Buddhist philosophy. The adherents of the Śākta and Śaiva cult today are the direct descendants of the Tāntric group of followers. With the decline of Buddhism, the Śākta cult came into prominence and even the *Vajrayāna* branch of Buddhism found expression in Bauddha-Tantra. It developed along with the Tāntric cult which had already taken deep roots in the soil. This is supported by a study of Śaivism itself, the rise of which is held by consensus to be the 6th century of the Christian era. The Bauddha-Tantra *(Vajrayāna* branch of Buddhism) also flourished along with the Tāntric principles in Kashmir. A study of the *Śaivaśāstra* reveals that the Tāntric literature that had developed much earlier in the sixth century was based upon the main principles of *Iśvarādvayavāda.* These principles have been explained at length in different forms in *Śaivaśāstra* and have been rightly characterised as *Trika-śāstra*. It took the name of Trika as it included the elements of *Āgama, Pratyabhijñā* and *Spanda Siddhānta. Āgama Śāstra* is included in the *Tantra-śāstra* which implies the description and analysis of a particular sectarian *śāstra.* Etymologically it has its roots in "*tanu*" with the termination : "*tra*" and gives the exposition of a particular religious cult or esoteric character of the rituals. *Āgama-śāstra* was in use much earlier than *Tantra-śāstra* and the noblest principles stated therein have found expression in a masculine form through the mouth of Lord *Śiva,* whereas the *Tantra-śāstra* confirms the expounded subject in the form of a male-female dialogue, viz. the *ākhyānas* dialogue between *Śiva* and *Pārvatī.*

The *Tantra śāstra* which concerns itself with the subject through *Parāśaktī* is called *Śākta Tantra* and the same *Parā-śaktī* is known as *Tripurasundarī* in *Tantra-śāstras.* All that was regulated in the world in three different manifestations was called *Tripurā* and the collective energy of *Brahma, Viṣṇu* and *Maheśa* was known as *Tripurā* or *Śri Tripurasundarī* which is also variously known as Mahāsarasvatī, Mahālakṣmī and Mahākalī.

During the mediaeval period in Kashmir much stress was laid on *Bhairava-yāga* and Bhairava worship. These are closely related to *Tantra śāstra.* But the texts dealing with them are now no longer available. *Ānandeśvara, Maṅgaleśvara, Hātkeśvara, Pūrnarāja Bhairava, Turṣkarāja Bhairava, Viśvaksena, Jayakasena* and *Mahākāla* – the eight Bhairavas and their worship was Tāntric in nature. *Bhairavayāmal Tantra, Ānandabhairava Tantra, Utśuśma Bhairava* and *Hātkeśvara Saṁhitā* etc. that are known to us through stray references only and could confirm the prevalence of the eight Bhairava cults are also not available. The *Rudrayāmal grantha* that deals with the source of hymns and thousands of names of the various gods and goddesses is available only in a fragmentary form. A fragmented but defective edition of this book has been published from Calcutta and a few incomplete Mss are preserved in the archives of Nepal, Varānasi and Kashmir. Like other Paurāṇic *parvas* (festivals), the Kashmiri Pandits had a number of Tāntric *parvas* too, which are now not existing. These included *Bhairavaparva, Matsyabali, Vāstuṣpatibali, Mārgaśīrṣabali* etc. A study of the Rājataraṅgiṇī reveals that other Tantras were also prevalent in Kashmir but the Pandits did not hold them in high esteem. The main subject of these was मारण (To kill), मोहन (To hypnotize), उच्चाटन (To apply witchcraft). The *Śatakapāla Ākhyāna* of Cakropala of *Akahāra* was Tāntric in character.

The Tāntric cult was in vogue in Kashmir before the spread of Buddhism, Śaivism and Vaiṣṇavism. Its literature is now not procurable. There is no gainsaying the fact that even before the prevalence of the Vedic religion, the Tantra cult was a dominant creed and this explains the existence of Tāntricism in the various activities of Vedic rituals. The sixth century saw the emergence of Śaiva philosophy which had its roots in the contemporary Tāntric literature and Bauddha Tantras. In course of time it led to the development of a refined and highly evolved *Śaiva-advaitavāda.* The main Tantras which fall under the group of Āgamas are : *Svacchanda Tantra, Mālinīvijaya, Netra Tantra, Vāmakeśvarī, Rudrayāmala* and *Vijñāna Bhairava.* The subject matter of these is closely related to the exposition of the Trika cult. Of these the *Svacchanda Tantra, Mālinītantra, Netra Tantra, Mṛgendra Tantra, Vijñāna Bhairava, Vāmakeśvarī Tantra* have been published by the Kashmir Research Department. Besides *Tantrāloka* based on *Advaita Śaiva-śāstra* has also been published by the same department in twelve volumes. A brief description of the published Tantrās is given as follows. The unpublished Tantra literature preserved in the Kashmir Archives is : (1) *Munimatamanimālā (Vāmadeva);* (2) *Subhagarcharatham;* (3) *Āgamakalpalatā (Yadunath)* (4) *Sivanṛtya* (5) *Kaula Kantahala,* (6) *Śakti-Sangam,* (7) *Yoga-ratnāvali* (Nagārjuna) (8) *Saubhāgya Ratnākara.* In *Svacchanda Tantra* a clear exposition of *Tantra-śāstra* is given in all its aspects of *'dīkśā', 'āsana' 'pañcakṛtya', 'pañcamukhas' mandala rudra, bhuvana, nārī,* guru-disciple, *mantra, sadadhvarnan* etc. These are *Āgamika Tantra śāstras* which have been published in six volumes by the Kashmir Research Department. The contents of *Āgamika-Tantra* deal with *Parmaśivasvarūpa Bhairava.* Like Tantrāloka, *Svacchanda Śāstra* is an encyclopaedia of *Śaiva-śāstra* and is in itself a standard manual. *Vidyārṇava Tantra* was written by Vidyāraṇymuni, the disciple of Pragalbhatāchārya (the disciple of Vishnu Sharma). Their tradition has come down to us from the Jagatguru Ādi Śankarācārya. A description of Tripurā of Tripurasundarī is given therein : the three main activities of creation etc. Paramaśiva has been eulogized and this represents the energy of Brahmā, Viṣṇu and Rudra. These, as mentioned above, are manifested in *Mahāsarasvatī, Mahālakṣmī* and *Mahākalī.* Thus in the form of a 'male-female' dialogue, a very apt description is given of Śiva-Śakti worship. Tripurasundarī is not only the *Sundarī* of three worlds but is also the sole directing force of the activities of the Trinity and of the five different kinds of forces to the east, west, south and north and the higher regions in the form of *Unmanī, Bhoginī, Kumbhikā, Kalikā* and Mahā-Tripurasundarī of the upper regions. The said *'grantha'* is in the form of hymns in worship of *Mahā-Tripurasundarī.* It has too large sections dealing with the numerous *mantras* अनुष्ठान etc. in praise of *Mahā-Tripurasundarī,* in her twenty different forms.

The date of composition of *Vidyāraṇa Tantra* is fixed at 1130 of Vikrama era corresponding to 1073 A.D. It is a huge compendium which draws freely from the following Tantras, most of which are not available now: *Agastya-Saṁhitā, Phetakarini Tantra, Dakṣināmūrti-kalpa, Yogaśāsta, Vāmkeśvar, Śārdā, Kalīmata, Tantra-rāja, Dakṣināmūrti Saṁhitā, Bhairavī Tantra, Siddha-Sārasvata Tantra, Uttar Tantra, Kulāraṇava, Pingalāmata, Śivayāmala, Brahmayāmala, Rudrayāmala, Kulaprakāśa Tantra, Nārada Pañca-rātra, Yogini Tantra, Vayāni Saṁhitā, Akṣa-śāstra, Śārada-Tilaka, Nīla Tantra, Śrikrama Nārāyanīya, Bṛhat Nārāyanīya, Śatātapa-saṁhitā* etc, regarded as an encyclopaedia of *Tantra-śāstra* and its literature. It was once published by the Kashmir Durbar but is now out of print. The original copy of it was available in the private library of Mahāraja Hari Singh and the MSS Library of Jammu Raghunath Mandir. I too had purchased a copy of it for the Research Library, Srinagar.

Devī-Rahasya

This is also a huge *grantha* of a kind of specific *Tantra-śāstra.* Along with it has been published *Uddhārkośa,* a *grantha* for *mantrodhāra,* quite unique as a type. The first half includes 25 *patalas* (paragraphs) and has been composed in the form of *Adhyāyas* (chapters) dealing mainly with the *bījamantras* of gods and goddesses, worship of the crematorium, *madya śuddhi* (purification of wine) and *madyapānavidhi,* (drinking method) etc. The other half, known also as *Rahasyayiya,* contains 35 chapters. The Pañcāngas mentioned therein are: *Jvālāmukhī,*

Śārikā, Mahārājñā, Bālā, Tripurā, Lakṣmī Sarasvatī, Tārā, Bhuvaneśvarī, Mātangī, Bhedā and the *bījamantras* releated to these goddesses and six other *mantras* of other goddesses. These are: *Bhadrakāli, Turī, Cchinamastā, Dakṣināmūrtī, Śyāmā, Kālarātrī.* All these goddesses are included in the pantheon of the Hindu goddesses. In the third section *Vārāhī, Vajrāyoginī, Kameṣvarī, Gaurī, Annapūṛnā, Śāradā* etc. are included along with basic *mantras* and *bījamantras.* The *mantras* of *Gaṇeśa, Vaṭuka Kumāra, Mṛtyunjaya, Kārtaviryārjuna, Sugrīva, Hanumāna* and those of *navagṛahas* are also included. Similarly, the basic *mantras* of *Varṇamālā* and the *mantras* of *navagrahas* as also those of *Bhavānī, Bagulāmukhī, Indrākṣī, Khecarī* too find a place therein. The *dhyāna-dhāraṇā* of these goddesses and *grahas* are also included. It appears to be a large section of *Rudrayāmala Tantra. Uddhārkośa* is in the form of a dialogue between *Dakṣināmūrtī* and his disciple *Akṣayya.* It is a publication of the Kashmir Reserch Department (1941).

Bṛhat Nīla Tantra

It is so called because it supplies every information in connection with the worship of *Nīla Sarasvatī.* The eleventh chapter of the Tantra describes at length how the Goddess of Wisdom became Nīla (blue).

The Tantra is written in the form of a dialogue in which *Mahākālabhairava* appears as the speaker and *Mahākālī* as the listener.

It contains twenty-four chapters. Contents of these are briefly mentioned in the first chapter. The Tantra is evidently later in composition than the *Gandharva-Tantra* to which it refers and the *Durgāsaptaśatī.*

In this tantra the Devī requests Bhairava to reveal the *Nīlatantra* as promised at the time the *Kālītantra* was revealed. The Bhairava redeems the promise and declares that the Tantra which he is to reveal should be duly preserved and concealed, as that leads to many blessings. Firstly, he briefly mentions the important topics of the Tantra and then begins the description of

Tārā in all her forms together with the way in which she is to be worshipped.

The *mantra* of *Nīla Sarasvatī,* consisting of five syllables, reads as उों ह्रीं स्त्रीं तूं फट्, of this Vasiṣṭha is the sage, *Vṛhatī* the metre, *Nīla Sarasvatī* the deity and the object, acquisition of poetic power. Practitioner of the mantra is advised to perform the bathing etc. in the right manner according to both forms, Vedic and Tantric.

A chapter describes the worship of the *Nīla Sarasvatī.* It is to be done in out-of-the-way places, such as deserts, cremation-grounds, jungles, hills and hillocks. Workship of the deities; *Gaṇeśa, Kṣetrapāla, Yoginī* and *Vaṭuka* with भां क्षां यां वां comes at the beginning. While entering the altar Brahmā and Vāstupuruṣa receive their worship. Devī is to be mediated upon as occupying the seat of jewels at the foot of the desire-granting tree. Water required for worship is to be purified with the mantra of उों वज्रोदके लूं फट् स्वाहा।

Gandharvatantra : It gives, with elaborate details, instructions in ritualistic worship purifications, *mantras, yantras, mudrās, āsanas* and the like. It also provides, in eleventh chapter, forms of mediations on *Kuṇḍalinī* and prescribes *Prāṇāyāma* as almost the panacea of all ills. This Tantra is extremely rich and predominately *Śākta* in nature and philosophically of Trika outlook.

Vijñāna Bhairava Tantra : This is commented on partly by Kṣemarāja and partly by Śivopādhyāya. This is a text of the *Tantra Śāstra* of Āgamic nature being a conversation between *Śiva* as *Bhairava* and *Śakti* as *Bhairavī.* The theme of the text is explained by *Śiva* himself. Main topic of the text is 112 yoga *dhāranās;* the forms of *Dhyāna* are elaborately mentioned therein. It is based on the famous *Rudrayāmala Tantra.*

Uḍḍāmareśvara Tantra : This Tantra is a book of magical formulas and also prescribes a number of medicinal drugs.

Vāmakeśvarī Mata Vivaraṇa : This is *Āgama Śāstra.* It deals with philosophical thought as well as rituals, mainly the latter.

It gives a clear explaination of *Śakti* as *Tripura-Sundarī,* whose worship, in various forms, it prescribes.

Mālinī Vijaya Tantra : This work belongs to Āgama *Śāstra* and according to Abhinavagupta is the most important Āgama treatise for Trika system of Śaiva philosophy. It is a conversation between *Śiva* and *Śakti.*

Mālinī Vijaya Vārtikam : This is a running commentary of above work by Abhinavagupta and is written ín simple Sanskrit in the *Anuṣṭup* meter.

Netra Tantra : (with a commentary of Kṣemarāja) is published in two volumes in a dialogue form between *Śiva* and *Śakti.* The conversation introduces a question from Śakti that all the eyes are full of water, how is that from thine eye, Thou Divine Lord, there sprang forth the great fire which burnt everything? The whole book is mainly as answer to this question.

Mṛgendra Tantra : It deals with an Āgamic nature of Tantra. There is a dialogue between sage *Ananta* and his disciple. It is depicting pluralistic thought of Śaiva School.

Besides these published Tantras, I had some rare unpublished Mss of Śaiva Tantras in my possession in Kashmir which are now lost to posterity because of the present disturbance in the valley.

* * * *

'What's in a name?' Kṣemarāja and the Doctrine of the *Svacchandatantra*

Dr. Eivind Kahrs

To a considerable extent intellectual endeavour in classical Indian traditions proceeded through the processing of authoritative scripture driven by a sharp application of hermeneutic tools. In memory of Pandit Jankinath Kaul, illustrious exponent of Kashmirian and other Sanskritic traditions, I offer here a small example from Śaiva Kashmir.

According to such authoritative scripture, the term 'Śaiva' refers to those who follow the teachings of Śiva.[1] In Kashmir towards the end of the first millennium CE a particular Bhairava cult had become what seems to have been the norm. But the deity of this cult, called Svacchandabhairava 'Autonomous Bhairava', was no longer the blood-thirsty deity associated with the Śaiva culture of the cremation grounds. This older Bhairava is known from south Indian inscriptions dating from around 400 CE as the object of an exclusive theistic cult. Among later evidence we find that iconographic features of Bhairava are mentioned in a *Tēvāram* hymn, the most famous portion of the *Tirumuṛai,* a collection of Tamil Śaiva hymns composed from the sixth century onwards. The Śaiva Kailāśanātha temple at Ellora (founded c. 775) contains a Bhairava shrine. Bhairava is clearly associated with Rudra, and is seen to hold a strong position among the Kāpālika (from *kapāla* 'skull') form of Śaivism. This non-dualistic Kāpālika Śaivism was based scripturally in the *Bhairavatantras,* a corpus of texts that have the form of Bhairava's teachings to the Goddess *Bhairavī* (*Devī*),

1. For an outline of Śaivism and the Tantric traditions, see A. Sanderson 1988.

but it embraced also the *Bhūtatantras,* concerned with control of various powers through the worship of Bhairava, and texts concerned with the worship of *Kālī,* the cult of whom was later considered the highest form of Śaivism with the incorporation of the goddess-worship adapted from the system known as the *Krama.*[2] At the time of Abhinavagupta (c. 975-1025 CE), however, we find Svacchandabhairava as a slightly domesticated and modified version of the wilder Bhairava, and worshipped together with his female consort *Aghoreśvarī.* This cult of Svacchandabhairava with his female consort was, and remained, the middle ground of Śaivism in Kashmir.

To the one side of this cult was the daulistic Śaiva Siddhānta, originally an esoteric system of Śaiva temple worship based on a well defined corpus of texts. Here Śiva is worshipped as Sadāśiva,[3] and Śaiva Siddhānta ritual is in general more congruent with the Vedic world. To the other side of the Śaiva midde ground, we meet with a cluster of charismatic cults based on the unorthodox *Bhairavatantras.* Here we find the gnostic non-dualism known as the *Trika* which Abhinavagupta and his followers tried to expound. In other words, we find an opposition between the dualistic *(dvaitācāra)* Siddhānta which confines itself to the dualities of the pure and the impure, the permitted and the forbidden, but most importantly to a dualistic view of the relations between their basic ontological categories, and the non-dualistic *(advaitācāra)* system of the *Trika* which transcends such

2. The term *Krama* refers to a number of esoteric cults of intense Kālī worship in a sequence (*krama*) of sets of divine Powers; the Krama conceives of ritual as a means of liberating insight, and the sequences consist in the worship of goddesses which represent the cycle of cognition from initial to final voidness.

3. In the early Kashmirian Siddhānta, Sadāśiva is worshipped without a consort. Then Manonmanī appears as his consort on some occasions but not as part of the regular (*nitya*) private ritual, normally only in the context of establishing external idols where the Śakti is the throne. Manonmanī is the highest of the nine Śaktis that form his consmic throne, and is placed in the centre (see H. Brunner-Lachaux 1963:167-75, 1977:590 and note 42). In the later Siddhānta she appears as Sadāśiva's regular consort.

limitations and formulates its ontological categories in terms of an absolute non-dualism. As a system of ritual Trika Śaivism sought to assimilate the power of a triad *(trika)* of three goddesses: *Parā, Parāparā,* and *Aparā,* the first mild and benevolent, the other two raging and terrifying. At the outset the Trika propagated the cult of these three goddesses alone, but this is not the only triad encompassed by the name. Indeed, it is the wide distribution of this model of triadic power which facilitates the ambition of Abhinavagupta's Trika to attain the state of a universal Śaiva exegesis by the process of assimilating the older triads to the metaphysical conceptions which it gives to its own.[4] This esoteric fringe sets itself up as a separate division, offering what it considered a superior way to salvation. It sought to incorporate the doctrines of the wilder Kaula[5] and Krama practices, concerned in ritual with impurity, sex, and death, and centered around the goddess Kālī and her emanations.

Primarily Abhinavagupta's exegesis is a rather narrow exegesis of the *Mālinīvijayottaratantra* which he takes to be the fundamental scriptural authority of the Trika.[6] He regards this as the summit and summation of all Śaiva traditions, and develops a theory which accomodates the rest of Śaivism within his own metaphysical system. Through his exegesis of the *Mālinīvijayottara* Abhinavagupta tries to cover a wide range of Śaiva scripture and to establish a basis of hermeneutics conceived of as the elucidation of the conditions that make knowledge possible. His task in exegesis was first and foremost to

---

4. A. Sanderson (e.g. 1988:164) suggests that we may speak of at least three major phases in the evolution of the Trika. The second phase sees the triad of the three goddesses subsumed within the goddess Kālī. Finally, there is the Pratyabhijñā-based Trika of Abhinavagupta with its two aspects, the first being the Kālī-based cult of the *Tantrāloka,* and the second the condensed cult of Parā as Solitary Heroine (*ekavīrā*).
5. Developing from within the Yoginī cults, the erotico-mystical Kaula Śaivism (*kula,* lit 'family; lineage' but later interpreted to mean 'body; totality') carried the Kāpālika cult of power through impurity into the Krama and from there got incorporated into the Trika.
6. See, e.g., *Tantrāloka* 1.17-18.

incorporate into the non-dualist Trika the cult of the goddess *Kālī* or *Kālasaṃkarṣiṇī, Kālī* as the destroyer of time.

However, the *Mālinīvijayottaratantra* lacks the doctrine of non-dualism so fundamental to the Trika, as has been convincingly demonstrated by A. Sanderson (1992). Moreover, the ritual and metaphysics of the *Mālinīvijayottara* lack the Goddess as well as the idea that the universe is a projection in and of consciousness. Still, it is on the basis of this text that Abhinavagupta seeks to establish that the various branches of Śaiva literature embody modes of consciousness which collectively form a structure that perfectly reflects and therefore, is the expression of the core of female powers which is inherent in Śiva/Bhairava and therfore, constitutes the essence of all phenomena.

Towards the end of the tenth century, then, Trika Śaivism found itself competing with the dualistic and more conservative Śaiva Siddhānta. Hence it tried to resurrect the wilder Bhairava within the cult of Svacchandabhairava, and to read a gnostic nondualism into a basically dualistic corpus of texts. Abhinavagupta's task, then, was to displace the dualistic exegesis of the Śaiva Siddhānta, as well as to incorporate the more heterodox elements of the teaching he sought to propagate, while at the same time offering an exegesis that was acceptable within a general system of shared beliefs.

There are, however, more direct ways of establishing one's desired ideology. When Abhinavagupta's pupil Rājānaka Kṣemarāja (fl.c. 1000-1050 CE) composed his commentary on the *Svacchandatantra* 'Tantra of the Autonomous', he wrote it to defeat the prevalent adherence to the dualistic Śaiva Siddhānta. The voluminous *Svacchandatantra* is in a form of a dialogue between Śiva as Svacchandabhairava 'Autonomous Bhairava' and his Śakti 'Power' as Bhairavī, and is mainly concerned with rituals of initiation and the desiderative practices of the Sādhaka. It is accordingly not particularly concerned with metaphysics, and no more non-dualistic than the *Mālinīvijayottaratantra.* In order to displace the dualistic exegesis of the text, Kṣemarāja enters straight into its very name *Svacchandatantra* to demonstrate that its doctrine *is* in fact non-dualistic. At the end of his subsequently authoritative commentary, the *Svacchandatantroddyota* 'Illumination of the Tantra of the Autonomous', Kṣemarāja writes (SvTU 6[15]:146,11-16):

नाम्नैव भेददृष्टिर्विधुता येनास्वतन्त्रतातत्त्वा ।
श्रीमत्स्वतन्त्रतन्त्रं भेदव्याख्यां न तत्सहते ॥
भेददर्शनसंस्कारतन्तुसन्ततमादितः ।
स्वच्छस्वच्छन्दचित्स्वात्मसतत्त्वं नेक्षते जनः ॥
गतानुगतिकप्रोक्तभेदव्याख्यातमोऽपनुत् ।
तेनाद्वैतामृतस्फीतः स्वच्छन्दोद्द्योत उम्भितः ॥

'This illustrious Tantra of the Autonomous (*Svatantratantra* = *Svacchandatantra*) cannot tolerate dualistic exegesis since dualism, the nature of which is lack of autonomy (*asvatantratā*), is eliminated by its very name. People do not see that their identity is pure, autonomous consciousness, since it is enmeshed from the beginning by the threads of their deep conviction of the truth of dualism. Therefore, this *Svacchandoddyota* (Illumination of the [Tantra of the] Autonomous) had been composed, rich with the nectar of non-dualism, in order to dispel the darkness of the dualistic exegesis propagated by the blind followers of tradition.'

Kṣemarāja thus leaves us in no doubt as to why he wrote his commentary on the *Svacchandatantra.* It is significant that according to him the very name of the text eliminates heteronomy, and so it cannot be subject to a dualistic interpretation. Kṣemarāja makes a similar statement towards the end of his commentary on the *Netratantra* (Ne TU 2[22]: 343, 21-22)[7] on which too, he imposed his non-dualistic exegesis.

Enmeshed by the threads created by his dualist view, the Śaiva Siddhāntin is unable to see his true identity, to see the infinite autonomy of his own self, which ultimately is Bhairava,

7. गतानुगतिकप्रोक्तभेदव्याख्यातमोऽपनुत् । पराद्वैतामृतस्फीतो नेत्रोद्द्योतोऽमुत्थितः ॥ For the reading *utthitaḥ* here, read *umbhitaḥ* as in the SvTV passage above.

as revealed by Kṣemarāja's non-dualist, idealist interpretation of the name of a text.

Bibliography

Brunner-Lachaux, Hélène (ed., trans., annot.): 1963, *Somaśambhupaddhati, première partie: le rituel quotidien dans la tradition śivaïte de l'Inde du Sud selon Somaśambhu (Publications de l'Institut Français d'Indologie* 25.I*)*, Pondichéry: Institut Français d'Indologie.

–:1977, *Samaśambhupaddati, troisième partie: rituels occasionels dans la tradition śivaïte de l'Inde du Sud selon Somaśambhu, II: dīkṣā, abhiṣeka, vratoddāra, antyeṣṭi, śrāddha (Publications de l'Institut Français d'Indologie* 25.III) Pondichéry; Institut Français d'Indologie.

NeTU *Netratantra,* with the commentary (*-uddyota*) of Rājānaka Kṣemarāja (*Kashmir Series of Texts and studies* 61), vol. 2, ed. Madhusūdana Kaul Śāstrī, Bombay, 1939.

Sanderson, Alexis: 1988, 'Śaivism and the Tantric traditions', in Stewart Sutherland *et al.* (eds.): *The world's religions,* London: Routledge, pp. 660-704. [Repr. in Friedhelm Hardy (ed.): *The world's religions: the religions of Asia,* London: Routledge, 1990, pp. 128-72.]

–: 1992, "The doctrine of the Ma-lini-vijayottaratantra", in Teun Goudriaan (ed.): *Ritual and speculation in early Tantrism: studies in honor of André Padoux,* Albany, N.Y.: State University of New York Press, pp. 281-312.

SvTU *Svacchandatantra* with the commentary (*-uddyota*) of Rājānaka Kṣemarāja (*Kashmir Series of Texts and Studies 56),* vol. 6, ed. Madhusūdan Kaul Śāstrī, Bombay, 1935.

* * * *

Śaivism and Vaiṣṇavism

Dr. Kapila Vatsyayan

The two words and the names of the two deities Śiva and Viṣṇu with a third Brahmā conjure up a multiplicity of responses for the devotee, philosopher, historian and the artist. For the devotee immediately the god Śiva or Viṣṇu appears in his mind's eye as icon to be worshipped at home or temple, pilgrimage to a holy sacred spot in the Himālayas, Kedarnāth or Badrināth, Kānchipuram or Tirupti, Varanasi, Ujjain or Dwarkā or Jagannātha Puri and Somnāth. For the philosopher both the terms and the names represent systems of thought which are clearly distinguishable and yet interpenetrative. For the historian the terms and the names of the two deities are indicators of the emergence of diverse cults in a chronological order conditioned by developments in pre and post agricultural societies, social organisation, rise of political power and relationships between people and ruler and amongst classes and castes. For the artist, writer, sculptor, painter, musician and dancer, they are both the content of his particular art as also the supreme symbol of creativity to which he surrenders his individuality and with which he identifies himself. This is evident from a vast body of literature, drama, poetry, hymnal composition, countless sculptures, icons, musical compositions and dance styles.

All this although apparently complex and belying easy definitions, evolves from a world view which conceives of the universe as a perennial phenomena of stillness and flux of the unmanifest and manifest, and of the one and the multiple in a continuous ceaseless movement of evolution and devolution of creation and destruction and of creation again. The juxtaposition of chaos and order and the maintainance of ecological balances of inorganic and organic life of matter and energy of the gross and subtle is its central theme couched as it is in a variety of expressions ranging from the most obstruse to the most popular, from the abstract to the concrete.

Thus in order to comprehend even simplicity the basic tenets of Śaivism and Vaiṣṇavism, it is important to remember the two systems of thought, philosophy, theology, religion and ritual are neither mutually exclusive, nor are they sects in the Christian sense of being two schools related to a single monolithic church or a single parent philosophic system. Nor are the schools of thought or the deities set up in opposition or confrontation. Both at the level of philosophy and religion as also myth and ritual they interpenetrate. Again, while the myths constitute the kernal of philosophic schools, the speculative thought provides the basis for the emergence of iconic forms and symbols and a complex system of rites and rituals. Śaivism and Vaiṣṇavism provide an excellent and typical example of the pan-Indian phenomena of the integral vision and the intricate coalescing of the mythical, philosophical, ritualistic, and the artistic each complimenting and enriching the other, indeed being cause and effect of the other.

Understandably many who have tried to outline these two sweeping movements have seen them in their dimension of either myths of cosmology or cosmogony or historicity or philosophic schools, or as ritual icons for worships of particular sects.

The origin of the philosophic schools have to be traced back to the Vedic and subsequent cosmology. Some archaeological evidence suggests the existence of pre-vedic prototypes of the deities if not the philosophic schools. The kernal of Śiva lies in the myth of Rudra in the Vedic hymns specially Ṛgveda: the kernal of Viṣṇu is also traced back to the same source in the myth of the origin of the universe and his taking three strides.

We outline below briefly the evolution of the myths as also the related philosophic schools, the religious centres and the artistic expressions of each. Indian myth, philosophy, religion and the arts particularly all that we generally understand by the term Hindu would be the poorer for their absence.

Śiva and *Śaivism*

First *Śiva* and *Śaivism.* Most accounts of Śaivism begin by drawing attention to the proto-Paśupati seal of Mehenjo-daro. One of these seals depicts a seated anthropomorphic figure seated in a yogic posture, his hands resting on the knees and his head adorning a headdress. Surrounding this figure are many animals which have been identified as a rhinoceros, a buffalo, a tiger and an elephant. In the lower most register there are two other animals identified as goats or deer. Over the last several decades scholars have tried both to establish and refute the relationship of this figure with the description of Rudra in the *Ṛg Veda.* Marshall, one of the earliest archaeologist considers the figure as the clear precursor of the god Śiva, the lord of animals and Kosambi refutes it. Other authorities Keith, Gonda, Dandekar have all dwelt on the subject. We may remember that the mythology of the Veda is itself an accretion of many movements and currents. The one underlying unifying principle that the conception reflects is an intrinsic man-nature, man-animal relationship. Both the representation on the seal as also the description of Rudra the precursor of Śiva in the Ṛgveda is related to the animal world and to aspects of nature, specially the wind and the storms. The word Rudra is itself derived from the known root *rud* to 'cry', to howl. Of course an alternate derivation has been suggested by drawing attention to the Dravidian root *rud* meaning to 'shine'. It is in the Yajurveda that a more full fledged portrait appears because now in the Śaṭarudrya hymns he is adressed as the mountain dweller lord of cattle (*Paśunām patiḥ*) wearer of animal hides and blue-necked. Many more appellations and names of Rudra begin to appear in the Brahmanas, specially the familiar names of *Bhava, Śarva, Ugra Mahādeva* and *Īśāna.* In course of time the god is known by either eight names (aspects) or five.

The first philosophic enuciation of Rudra Śaiva or Śaivism in its incipient form appears in the *Śvetāśvatara Upaniṣad* a late Upaniṣad often called a *Śaiva Bhagvadagītā.* Here Rudra is addressed as the one god (*eka deva*) the cause of all *brahman* itself and names *Hara,* Īśa, *Mahāpuruṣa, Īśāna, Bhagavat, Śiva* and *Maheśvara* appear. The Upaniṣad is also closely related to the philosophic schools of *Sāṁkhya* and *Yoga.*

The myth and the metaphysics evolve concurrently while the Rudra-Śiva theme gives rise to a variety of myths, popularly narrated as Śiva appearing in the 'sacrifice' of Dakṣa as the hunter who gives the weapon to Arjuna in the Mahābhārata as the *yogi* and as the mendicant and the destroyer of the three cities of (Tirupurankakara) the philosophic schools evolve a kind of monotheism.

By the time of Patañjali (C. 150 BC) there appears to have been a cult of Śiva and the first icon of Śiva as *liṅga* appears in the Gundimallam image of the same period. Judging from archaeological evidence of the Kushanas and later the Guptas it is clear that Śiva worship or the Śaiva cults were known to practically all parts of India. But the seventh century it is a dominant current in the North in Kashmir as also in the South. Between the seventh to the eleventh century great temples are built and many dynasties of political power patronise Śaivism, the Pallavas, Cōlas and Cālukyas in the south, the Chandelas and Gurjara Pratiharas in the Central India and the North.

During roughly the same period many *Purāṇas* are composed. These elaborate on the myths of Śiva especially the Śiva Purāṇa, Skandapurāṇa and the three or more doctrinal schools of Śaivism emerge. In the south a distinct school of Śaiva Siddhānta evolves both a philosophy and a theology. Its canonical literature comprises eleven or twelve books collectively called *Tirumurai* and the fourteen *Meykantaśāstra.* These were composed by the *Nayanara* and the *Vellala* both eschewing distinctions of class, caste, creed or sex. Śaiva Siddhānta in all its diverse shades and varities asserts that the world and individual souls are real entities and that final release depends on the grace of Śiva. Little wonder that the *Tirumurai* comprises devotional hymns of brahmans and toddy drawers alike in which saint after saint outpours with intensity his personal experience of god this Śiva.

"The ignorant say that god and love are different when they

know that love and god are the same, they rest in gods love" says Tirumalai. And again:

"They have no love for god who have no love for mankind."

Appar a seventh cetury saint reminds himself and others repeatedly that inward and spiritual worship is the essence of religion. Śiva indwells in all creatures in a subtle form and manifests himself to his devotees. Manikkavacakar yet another saint of the ninth century speaks of the journey of the soul from bondage of ignorance and desire to the salvation of love and light.

The theology of Śaiva Siddhānta is propounded by Maykanda in his *Śiva jñānabodham* a semi-philosophic work. He emphasises the prime importance of Divine grace (*arul*) which alone is the remedy to ignorance (*irul*). There are according to Śaiva Siddhānta three real substances, god (*Pati*), souls (*Paśu*) and bondage (*Pāśa*). Śiva is immanent in everything and yet he transcends everything. Umāpati Śivacārya sums it up beautifully:

"A subtle Trickster is he who fills the worlds
And all the cardinal points with his light."

"He stands at the roof of all; the seed as well; he is the body and the *tanmātras.* The elements and the pure space of zero. The void and the things beyond the void."

Out of his love and compassion, Śiva grants the individual an ability to attain his own state of all pervasiveness. He is above all pure being, pure consciousness and pure bliss. Several analogies are given to bring home Śiva's immanence as also his relationship to the individual souls. Just as eyes cannot see but for the light of the soul, the soul cannot know but for the light of god. God and souls are one in the sense that they cannot be disjoined. Love and grace are fundamental to Śaiva Siddhānta, although many paths to salvation and release from bondage are suggested such as service (*caryā*), worship (*kriyā*) and meditation (*yoga*). Beautifully the lord dances eternally in the Mahasabha in Tillai.

Far off in the North developed other forms of Śaivism. Some precursors, other co-evel and other later than Śaiva Siddhānta.

Of these, the principle ones are known as Krama Śaivism and Trika Śaivism. These were related but in clear contrast to the dualism propagated by Śaiva Siddhānta. Kashmir Śaivism in its fully developed forms is seen in the monumental works of Abhinavagupta and his pupil Kṣemrāja (1000-1050). His precursors were Vasugupta and his pupil Kallaṭa and Somānanda (900-950). The distinguishing feature of Kashmir Śaivism is its exposition of the philosophy of non-dualism. The three streams of Krama Śaivism, Trika and Pratyabhijñā have to be seen in relation to each other and also as distinct developments. Krama Śaivism refers generally to a number of closely related cults of the goddess Kālī, and her emanations. The rituals are designed to induce the liberating intrinscism through the assimilating worship of Kālī (the true self). These are structured as sequence (*Krama*) of worship of various deities each symbolising different states of consciousness. The goal is to make the initiate fully self-aware that his individualised consciousness is but the play of an universalised consciousness. Without elaborating further on the religio-mystical system of Krama, suffice it to say that this Krama Śaivism influenced Trika soteriology of Kashmir. Trika Śaivism is defined by a system of ritual which aims at the assimilation of the power of a triad (*trika*) of a goddess (*śakti*), *parā*, *parāparā* and *aparā,* the first benevolent, the other two wild and terrifying. The three also refer to *Śaktis* viz. *icchā* (will), *jñāna* (knowledge) and *kriyā* (activity) and the three states or movements of *sṛṣṭi* (creation), *sthiti* (preservation) and *samhāra* (destruction). Later in the hands of Abhinavagupta rituals are inward and not outward, in short the initiate has to face and make self aware of the forces, tendencies within him. In the final phase of the development of Trika Śaivism stress was laid on the co-essentiality of the trial (*trika*), of the individual (*anu* or *nara*), cosmic power (*śakti*) and the ground of *śakti* (Śiva). The stress is on unity. Krama and Trika Śaivism are closely connected with the philosophic school of Kashmir Śaivism known as *Pratyabhijñā.* Literally translated as 'recognition' it alludes to knowledge (jñāna) of an object to which one turns back (*prati*) and which then faces (*abhi*) the knower. It is knowledge regained of the identity of the individual self and of the world with the supreme source of all. Kṣemrāja, the great exponent of the school says "It is the divine consciousness above self shining absolute free will that flashes within the form of the multitudinous universe." It is the unique cause, the inner reality and the substratum of cosmic manifestation which it projects as a shining path (*ābhāsa*) on itself as on a screen. This consciousness Śiva is the one absolute reality. The world as if is hidden or is a kind of cosmic oblivion and it is through recognition through which the forgotten truth is re-discovered. It is not re-discovered through memory instead through an activity of the mind which destroys the misconception veiling the real nature of the supreme self and finally brings one to realise the truth. "I am Śiva the only true consciousness, omniscient, the only active power of the universe." Śaiva Siddhānta had altered *'Om Namaḥ Śivāya'*. Kashmir Śaivism says "*Śivohaṁ*". Love and grace were the key words of Śaiva Siddhānta. Immanence was the principal attribute. In Kashmir Śaivism, knowledge, intense spiritual concentration (*bhāvanā*) are the exacting demands, not under estimating the role of the necessary help of god's grace (*anugraha* or *śaktipāta*). The yogi attains the state of Samādhi where he experiences a merging (*samāvesa*) or a unifying contemplation of (*samapatti*) the supreme. At this moment it shines in a flash an intutive vision (*pratibhā*) and destroys all misconceptions and illusions. The yogi is freed from all bondage (*pāsa*), is identified with Śiva, experiences cosmic bliss and release and is free in life this moment here and now and is a *jīvanmukta*.

While there are very fundamental differences between Śaiva Siddhānta and the most developed forms of Kashmir Śaivism, it is obvious that for both the goal is freedom from bondage. One attains it through *bhakti,* pujā, song and dance. The other through spiritual concentration, knowledge, awareness and deep inward meditation.

Understandably many sects, subsects, and religio-social

organisations developed in different parts of India in different periods. These range from Vīraśaivities of the South, to the Pāśupatas of Western India and many others. However the essence of Śaivism is its vision of an unifying principle of cosmic creation, preservation and destruction and its call to the devotee and the yogi alike to free himself from the bondage (*pāśa*) of the so muchness, the thingness of life of the individualised narrow self and to unite itself with that infinite cosmic self which is both immanent and ominiscient. It is given to one to attain transendence here and now if he/she wills it.

The myths and ritual, the philosophy and the socio-religious sects, each interpenetrate. While the myths of Rudra, Śiva give rise to the visual imagery of *liṅga* a subject too vast to be treated here, other myths are interpreted in stone, bronze, painting giving rise to a mighty pantheon of Śiva, the unmanifest but the embodiment of the five elements (space, air, fire, water and earth) as the *liṅga* and to varied forms as *Ardhanārīśvara, Bhikṣātana, Bhairava,* as *Kalyānasundar* as *Gangādhara,* as *Andhakasuravadhamurti,* as *Ravananugrahamurti* and finally as *Naṭarāja*. Each symbolises an aspect of one supreme consciousness which in fact resides within the inner most lotus of the heart. If one worships the concrete image with thought "I am He" one will attain release and bliss.

Viṣṇu and Vaiṣṇavism

Viṣṇu is the other deity who was and is venerated and Vaisṇavism the other religio-philosophic movement which spread throughout India. The origins of Viṣṇu have been traced to the Ṛg veda by some scholars and to non-vedic religion and cults by others. Whatever the origins it is clear that very early in Indian history, there was recognition, acceptance of an attitude which gave prime importance to exclusive devotion to a personal divinity. Today we recognise it by the generic word *bhakti*. In the *Ṛg Veda* Viṣṇu is clearly mentioned, whether or not as minor or major importance. The word Viṣṇu is derived from the root *viṣ* to mean 'asunder'. Viṣṇu's first attribute is his pervasivness which forms the central feature in the vast complex of ideas and philosophy denoted by Viṣṇu. The *Ṛg Veda* speaks of him (Viṣṇu). "He who pervades the universe and measured the universe with his three strides." The three strides and steps are interpreted at many levels cosmological, psychical and spiritual. The myths of Vāmana and *Tṛivikrama* owe their origins to these descriptions. Viṣṇu in the Ṛg Veda is also the primeval germ of the cosmic order. He generates the sun, the dawn and fire for the purpose of sacrifice. He is preserver and protects unfailingly his devotees. The association with sun and the rays is also an enduring epithet. In time, it crystalises as the emblem of discus which Viṣṇu holds. Also, he assumes different forms concealing his affulgent form.

In ancient Tamil literature specially the *Tolakappiyam* is the description of a deity called *Mayon.* He is the god of the pastoral region and is considered a counterpart of Viṣṇu.

The *Ṛg Veda* and the *Śatapath Brāhmana* and other non Vedic sources all point at the fact that very early the Indian mind conceived of a power or force which was pervasive and protecting and one which was connected with the earth, pastoral life and the sun.

Historically the precursors of Viṣṇu and Vaiṣṇavism were Vāsudeva and Vāsudevism. They are the earliest known phases. Pāṇini (5th, 6th century BC) explains the word *Vāsudevaka* as *bhakta* or devotee of the venerable god Vāsudeva. The god Vāsudeva, it is said, belonged to a tribe called Vṛṣnīs. This is borne out by references in Patañjali's *Mahābhaṣya* and other texts. Inscriptions dating back to the 2nd century BC particularly the Garuda column of Besnagar refer to Vāsudeva as god of gods. There are other references in Magesthenes (4th century BC), the Buddhist Niddesa and of course the *Gītā* itself. Cōeval was the existence of a movement called *bhāgavata.* This is clear from the sources mentioned above. In the Besanagar inscription on *Garudadhvajā* (pillar) Heliodoros the native of Taksasila declares himself a *bhāgavata* dedicating the pillar to Vāsudeva. So also Pāṇini and Patañjali. A sub-school of the Bhāgavatas was possibly of the *Pañcarātrikas*. There is however still considerable unaniminity regarding the origins and development of the P*añcarātrikas*. However devotionalism is also their principal tenet.

A third trend is the emergence of Kṛṣṇa. Some scholars are of the view that Vāsudeva and Kṛṣṇa were two distinct personalities. While Vāsudeva is related to the Vṛṣnis, Kṛṣṇa is associated with the Yadavas, particularly as Devakīputra. Kṛṣṇa who is the pupil of Ghora Angirasa a sage mentioned in the *Chāndogya Upaniṣad*. In course of time the two merged to form the conception of Vāsudeva-Kṛṣṇa. A fourth stream was also evident in the form of the cult of Gopāla-Kṛṣṇa of the Abhiras. Gradually it would appear that Vāsudeva of the Vṛṣṇis, Kṛṣṇa of the Yadavas and the Gopal of the Ābhiras were integrated into a single mythological image we recognise as Kṛṣṇa.

This seemingly complex history of the conception of Viṣṇu and Kṛṣṇa, the movements of Bhagavatas and the *Pañcarātrikas* points to the multiple layers of the emergence of both the conception of the deity as also the movement and cult.

Despite the monumental scholarship on the subject by Indian and foreign scholars there is lack of certainity and definitiveness at the level of history, that is on the how and when of the development of Viṣṇu and Vaiśṇavism.

Nevertheless there is both unanimity as also clarity in regard to the nature of the deity, god and movements. The *Bhagavadagītā* expounds a world view which leaves little room for doubting the existence of a basic or incipient Vaiśṇavism. The *Mahābhārata* incorporated thc *Bhagavatagītā,* the *Narayanīya* and the *Harivaṁśa*. The three together lay the foundation of pervasive movement which we recognise as Vaiṣṇavism. As in the case of Śaivism, once the form of the deity emerged and cults identified, there was further proliferation and development of the myth, the philosophic schools and the socio-religious movements. The myth was elaborated in many *Purānas* called the *Vaiśṇava Purānas* principally the *Viṣṇu, Nārada, Bhāgavata, Garuda, Padma* and *Varāha*. The *Saṁhitas* specially of the *Pañcarātrikas* on the other hand were theological texts which dealt with *jñāna* (knowledge), *yoga* (psycho-physical discipline), *kriyā* (action) and *caryā* (personal behavior). In contrast *āgmas* lay down the rules of worship. Important philosophic schools called the Vaiṣṇava Vedānta emerged and a vast body of literature, poetry, hymns, drama and music is inspired by and devoted to Viṣṇu and Kṛṣṇa.

The Mahābhārata and its appendix the *Harivaṁśa* reveal two different but related Kṛṣṇa's each an aspect of Viṣṇu. Kṛṣṇa of the *Bhagavadagītā* is without a re-incarnation of Viṣṇu. He appears again and again to establish order whenever chaos and disequilibrium prevails. He establishes *dharma* (order, justice, righteousness) whenever disorder thrives.

The *Gītā* becomes a basic articulation of a world view which relates man-god and insists on the necessity of maintaining a balance between action, knowledge and devotion. It expounds the three paths of *Karma, Jñāna* and *Bhakti.* In the eleventh chapter Viṣṇu reveals his cosmic form, the *Viśvarūpa* and in the twelfth the *Bhaktiyoga* is expounded. Throughout the *Gītā* no matter from which view point it is considered as philosophy or poetry, religious text or moral teaching, it demands the need for a balance and equanimity from the 'human' if he wishes to know the Divine. The emphasis is on the relation of the human and the divine, of the inner and the other, the unexpressed, undefinable and the *avyakta* (unmanifest indiscrete). The *vyakta* (manifest), the unchanging immutable and the changing. The supreme in who all beings are and who has manifested himself in these diverse forms is to be attained by single residue devotion, *bhakti*.

Although hundred of commentaries on this little great book have been written and sages, scholars, philosophers, historians and sociologists have interpreted and re-interpreted the text, it holds meaning and challenge to any individual. It transcends any sectarian or denominational affiliation. The Gītā itself incorporates the speculative thought of the Upaniṣad particularly the Kathopaniṣad and by some accounts also the Saṁkhya and

Yoga philosophy.

In turn it gives rise to both philosophic schools as also socio-religious cults.

The *Harivaṁśa,* the appendix to the Mahābhārata, recounts the myth of the child and adolescent *Kṛṣṇa* which finally culminates in the massive *Bhāgavatapūrāṇa* attrituted to the eighth to tenth century A.D.

Historically, there is a gap of many centuries between the first inscriptional evidence of *Garudadhvaja* mentioned above and epigraphical and sculptural evidence of the Gupta period (5th century AD). Important amongst the sculptures is the four armed image probably of Viṣṇu in Udayāgiri (400 AD). In Udayāgiri again we find the monumental image of Viṣṇu Varāha rescuing Pṛithvi. A little later on the Deogarh temple of Lalitpur there is a magnificent relief of Viṣṇu lying on the cosmic serpent *Ananta.* Not he is *Seśāśaī.* Other evidence, epigraphical and sculptural follows in quick succession throughout the sub-continent. Monumental sculpture is carved in cave temples in the North and South. Mammallapuram and Ellora temples are erected to consecrate one or another form of Viṣṇu. Throughout the varied forms of this god runs the dominant theme of Viṣṇu as associated with solar system and as preserver, sustainer, the maintainer of the universal order *dharma.* Logically it leads to the conception of the *avatāras* where Viṣṇu descents to earth as animal or man on diverse occasions to maintain the order. In the *Gītā,* Arjuna had seen for a moment the *Virātapuruṣa,* the visual counterpart is the Viśvarūpa. The omniform of the Universe made manifest.

The *Alvaras* of South India were the first to sing the praise of Viṣṇu like their Śaivite counterparts the Nayanaras, they eschewed class-caste distinctions, stressed *bhakti* as a self validating outpouring of emotion and an assertion of the intrinsic relationship of the human and the divine. The Śaivites composed *Tevaramas,* the *Ālvaras,* the *Divya Prabhandas*. The *Ācarayas* of Vaiṣṇavism instead expounded theories, established systems and schools of interpretation. Rāmānuja is the towering figure amongst these. Author of many works and commentaries he is best known for enunciating the three eternal principles; the individual or animal soul (*cit*), the insensate world (*acit*) and the supreme soul (*Īśvara*). According to him the first two are subsumed in the third. The Bhāgavata Purāṇa is composed sometime between the eighth to tenth century, possibly in the south in the culmination of the Kṛṣṇa theme. It becomes the fountainhead of both myth and ritual, philosophy and religious sects. At the level of myth it recounts the life of Kṛṣṇa from a child to adulthood. Although the *Harivasṁśa* and *Viśnu Purāṇa* had spoken of the cowherdess, the gopis. The *Bhāgavatapūrāṇa* elaborates upon the theme. The *Daśamaskanda* gives a vivid account of the dance of Kṛṣṇa with the gopis. At the symbolic and philosophic level, its essence is the love of the human for the divine and the divine for the human. Devotion (*bhakti)* is its theme. The grace of god is compared to the love of the cow for its calf. His grace is perennial. Spontaneous and impartial the love of the human and the divine can be *dāsya* (service), *vātsalya* (maternal), *sakhya* (friendship), *kānta or mādhurya* (of the lover and beloved). It can be in separation or union (*viyoga* or *sambhoga*). All stories are meant only to illustrate the principles and way of life of the people who see god in everything and surrender to him.

Firm and pervasive foundations of Vaiṣṇava *bhakti* are laid and the movement spread throughout India. Its ramifications were many each distinct and distinguishable but with an unflinching conviction and faith in devotion (*bhakti*) and worship.

In Maharashtra there was *Jñānesvara* who formed or reformed the Varakari order and Namadeva (12th to 14th century) who celebrated the inner quest for purity of spirit and direct communication through recitation of the holy names. They were followed by Eknatha and Tukaram (16th and 17th century). Each stressed personal worship with or without image. Kṛṣṇa for them was the faithful husband of Rukmini who embodied Kṛṣṇa's dynamic nature.

In contrast in the East, Jayadeva wrote the *Gitā Govinda*

which celebrates the love of Kṛṣṇa and Rādhā. Subsequently Kṛṣṇa and Rādhā became central to the many sects founded by Nimbarka, Vallabha and Caitanya. Each inspired poetry and special forms of ritual. Sūrdās and others of the *Ashtechhays* schools sang with emotional fervour. Others followed. Each longed for Kṛṣṇa. The Vallabhāchāryas established a special mode of worship, recognised as the Nathadvara cult.

The followes of Caitanya were the Goswamis who established the distinct school of Gaudīya Vaiṣṇavisṃ. Here Rādhā and Kṛṣṇa are worshipped in their *yugalarūpa* (together as pair). The Goswamis propounded a theology in works like *Neelujvalamani* and others. It spread to Manipur and other places.

In Orissa grew the mighty and complex cult of Jagannath and in Assam there was Śankaradeva and his followers. In Kerala, Guruvayoor temple was established and in Karanatka, the Udupi temple, in Andhra Tirupati. From the thirteenth to eighteenth century, the entire country reverberated with the poetry, music, dance and painting revolving around the divine player Kṛṣṇa and his divine play. The calendar was punctuated with the renactment of his life; Janmāṣthmi, Holi, the rāsa dances of spring and autumn. The myth ritual philosophy coalesced as they do today. The *līlā* (the play) continue and lives. Breft of the two great gods Śiva and Viṣṇu their myths and the philosophic schools and the celebration of life they inspire the Indian landscape, outer and inner, the seasons and the annual cycle would be the poorer and of art of all genres little would be left.

Each age and period, each region gave the two gods and their philosophies a specificity of period and place a distinctiveness of style and form and yet without ever eschewing the perennial immutable principle of the love of the human for the divine and divine for the human, each incomplete without the other.

Śiva dances in Tillai, the hearts, Kṛṣṇa's dance in Vrindābana is also the inner landscape of the human psyche. Śiva is the one with latency and potency of creational. Kṛṣṇa is the eternal play of the one and the many. The mythical world in the psychical world and the devotee surrenders in love and devotion to that which is within and without all pervading.

* * * *

Re-Accessing Abhinavagupta*

Dr. Navjivan Rastogi

Some twenty five years ago I wrote an article on the contribution of Kashmir to Indian philosophy, thought and culture.[1] An effort was made, in that paper, to highlight the fact that the cultural history of India would ever remain incomplete if it fails to take into consideration the enormous contribution made by Kashmir in practically all areas of Indian Culture and all realms of Indological studies.[2] Today when we sit again to reappraise the whole scenario we find Abhinavagupta emerging as the single most potential and creative factor in the centre of total Kashmirian contribution to the history of Indian metaphysical speculation and as one of the most potent sources of the Indian contribution to the world thought.

Tradition has its own way of appraising such epoch making personalities. Abhinavagupta was hailed as an incarnation of

---

* This paper was written about five years back for the Vāṅmayī, the research journal of the Sanskrit Depatment, Lucknow University. Realizing that the issues raised in the paper have become all the more relevant calling for urgent concerted attention of the larger academy of sholars it is being reproduced, with requisite changes, as my humble tribute to the sacred memory of Pt. Janakinath Kaul 'Kamal'.

1. Paper entitled "Contribution of Kashmir to Philosophy, Thought & Culture" read at the International Sanskrit Conference, New Delhi, 1972, *Proceedings,* Vol.-1, part I, pp. 258-266. Later published in *ABORI,* Vol, 1975.

2. In people's mind, down the passage of history, Kashmir was perceived as the citadel of the Goddess of Learning and a testing ground of the persons claiming to be the scholars. As Jayaratha rightly observes in one of the closing verses of his *Tantrāloka-viveka* (verse no. 4)
   युक्ता बोधप्रधाना स्थितनिजमहसा शारदा पीठदेवी।
   विद्यापीठे प्रथीयः प्रथितनिखिलवाग्यत्र काश्मीरनाम्नि॥

Śeṣanāga,[3] as the Patañjali-incarnate,[4] as a wordly embodiment of the Lord Dakṣiṇāmūrti i.e., Śiva,[5] as the progeny of the parents established in the divine essence of Bhairava[6] (i.e., Yoginībhū), as the person initiated by his own deified awareness[7] and as a scholar whose name alone spelt authentic authoritativeness.[8] In fact, from all available data, Abhinavagupta was not his real name but a title earned by him from his teachers in recognition of his outstanding intellectual and spiritual accomplishments.[9]

All these descriptions may however be dismissed by a modern student as being purely holistic and eulogistic in content. It will, therefore, be necessary for us to demonstrate the factum of these statements and in the process to re-discover and reassess the personality, contribution and contemporary meaningfulness of Abhinavagupta. It has become imperative for two reasons.

Our first concern for reappraising Abhinavagupta is rooted in the general surveys of the contemporary Indological scene the world over. During the last fifty years a gradual, but increasingly accelerated, shift is discernible in the focal areas of interest of transnational Indological scholarship – from Vedas, Linguistics and Philosophy to Buddhism, Tantras and Abhinavagupta. The last one occupies centre-stage because of the path shown by Pandey in the first place and because of the multinational craze to explore the unfathomed intellectual depths of Abhinavan thought in a second. In the stark contrast, back home, the studies on Abhinavagupta have slackened and classics like Pandey's *Abhinavagupta and Comparative Aesthetics,*

3. *Abhinavagupta: An Historical & Philosophical Study, P.10-11*
4. *Ibid.*
5. श्रीमान्नः पातु साक्षादभिनववपुषा दक्षिणामूर्तिदेवः। *Gurunāthaparāmarśa,* verse no. 4
6. तादृङ्मेलककलिकाकलिततनुः कोऽपि यो भवेद्गर्भे॥
   उक्तः स योगिनीभूः स्वयमेव ज्ञानभाजनं रुद्रः। *Tantrāloka* 29.162-63. Also see *Tantrāloka-viveka,* VIII, p. 137
7. अभिषिक्तः स्वसंवित्तिदेवीभिर्दीक्षितश्च सः। *Tantrāloka,* 4.42-43
8. अभिनवगुप्तस्य इति सकललोकप्रसिद्धनामोदीरणेनापि आप्तत्वमेव उपोद्बलितम्। *Tantrāloka-viveka,* Vol. 1, p. 34
9. अभिनवगुप्तस्य कृतिः सेयं यस्योदिता गुरुभिराख्या।

Shankar Chaitanya Bharati's *Darśanasarvasva* and Kalidas Bhattacharya's *Gopinath Kavirāj's Thoughts-Towards a Systematic Study* are gradually, but conspicuously becoming a rarity. The Lucknow University did produce a few good studies in the cognate areas but with the exit of second generation scholarship, this too is likely to wither away soon. It calls for an immediate in-depth analysis of the reasons for the creeping loss of interest in Abhinavagupta. One may be confronted with the mushrooming of literature on Abhinavagupta in India in order to belie the above contention, but a close look does not fail to tear apart the deceptive veneer that covers the so-called studies. One reason may be that over these years we have failed to generate supportive tools and adequate groundwork necessary for sustained deepening of our insight into Abhinavan thought.

Our second concern flows from the second. Besides Pandey at Lucknow, there were quite a few other centres of spirituo-academic activity totally dedicated to the pursuit of Abhinavan thought, namely Gopinath Kaviraj, Lakshman Joo, Jai Shankar Prasad, S.K. Das, Amrit Vagbhava closely followed by R.K. Kaw, Jaidev Singh and B.N. Pandit. With the exit of all these scholars except the last one, the serious studies on Abhinavagupta on the home front are almsot extinct and there is every danger of loosing our moorings in the field of serious investigations in the area. Chances are that we might even loose our identity when viewed agaisnt the global backdrop. Because in the West as well as in the Far East, strong centres of deep academic interest synchronizing with the currents of neo-spiritualism have surfaced churning out first class studies on the different aspects of Abhinavan thought. France, Oxford, USA, Italy, Mexico, Japan, inter alia, have produced remarkable works in this special area. With the ever-growing appetite outside India for exploring Abhinavagupta more and more, our complacence may prove suicidal and self-effacing in a field that was pioneered and nurtured here. This explains urgent need for reappraising our academic priorities and reassessing the potential of Abhinavagupta.

By whatever method or in whatever way we may access Abhinavagupta as a philosopher, aesthetician, art-critic, dramaturgist, tantric, sādhaka, yogin, master of performing arts, metaphysician, devotee, researcher, historiographer, author, editor, commentator-all his pursuits are characterized by one common mission: they are palmbearers of a unified essence. He defines his vision as non-dualism (*advayavāda*). '*Advaya*' to him means fullness, harmony and integrality (*pūrṇatā, sāmarasya and sāmaṣtya*). Though conveying different connotations all the three terms stand for a single denotee clearly underlining the fact that the changing universe of discourse and the fleeting variety of the phenomena are nothing but the real manifestations of a single essence which for want of a better English equivalent may be rendered as self-referential awareness. The fullness, and for that matter, the harmony and the integrality lie in exploring the real identity between the phenomena and the ultimate unitary essence. This identity is realized not through the mechanism of a logically constructed superimposed entity but through the dynamism of the Reality's inherent agency. This unified essence, as a sequel, refuses to remain a mere simple unity, but a unity, a unified essence, filled by a rich self-unfolding content. While this presentation describes Abhinavagupta's philosophy, it also sums up his personality because his personality is a living realization of his vision. His is a total yet constantly and consistently unfolding personal identity.

If this were the tenable assessment, the enigmatically multidimensional personality of Abhinavagupta must cease to baffle us. In its own characteristic manner analogy of a *puruṣa* (person) is quite often resorted to in the Indian parlance to lend a semblance of life and to inject an element of wholeness into the idea by personifying the same. Like *kāvyapuruṣa or vedapuruṣa,* Abhinavagupta may be conceived as *prajña-puruṣa* embodying the essential features of *Sarasvatī* and *Naṭarāja* fused into one. The very notion of *prajñāpuruṣa* symbolizes the attempt to visualize knowledge as a whole (*avayavin*), that is, to adopt an integrated approach to knowledge. Abhinavagupta's whole personality is thus structured as an encyclopaedic thinker who not only displays an encyclopaedic fervour in whatever he touches, but he in the process also emerges as a nodal point where almost all the streams of Indological studies tend to converge. Let us see how.

Abhinavagupta appears as the tallest intellectual figure of medieval India by virtue of his all-encompassing genius. Beginning on the basis of relatively more known facts, Abhinavagupta's first impression is that of a philosopher. Generally we know him as a first rate metaphysical thinker of the Kashmir Śaivism. The Kashmir Śaivism literally stands for all the offshoots of Śaiva and Śākta speculation that grew or got matured in the valley. The modern usage of the term, however, has a slightly restrictive signification. The term now represents a sort of loose conglomerate of all monistic strands of thought pertaining to Śaiva-Sākta combine, the Pratyabhijñā and Trika Schools being the main and most popularly known systems. Remarkable as it may sound, Abhinavagupta contributes to both the segments. Under the second segment within the realm of Pratyabhijñā the two of the five core texts,[10] namely the *Īśvarapratyabhijñā-vimarśinī* and *Īśvarapratyabhijñā-vivṛtti-vimarśinī,* are from his pen. It is a matter of pity that till this day we have not been able to critically edit the text of the *Īśvarapratyabhijñā-vivṛti-vimarśiṇī* or translate the same in any language. It is a great scholastic work running over about 1200 finely printed pages and is comparable to the glosses of Vātsyāyana, Śabara or Saṁkara in their respective systems in scholarship. In the Trika system his versicular commentary called the *Malinī-vijaya-vārtika* on the *Mālinīvijayottaratantra,* the source text of the Trika system, is a pathsetter text and has met with a similar fate. A critically edited text and its translation into any language has so far eluded us. In the realms of the Kula system his *Parātriśikā-vivaraṇa* is a work of substantial merit.

10. सूत्र वृत्तिर्विवृत्तिर्लघ्वी बृहतीत्युभे विमर्शिण्यौ।
प्रकरणविवरणपंचकमितिशास्त्रं प्रत्यभिज्ञायाः ॥ *Sarva-darśana-saṁgraha* (chapter on pratyabhijñā, p.349)

In the Krama system, though his major work *Kramakeli* is now lost to us due to vagaries of time, his minor works such as the *Kramastotra* have survived the atrocities of time. He is equally famous for his immense contribution to the fields of literary criticism and aesthetics. His celebrated *Locana* on the *Dhvanyāloka* is a landmark in the history of Sanskrit literary criticism in general and in the history of Dhvani school in particular. What is important, Abhinavagupta establishes an inner chord between literary criticism and aesthetics. His illustrious commentary *Abhinavabhārati* on Bharata's *Nāṭyaśāstra* is a work of monumental value seminal to our current insight into Indian aesthetics. We must be grateful to Ramchandra Kavi who has afforded to us an edited text of the *Abhinavabhārati.* The four volumes of this enormous text comprise about 2000 pages. Again the irony is that this work too needs critical edition and an authentic translation. Except a few sporadic efforts towards editing the *Abhinavabhārati* pertaining to the *Rāsa-sūtra,* we are ill-equipped to grapple with this gigantic text. While commenting upon the *Nātya-Śāstra,* which is patently a text on dramaturgy, Abhinavagupta attempts a subtle transition from dramaturgy to aesthetics eliciting support from his master Bharata himself who views drama as the primary art-form and the other art-forms such as music, dance, sculpture and architecture being subordinate. Besides, by strongly substantiating the role of *vyañjanā* as a vehicle of transmission of art-experience in the *Locana* and by advocating the immediacy of art-experience being common to poetry and drama he demolishes the divider between poetry and drama and thus paves his way for smooth and purposeful foray into the realm of fine arts. In the field of Tantra perhaps there is none to match his standing in the entire history. His *magnum opus Tantrāloka,* which alongwith Jayaratha's commentary *Viveka* covers about 12 volumes extending over 3500 pages, is a text of matchless genre. Though purporting to be a commentary on the *Mālinivijayottara-tantra* the work remains thoroughly original in content, design and treatment. The work by itself is an enclyclopaedia of the tantric literature, ritual and praxis. This work too, though translated into Italian by Gnoli and into Hindi by Parama Hans Misra, needs a critico-textually edited text. I want to put this point across with a sense of added responsibility owing to my personal association with the text by way of bringing out an enlarged edition and also attempting a sizable introductory study. This text was later summarized by Abhinavagupta himself into growingly smaller *avataras* e.g., *Tantrasāra, Tantroccaya* and *Tantravaṭadhānikā.* Toeing the traditional Indian line, Abhinavagupta is not satisfied with his forays into the realm of knowledge and spirituality (*jñāna*); he is equally determined to make deep strides in the paths of devotion (*bhakti*) and action *(kriyāyoga)*. While he views all his works as constituting homage to the Divine (*stuti*) he has written several devotional poems (*stotras*)[11] as well, in which he pours his heart underscoring his roots in the tradition presided over by Bhaṭṭa Nārāyaṇa and his own grand teacher Utpala. Despite the descent of any specific text on yoga from his pen till date, it does not deter us from having a peep into his unique brand of yoga. His deep insight into *ānanda-yoga,* a term coined by him to mark his own approach, is abundantly noticeable in the *Mālinīvijaya-vārtika, Tantrāloka* and *Parātriśikā-vivaraṇa.* In addition, Abhinavagupta distinguishes himself from the general tenor of Indian philosophers. Here he finds himself in the coveted company of a great philosopher like Bhartṛhari. While the whole of Indian philosophy treats reality as 'meaning' (*artha*) or 'meaning of word' (*Padārtha*), the entire monistic Śaiva tradition of Kashmir perceives reality as 'word' (*śabda*) also. To be accurate, reality is a synthesis of word and meaning both. Abhinavagupta differs from Bhartṛahari in the sense that the latter views the meaning as an evolute of the Word Principle. A substantial block of the Mīmāṁsists too propounds the philosophy of language taking the meaning as a priori anticipation of facts represented by the pure word. While Abhinavagupta

11. A study of these *stotras* and other minor devotional works was done by me way back in 1959 while presenting a dissertation for my postgraduate degree. Later Lilian Silburn also published a work on these in France.

agrees with the Mīmāṁsaka stand, he finds pure word identical with pure awareness unlike the Mīmāṁsaka. Thus according to Abhinavagupta, objects and images are not contingent, they are self-concretizations of the pure word. Thus the linguistic evolution, like its parallel objective evolution, is a real symbol of the creative process. Abhinavagupta's linguistic thesis projects him as a philosopher of language par excellence and lays bare the subtle inner linkage obtaining between his theories of word, meaning and conveyance of art-experience.

Not only the mammoth canvas betrays the extent of his encyclopaedic mind, his treatment of the subject-matter too reveals the encyclopaedic functioning of his intellect. As seen above, Abhinavan genius is integral. In fact it is not just integral; it is 'integrating' also. To him, all the different disciplines he has worked on are various expressions of an underlying common essence. As he has emphatically demonstrated in the case of the *Tantrāloka* he views all his works – be it a work on literary criticism or a treatise on philosophy, a devotional poem or a manual of tantra – share identical structural pattern. All the texts, are designed as a compendium (*saṁgraha-grantha*), a procedure manual (*prakriyā-grantha*), a systemal text (*Śāstra-grantha*) and a devotional work (*stuti-grantha*). This fact is amply borne out by the benedictory and concluding verses of the respective works. By embracing such a structural organization he procures and preserves all the relevant information pertaining to ideas, literature and practices, followed by their organization into a systematic framework propounding the methodology to be adhered to and thereby spiritually sublimating everything as an offering to the Divine. A level below the structural fundamentalism is the next level of textual integration. For example the study of the *Tantrāloka* as an individual text is not advocated by Abhinavagupta. He visualizes the *Mālinīvijaya-vārtika, Tantrāloka* and *Parātrīśikāvivaraṇa* as forming a consistent whole and urges the reader to approach them as complementary texts. Similarly he perceives a logical integration between the *Locana* and the *Abhinavabhārati* on the one hand

and between the *Īśvarapratyabhijñā-vimarśinī* and the *Vivṛti-vimarśini* on the other; and then integrating the two sets from two separate disciplines he prepares the ground for integration at a larger and higher scale. A subsequent level of integration is seen within the schematization of the subject-matter of a given text. This process is visibly at work in all the major works such as the *Tantrāloka*, the *Īśvarapratyabhijñā Vimarśinī*, the *Vivṛti Vimarśinī* and the *Abhinavabhārati*. In all these texts Abhinavagupta aims to integrate vertically as well as horizontally. In the *Tantrāloka* by introducing the twin notions of the *tantra-prakriyā* and *Kulaprakriyās* and by subsuming all the systems under them and by interacting the two classes of systems he vertically integrates all the monistic Śaiva systems on the one hand; and on the other, he integrates all the Śaiva systems of nonmonistic shade also as emanating from *trayambaka* and non-*trayambaka mathikās* and constituting a single progressively assimilative channel. He is then able to produce a comprehensive manual on all the tantric systems placing them in a logically cohesive sequence. In the *Abhinavabhārati* he unearths a logically ordered whole of all the theories of *rasa* as an experience as well as an object and all the forms and variants of other art-forms and traditions and puts up a virtual store house of all previous as well as prevalent theories and practices at our disposal. In the *Īśvarapratyabhijñā-vimarśinī* and *Īśvarapratyabhijñā-vivṛti-vimarśinī* his integrating faculty wears a different mantle. Here he is ranked amongst the systematizers or systembuilders, portrayed as तर्कस्य कर्तारः by Jayaratha, like Somānanda and Utpala. Here he not only integrates but rationalizes, systematizes and reconstructs the loose ends into a well orchestrated cogent system of thought. It is Utpala, Abhinavagupta's grand teacher who introduces the four-fold division of the *Pratyabhijñākarikās* and integrates knowledge, action and *āgama* as belonging to the supreme subjectivity and discovers the principle of recognition as operating through each of them. Each cognitive variant and functional diversity of the subject is nothing but a recognitive mode of self-discovery. Thus *rasa*-experience is nothing but a recognitive mode of self-discovery through art. Meaning is nothing but a recognitive mode of self-discovery through word. The list is endless.

There is one more dimension to his encyclopaedic vision. It is the historical genius and keen historical sense that is evident in all the works of Abhinavagupta. The Indian notion on beginningless time and endless worldly cycle (*anādi* and *ananta*) happens to be a great deterrent of any historical activity in the modern sense of measurable time. Thus the rise of Kalhaṇa should be viewed as an exception, not as a rule. Against this backdrop Abhinavagupta indulges in a real historical activity. He dates at least his three works in precise terms of date, month and year. Goudriaan treats Abhinavagupta as one of the three concrete sources for dating the tantric texts. Abhinavagupta's historical sense transcends beyond this. He furnishes valuable information about his ancestral and preceptorial lineages. Everywhere he tries to point out and, if feasible, to restore the missing links in the tradition. It is possible to conclusively show that Abhinavagupta utilizes the entire pre-Abhinavan source material and imparts to them a chronological order. Modern researches have authenticated the vast material in manuscripts used by Abhinavagupta while writing his *Tantrāloka.* A study into the source-material of the *Tantrāloka* offers a very fascinating scope for future research. Exactly a similar phenomenon one comes across in the *Abhinavabhāratī,* where Abhinavagupta undertakes a stupendous task of collecting text-books, technical data, forms variants and modes of literary, dramatic and other performing arts. As a glaring and popular example *Abhinavabhāratī* remains till this day our only source of knowledge on various theories and theorists of *rasa.* Abhinavagupta's works offer an extremely rich sources for various aspects of Indian cultural history. The *Tantrāloka* and *Īśvarapratyabhijñā-vivṛti-vimarśinī* are replete with several informations on Buddhism, Tantric Buddhism and other systems of Indian philosophy which are now extinct in their own respective systems. For example, sixteenth Āhnika of the

Tantrāloka contains valuable information on *kālacakra,* the *Iśvarapratyabhijñā-vivṛti-vimarśinī* refers to and quotes from a sub-sect of Buddhists called *Dharmottarīya,* about which little is known from Buddhist sources.

Bound with this is Abhinavagupta's role as an editor and an exemplary research scholar in the modern sense of the term. He subjects his data to most vigorous historical, theoretical, chronological and logical scrutiny before utilizing the material. Abhinavagupta shares his problems and difficulties while negotiating his source text. He takes his reader into confidence about the precise norms of the methodology used by him. he throws copious hints to show that many texts had corrupt readings and several texts were incomprehensible and as such he had to edit them before he was able to use them. Utility, relevance, authenticity and consistency are his proclaimed norms which he scrupulously adheres to. When he finds his source text silent, he seeks guidance from the cognate texts from the allied fields, even when he does not subscribe to them.

Few would know, fewer would believe, that Abhinavagupta impresses us as an excellent musician. We do know that he was a philosopher of music. His treatment of the complexities of music, both vocal and instrumental as well as systemal, found in the *Tantrāloka, Abhinavabhāratī* and *Īśvarapratyabhijñā-vivṛti-vimarśinī,* presents a scientific as well as a philosophical account of music. The merit of Abhinavagupta lies in one more aspect that his *Abhinavabhāratī* also comes up an additional and complementary source of exposition of Bharata's contemporary or successor, Dattila, a great exponent of Gāndharva music. What is more remarkable that he is a great performing artist and ranks at par with *Nārada, Udayana* and *Tumbura* in tradition. In a pen-picture drawn by his contemporary and a senior pupil, *Madhurāja Yogin,* he is portrayed as playing on *Nāda-vīṇā.*[12]

He also impresses as a creative and thoughtful art critic. The way he subjects various poems to critical analysis in the *Locana, Abhinavabhāratī* and the fine nuances he brings to bear upon his

12. वामश्रीपाणिपद्मस्फुरितनखमुखैर्वादयन्नादवीणाम् । *Gurunāthaparāmarśa,* verse no.4

critical appreciation are landmarks in the field of practical literary criticism. Attention may specially be drawn to his critical analysis of a few verses from Kālidāsa[13], during the course of his build-up of the metapsychology of *rasa* and creative art process involved in the intuitive experience of a connoisseur of art (*sahṛdaya*), that is remarkable for its depth, range and originality and is sure to stay as a model of innovative practical art criticism.

Abhinavagupta defies his categorization among the known classes of Indian philosophers. Philosophy in general is supposed to be a system of thought which offers a rational explanation of the apparent intricacies confronted by us in our understanding of the phenomenal world and also how it paves way for the spiritual realization. Theories of knowledge, reality, relation and value etc. are the natural off-shoots of the metaphysical reasoning. But to Abhinavagupta, philosophy is much more than a mere speculative thought, its commitment to life as we live it is deeper and, therefore, it must be applied to explain those areas also. From metaphysics he transgresses into applied metaphysics. He is the only thinker of his kind who applies his philosophical thesis to the realms of art-experience, dramatic presentation, tantric praxis, yogic transcendental realization of the self and mundane sensual ecstacy specially marking the sex-experience viewing them all as the various expressions of the ultimate self-experience, their mutual difference being caused by the specifics of the medium or the instrument employed.

Abhinavagupta as a part of his two-way strategy utilizes these varied experiences as exemplifying and substantiating his metaphysical thesis. These constitute a sort of argumentation and support systems establishing the authenticity, validity, tenability and intelligibility of his theories bridging the seeming gulf between the existential, the experiential and the spiritual on the one hand and between the wordly and transworldly on the other. Thus while his metaphysics of recgnition offers a most

---

13. ग्रीवाभङ्गाभिरामं मुहुरनुपतति स्यन्दने बद्धदृष्टिः....... *Abhijñāna Śākuntalam*, 1.7
रम्याणि वीक्ष्य मधुरांश्च निशम्य शब्दान् *Ibid.*, 5.2
हरस्तु किंचित्परिलुप्तधैर्यश्चन्द्रोदयारम्भ इवाम्बुराशेः। *Kumāra-sambhavam*, 3.67

cogent known Indian explanation of the aesthetic experience, the art-experience brings the immediacy of transworldly intuitive realization within our reach. According to Abhinavagupta, the art- or aesthetic-experience is self-recognitive experience which reflects fullness of joy because of its freedom from the conditionalities of medium, time and space. In plain words, it is an aesthetic rehearsal of spiritual self-recognition. This recognitive art-experience is communicated and thereby re-created in the aesthete by employing the suggestive power of language. It should be clear that power of suggestion as developed by Abhinavagupta can be described as a theory of transcendental recognition. Like Bhartṛhari, Abhinavagupta's understanding of the revelatory unity of reference allows us to the higher level of language through *pratibhā* and communication is successfully effected through its revelation (*sphoṭa/dhavani*). Abhinavagupta's description of the Supreme Word (*parāvāc*) as the absolutic self-recognition (*ahaṁpratyavamarśa*) makes it essential to the very structure of experience and thereby again removes the gap between experience and expression (*rasānubhūti* and *rasābhivyakti*). One cannot miss that the process of *rasa-niṣpatti* as being concomitant to *rasanā* (*vyañjanā*) offers the poetic epistemological argument in support of Abhinavagupta's philosphy of language whereby the self is both revealed and enjoyed. Amongst all art-forms Abhinavagupta accords the highest status to drama because of the analogical character of the Absolutic enactment of the world and the actor's enactment of a character in a drama. As Śiva is portrayed as a cosmic actor (*naṭa/śailūṣa*) and the cosmic arena as a huge dramatic stage where, by assuming roles of individual subjects, He enacts the world-drama and after conclusion gives up the assumed identity and reverts to Himself. Thus the myth of the absolutic descent and return to its original being is symboised by the dramatic art-form where the actor, under the assumed identity, becomes a part of the dramatic action and reverts to himself when the drama is over. There is a subtler similarity too. The actor by identifying himself with the focus of dramatic situation, even though enacting an assumed character, experiences the aesthetic relish due to intuitive self-realization resulting from the process of universalization (*sādhāraṇīkaraṇa*). The absolute too, likewise, even while discharging the worldly role, has a beatific self-experience due to self-recognitive universalization. By substituting dramatic art with ritual and praxis, Abhinavagupta extends application of his theology to the field of tantras. Abhinava attempts philosophical rationalization of the Śaiva monist's central soteriological doctrine of the Absolutic agency symbolically internalized by tantric praxis and rituals (*kriyā, caryā*) duly re-inforced by his assertion that he himself was conceived in a tantric riutal. In the Kashmir Śaivist terminology Śiva is conceived as the supreme agent (*kartā*) and everything else is his agency or act (*kriyā*). The tantric phraseology replaces it by the paradigm of the 'powerful' and the 'power' (*śaktimān* and *śakti*). The world is nothing but the self-actualization of *Śaktimān* through its own agency in the phase of expansion (which is also a literal meaning of the term 'tantra') and reabsorption of the world within self by deactivating this agency. The plethora of tantric practices and ritual are the tantric enunciation of the divine functionalism by undertaking which the Godhead unfolds and enfolds itself. The situation bears close analogy to the aforesaid dramatic performance. We reach this tantric unity of Śiva and Śakti by another route also. The overall pattern of the spiritual practices corresponding to the broad tantric mythical structure is the recourse to the sexual rituals, physically and alternatively by mental visualization, to manifest or reintegrate "the cosmogonic sexual unity of Śiva and Śakti."[14] The fundamental thrust of the argument consists in the adept's achieving complete identification with Śiva in the enjoyment of the world as Śakti, both as his 'power' as well as 'consort'. The various rites comprising *caryākrama, rahasyaprakriyā* or *ādiyāga* (primal rite) are typical examples of such tantric praxis. The homology between the dramatic experience and the tantric

14. Arguments and the Recognition of Śiva, David Peter Lawrence, p.38

experience of the self lies in the role of Śakti or agency which consists in self-referential integration or self-recognitive awareness where connoisseur of art (*sahṛdaya*) or the actor (*naṭa/ anukartā*) is akin to Śiva and his experiencing capacity to *pratibhā* or intuitive power (*Śakti*) which is nothing but the self-referential awareness. In this extended sense the sexual experience includes all the sensual experiences, their self-sublimating or self-refining potential being constituted by Śakti or power. Thus intrinsic nature of aesthetic, sexual or sensual experiences are homologous to and practically approximate to the monistic Śaiva soteriological realization.

The greatest feature of Abhinavan contribution lies not in his extreme originality, nor in his capacity to rise way above the past tradition or break with the tradition, but in his contemporaneity and futuristic potential towards opening up new vista for the Indian thinking.

While taking stock of the social margins of the Abhinavan thought viś-a-vis contemporary content and futuristic expectations our attention is arrested by five important features of his approach:

(a) Out of the two basic strands of Indian thought- analytical (*Adhyavasāyātmaka*) and synthetical (*anusaṁdhānātmaka*), Abhinavagupta sides with the latter. The process of analysis implies an exclusivist (*vyāvṝttimūlaka*) or negative approach towards life, undermining its value, opting for congnition which is based on 'pick and choose' Selectivity and dividing society in compartments of language, caste, creed and gender. As against this the process of synthesis is based on life-affirmation, recognizing life as a value, embracing recognition on unilocality of time and space and advocating inclusivism (*anuvṛtti*) rejecting artificial pigeon-holes of humanity created by caste, creed, gender and language. According to Abhinavagupta those who subscribe or sympathize with the social fragmentation are bent upon insulting the Divine and are prone to make themselves laughing stock.[15] This idea of Abhinavagupta is buttressed from another source of his. His metapsychological enunciation of the process of universalization (*sādhāraṇikaraṇa*) in the artistic consummation is a bold statement of such a radical reasoning.

(b) Abhinavagupta's life-embracing approach is a direct outflow from his doctrine of totality and complete integration (*pūrṇatā/sāmarasya*) which is reflected in the ecclectical value-structuring and acceptance of all finite truths as human truths. This is indicative of Abhinavagupta's fundamental belief in the possibility of countless modes of the ultimate Reality's manifestation. Abhinavagupta's direct student, Kṣemarāja, gives an exquisite vent to it in his famous aphorism.[16]

(c) Abhinavagupta joins the main stream tantricism in projecting 'power' as the special theme of the tantric myth, symbolism and practice. The entire tantric ritual mechanism is geared to realize this 'power'. Through ideological rationalization, the sole direction of the cognitive activity, which is recognitive *per se* is said to 'discover'/'rediscover' this power[17] and that of agential activity (*kartṛtā*) is to 'actualize' this power at the level of experience. By valuation of power over other considerations in our thought and conduct both, a stage is set to elevate human independence or self-instrumentality towards energizing inherent potential.

(d) Abhinavagupta's equation of microcosm with macrocosm, of *yogin* with *Parama Śiva,* of individual consciousness with universal consciousness is obviously

---

15. ते हि भगवतः सर्वानुग्राहिकां शक्तिं मितविषयतया खण्डयन्तः तथा परमेश्वरस्य परमकृपालुत्वमसहमानाः, भगवत्तत्त्वे भेदलिङ्गं बलादेवानयन्तः, मात्सर्यावहित्थलज्जा-जिह्मीकृतावाङ्मुखदृष्टय इति हास्यरसविषयभावम् आत्मेति आरोपयन्ति इति। *Bhagvadātārthaśaṁgraha* on Gītā 9.35

16. तद्भूमिकाः सर्वदर्शनस्थितयः। *Pratyabhijñā-hṛdayam,* Sūtra 8

17. स्वशक्त्याविष्करणेनेयं प्रत्यभिज्ञोपदर्श्यते। *Īśvara-pratyabhijñā-kārikā,* 1.1

aimed at viewing the man as an end in himself and thereby paving the way for exploring the ultimate possibilities of his growth.

(e) Abhinavagupta views the mundane as an extension of the transmundane or the Divine. His total being is fully disposed towards discovering a deep mutual level of dependence between the objects. This proclivity consists in innate realization of the basic unity inherent in diversity. Abhinavagupta has repeatedly declared that this world of discourse marked by unity-in-diversity carves out gateway to the spiritual awakening.[18]

Laced with the foregoing overview of Abhinavan theology and its quintessential premises a modern student of Abhinavagupta will instantly catch hold of a fertile ground in Abhinavagupta towards reconstructing a new system of Indian thought whose immediate central concern will be to transgress the artificial barriers eroding the social cohesion, to uphold the cause of 'power' as a real tool of exercising one's agential freedom, to offer a congenial atmosphere for achieving ongoing divination of man and, in the sum total, for attaining a joyous existence as the celebration of life.

Before winding up, attention must be drawn towards political significance of no mean order of Abhinavan contribution. Kashmir constitutes a burning test of our secular credentials and Hindu-Muslim unity. If we fail to retain Kashmir, we loose the battle of secular Indian polity. The best of Kashmir is embodied in and represented by Abhinavagupta. As the tradition has it, his birth in Kashmir was by his own compassionate choice.[19] It is, therefore, our sacred duty not to allow Abhinavagupta to die in the land of his birth.

With the foregoing statement of rationale, I invite the scholarly world to re-access and re-assess Abhinavagupta for

18. सर्वथा तावदत्र प्रमेये भगवत एव भेदने च अभेदने च स्वातन्त्र्यं घटगताभासभेदाभेददृष्टिरेव परमार्थाद्वयदृष्टिप्रवेशो उपायः समवलम्बनीयः, न तु व्यवहारोऽपि अयं परमेश्वरस्वरूपानुप्रवेश-विरोधी *Īśvara-pratyabhijñā-vimarśinī* II,p. 129

19. श्रीकण्ठेशावतारः परमकरुणया प्राप्तकाश्मीरदेशः । *Gurunāthaparāmarśa* verse no. 4

answering our basic concerns of cultural identity, radical secular commitment, nodal centrality of Indological persuits and divining a fresh sociophilosophical thinking with contemporary humanistic ethos.

Bibliography

1. *Abhinavagupta :* An Historical & Philosophical Study K.C. Pandey, Chowkhamba, Varanasi, 1935, 2nd revised edition, publisher same, 1963.
2. *Abhinavagupta Ke Stotra : Eka Adhyayana* (unpublished) Navjivan Rastogi, dissertation submitted to the Lucknow University for partial completion of M.A. final examiniation 1959.
3. *Arguments and the Recognition of Śiva : The Philosophical Theology of Utpala Deva and Abhinavagupta* David Peter Lawrence, Ph.D. dissertaion, University of Chicago, 1992; now published as *Rediscovering God with Transcendental Argument,* SUNY Series, Albany (U.ṢA.), 1999.
4. *Bhagvadagītārthasaṁgraha* Abhinavagupta, commentary on *Gītā,* ed. Pt. Lakshmana Raina, Srinagara, 1933.
5. *Comparative Aesthetics* Vol. I (Indian Aesthetics) K.C. Pandey, Chowkhamba, Varanasi, 1950. 2nd revised edition, publisher same, 1959.
6. *Comparative Aesthetics* Vol.II (Western Aesthetics) *K.C. Pandey, Chowkhamba,* Varanasi, 1956.
7. *Gurunāthaparāmarśa* Madhurāja Yogin, ed. V. Raghavan, *Bulletin of the Government Oriental MSS Library,* Madras, vol.II-I, 1949.
8. *Introduction to the Tantrāloka; A Study in Structure* Navjivan Rastogi, Motilal Banarsidas, Delhi, 1987.
9. *Īśvarapratyabhijñāvimarśinī* (with the *Īśvarapratyabhijñā-Kārikās* of Utpala) Abhinavagupta, edited with Bhāskarakaṇṭha's commentary by K.A.S. Iyer and K.C. Pandey under the title *Bhāskarī,* Reprint, Motilal Banarsidas, Delhi, 1987.
10. *The Krama Tanricism of Kashmir* Vol. I Navjivan Rastogi, Motilal Banarsidas, Delhi, 1979.
11. *Nātya Śāstram* (with the *Abhinavabhārati* by Abhinavagupta) Bharata Muni, ed. Ram Krishna Kavi, Baroda, 4 vols. 1926, 1934, 1954, 1964.
12. *Pratyabhijñāhṛdayam* Kṣemarāja, English trans. and notes by Jaidev Singh, Motilal Banarsidas, Delhi, 1963.

13. *Tantrāloka* (with the *Viveka* of Jayaratha) Abhinavagupta; republication, edited by R.C. Dwivedi and Navjivan Rastogi, Motilal Banarsidas, Delhi, 1987.
14. *Sarvadarśanasaṁgraha* Hindi translation by S. Sharma 'Rishi' Chowkhamba, Varanasi, 1964.

* * * *

Grace

Dr. Bettina Bäumer

Grace is always unexpected, undeserved, full of surprise. It cannot be earned, not even desired. It is useless to sit and wait for it to happen. Like any real gift, it is given freely. But when it comes, it fills the whole being of the receiver with light, peace and joy, with a new vision and new energy. To this description both, Śaivas and Christians can agree.

This brief outline of the topic takes a comparative approach. It is precisely in the meeting of their mystical dimention that different religions can come to an understanding.

I. Generally three terms are used to denote 'grace' in Kashmir Śaivism: *anugraha* which means more favour, divine kindness, *prasāda,* which means transparency and clarity, and which Abhinavagupta describes in the following way : "Divine favour is a state of purity of the nature of fullness, in which Śiva is resplendent in all his fullness together with the limited self" (Tantrāloka XIII. 286). These two terms are common to other systems also. The third term, *śaktipāta,* lit. "descent of the divine Energy" is very much favoured by Abhinavagupta. My question, which I am supporting by some texts, is whether *anugraha* refers to the general grace which is theologically/ontologically available to all human beings, and *śaktipāta* to the specific grace, also related to initiation, bestowed on yogis or highly advanced souls, which we could call mystical grace.

Regarding "general grace", *anugraha* is one of the five acts of Śiva which are continuously going on in the universe and in the soul, but this is his foremost act. Abhinavagupta says at the beginning of the Parātrīsikā Vivaraṇa : "The Highest Lord ever brings about the five-fold act. He is in fact the very Grace itself, being always equipped with His Supreme Divine Energy whose very nature is Grace. This Śakti which is full of the thought of Grace for the entire world...." (*Sā ca śaktiḥ lokānugrahavimarśamayī,* p. 2). A little further he says: "Thus the power of grace of the Divine is always and in all experients uninterrupted" (*eveṃ ca anugrahaśaktiḥ satataṃ sarvapramāṭṛṣu anastamitaiva,* p.4). "Therefore she (the power of Grace) alone, the life and soul of Trika Śāstra, constitutes the highest relationship (*para sambandha*)". When he states the purpose of the scripture, we find a phrase combining the general with the specific grace : "The aim or purpose of the Śāstra is liberation of all experients in life-time, experients who have become entitled for this knowledge of the unsurpassable *(anuttara)* derived from grace in the form of excellent descent of divine Śakti" (*paraśaktipāta-anugrahavaśa-utpanna...* p. 6). If we agree that there is such a difference between general grace that is available to all subjects and the actually experienced, liberating grace, there is one more question involved: If grace is the very nature of the Divine and potentially available to all, what is the need of making any spiritual effort? This could lead to a quietistic attitude, letting oneself go with the idea that in any case it is God's will, whatever may happen. Abhinavagupta takes this view as a *pūrvapakṣa* and makes it quite clear that the doctrine of ever-present divine grace does not mean laziness : "If it is said that God's will is perfect, it is not open to discussion, then enough of useless efforts like reading and concentrating on books, exposition, discussion etc. This heavy burden should certainly be abandoned. One should then sit quietly, God's will alone would save one who is to be saved. It is His merciful will that makes one depend on such thought.

By no means should people remain stretching their legs and lying with ease, indulging in enjoyment, without deliberating for themselves, nor should people sit idle, averse to the constant application of the competent intellect for the subtlest deliberation, brought about by intense and intenser grace of the Lord which appears in accordance with one's *sādhanā...*" (PTVi pp. 105-

108 transl. Jaideva Singh).

The exact relationship between the readiness of the disciple or sādhaka and the degree of *śaktipāta* is precisely described in the 9 grades of intensity of grace in Tantrāloka XIII.

Coming to *śaktipāta* as mystical grace, we may refer to a very moving verse in Utpaladeva's *Śivastotrāvalī* :

śaktipātasamaye vicāraṇaṃ
prāptamīśa na karoṣi karhicit ।
adya māṃ prati kimāgataṃ yataḥ
svaprakāśanavidhau vilambase ॥

XIII.11

Lord, although it is fitting,
You never discriminate
When bestowing grace.
What has befallen me now that you delay
In revealing a glimpse of yourself?

Abhinavagupta uses this verse to give a beautiful definition of grace : he explains the words "never" and "proper" by saying that grace is not dependent on anything (*anapekṣitvam*), and that the Lord who bestows it is impartial (*arāgitvam*). (TĀ XIII.291) He also calls this power of the Lord a "revealing" or "opening" grace (*unmīlinī,* V. 294).

I think all these characteristics of *śaktipāta* agree perfectly with a Christian understanding of grace.

II. Let us come to the second point, the Christian understanding of grace. The Greek word *Xaris* has a natural and a supernatural meaning. Gregory Palamas gives the following meanings : "Sometimes it is the object given gratuitously which is called grace, but sometimes it is the very act of giving; at other times neither of these senses apply to the word "grace" which designates, so to say, the beauty, the beautiful appearance, the ornament and the glory of each nature..." (Against Akindynos III, 9, quoted from John Meyendorff, A Study of Gregory Palamas, p. 163). Theologically it is clear that without divine grace there is no salvation, because man is not able to reach

God with his own powers. Grace means participation in the divine life. Of course, we cannot go into the subtle distinctions of the theology of grace in such a short note. I only want to mention one doctrine of grace which I found strikingly close to that of Kashmir Śaivism.

St. Gregory Palamas, great mystic and theologian of the Eastern Church in the 14th Cent. (1296-1359), has already two important teachings in common with Trika : one is that he speaks of the "Divine Energies" through which God is acting in the world. The other is that he defends the role of the body in spiritual practice, against such teachers (esp. Barlaam) who deny any positive role of the body in spiritual life. According to orthodox doctrine, Palamas also accepts the idea of the "obscuring" of the divine image in man, and of grace as removing the veil and bestowing illumination – corresponding to the *tirodhāna* and *anugraha* aspects of Śiva's activity. Not only that, he also distinguishes between two types of grace, 'created grace' and 'uncreated deifying grace'.

In Gregory Palamas' teaching, God's deifying grace or energy is not only itself uncreated, but renders uncreated those who share in it. Insofar as man does not partake of deifying grace he remains a created consequence of God's creative energy, in which case his relationship with God is confined to one of creature to Creator. But when man shares the uncreated divinizing gift, he acquires supranatural attributes. Without ceasing to be created as regards the nature, he is nevertheless placed beyond the category of created things because of the grace within him. He is now in possession not only of his created nature but of an uncreated and indwelling grace, and he can be defined not only according to his natural characteristics but also according to the qualities of the grace dwelling within him :

"He who achieves deification is fittingly defined by both : he is on the one hand unoriginate, eternal, and heavenly, as we heard just above, on account of the uncreated grace that eternally derives from the eternal God; he is on the other a new creation and a new man and things similar to these, on account of himself and his own nature."[1]

New-made by the regenerative power of divine grace, man is not merely a product of God's creative energy but shares in His uncreated life which is without beginning and without end.

(G.I. Mantzaridis, *The Deification of Man,* New York, pp. 111-112).

The passing from the state of creature to the divine state by means of grace reminds us of the transformation of the *paśu* into *pati* in Śaivism. Palamas speaks also of *Synergy,* that is the "collaboration" of man with God's action, of grace and human effort. The effect of grace is nothing less than the complete deification of man. This is possible because of Incarnation, for "God became man, so that man may become God." "Grace is therefore not a 'thing' which God grants to nature either to 'complete' its deficiencies, or simply to 'justify' it, or to 'add' to it a created supernatural, but it is the divine life itself." (John Meyendorff, *A Study of Gregory Palamas,* Aylesbury, Bucks, 1964, pp. 163-164).

III. Coming to practical experience, I would like to put the following question. There is no doubt that there exist different degrees of intensity of grace, as described by Abhinavagupta. There is also no doubt that these degrees do not depend on the whimsical will of God, because in Him there is no difference possible, but they rather depend on the purity and readiness of the receiver. Abhinavagupta relates his nine degrees to different people, their different dispositions and the effect of grace on them. But if we follow our experience, I find that the same person experiences in his or her lifetime moments of grace which are different in intensity. Somethimes the initial grace, which puts a person on the spiritual path, which Christians would call 'conversion', better *metanoia,* is very powerful. Then the *sādhaka* may be left in a kind of desert for long periods, without experiencing this kind of grace. At other times he or she may receive grace of a lesser degree. As far as my experience goes,

1. *Anwser to Akindynos* 3, 6, 15, *Works* 3, p. 172; cf. Maximus Confessor, Ambigua, PG 91, 1141A-1144D.

there is no direct relationship between what we may call preparedness and the flowing in of grace. We may receive it when we are least prepared, not only consciously but even unconsciously. One may be in a state of crisis, or depression, or sickness, and there it is suddenly: a new clarity, a sense of lightness, of deep peace. This is also independent of any time and place where one would "expect" such an experience or not expect it. As Swami Lakshman joo says often: "It will not happen to you during your meditation, in your prayer room, it will happen to you in the middle of the bazar, while you are cleaning utensils or going to the bathroom."

There is another question connected with this unexpectedness of grace : Many people experience it without knowing what it is, and without being able to hold it or make it fruitful for their lives. And here of course a conscious effort, meditation, reflection, understanding etc. is necessary, otherwise the precious pearl which has been received freely may be wasted or lost. Here a guru or spiritual tradition is necessary.

But coming back to the question of the degrees, can we relate the different intensities experienced during a life-time to our weakness, purity or impurity? Also, how can we make full use of an intense grace? – without, of course, trying to hold it in the fist of our hands. It would be like trying to catch a butterfly or a bird.

Another last point concerns the "sharing" of grace. If Abhinavagupta relates the three degrees of the highest *śaktipāta* to the creation of masters, and the middle and lower intensities to the creation of disciples, it is clear that the stronger the grace, the more permanent the inner transformation, the more it has the capacity to radiate on others, to transform others. But let alone *jīvanmuktas* like Ramana Maharshi, I believe that even on a much lower level, the transforming power of grace can be passed on. It is like the lighting of a lamp with the help of another lamp, as Abhinavagupta says about the passing on of the experience from guru to disciple.

* * * *

Āgamādhikāra of Ācārya Utpaladeva

Dr. Koshalya Walli

(Among the four adhikāras of the Īśvarapratyabhijñā-kārikā Āgamādhikāra is the third one. – Eds.)

According to the *Vimarśinī* of *Ācārya Abhinavagupta, Āgama* in its essence is simply the determinate knowledge (*Vimarśa*) of the Highest Lord who is unlimited pure light of knowledge. Hence, nothing is beyond Its view. The teacher is to explain the exact nature of the dejective world so as to enable the people to understand that state which is transcendental and is attained by making the universe an object of knowledge (i.e., Knowing in reality what it is). To attain this objective, the third *adhikāra,* called *Āgama Adhikāra* begins.[1]

Thus action is free conscionsness, manifesting internallly and externally, in accordance with the temporal order, hence action really belongs to the subject. Thus the power of knowledge and action are mutually inseparable. Knowledge is enlivened by *Vimarśa* and *Vimarśa* is action.[2]

It is not possible for a person without knowledge to be associated with action. This catagory is known as "*Śiva*", being characterised by both powers of knowledge and action. Through the power of action, it is capable of bearing the reflection of the innumerable creation and destruction of the entire mass of *Tattvas* and which though it appears in meditation and instruction as mere appearance "*Ābhāsa*", is not *Ābhāsa*.

---

1. आगमस्त्वपरिच्छिन्नप्रकाशात्मकमाहेश्वरविमर्शपरमार्थः किं न पश्येत्, इति तदनुसारेण पदार्थनिर्णयविश्वप्रमेयीकरणप्रतिलब्धतद्विश्वोत्तीर्णप्रमातृपदहृदयमङ्गीकाराभिप्रायेण निरूपयितुमाचार्य आगमाधिकारं तृतीयमारभते। (आगमधिकारः, विमर्शिनी, तृतीयमारभते।)
2. न च ज्ञानशक्तिविहीनस्य क्रियायोग इति। तदेतदवियुक्तज्ञानक्रियारूपं क्रियाद्वारेण सकलतत्त्वराशिगत सृष्टिसंहारशतप्रतिबिम्ब सहिष्णु यत् तदुपदेशभावनादिषु तथाभासमनाभासमपि वस्तुतः शिवतत्त्वमित्युक्तं भवति। (विमर्शिनी – III.1.1)

All the categories rest on pure consciousness, thereby having no scope for any succession, as there is no temporal or spatial difference amongst them.

First of all *Sadāśiva* comes into being on account of the rise of the internal aspect – the power of knowledge to prominence and then there comes into existence *Parameśvara Tattva* when the external aspect comes into predominance. As the *Sādākhya* is so called because here the consciousness of being arises for the first time. *Sādākhya* is synonymous with *Sadāśiva.* External aspect consists in the power of action. *Parameśvara* is *Īśvara Tattva.* It's manifestation is after the *Sādākhya Tattva.*[3]

"*Tattva*" is the essential nature of that which shines undivided in the various groups of things with distinctive features that serves as the cause to justify their being represented as belongings to one class. Mountain, tree, rock are earth in their essential character. *Sadāśiva Tattva* is concretization of *'Cit'* – Consciousness. It consists in "this-consciousness" of the mass of dejects on the part of sentient beings who are pure consciousness and technically called *Mantramaheśvaras.* This mass of objects shines like a reflection on them. It is very dim like that which shines as the object of inner sense only in the new creation (the first descent from the state of free consciousness or *Savimarśa Caitanya*). It is like an extremely dim outline of a picture. It may also be compared to the mass of objects which it is on the point of absolute annihilation at the time of the dissolution of the universe and hence is extremely dim. But to the sentient beings, universe, that has attained a stage of clarity, similar is that of the objects of on external cognition, shines almost in a reflection. The category, technically called *Mantreśvara,* the universe which has attained a stage of clarity, similar to that of our cognition, shines almost as a reflection. The category technically *Īśvara* is nothing but the shining of it. But the *Sadāśiva* and *Īśvara* are the objects of contemplation and worship. They are like *Brahmā* and *Viṣṇu.*[4]

3. किन्त्वान्तरदशोद्रेकात्सादाख्यं तत्त्वमादितः ।
बहिर्भावपरत्वे तु परतः पारमेश्वरम॥ (Ī.P.V. – III.1.2)

4. Vimarśinī – III.I.2

Īśvara manifests the outer world and *Sadāśiva* closes up the external world. The light of consciousness rests on itself alone as activity (*Vimarśa*), characterised by resting on self-luminousness, perfectly independant of all others, is represented as *'Ahaṁ'*. And the consciousness that is dependent upon another is represented as "*Idaṁ.*" The latter in reality rests on that which is self-luminous and is perfectly independent of others. The first consciousness is *Śiva Tattva* and the second is *Videyeśa.*[5] In *Śuddha Vidyā* things are essentially of the nature of I-consciousness and they are conceived as they really are. '*Avalokana*' means knowing conceiving. These words are synonymous with *Vidyā.* Correctness of knowledge consists in its following the true nature of a thing. The purity of *Vidyā* is in the fact that it remains contradicted. '*Bodha*' – the light of consciousness, the essence of which is the self consciousness, free from dependence on any other - is the essence of all the objects, which are correctly conceived as 'this'. As they have assumed the state of being the objects of knowledge. "अहम्-इदम्" – "I-This", because it rests on ultimately true nature of the objects.[6]

In *Sadāśiva* and *Īśvara,* the objects are not only in the state of imperfection (*Aparatvam* – अपरत्वम्) because they shine as not-self, but they are also in the state of perfection (परता – *Paratā*). They are covered by I-consciousness (आच्छादत – *ācchādata*), because they shine as identical with the self. For, the *Sadvidyā* is common to the category of the *Sadāśiva* and *Īśvara* as *Parāpara Daśā.*[7]

---

5. ईश्वरो बहिरुन्मेषो निमेषोऽन्तः सदाशिवः।
सामानाधिकरण्यञ्च सद्विद्याहमिदंधियोः॥ Ī.P.V. – III.1.3

6. इदं भावोपपन्नानां वेद्यभूमिमुपेयुषाम्।
भावानां बोधसारत्वाद्यथावस्त्ववलोकनात्॥ Ī.P.V. – III.1.4

7. अत्रापरत्वं भावानामनात्मत्वेन भासनात्।
परताहन्तयाच्छादात्परापरदशा हि सा॥ Ī.P.V. – III.1.4

According to same, *Vidyā* is nothing but the distinct consciousness which is similar to that which is brought about by the power of *Māyā*. Such a consciousness is found in *Vidyeśvaras* – the subjects.[8]

Vidyā Śakti reveals the real nature of the Lord in the state of *Paśu. Māyā Śakti* obscures the reality.[9] An undiluted diversity is manifested by the power of *Māyā*. She identifies the *Śūnya, Buddhi* and *Prāṇa* etc. with the self.[10]

The limited subject *Śunya* etc. knows the limited objects that are separated from it and is really an object and as such is limited by *Kāla* (time), *Kalā – Limited action, Vidyā* – limited knowledge, *Rāga* – attachment with something to the exclusion of other things, *Niyati* – is that limiting condition which is responsible for the attachment to a certain fixed object.[11]

As regards the essential nature of the subject, according to Utpaladeva, a subject blinded by *Māyā* is limited by five *Kañcukas* and thinks that *Karma* binds him, thus he is transmigratory. When he is made to recognise his powers by true knowledge, he becomes purc *cit* and is spoken of as liberated.[12] He is called Lord (*Pati* – पति) when looks upon the objects as non-different from himself. He is called *Paśu* – limited subject, when objects are manifested, separated from him by *Māyā* and he is defiled by troubles (*Kleśas*) and actions (*Karmas*).[13]

---

8. भेदधीरेव भावेषु कर्तुर्बोधात्मनोऽपि या।
मायाशक्त्येव सा विद्येत्यन्ये विद्येश्वरा यथा॥ *Ibid* – III.1.6
9. तस्यैश्वर्यस्वभावस्य पशुभावे प्रकाशिका विद्याशक्तिः ....
...... तिरोधानकारी मायाभिधा पुनः॥ *Ibid* – III.1.7
10. भेदे त्वेकरसे भातेऽहंतयानात्मनीक्षिते।
शून्ये बुद्धौ शरीरे वा मायाशक्तिर्विजृम्भते॥ *Ibid* – III.1.8
11. यश्च प्रमाता शून्यादिः प्रमेये व्यतिरेकिणि।
माता स मेयः सन्कालादिकपञ्चकवेष्टितः॥ *Ibid* – III.1.9
12. एष प्रमाता मायान्धः सन्सारी कर्मबंधनः।
विद्याभिज्ञापितैश्वर्यश्चिद्घनो मुक्त उच्यते॥ *Ī.P.V.* – III.2.2
13. स्वाङ्गरूपेषु भावेषु प्रमाता कथ्यते पतिः।
मायातो भेदिषु क्लेशकर्मादिकलुषः पशुः॥ *Ibid* – III.2.3

Āgamas describe three kinds of *Malas* (ignorance) with regard to *Paśus* (human beings with limited powers) – Loss of *Bodha* (wisdom) due to loss of freedom, ignorance about the essence of *Svātantrya* (freedom). Thus *Āṇavamala* is of two types. This *mala* results in the loss of knowledge of ones essential nature. *Māyīyamala* is due to the consciousness of the object as distinct from the subject. Birth and subjection to the furits of Karma are due to the *Māyīyamala.* Not having the knowledge about the actions to be done or not to be done – *māyā śakti* is the root of these three *malas* (as described above).[14]

Those who are pure consciousness but devoid of the freedom of action are formed different from Himself by the Highest Lord, for want of freedom in action in them.[15] *Vijñāna Kevalas* with no difference in respect of omniscience, eternity and omnipresence, have consciousness without freedom as essential characteristics. On account of the Lord's will to shine differently *Vijñāna Kevalas* are different from each other.[16] *Pralayākalas* are essentially insentient like *Śūnya* etc. They have the impurity of *Kārmamala* also. But the impurity of *Māyā* they may be in possession of or not – it is optional.[17] *Vidyeśwaras* are the subjects identifying themselves with pure consciousness and omniscient and omnipotent as a result of the destroyers of the impurity of *Karma*. But body, senses and *Bhuvanas* etc. shine as

---

14. स्वातन्त्र्यहानिर्बोधस्य स्वातन्त्र्यस्याप्यबोधता।
द्विधाणवं मलमिदं स्वस्वरूपापहानित: ॥ *Ibid* – III.2.4
भिन्नवेद्यप्रथात्रैव मायाख्यं जन्मभोगदम्।
कर्तर्यबोधे कार्मं तु मायाशक्त्यैव तत्त्रयम् ॥ *Ibid* – III.2.5
15. शुद्धबोधात्मकत्वेऽपि येषां नोत्तमकर्तृता।
निर्मिता: स्वात्मनो भिन्ना भर्त्रा ते कर्तृतात्ययात् ॥ *Ī.P.V.* – III.2.6
16. बोधादिलक्षणैक्येऽपि तेषामन्योन्यभिन्नता।
तत्रेश्वरेच्छाभेदेन ते च विज्ञानकेवला: ॥ *Ī.P.V.* – III.2.7
17. शून्याद्यबोधरूपास्तु कर्तार: प्रलयाकला:।
तेषां कार्ममलोप्यस्ति मायीयस्तु विकल्पित: ॥ *Ībid* – III.2.8

separate from them, hence are possessed of *māyīya mala.*[18] All the gods and human beings are enveloped by all the three impurities, but, chief impurity is *Kārma mala* – the main cause of birth and rebirth.[19]

Citatva – free consciousness is full of power of action – *Kartṛtvamayam.* It is revived by the power of *kalā* and constitutes the subjective aspect of *Śūnya* etc. These are in reality devoid of sentiency, free consciousness is limited i.e., of the nature of am object, as it occupies a subordinate place i.e., 'I' element is subordinate to 'this' element.

Jñāna – innate true knowledge – is the most essential characteristics of liberation, consists of the equal predominance of *Bodha* consciousness and *Kartṛtva* (freedom). Consequently *Śunya* etc. is subordinate to *cit.*[20]

The absence of object of knowledge characterises the *Śūnya Pramātā* who is nothing more than not being of *Buddhi* etc. and who experiences subjectively as 'I' which is related only to the vague and absolutely formless residual trace.

Power resides in the *Śūnya.* It sets vital air etc. in motion and is the internal activity of the senses (*Indriyas*). This power is called *Jīvana* (life). Another view of 'life' is that it is nothing out but self consciousness, identified with vital air (*prāṇa*) which is identical with the group of eight (*Puryaṣṭakas*).

Deep sleep consists of the rest of self consciousness in *Śūnya* or *Prāṇa.* It is like the state of dissolution. It is of two types –

---

18. बोधानामपि कर्तृत्वजुषां कार्ममलक्षतौ।
भिन्नवेद्यजुषां मायामलं विद्येश्वराश्च ते॥
सर्वज्ञाः सर्वकर्तारश्च ते विद्येश्वराः, किन्तु तनुकरणभुवनादि यदेषां वेद्यतया कार्यतया च भाति ---- भिन्नमेव सत् इत्यस्ति विद्येश्वराणां मायाख्यमलयोगः। *Ibid* – III.2.9

19. देवादीनां च सर्वेषां भविनां त्रिविधं मलम्।
तत्रापि कार्ममेवैकं मुख्यं संसारकारणम्॥ *Ī. P. V.* – III. 2.10

20. कलोद्वलितमेतच्च चित्तत्त्वं कर्तृतामयम्।
अचिद्रूपस्य शून्यादेर्मितं गुणतया स्थितम्॥
मुख्यत्वं कर्तृतायास्तु बोधस्य च चिदात्मनः।
शून्यादौ तद्गुणे ज्ञानं तत्समावेशलक्षणम्॥ *Ibid – III.2.* 11-12

a) That in which the objective consciousness persists. b) That in which there is no objective consciousness. In the former the subject has the impurity of *Māyā,* but in the latter, he is free from it.[21]

In the state of dreaming, the objects in mind only (*manas*), shine as clearly as they do when they are related to external senses. This is an illusion. In the wakeful state of the subjects, the creation (of object) is common to all subjects, is stable, and, is external because it is the object of all senses.[22]

These three states are to be given-up on account of the dominance of *Prāṇa* and subordinate position of power of freedom (*Kartṛtā*) in them. There is pleasure or pain in them, according as the predominance of this power of freedom increases or decreases.[23]

The question arises – if the first three states are to be given up because of the predominance of *Prāṇa* etc. (vital air) in them, which is not predominant in *Turīya* etc., how after entering into *Turīya* state, there is rise again of *Vyutthāna.* Ācārya Utpala while replying says that in waking and dream states, *Prāṇa* – the vital air – manifests itself primarily in inhaling and exhaling. It is given the name of *Samāna* in the state of deep sleep, the most essential feature of which is the non-manifestation of *Prāṇa* in the form of inhaling and exhaling. *Samāna,* as such is

---

21. शून्ये बुद्ध्याद्यभावात्मन्यहन्ताकर्तृतापदे।
अस्फुटारूपसंस्कारमात्रिणि ज्ञेयशून्यता॥
साक्षाणामान्तरी वृत्तिः प्राणादिप्रेरिका मता।
जीवनाख्याथ वा प्राणेऽहन्ता पुर्यष्टकात्मिका॥
तावन्मात्रस्थितौ प्रोक्तं सौषुप्तं प्रलयोपमम्।
सवेद्यमपवेद्यं च मायामलयुतायुतम्॥ *Ī.P.V.* – III.2. 13-15

22. मनोमात्रपथेऽप्यक्षविषयत्वेन विभ्रमात्।
स्पष्टावभासा भावानां सृष्टिः स्वप्नपदं मतम्॥
सर्वाक्षगोचरत्वेन या तु बाह्यतया स्थिरा।
सृष्टिः साधारणी सर्वप्रमातॄणां स जागरः॥ *Ibid* – III. 2. 16-17

23. हेया त्रयीयं प्राणादेः प्राधान्यात् कर्तृतागुणे।
तद्धानोपचयप्रायसुखदुःखादियोगतः॥ *Ibid* – III. 2. 18

compared to the time – (*Viṣuvat* i.e., equinoctial time). It is characterised by the movements of *Prāṇa* and *Apāna* and the rest of the *Prāṇa* in the cavity of the heart i.e., not moving to the left or right for a while, like the time *Viṣuvat,* characterised by the equality of the duration of the day and of the night and stoppage for a very short time of the sun towards the south or the north i.e., its being at the equator.

In the state of *Turya,* it moves up through *Suṣumnā* – mid-passage, and, as such is called *Udāna.* Here starts destruction of the objective world. This state is from *Vijñānākala* to *Sadāśiva* and *Īśvara. Turīyātīta* state is the state of *Parama Śiva,* characterised by the working of *Vyāna.*[24]

Thus the Highest Lord is *Prāṇa, Apāna, Udāna, Samāna* and *Vyāna.* The universe comprising thirty six tattvas is Lord's power of *Prāṇa* etc.

* * * *

---

24. प्राणापानमयः प्राणः प्रत्येकं सुप्तजाग्रतोः ।
तच्छेदात्मा समानाख्यः सौषुप्ते विषुवत्स्विव ॥
मध्योर्ध्वगोप्युदानाख्यस्तुर्यगो हुतभुङ्मयः ।
विज्ञानाकलमन्त्रेशो व्यानो विश्वात्मकः परः ॥ *Ī.P.V.* – III.2. 19-20

Abhinavagupta's Anuttarāṣṭikā

(Eight Verses on the Unsurpassable)

Translation and Commentary by Dr. Bettina Bäumer

अनुत्तराष्टिका

संक्रामोऽत्र न भावना न च कथायुक्तिर्न चर्चा न च
ध्यानं वा न च धारणा न च जपाभ्यासप्रयासो न च।
तात्किं नाम सुनिश्चितं वद परं सत्यं च तच्छ्रूयतां
न त्यागी न परिग्रही भज सुखं सर्वं यथावस्थितः ॥१ ॥

There is no need of sprititual progress,
nor of contemplation, disputation or discussion,
nor meditation, concentration nor even the effort of prayer.
Please tell me clearly: What is supreme Truth?
Listen: Neither renounce nor possess anything,
share in the joy of the total Reality
and be as you are!

संसारोऽस्ति न तत्त्वतस्तनुभृतां बन्धस्य वार्तैव का
बन्धो यस्य न जातु तस्य वितथा मुक्तस्य मुक्तिक्रिया।
मिथ्यामोहकृदेष रज्जुभुजगच्छायापिशाचभ्रमो
मा किंचित्त्यज मा गृहाण विहर स्वस्थो यथावस्थितः ॥२ ॥

In reality no world of transmigration exists,
so how can one talk about 'humans in bondage'?
To try to liberate one free already
is futile, for he was never in bondage.
All this just creates a delusion like that
of the shadow of a ghost or a rope mistaken for a snake.

So neither renounce nor possess anything.
Enjoy yourself freely, resting in your self,
just as you are!

पूजापूजकपूज्यभेदसरणिः केयं कथानुत्तरे
संक्रामः किल कस्य केन विदधे को वा प्रवेशक्रमः
मायेयं न चिदद्वयात्परतया भिन्नाप्यहो वर्तते
सर्वं स्वानुभवस्वभावविमलं चिन्तां वृथा मा कृथाः ॥३॥

What words can describe the Unsurpassable? In the Absolute
can there be any distinction between the worship,
the one who worships and the object of worship?
How and in whom can there be spiritual progress?
What are the degrees of absorption?
Illusion itself is ultimately the same
as non-dual Consciousness, all being the pure
nature of the Self, experienced by oneself-
so have no vain anxiety!

आनन्दोऽत्र न वित्तमद्यमदवन्नैवाङ्गनासङ्गवत्
दीपार्केन्दुकृतप्रभाप्रकरवन् नैव प्रकाशोदयः।
हर्षः संभृतभेदमुक्तिसुखभूर्भारावतारोपमः
सर्वाद्वैतपदस्य विस्मृतनिधेः प्राप्तिः प्रकाशोदयः ॥४॥

This bliss is not comparable to that which is experienced
through riches or wine or even union with the beloved.
The dawning of that Light is not to be compared
with the light of a lamp or that of sun or moon.
The joy that is felt when one is freed from the burden
of accumulated differences[1] can only be compared
to the relief felt while setting on the ground a heavy weight.
The dawning of the Light is like finding a lost treasure:
the state of universal non-duality.

1. Bheda: divisions, separation, duality.

रागद्वेषसुखासुखोदयलयाहंकारदैन्यादयो
ये भावाः प्रविभान्ति विश्ववपुषो भिन्नस्वभावा न ते।
व्यक्तिं पश्यसि यस्य यस्य सहसा तत्तत्तदेकात्मता-
संविद्रूपमवेक्ष्य किं न रमसे तद्भावनानिर्भरः ॥५॥

All states of mind like love and hatred, pleasure and pain,
arising and disappearing, to you appear distinct.
They are, however, part of the universal body,
their nature is not separate. Whenever you observe
any one of them arising, at once become aware
of their oneness: contemplate in them the form of pure Consciousness.
Filled with this contemplation, will you not experience joy?

पूर्वाभावभवक्रिया हि सहसा भावाः सदाऽस्मिन्भवे
मध्याकारविकारसङ्करवतां तेषां कुतः सत्यता।
निःसत्ये चपले प्रपंचनिचये स्वप्नभ्रमे पेशले
शङ्काकङ्कलङ्कयुक्तिकलनातीतः प्रबुद्धो भव ॥६॥

The non-existent suddenly is brought into existence;
such are always the states of being in this world.
How, being intermingled due to deformation
of the intermediate state, can they possess any reality?
How find reality in the unreal, unstable,
in multiplicity of worldly things, a dream's confusion
or in deceptive beauty? Transcend the impurity
that causes doubt and fear and awaken!

भावानां न समुद्भवोऽस्ति सहजस्त्वद्भाविता भान्त्यमी
निःसत्या अपि सत्यतामनुभवभ्रान्त्या भजन्ति क्षणम्।
त्वत्संकल्पज एष विश्वमहिमा नास्त्यस्य जन्मान्यतः
तस्मात्त्वं विभवेन भासि भुवनेष्वेकोप्यनेकात्मकः ॥७॥

It is not the Innate Being that gives rise to these various
states. They appear, created by you. Though unreal,
they become real through a momentary confused perception.

The glory of this universe is born from your will.
It has no other origin. Therefore your glory
shines in all the worlds. Though one You have many forms.

यत्सत्यं यदसत्यमल्पबहुलं नित्यं न नित्यं च यत्
यन्मायामलिनं दयात्मविमलं चिद्दर्पणे राजते[१]।
तत्सर्वं स्वविमर्शसंविदुदयाद् रूपप्रकाशात्मकं
ज्ञात्वा स्वानुभवाधिरूढमहिमा विश्वेश्वरत्वं भज ॥८॥

Both the real and the unreal, the simple and the complex,
the eternal and the temporal, that which, due to illusion,
is impure and also the purity of the Self-
all shine in the mirror of Consciousness. All this
is seen as having the nature of pure light,
as consciousness arises in self-awareness.
Recognising your glory rooted in your own experience,
share in the universal power of the Lord!

इति श्रीमदाचार्याभिनवगुप्तपादैर्विरचितानुत्तराष्टिका समाप्ता।

Commentary[2]

Anuttara, the Unsurpassable, Transcendent, Ultimate or Absolute is neither the object of devotion of this mystical Stotra, nor is it described philosophically. Rather, Abhinavagupta is moving here in a mystical state which can only be described negatively as "that which has nothing beyond it", *anuttara.* The word occurs only once, in verse 3, and there too it is called indescribable. In fact, it is not surprising that Abhinavagupta gives as many as 16 definitions of the word *anuttara* in his Parātrīśikā Vivaraṇa on the very first verse of the Tantra.

In his Stotras he is free from any literary, devotional or philosophical restrictions and he allows his mystical inspiration a free flow. Here he describes both the highest state possible to be reached by a spiritual being, and he instructs his most

1. Bheda: divisions, separation, duality.
2. Abhinavagupta's Stotras have been translated and commented upon in French by Lilian Silburn and in German by myself.

advanced disciples in experiencing such a state. The first three verses and verses 5 and 6 end with a personal address which can go directly to the heart of the disciple/listener/reader. Only a Master like Abhinavagupta can utter such mystical instructions, and only advanced disciples can receive them. He removes their doubts and worries.

In the case of immature disciples these instructions could prove dangerous, since they negate everything that belongs to spiritual practice: meditation (*dhyāna*), contemplation (*bhāvanā),* reflection or discussion *(carcā*), concentration (*dhāraṇā*) or recitation of mantras (*japa*) (verse 1). The very idea of moving on a spiritual path and progressing on it is denied *(saṃkrāma,* verses 1 and 3). For spiritual practice only has meaning if there is a state of bondage from which one wants to be liberated (verse 2), but Abhinavagupta denies that ultimately such a bondage exists. And if there is no bondage in *saṃsāra,* what is the use of the action of liberation? What is then to be done?

Nothing, for every action, practice or effort is only a sign of the limited being and is not fit for the *anuttara.* Thus both acts or attitudes have to be abandoned: renunciation and possession *(natyāgī na parigrahī,* verse 1, *mā kiṃcit tyaja mā gṛhāṇa,* verse 2). What remains then? The joy of being as one is and having a share in the totality. Not by chance Abhinavagupta uses the imperative *bhaja* in the first and last verse, because the one who is established in his natural state *(sahaja,* verse 7) shares in the divinity, in universality and universal lordship *(viśveśvaratvam*, verse 8). The injunction "be as you are" is not an invitation to egoism, but a reminder of our Divine and universal nature.

What is it then that separates us from this spontaneous state of being if there is no bondage in reality? It is only the illusion of not being free already, but an illusion which is not substantial, which is nothing but the shadow of a ghost (verse 2). But since illusion has no independent reality, it is also ultimately not different from non-dual Consciousness. Therefore even the fear of being in illusion has no basis and one should be free from the worry of not having realized one's true nature (verse 3). Nothing could be more liberating to the troubled mind but these condensed verses.

What Abhinavagupta says here in very personal terms is expressed more theologically in the Spanda Kārikā:

"Inasmuch as nothing can veil His nature, there cannot be any obstruction of his in whom all this world rests and from whom it has come forth." (I.2)

In his Parātrīśikā Vivaraṇa, he comments on this: "Even if He (Śiva) is supposed to be obstructed by a cover, He still shines by His freedom in the form of that cover itself, and thus the Lord is always of the nature of knowledge and activity." (transl. Jaideva Singh, p. 79).

Therefore Abhinavagupta concludes in the last verse (8) that everything, even the so-called impure, the temporal, illusory and unreal, belongs to the one, pure light of Consciousness. It is Consciousness alone which creates all these states and conditions, and one should see only its glory shining in everything (verse 7).

But is there a way of piercing through this veil and discovering its oneness with universal Consciousness? Starting from the ordinary experience of the disciple which is always an experience of dualities, like pleasure and pain, love and hatred, Abhinavagupta points out a very subtle method in verse 5:

Since all the opposite mental states are aspects of the same Consciousness, one should fix one's awareness on the moment of arising of any emotion or experience.

By catching hold of this initial moment, called *prathamakoṭi,* one enters into the oneness of Consciousness. In this way one experiences a bliss and freedom which cannot be compared with any wordly joy (verse 4).

If there has been any burden, it was the burden of separation of living in duality and fragmentation *(bheda),* but the moment one is freed from this, there is a relief as by putting down a heavy load from one's head. This is a moment of enlightenment, like finding of a lost treasure, the treasure of the non-dual state (verse 4).

This awakening to one's own original glory makes one share in the universal Divine Power (*viśveśvaratva,* verse 8).

Thus the entire hymn glorifies the unsurpassable state - *anuttar* - and leads the disciple from duality to non-duality. By the powerful expression of pure spontaneity Abhinavagupta achieves a liberating effect.

* * * *

Section-B

Cultural and Philosophical Studies

Cultural and Philosophical Studies

This Section of Part II is titled as Cultural and Philosophical studies. Here we have twelve articles by eminent scholars, which lay down the basics of our culture. The section opens with Prof. Gangadharan's article titled 'Gleanings from the Purāṇas.' These gleanings have been done with a purpose. They spell out Hindu Culture. Prof. Gangadharan has presented here a bird's eye view of all the major Purāṇas. The essay orients readers to overall Purāṇic studies.

Mokṣa is the *carama Puruṣārthă* in Hindu tradition. Dr. G. Mishra, expounds *Jīvanmukti* in the light of the philosophy of Vidyāraṇya. The concept of *cinmātra, vāsanā, manonāśa* are lucidly explained by Dr. Mishra. The other two depicting the essentials of Nyāya-Vaiśeṣika philosophy follows this article. Prof. V.N. Jha is very pithy in explaining *Śakti* and *Tātparya*. He says that the one is the desire of God and the other is the desire of the speaker. Prof. Jha has pointed out distinct functions of both, *Śakti* and *Tātparya*, in a mathematical way.

In an article on *Alankāraśāstra* Dr. Rajendran traces the influence of *Nyāya-Vaiśeṣika* philosophy on this *śāstra*. He cites Bhāmaha, Mahimbhatta and Jagannāth and traces the principles of *Nyāya-Vaiśeṣika* in the exposition of *Rasa* theory. He analyses the logical structure of a few *alaṅkāras* and points out the cause-effect relationship that adds beauty to description.

Mind is an ever eluding subject and a challenge to all philosophers. We could not so far ascertain the nature of mind. Dr. Dalai gives here 'Jain Concept of Mind'. He conceptualizes mind as per the references in the literature, ancillary to Jain texts and conjures before readers an invisible picture of mind. He further scrutinizes mind in relation with other sense organs. All this is laid down in the terminology of Jain texts. Dr. Dalai says emphatically that among the systems of Indian philosophy, only the Jain philosophy has developed such an advanced concept of mind.

In a brief article on *Navya Nyāya* Prof. K.C. Dash has laid down the basic assumptions of *Nyāya* and has pointed to the theories, in this system which deal with Epistemology, Ontology, along with Metaphysics and Ethics.

Prof. Nagaraja Rao narrates how Sri Ramana Maharshi, even as a boy overcame the fear of death and how he lived in the Self since then. He was a living example of a pure life merged in *advaita*. This realization permeated his actions and word.

After describing, *anicca, dukkha* and *anatta* Dr. O.P. Pathak introduces *Vipassana* Meditation to overcome these. Though this is an old Buddhist technique of meditation, it is still practised in the modern world, individually and collectively, at retreats and in certain institutions including jails. The *Vipassana* Meditation has changed the lives of many and is thus helping social regeneration.

In a long article, on 'Sanskrit and Cultures of the World,' Dr. Lokesh Chandra presents a world scenario in the context of Sanskrit language. He traces the origin of a number of European languages to Sanskrit. Sanskrit studies gathered roots in Germany, a couple of centuries before and since then that country is in the forefront of Sanskrit Studies. Dr. Lokesh Chandra has travelled extensively, both in the East and in the West and has presented here the worldview of the historic language. Many a new fact in the history of Sanskrit Language has been presented here.

Dr. A.D. Mathur surveys the '*Nītikāvya* literature in Sanskrit.' The word *nīti* was associated early with politics, *rājanīti*. But essentially *nīti* is a way of life and touches a number of human activities. Dr. Mathur particularly mentions Cāṇakya, Bhartṛhari and Kṣemendra. Other minor works on *Nītiśāstra* have also been covered in the article.

This section ends with two essays on Kālidāsa. One by Dr. T.V. Vāsudeva examines 'Life and Death in the *Mahākāvyas* of Kālidāsa.' The concepts of life and death, lead one deep in philosophy. It is interesting to note how the great poet in his masterpieces deals these philosophic concepts namely *Kumārasambhava* and *Raghuvamśa.* Dr. Vasudeva has drawn a parallel with a number of acknowledged philosophical works. This helps the reader in understanding the base of Kālidāsa's poetry.

The last article in this section is by Prof. Jadhab. Kālidāsa is undisputedly regarded as a Master of Similes. Simile is no doubt, a significant characteristic of a great poetry. But Prof. Jadhab points here, Kālidāsa's superb use of *arthāntaranyāsa,* a form of embellishment of poetry. The rhetoricians have explained this form of literary embellishment in a number of ways. Prof. Jadhab scrutinizes these definitions and points out the apt handling of this *alaṅkāra* by Kālidāsa in *Kumārasambhavam.* The essay presents one more facet of Kālidāsa's marvelous poetic genius.

This is the richest part of this Commemoration Volume and it touches all the topics, which were dear to Prof. Jankinath Kaul. The Śaiva studies were not merely an academic pursuit for him, but they formed a very basic of his life. All the spiritual values he cherished had their source in Kashmir Śaivism. We are happy we could collect and present these essays here as a fitting tribute to Prof. Kaul.

The twelve articles in the second section of this part will also go a long way in stimulating the Indologists and may motivate them for further research.

– Editors

Hindu Culture – Gleanings from the Purāṇas

Professor N. Gangadharan

Culture denotes the cumulative ideas immortalized in the literatures, histories, biographies and scientific and philosophic expressions. It is differentiated from civilization by its existence all through the ages. Hindu culture has survived for four thousand years in spite of numerous hordes of foreign invaders. It is noteworthy that these foreign elements have also been absorbed into Hindu culture. The Hindu culture has spread far and wide and its influence is still noticed in the distant Bali islands in the Far East.

The noteworthy features of Hindu culture are – 1) the firm faith in the existence of a Supreme Reality that sustains the world and its beings, 2) tolerance and freedom of thought and pursuit, 3) holding the integral nature of the Supreme Being and his creations, 4) the spiritual and religious debts a person owes to the sages, gods and ancestors and 5) the institutions of *varṇa and āśrama.* Another important feature is the formulation of a scheme of life based on the fourfold goals of human existence – righteous living (*dharma*), acquisition of wealth by righteous methods (*artha*), utilizing it for good living (*kāma*) and gaining liberation from human existence (*mokṣa*). The first three goals constitute the path of involvement, gradually leading to the last one, the cessation of all activities. We notice this feature permeating the last one, the cessation of all activities. We notice this feature permeating the Epics and Purāṇas in the form of ideal types of characters portraying the virtues.

The institutions of *varṇa* and *āśrama* enabled to a great extent in the efficient functioning of the Hindu society catering to the needs of the different layers of the society. The *varṇa* system was based on the aptitude and the ability of an individual. When it was formulated it was not based rigidly on one's birth as it grew to be in later days. The *āśrama* system on the other hand governed the functioning of different stages of life: as a student, householder, forester and an ascetic. There was perfect coordination among the different elements forming part of these two systems.

The Vedas are traditionally believed to be not by any human agency and enjoy a hoary antiquity. Next to the Vedas, the Purāṇas are also recognized as a valuable source for understanding Hindu culture. Moreover according to a statement found in the ***Mahābhārata***[1] the Vedas are to be amplified with the help of the Purāṇas. The Purāṇas are voluminous in nature and have assimilated diverse material in the course of several centuries and hence are good source material for understanding the Hindu culture. The statement relating to the ***Mahābhārata*** that whatever is found in it is found elsewhere and whatever is not found in it is found nowhere is very well applicable to the Purāṇas. Though the Purāṇas are mainly devoted to the explanation of the principles governing the practice of *dharma* and other related topics, there are many other secular topics throwing light on the Hindu culture.

The Purāṇas are reckoned as eighteen and their names are almost the same except that some Purāṇas read ***Śivapurāṇa*** in the place of ***Vāyupurāṇa***. The ***Devībhāgavata***,[2] a minor, contains a couplet indicating the names of the eighteen Purāṇas by means of the first letters in the respective Purāṇas. These Purāṇas are classified into three groups as *sāttvika, rājasa* and *tāmasa* on the basis of their subject matter relating to one of the three deities of the Hindu pantheon of gods. There are other methods of classification of the Purāṇas on the basis of the material found in them. Accordingly the ***Garuḍa purāṇa, Agni purāṇa*** and ***Nārada purāṇa*** are classified as encyclopaedic on account

1. I.1.208.
2. I.3,2.

of the diverse branches of learning described in them.

The Purāṇas advocate three pathways for visualizing the form of god – knowledge, action and devotion. The salient features of the path of knowledge may be described. The fundamental philosophical background in the Purāṇas is theistic Sāṅkhya. Besides the twenty-four categories of the Sāṅkhya system we find the reference to the twenty-fifth category as the worshipper and the twenty-sixth as Śiva, Viṣṇu or Devī as the case may be.[3] The Purāṇas describe the process of creation according to the Sāṅkhya system. Yoga with its eight constituents is described in detail in almost all the Purāṇas. We find description of the tenets of the Advaita system in several passages of the Purāṇas. Accordingly Brahman is spoken as the single reality, self-luminous, eternal, non-decaying, non-dual, devoid of limiting adjuncts, omniscient, omnipresent and omnipotent. The individual is identical with the Supreme Brahman. In order to realize this identity one has to seek the aid of the scriptures that have incorporated the direct revelation of the seers as well as cogent logic. The reality and eternal nature of the self is known from its existence through the three states of waking, dreaming and deep sleep. Grief arises from holding the concept of the self with reference to that which is not the self and the sense of possession in respect of things not belonging to one.

The second path comprising the practice of virtuous acts laid down in the scriptures is dealt with extensively in the Purāṇas. These are the performance of the austerities, making gifts and performance of sacrifices and practising virtues. The different kinds of austerities have to be practised on the different days of a lunar fortnight in different months.[4] Sixteen great gifts are described in detail in the Purāṇas reflecting the economic conditions, which prevailed in those times. Gold played a significant part in these great gifts.[5] The Purāṇas describe the

3. See ***Liṅgapurāṇa*** I.28, 7-9a.
4. See ***Garuḍapurāṇa*** I.117-25 and 130-37. See also Kane, ***History of Dharmaśāstra*** V. pp. 255-462.
5. See ***Matsyapurāṇa*** chs. 274-89 and ***Liṅgapurāṇa*** II. 28-44.

different kinds of atonement for violating the principles of dharma. They mainly consist of regulating one's food. *Kṛcchra* is the general term denoting expiation. There are other expiations based on the phases of the moon such as the Cāndrāyaṇa, Parāka, Sāntapana etc. Shaving, bathing, offering of oblations and worship of gods and fasting are common for all the expiations.[6] Besides pollution caused by birth and death there are other kinds of pollution arising from contact with impure things. The Purāṇas lay down remedial measures for the removal of pollution. The belief in the cause and effect made men believe in the existence of different hells in which sinners had to undergo sufferings proportionate to their sins. Hell was considered to be the opposite and counter-part of heaven. The Purāṇas mention the names of the different hells and the sufferings one has to undergo in them.[7] Some Purāṇas describe in detail about the life after death and describe vividly different hells.[8] The Purāṇas deal with the forty sacraments (Saṁskāras) prescribed in the Codes on *dharma*. These are to be performed at the appropriate time in the course of different stages of the growth of a person commencing with the conception. We find the general rules governing the functioning of the four stages of life as a student, householder, forester and ascetic. Some Purāṇas deal with general maxims on themes like making friendship with pious men, the practices one should avoid, the practices leading to one's fall, the role played by time, the need for offering worship, virtues of good rulers, selections of a servant etc.[9]

Allied to the Dharmaśāstra the Purāṇas deal with Jyotiṣa mainly for the purpose of practicing the austerities at the appropriate time.[10] The observation of the eye, the scriptures, water, written document and calculation are the five means for deciding the measurement of the luminaries.[11] There are different

6. See ***Garuḍapurāṇa*** I. 214, 25-65 and ***Liṅgapurāṇa*** I.89, 12-12.
7. See ***Viṣṇupurāṇa*** II.6, 1-34.
8. See ***Garuḍapurāṇa*** II. 1-35.
9. See ***Garuḍapurāṇa*** I.108-115. See also ***Agnipurāṇa*** ch. 238 ff.
10. See ***Viṣṇupurāṇa*** II. Chs. 8-12.
11. See ***Liṅgapurāṇa*** I.61, 53.

systems of reckoning the *daśā* periods of the planets. The ***Garuḍapurāṇa*** describes the rather unfamiliar *daśā* system known as the Aṣṭottarīdaśā giving the duration of the *daśā* periods of the different planets – Sun (6 years), Moon (15 years), Mars (8 years), Mercury (17 years), Saturn (10 years), Jupiter (19 years), Rāhu (12 years) and Venus (21 years) totaling 108 years. It is to be noted that the period for Ketu is omitted in this reckoning and the periods mentioned for each planet is different from the familiar *daśā* system.[12] Among the Purāṇas the ***Nāradapurāṇa*** is unique in that it treats elaborately the Jyotiṣa in its scheme of its three branches – Astronomy (*Gaṇita*), Horoscopy (*Jātaka*) and Natural Astrology (*Saṁhitā*), the first one dealing with arithmetical operations and calculation of planetary positions etc., the second one with matter relating to horoscopy and the third one with varied matter relating to natural astrology.[13]

The animals and birds are believed to possess some natural instinct and indicate something foreboding by means of their extra-ordinary behaviour. The Purāṇas describe the auspicious and inauspicious periods for travel based on the movement of animals and birds.[14] Some Purāṇas describe the indications foreboding one's death after a specific period and the remedial measures one has to take after knowing about the impending calamity.[15]

The vastness of the phenomenon of time is a popular theme in the Purāṇas. The concept was based on the Vedas and elaborated in the Ahorātra school. It is one of the doctrines reckoned in the Nāsadīya Sūkta of the ***Ṛgveda***. The mutually opposed units of the Ahorātra were expanded into a month consisting of the dark and bright lunar fortnights (pakṣas), year consisting of two six-monthly periods (ayanas), yuga and manvantara. It is started that 1, 96, 08, 53, 097 years have

12. See ***Liṅgapurāṇa*** I.60, 1-2.
13. See ***Nāradapurāṇa*** I.54-56.
14. See ***Garuḍapurāṇa*** I.60, 12-14.
15. See ***Liṅgapurāṇa*** I.91, 1-44.

elapsed since creation. Some Purāṇas describe the division of time commencing with *nimeṣa* and concluding with the day and night of Brahmā.[16] The ***Bhāgavatapurāṇa*** records the minute divisions of time further below the day and night.[17] Similarly linear measures – *pradeśa, vitasti, gokarṇa, ratni, hasta, tāla, kiṣku, gavyūti* and *yojana* are also mentioned.

We have described the path of knowledge at first. What we have described above may be taken as representing the path of action among the three ways – path of knowledge, path of action and path of devotion. Now we may deal with the path of devotion. Action leads to devotion and knowledge arises from devotion leading to release from bondage. The path of devotion is commended as the best for the present Kali age. The Purāṇas refer to the well-known division of devotion into nine types.[18] There are other methods of classifying devotion. Devotion is divided into three – best, middling and inferior based on the three characteristics.[19] Devotion is differently divided into three as intimacy, equality and tranquility.[20]

In the scheme of four-fold goals of human existence we have so far dealt with the topics, which may represent *dharma* and *mokṣa*. We may now deal with the topics, which may represent *artha* and *kāma*. The Purāṇas contain abundant material relating to secular topics. Since it may not be possible to describe these topics in detail we may just mention the topics pointing out briefly the salient features in each one and making reference to the Purāṇas which deal with those topics.

Physiognomy[21] provides the indications of the physical features of men and women. We may mention the thirty-two characteristics – 1) five minutes comprising the skin, hair (on

16. See ***Matsyapurāṇa*** 141, 4-37 and ***Viṣṇupurāṇa*** I.3, 8-27.
17. See III. 11, 3-10.
18. See ***Bhāgavatapurāṇa*** VII.5, 23.
19. See *ibid.* III.29, 7-10 and ***Padmapurāṇa*** VI.126, 4-11.
20. See ***Nāradapurāṇa*** I.16, 31-35.
21. ***Skandapurāṇa*** IV.11, 55 ff and ***Garuḍapurāṇa*** I.64 and 65. For a detailed description see Dange, S.A., ***Encyclopaedia of Purāṇic Beliefs and Practices*** V. pp. 1599-1605.

the body), fingers, teeth and the parts of the finger, 2) five long one such as arms, eyes, jaws, knees and noses, 3) seven that are reddish such as palms, ends of the eyes, palate, tongue, lips and nails, 4) six elevated such as the chest, belly, hair (on the head), shoulders, hand and mouth, 5) three large – fore-head, waist and chest, 6) three short – neck, shanks and the penis and 7) three deep-voice, navel and prowess.

Formation of the foetus and its subsequent growth[22] is an interesting topic. Soon after the formation of the foetus the fluid in the womb encircles it. It is in the form of the male seed for the first two months. It is gradually endowed with the limbs in the third month deriving the different faculties like hearing from wind, heat, light, water and earth. The desire that arises during pregnancy has to be gratified for the sake of the proper development of the foetus without any deformity. The limbs get settled in the fourth month, blood is formed in the fifth, strength, colour, hair and nails gained in the sixth, the mind begins functioning in the seventh and the development of the skin and memory take place in the eighth. Birth of the child in the eighth month is fatal. The force of the inner winds causes the natural delivery of the child in the ninth or the tenth month.

Vāstuśāstra, Architecture and Sculpture[23] is extensively treated in some Purāṇas. The term *vāstu* denotes a piece of ground on which structure is to be raised. The presiding deity of such a place to be worshipped before commencing any construction is known as the Vāstupuruṣa represented as having contracted hands, resembling an *asura*, down-faced, hands folded on his chest, knees facing the north-west quarter, elbows to the south-east and face towards the south. Before raising any structure the ground is divided into sixty-four or eighty-one or hundred squares for assigning and worshipping Brahmā at the centre and other gods around him. Temples are broadly classified

22. See Dange, ibid. IV. pp. 1099-1100.
23. See ***Agnipurāṇa*** 38-39.42. 44-6. 49-57.67.104-6; ***Garuḍapurāṇa*** I.46-47; ***Liṅgapurāṇa*** I.77, 1-22; ***Matsyapurāṇa*** 252-70; ***Viṣṇudharmottara-purāṇa*** 42-86.

into three as representing the northern style, middle region and southern style. The general plan of the construction of temple, the division of the ground, the number of doors, the walls to be raised, the dimensions of pedestals and pillars, the projections of the pedestal proportionate with the sanctum sanctorum, the base pedestal and quadrangular moulding are briefly described. Temples are constructed proportionate with the length of the image of the deities or proportionate with the length of the door or proportionate with the dimension of the ground. We get details about different kinds of house and the general characteristics of a divine edifice.

Among the entire Purāṇic literature the ***Viṣṇudharmottarapurāṇa*** stands unique in that, it treats the Art of painting[24]. Painting is glorified as the foremost among the arts. The poses of a person, environment, sweetness, symmetry, similarity and grandeur of different limbs are the requisites of good painting. We may note that these features are valid for even for the modern times. There are different views about the constituents of an excellent painting. The masters commend the excellence of lines, experts the variegated colours, women the decoration and the common man the richness of colours. The prominent defects in painting are – not having a good location, getting faded, not looking lively and stained. A good picture is expressive, lively and exhibiting the characteristics remarkably. The general principles governing painting are – taking great care for determining the location, application, seat, bed and vehicle.

It is appropriate to describe music and dancing after describing painting. Theoretical explanation of music, detailed information relating to the seven musical notes, the different defective form of singing, the voice modulations and the different musical instruments are noticed in the ***Nāradapurāṇa***.[25] Besides reference to the technical terms relating to music and dancing,

---

24. ***Citrasūtra*** section chs 35-43.
25. See Nambiar, Damodaran K., ***Nāradapurāṇa A study*** pp. 335-36; ***Liṅgapurāṇa*** II. 1-3;

the ***Agnipurāṇa***[26] explains the different terms associated with a dramatic representation.

Lapidary science is dealt with in the ***Garuḍapurāṇa***[27] and the ***Agnipurāṇa***[28]. The treatment of the topic is longer in the former while it is very brief in the latter. The former deals with the diamond, pearl, ruby, emerald, sapphire, lapis lazuli, topaz, *karketana, bhīṣmamaṇi, pulaka, rudhira,* crystal and coral. The latter describes briefly in fifteen verses the salient features of different gems. Since there are good and bad features in the jewels one has to take care in their acquisition in general. Experts should first examine the shape, colour, quality and defect of the gems and find the value.

The section of Rājadharma[29] deals with the personality, character, duties and ideals of an anointed king and how the king takes the assistance of the ministers. There was a council of ministers headed by a chief minister with whom the king held deliberation. The ministers were required to possess certain noble characteristics. There were other members of king's council such as the Commander of the army (Senāpati), Minister for peace and war (Sāndhivigrahika), Ambassador (Dūta), A person in charge of revenue (Deśarakṣita) and Upholder of justice (Dharmādhikārin). We may mention some of the codes of conduct for the Government servants. He should not speak against the ruler in public, but if required he should tell the ruler in privacy. All duties should be done at the right time. Government money should not be wasted in a heartless manner. The six kinds of expedients are explained. Fortification, formation of arrays and archery are some of the other topics in this section. The section on medicine (Āyurveda)[30] covers the diagnosis and treatment of

---

26. See ***Agnipurāṇa*** 341, 1-20 and 360,70-76.
27. See ***Garuḍapurāṇa*** I. chs. 68-80.
28. See ***Agnipurāṇa*** 246, 1-15.
29. See ***Matsyapurāṇa*** chs. 215-228 and ***Agnipurāṇa*** chs. 218-45.
30. See ***Garuḍapurāṇa*** I.146-193; ***Agnipurāṇa*** chs. 279-81; ***Brahmavaivaartapurāṇa*** I.16, 11-78.

different ailments. The section on veterinary science[31] deals with the treatment of the diseases of the horses and elephants.

We may conclude this survey with the statement[32] of mother Earth that she feels distressed with the persons – who hate to perform duty towards their fellow beings and engage in selfish pursuits, who do not perform some rituals for the purification of their minds.

Thus the foregoing brief survey explains the utility of the Purāṇas in understanding our cultural heritage.

* * * *

31. See ***Agnipurāṇa*** chs. 287-92.
32. See ***Brahmavaivaartapurāṇa*** IV. 4, 206-28

Jīvanmukti and Jīvanmukta

Transcending I and Mine – Exploring an Ontological Hermeneutic for Advaitic Liberation

Dr. G. Mishra

निःश्रेयसस्य खलु साधनमुक्तमेव-
मेतत्परेण गुरुशास्त्रवचो विचार्य।
तच्चापि जीवपरयोः परमाद्वयार्थं
युक्त्या तदर्थमधिगत्य कृती भवाशु ॥ 42 ॥

The means to attain the supreme reality has been spoken of in this manner. Hereafter, by contemplating on the teachings of the preceptor and the scriptures, that too after knowing the non-dual reality through reasoning may you become successful in you endeavour soon. (*Anubhavavilāsa* of Hariharatirtha, Verse – 42.)

Introduction

In Advaita, the liberation consists of being in the state of Brahman, i.e. *brahmabhāva eva mokṣaḥ*. The *saṁsāra* is a product of *avidyā* i.e. illusion. Liberation means redeeming oneself from this illusion, which is simultaneous with the advent of the knowledge of the Self. According to Advaita, mutual superimposition between the self and the not-self is bondage.[1] This superimposition is caused by ignorance of the real nature of the Self. Removal of this ignorance results in the knowledge

1. When one says "I am six feet high" and "the body is conscious" there is mutual erroneous identification between the self and the body. The consciousness which is present in the body belongs to the self and the height of six-feet, which is attributed to the self, belongs to the body. See *Adhyāsabhāṣya* of Śaṅkara.

of the Self. Knowledge being the sole means to liberation there is no intrinsic difference between the two types of ***mukti***, i.e. ***jīvanmukti*** and ***videhamukti*** as far as the content of *mukti* is concerned. The difference lies only in the state in which the liberation takes place, whether it is in the state of living or at the time of the fall of the body *(videhamukti)*.

There are two views prevalent in Advaita with regard to the direct cause for attaining immediate knowledge ***(aparokṣajñāna)***. The ***Vivaraṇa*** school holds the view that hearing *(śravaṇa)* the *mahāvākyas* is the direct cause. The ***Bhāmatī*** school of ***Vācaspatimiśra***, on the other hand, holds that listening to the *mahāvākyas* can only give indirect knowledge and only through reflection *(manana)* and meditation *(nididhyāsana)* upon that knowledge, the mediate knowledge *(parokṣajñāna)* evolves into immediate knowledge *(aparokṣajñāna)*.

Definition of Jīvanmukti

In his *Jīvanmuktiviveka,* Vidyāraṇya defines the state of *jīvanmukti* as follows:

Bondage consists in attributes of the mind such as *kartṛtva* (doership) and *bhoktṛtva* (enjoyership), pleasure and pain which is because of the very nature of the bondage. The removal of such a state is Liberation while being alive.[2]

The definition asserts that the attributes of the mind constitute the bondage as they represent different forms of pain. The attributes of the mind denote the modes *(vṛtti)* of the mind. They are of two kinds 1, subjective mode or, *ahaṁvṛtti* such as doership and enjoyership, and 2, objective or *idaṁvṛtti* such as pleasure and pain. In his *Pañcadaśī,* Vidyāraṇya explains these two as the representatives of all other mental modes.[3] In the case of a jīvanmukta, the mind and its attributes are present but do not bind him because they are understood as not real, and hence they do not afflict him. It is implied that the attributes

2. *JMV*, p.10.
3. *Pañcadaśī,* 6.70.

afflict the *vividiṣāsannyāsin* or a *vidvatsannyāsin* but not a *jīvanmukta*.[4]

Dialectics of Jīvanmukti

As regards jīvanmukti, there are two views. Maṇḍana[5] and Sarvajñātman[6] hold the view that *jīvanmukti* is not possible. This view is based on the *Muṇḍakopaniṣad* text, which says: "the knot of the heart is cut and all his doubts are dispelled and his *karmas* get terminated when he sees the lower and the higher.[7] The word *karma* in this passage refers to all *karmas* and since the present body is a product of *prārabdhakarma*, it will also disappear along with ignorance and other *karmas*. Hence he will get only *videhamukti*, which is known as *sadyomukti*.[8] The other view which is advocated by the adherents of the **Vivaraṇa** school is that the future bodies are destroyed alongwith ignorance by knowledge of Brahman but not the present body. The present body is the result of *prārabdhakarma* and hence it will not disappear immediately after the rise of the knowledge. When the fructified deeds are exhausted, the body, which is a product of them, will disappear. But the person who has attained the state of Brahman will continue to live in this world with the body-mind complex, and this is known as *jīvanmukti*. There are two views in Advaita with regard to the sustenance of body. The

4. On the basis of the *Kaholabrāhmaṇa* of the *Bṛhadāraṇyaka Upaniṣad,* 3.5.1., Vidyāaraṇya tries to show thc state of jīvanmukti to be higher than that of vidvatsannyāsa. The text goes thus: "Having realized that Ātman, Brāhmaṇas renounce all desires for offspring, wealth and the worlds and go about as mendicants. Here the word *viditvā* (having known) implies vidvatsannyāsa. For this he has the basis of the later Upaniṣads. *JMV.*, p.5.
5. *Brahmasiddhi,* p.130, See R. Balasubrahmanian, *Advaitavedānta* 1976, p. 266
6. *Saṁkṣepaśārīraka,* 4.38 See N. Veezhinathan, 1964, p.140.
7. *Muṇḍaka upaniṣad,* 2.2.8
8. While commenting on the Smṛti text,*"jñānādeva tu kaivalyam prāpyate yena mucyate"* Vidyāraṇya says *"kevalasyātmano bhāvaḥ kaivalyam, dehādirahitatvam, tatca jñānādeva prāpyate." JMV,* p.45. See *sadehatvasya ajñānakalpitatvena jñānaikanivartyatvāt samyag darśananiṣṭhānām sannyāsīnām sadyaḥmuktir uktā,* SB on *Gītā,* 5.26.

first view is that it is a *saṁskāra* of ignorance which sustains the body-mind complex. When ignorance is removed, its residuum, *avidyāsaṁskāra* continues to exist for sometimes and it sustains the body till the exhaustion of the *prārabdhakarma*. It is like the fragrance of the flower, which remains in the flower-vase even after the flowers are removed. The second view is that it is *avidyāleśa* (a portion of *avidyā*) which sustains the body and mind. *Avidyā* is known to have two powers, namely, *āvaraṇaśakti,* concealment and *vikṣepaśakti*, projection. At the dawn of knowledge, the *āvaraṇaśakti* disappears and *vikṣepaśakti,* which is the *avidyāleśa* sustains the body and mind, till the *prārabdhakarma* gets exhausted.[9]

Vidyāraṇya is insistent upon the idea that by the obliteration of latent impressions and the dissolution of the mind alone one cannot attain the state of *jīvanmukti.* Both these have to be simultaneously practised with the knowledge of the identity of Brahman and Atman through the impartite mode of the mind *(akhaṇḍakāravṛtti)* brought about by the right understanding of the *mahāvākyas.*[10]

Jñāna Versus Vṛttijñana – A Hermeneutic of Akhaṇḍākāratva

In Advaita as we have so far seen, nothing that exists can be wholly annihilated; However, knowledge *(jñāna)* destroys ignorance *(avidyā)*; since the phenomenal world due to *māyā* is annihilated in the state of liberation, *māyā* is equated with *avidyā.* Since *jñāna* alone can destroy *avidyā, jñāna* is claimed to be the sole means of release.

There are difficulties in accepting *jñāna*, which is non-different from Brahman as the means to knowledge. In other words, *jñāna* in the sense of *svarūpa-jñāna,* the consciousness

9. *Siddhāntaleśsaṅgraha* of Appayyadīkṣita, Ed. S. Krishnamurthy Sastri and N. Veezhinathan, 1973, pp. 365.
10. In *Advaitasiddhi,* Madhusūdana Sarasvatī holds the view that the nature of Śuddha Brahman is transcending the modal knowledge of Brahman generated through *akhaṇḍākāravṛtti.* The speciality of *akhaṇḍākāravṛtti* is that it not only destroys nescience but also destroys itself, i.e. its aspect of being a mode. *Advaitasiddhi,* p.234.

that is Brahman, is identical with release; but it is not a means to release, as it is the substratum of *avidyā.* The *jñāna* which is on the other hand claimed to be instrumental for liberation is *vṛtti-jñāna* a modal-knowledge intuiting the impartite. This knowledge is the result of study of the Vedānta, reflection and profound contemplation. It is a function of the internal organ. Though itself a product of nescience, it has the capacity to destroy all lower states of the mind which apprehend the finite, the relational and the diverse, and finally to annihilate itself.

What exactly does this final mental mode *(vṛtti)* do to the lower *vṛttis?* It is said, it destroys the latter. Again, such a view is inconsistent with the Advaitin's own position regarding the nature of *avidyā:* that it is a positive entity. If, *avidyā* is indeed positive, how can it be destroyed? It is true that knowledge and nescience cannot apparently co-exist. This is, however, not an absolute position; for, apart from the co-existence of *avidyā* and *svarūpajñāna,* the advaitin himself shows the co-presence of knowledge and ignorance in such experiences as "*tad-uktam artham na jānāmi*". It may be asked whether with the development knowledge does not replace ignorance and in that sense destroy the latter. Suryanarayana Sastri suggests that it is the ignorance itself, which has developed into knowledge, instead of being replaced by the latter.[11] The process is not self-contradictory since both are *āvidyaka*, of the nature of indeterminable māyā. The real cannot change; nor can the unreal; but the ignorance that was and the knowledge that now is, both are *anirvācya* neither real nor unreal, neither *sat* or nor *asat.* The coming into being of harmony is unintelligible in the last resort, except as a manifestation of the non-difference that is eternal. This when realised immediately *(aparokṣatayā)* constitutes the final mental mode *(caramavṛtti),* or knowledge.

The unintelligibilty of the world has been discussed at a great length by the opponents of Advaita, as "*dṛk-dṛśya-sambandhānupapatti.*" Because of such *anupapatti* there comes

11. Collected Papers of S.S. Suryanarayana Sastri, Ed. By T.M.P. Mahadevan, University of Madras, 1961, p.240.

the realisation, primarily mediate *(parokṣa)* that *seer* and *seen* are alike superimpositions on the *sight* (consciousness). If analysis thus reveals the failure of the relational concept in the field of knowing, does it not, one can ask, reveal a similar defect in the fields of conation and emotion? In every case, we have to rely on the concept of relation, and it does not, on analysis, reveal greater capacity in some cases than in others. Men do not act unreflectingly any more than they can cognise inactively. The difference in analysis is one of degree, not of kind. The saintly man in action may conceivably have arrived at a mode of action which reflects non-difference, not because of a metaphysical discipline, but because of a practical discipline leading to harmony. He gives no reward other than his own realisation, a mode of life radiating sweetness, imbued with love and inspired by sacrifice. Reflecting on this issue Suryanarayana Sastri remarks:

> 'The truth is one; but we live in a world of truths, which are but half true. The good is one; we act in a world of goods, none of which is wholly good. Love is one; we move and suffer in a world of loves, none of which transfigures the whole. Self-realisation comprises two stages, the realisation of the partial and imperfect nature of what we have, and the manifestation of the perfection but for which the imperfect would neither be nor be known. The first of these stages requires reflection and analysis, which may if desired be treated as cognitive or emotive. The service of the saint and the devotion of the *bhakta* are not necessarily inferior to the wisdom of the sage, if by wisdom we mean a function of the internal organ. If, however, we mean the wisdom that is *caitanya,* there the need to distinguish will not arise, since all three will have arrived though by slightly different paths.'[12]

It is often asked whether sages are doing the proper thing in the world by living in retirement. The assumption underlying

12. Ibid, p.241

the question is that perfection is possible for the sage alone and that if he retires from the world, the world will not have the benefit of the realisation. But, in fact sages may be quietly exercising an occult influence over the rest of creation. That apart, they certainly serve as noble exemplars and inspirers. They are specially of service in this way, when they are easily accessible like Bhagavān Ramaṇa or Ramakrishna Paramanhansa. Even if such sages do not mingle with the world it does not distract them from the advaita ideal of perfection, which may be attained by the saint in action as much as by the sage in wisdom.

The *Brahmī-bhāva* of a sage implies his attainment of *Īśvara-bhāva.* Hence Maṇḍana Miśra wisely advocates *jñāna-karma-samuccaya,* holding that the wise man's performance of *karma* accelerates release, just as the use of a horse accelerates one's arrival at one's destination. Much of this, however, has to remain as speculation; for we are all too human, while what we discuss is how *Īśvara* will act. Will the enlightened function as a great knower or a great doer or a great lover? We know only this much, that it would be the height of presumption to deny Him any or all of these roles, whether simultaneously or in succession.

Prārabdha and Pauruṣa (Personal Efforts)

After defining *jīvanmukti* as having the removal of the attributes of the mind, as one of direct causes of liberation Vidyāraṇya establishes the possibility of removing the attributes. He deals with the idea of "removal" (*nivārana*) in this context and shows the relationship between *prārabdhakarma* and personal efforts which is implied in the practices of Yoga. Thereafter, he relates personal efforts to the obliteration of latent impressions. Vidyāraṇya perceives two impediments in realizing *jīvanmukti;* external – in the form of *prārabdhakarma,* and internal – in the form of force of *vāsanā.* Vidyāraṇya says that the word 'removal' in the expression *"tasya nivāraṇam"* (in the definition of *jīvanmukti*) does not mean *"nāśa"* or the destruction of the mind but only the subduing of the mental attributes (*abhibhava*). He examines two alternatives for this, whether the bondage is to be removed from the witness self or from the mind. It cannot be from the witness self since it has been already removed by knowledge at the stage of *Vividiṣāsannyāsa* and hence it need not be removed again. It cannot be the second, because it is impossible to remove attributes from the substance without destroying the substance. The fluidity of water cannot be removed without destroying water. Similarly, the state of heat cannot be removed from fire without destroying the fire. In a similar fashion, the *kartṛtva* (doership) etc. cannot be destroyed without causing the mind to disintegrate. And if we held such a position it would amount to *videhamukti* and not *jīvanmukti*. Hence even if the definition talks of the removal of the attributes, such removal in the sense of destruction is not possible. Here Vidyāraṇya explains that the attributes of the substance cannot be destroyed but they can be subdued without destroying the substance just as in the case of water the fluidity can be subdued by the admixture of clay. The heat of the fire can be controlled through incantation or by the application of a gem. In the same way, the attributes of the mind need not be destroyed but can be controlled by practices of Yoga.

Jñāna or Cinmātra-vāsanā

Vidyāraṇya gives a *prima facie* view with regard to the applicability of the definition of *vāsanā* to the pure *vāsanā*. It has been stated that the absence of enquiry into the past and future is one of the criteria of *vāsanā*. Hence the given definition cannot be applied in the case of *vāsanā* of *tattvajñāna*. This objection is answered by explaining that there is absence of enquiry because of a strong impression. The impressions, result of long-standing practice such as anger, appear suddenly, without enquiry into past or future. In the same way *brahmajñāna*, is also contemplated for a long time, and such practice creates a strong impression of *Brahmajñāna*. Once such an impression is created, one need not pursue any further enquiry. Hence the definition of *vāsanā* becomes applicable to pure *vāsanās* such as Brahman-knowledge also.

Adhyātmavidyā to Achieve Manonāśa

Such Brahman knowledge denotes the understanding that the self alone is real and the entire non-self is not real. The entire non-self can be known and can be made the object of one's knowledge, whereas the self cannot be known or cannot be objectified. After being convinced of this, the mind recedes to its source like the fire when fuel is absent. The mind, Vidyāraṇya feels, owns objects if they are knowable and pragmatic. It does not objectify things, in the case of shell-silver or cold-fire etc. When the limitation of wrong cognition is noticed, a person gets convinced of the limitation of the not-self and of the permanence and non-objectifiability of the self.[13] Vidyāraṇya says that the non-objectifiability of the self is because of the inability on the part of the mind. When this fact is understood the mind recognises its own defects and recedes to its source. This is the inward journey of the mind. Without any application of force, it gets dissolved effortlessly.

In his *Upadeśasāhasrī,* Śaṅkara explains : "'This highest (Brahman) – which is of the nature of seeing, like the sky, ever shining, unborn, one alone, imperishable, stainless, all-pervading, and non-dual – 'I am is ever released. I am seeing, pure and by nature changeless. There is by nature no object for me. Being the Infinite completely filled in front, across, up, down, and in all directions, I am unborn and abiding in myself."[14]

Vidyāraṇya deals with two states of experiences leading to the state of a *jīvanmukta*. For the first, there is the experience of the world of duality with the recognition that it is unreal. This state is spoken of as *dvaitamithyātva*. The other is the state of absence of the experience of duality, which is *dvaita-apratīti* or *dvaitapratibhāsa-abhāva*. In the *Bhagavadgītā,* we notice the description of these two stages in the terms *"sthitaprajña"* (the person whose self-knowledge is firm) and "*samādhistha*" (the knower of truth who is established in *samādhi*). Vidyāraṇya,

13. *sā ca vidyā dṛśyamithyātvaṁ dṛgvastunaḥ svaprakaśakatvaṁ ca bodhayati.* Ibid, p. 89.

14. *Upadeśasāhasrī,* 10. 1-2.

though he recognises the role of *dvaitamithyātva,* favours *dvaitapratibhāsābhāva* as the superior state of the knower of the truth.[15]

Conclusion

To conclude, it may be said that Advaita attaches great significance to the concept of knowledge as a means to liberation. Vidyāraṇya draws upon examples from the dialogues of Rāma and Vasiṣṭha to substantiate this traditional viewpoint. His contribution lies in analysing the concept of *jñāna* in the context of *jīvanmukti* and *videhamukti,* and equating these two concepts on the basis of knowledge. Since knowledge is the sole means to *mukti*, there cannot be any gradation in *mukti* as superior or inferior. Nevertheless, in keeping with the stage in which it occurs, it can be divided into liberation after the fall of the body *(videhamukti)* and liberation attained when one is alive *(jīvanmukti)*. He treats the two as synonymous, as *jīvanmukti* involves the absence of *sañcita* and *āgāmi* bodies and not the body functioning under the influence of *prārabdhakarma.*[16] The *Śruti* text, "the liberated become liberated"[17] sanctions the two states of the *mukta* and thereafter he elaborately deals with the ideas of *vidvatsanyāsa* and with the process one goes through to become a *jīvanmukta*. Vidyāraṇya asserts that even a great *vidvatsanyāsin* like Yajñavalkya renounces the world to become a *jīvanmukta.*[18] In explaining the means to *jīvanmukti,* he states clearly that *vidvatsanyāsa* causes *jīvanmukti* through the dissolution of the mind and obliteration of impressions. Here lies the special contribution of Vidyāraṇya. He asserts that

15. In *JMV,* Vidyāraṇya extols the *brahmavidvariṣṭha* type of *Jīvanmukta* as superior to all other kinds. He is superior because he never experiences duality at all.
16. In a different context, Vidyaranya says that *videhamukti* occurs even before the fall of the present body. He says the condition of *videhamukti* comes about the very moment knowledge appears. For him the word *'deha'* in the term *'videhamukti'* refers to only future bodies and not to the present body. *JMV,* p.45.
17. *Kaṭhopaniṣad,* 5.1.
18. *JMV,* p.72.

prārabdhakarma is more powerful than knowledge which human efforts in the form of practice of Yoga are more powerful than *prārabdhakarma.* The whole endeavour of Vidyāraṇya is to clearly spell out the possibility and practiciability of the *Jīvanmukti.* He excels in this endeavour in an outstanding way.

Even in our recent past we had great spiritual personalities who attained *Jīvanmukti.* Following is an example of Ramakrishna Paramahamsa, who tried to keep awake in the lower plane in order to get rid of the state of *laya* lascitude and to be available to others and to perform the day to day activities.

> 'One day I (Swami Turiyananda) arrived at Daksineswara when the master was having his dinner. A number of bowls containing various food items were placed before him. Someone might have thought this as unbecoming luxury, fit only for *rājasic* life. The Master at once said: "Well, the tendency of my mind is always towards the infinite. It is by such *rājasic* devices that I hold it down to the lower plane. Otherwise, I could not talk to you.'[19]

Here is a case where Ramakrishna, whose mind is withdrawn from its objects for the purpose of restraint, becomes prone to lassitude or sleep due to habit. In order to be beneficial to others he tried to keep it active by effort or by keeping off the causes of sleep. Ramana Maharshi of Thiruvanamalai was having the similar type of experience and he had the natural endowment of self knowledge even without the *śravaṇa,* hearing of the *mahavakyas* and he reveled in absolute bliss. Once he is reported to have told :

'At Thiruvannamalai as I listen to *Ṛbhugītā* and other works I .... discovered that these books were analysing and naming what I had personally felt intuitively without analysis and name. In the parlance of the books, I should describe my mental or spiritual condition after the awakening as *Śuddha manas* or *vijñāna* i.e. the intuition of the illumined.'[20]

19. *Ramakrishna as we saw Him,* Ed. by Swami Chetanananda, Advaita Ashram, Calcutta, 1992, p.191.
20. *Self Realisation,* by B.V. Narasimhaswami, Published by Ramanasramam, Tiruvannamalai, 1976, p. 24.

The above passage testifies the fact that in a living liberated person too, there is the presence of a minutest amount of ego which helps him to reach to the people and share his being with others who are in the world of *avidyā* during this state of *vyutthāna*, i.e., when he comes out of the state of *samādhi*. We may quote Ramakrishna Pramahamsa on this, who said :

'A man cannot get rid of the ego and the consciousness that the body is the soul. The ego of the incarnations returns to them when they come down from the plane of *samādhi,* but then it is the ego of knowledge or the ego of devotion. Through the ego of knowledge they teach men. Śaṅkarācārya kept the ego of knowledge.'[21]

In his *Jīvanmuktiviveka,* Vidyāraṇya seems to have unraveled the mystery surrounding this idea of living liberated. He shows that such an idea is not utopian or wishful thinking and that it has the sanction of the *Śruti* and can be experienced transcending the ordinary states of 'I' and 'mine'. In his *Brahmasūtrabhāṣya,* Śaṅkara reiterates the idea of *jīvanmukti* saying that there should not be any difference of attitude whether a knower of Brahman lives in the world or not. Even though the falsity has been sublated, the impressions continue for a while. How can the realisation of a person in the form of self knowledge and his having the body be questioned by another person?[22] Hence the incomprehensibiliy of the state of *jivanmukti* is very natural to the persons who have not understood the greatness of such a state which can be attained only through relentless practice of *viveka* (discrimination) and *vairāgya* (renunciation).

* * * *

---

21. *The Gospel of Sri Ramakrishna,* Chennai, 2000, p. 700.
22. *Bādhitamapi tu mithyājñānaṁ dvicandrajñānavat saṁskāravaśāt kiṁcitkālaṁ anuvartata eva. apica naivātra vivaditavyaṁ brahmavidā kiṁcitkālaṁ śarīraṁ dhriyata vā na vā dhriyata iṭi Kathaṁ hyekasya svahṛdayapratyayaṁ dehadhāraṇam cāpareṇa pratikṣeptuṁ śakyate. Brahmasūtrabhāṣya of* Śaṅkarācārya on *Anārabdhādhikaraṇa,* 4.1.15.

Functions of *Śakti* and *Tātparya* in *Nyāya-Vaiśeṣika*

Professor V.N. Jha

The Problem

In the process of verbal understanding *Śakti* and *Tātparya* are considered to be very important and essential factors by the *Nyāya-Vaiśeṣika* systems of Indian Philosophy. *Śakti* is identified as desire of God or man[1] and *Tātparya* is identified as the desire of a speaker.[2] Both being of the nature of 'desire' a doubt is often raised in the other systems against the *Nyāya Vaiśeṣikas* acceptance of both *Śakti* and *Tātparya* as distinct factors in the process of *śabdabodha*. In this paper an attempt is made to clarify the distinct functions of both *Śakti* and *Tātparya* in the same process.

The Context

Let us first look at the process of a *śābdabodha* as presented by the *Nyāya Vaiśeṣika* system.[3] Suppose there is a sentence:

(1) *Devadattaḥ odanam pacati 'Devadatta* cooks rice'. It consists grossly of six morphemes (*pada*) namely, *Devadatta* –

---

1. ईश्वरसंकेत: शक्ति:-शक्तिवाद of गदाधर,
Chowkhamba Edition, 1984, pp. 5-6;
शक्तिश्च पदेन सह पदार्थस्य सम्बध:।
सा च अस्माच्छब्दादयमर्थो बोध्दव्य: इतीश्वरेच्छारुपा,
भाषापरिच्छेद: of विश्वनाथ with the commentary of Pananan Bhattacharya, Calcutta, 1884, pp.195-96,
2. वक्तुरिच्छा तु तात्पर्यम्, भाषापरिच्छेद *Ibid*, p. 226.
3. पदज्ञानं तु करणं द्वारं तस्य पदार्थधी:।
शाब्दबोध: फलं तत्र शक्तिधी: सहकारिणी॥
भाषापरिच्छेद *Ibid*, शब्दखण्ड verse no.81

, nominative suffix – *ḥ, odanam,* accusative suffix – (a) m, the root *pac* – and the personal suffix-*ti.* This sentence is the string of these morphemes, which may be put as follows:

(2) *devadatta* + *ḥ* = *odana* + (a) m + *pac* + *ti* let us say that *Devadatta* is called 'a', – b as *'ti', odana* as 'c', – (a) m as 'd', *pac*-as 'e' and – *ti* as *'f'.* Thus (2) can be written as

(3) a + b + c + d + e + f

The listener or reader of this sentence who knows Sanskrit language, thus, has identified the constituent units of the sentence. This is what the *Nyāya-Vaiśeṣika* calls the *pada-jñāna,* the beginning of the process to know the meaning of this sentence.

In the next stage he will remember all the meanings of all these constituents a, b, c, d, e and f. They are *Devadatta* + *va – viśiṣṭa* from 'a', ekatva from 'ti', *odanatva-viśiṣṭa* from 'c', *karmatva* from 'd', *paka* from 'e' and *kṛti* from *'f'.* This stage can be written as

(4) a +b +c +d +e +f

| | | | | |

Devadattatva-viśiṣṭa ekatva odanatva-viśiṣṭa karmatva pāka kṛti of *devadattatva-viśṣṭa is* represented as *a', ekatva* as *ti, odanatva-viśiṣṭa* as *c', karmatva* as *d', pāka* as *e',* and *kṛti* as *f',* the stage will look like the following :

(5) a + b + c + d + e + f

| | | | | |

a' b' c' d' e' f'

This stage (5) is identified as *padārthasmaraṇa.*

In the next stage if a *pada* is polygamous, the intended meaning is decided by knowing to *Tātparya* 'speaker's desire or intention'.

Thereafter, the verbal understanding occurs as follows:

(6) odana-niṣṭha-karmatva-nirūpaka-janaka-kṛtimān devadattaḥ

'Devadatta possesses the volition which produces cooking which determines the objecthood of the rice'.

The *Nyāya-Vaiśeṣika* has further claimed that (4) above needs the half of the factor called *Śakti-jñāna,*'the knowledge of the relationship between a *pada* and its referent.[4]

While defining *Śakti,* they say that it is God's desire in the case of words, the origins of which are not known and even human desire[5] in the case of words, the origins of which are known. To bring uniformity in the theory they held that *Śakti* is 'desire'. Similarly *Tātparya* was explained as *vaktuḥ icchā,* 'speaker's desire. Thus, *Śakti* is needed for remembering meaning of a *pada* and before reaching the verbal understanding the knowledge of *Tātparya* is required.

The Objection –

Śakti is human desire, *Tātparya* is also human desire and hence one becomes redundant and hence let *Śakti* be there, but *Tātparya* be dropped.[6]

Reply

The *Naiyāyikas,* then, point out to the functions these two factors perform in bringing about the verbal understanding.

Function of *Śakti*

One can see in the section titled 'The Context' above that (4) can emerge only with the help of *Śakti. Śakti* is the primary relation between a morpheme and its referent. Unless the listener or hearer knows this relationship he cannot remember meanings or from respective *padas* to help the listener in remembering the meaning or meanings of a morpheme. *Śakti* is, therefore, a *Vṛtti* and meaning, thus, is defined as *vṛtti-jñānadhina-padajñāna-janya-smṛti-viṣaya* 'an object of a remembrance caused by the knowledge of *pada* provided there is the knowledge of

4. शक्तिधीः सहकारिणी loc. cit.
5. Called आधुनिकसंकेत or परिभाषा.
6. न च आधुनिकसंकेतस्य वृत्तित्वे तात्पर्यस्यापि तथात्वप्रसङ्गः, तस्यापि बोधकत्वेन पदविषयकतया संकेतरूपत्वात्।

relationship between the *pada* and its *artha*'.[7]

Function of *Tātparya*

The section titled 'The Context' above has also demonstrated the context of *Tātparya.* The knowledge of *Tātparya* or speaker's intention is required after the meanings of the *pada's* are presented to the mind. Through the knowledge of *Tātparya* a listener or a reader wants to decide with what meaning in mind the speaker has uttered that word.

Thus, *Śakti* presents the meanings and *Tātparya* confirms the intended meanings.[8] It is only after the knowledge of the intention of the speaker one can claim that he has understood the sentence meaning.[9]

Conclusions

Speaking in an intentional act. Therefore, it is necessary to understand a sentence-meaning in terms of the intention of the speaker (*Tātparya*). But to decide the intended meaning of the sentence, it is necessary that *Śakti* presents the meanings to the mind. Thus, the function of *Śakti* is to remind the meanings of the respective morphemes of a sentence and after the meanings are remembered it is the function of *Tātparya* to identify the intended meaning of a *pada*, which facilitates proper verbal understanding.

* * * *

7. वृत्तया पदप्रतिपाद्य एव अर्थ इति अभिधीयते - शक्तिवाद *Ibid,* p. 4.
8. पदार्थोपस्थितिनियामक: संकेतो वृत्ति: ।
   तात्पर्यज्ञानं च साक्षादेव शाब्दबोधोपयोगी
   न पदार्थोपस्थितिद्वारा; वृत्युपस्थापितपदार्थ एव
   प्रकरणादिना वक्तृतात्पर्यावधारणात् - शक्तिवाद *Ibid,* p. 14.
9. नागेशभट्ट gives two definitions of तात्पर्य – (i) as a primary relation called *Śakti* which is God's desire (एतद्वाक्यं पदं वा एतदर्थबोधाय उच्चारणीयम् इति ईश्वरेच्छा तात्पर्यम्) and (ii) as speaker's intention (नानार्थस्थले लोके तात्पर्यं तु-एतत् पदं वाक्यं वा एतदर्थप्रत्ययाय मयोच्चार्यते इति प्रयोक्तु: इच्छारूपम्)—see परमलघुमञ्जूषा, Chawkhamba Edition, 1935, pp. 39-40.

Influence of *Nyāya-Vāiśeṣika* Philosophy on *Alaṅkāraśāstra*

Dr. C. Rajendran

It goes without saying that all types of scientific discourses, whether old or new, require a vigorous methodology for conceptualization and presentation of their precepts and principles. Logic is the firm foundation on which our methodological principles rest. Hence, logic has been acclaimed as an indispensable tool in all classical traditions, Eastern and Western. In India, the logical system variously designated as *Ānvīkṣikī, Nyāya-Vaiśeṣika* and *Tarka,* at different points of time, has been always recognized as an absolute must in education. Kautilya elevates *Ānvīkṣikī* to the status of a lamp lighting up all *Śāstras*; the saying *kanādam pāninīyam ca sarvaśāstropakārakam* brings forth the importance of *Nyāya-vaiśeṣika* on all types of scientific discourses.

The *Nyāya-vaiśeṣika* system has undergone remarkable transformations several times in the course of its development. In the earlier phase, *Vaisesika's* orientation was ontological and it tried to map the entire universe through its *padārtha* categorization. Side by side, the *Nyāya* philosophy also emerged, more as an instrument of argumentation than as an independent school of philosophy. Later, with the advent of *Gangeśopādhyāya* and his *Nyāyatattvacintāmaṇi,* there was a sea-change in the methodology of the *Nyāya* thought; epistemological issues came to the foreground and philosophy itself became armed with a sophisticated language with *avacchedakas* and *avacchinnas* to express sophisticated shades of thought in an accurate manner; yet a third phase in the history of *Nyāya-vaiśeṣika* thought witnessed the convergence of both the systems into a *Tarkaśāstra*.

All these strains of thought have had their impact on *Alaṅkāraśāstra*.

II

We find that it is *Bhāmaha* who has made use of the insights of the early *Nyāya-vaiśeṣika* thought in poetics. *Bhāmaha* prefaces his discussions with the observation that even *Śāstraic* knowledge, intermingled with the *Rasa* of poetry becomes palatable. People consume even bitter medicine after taking honey. *Bhāmaha* maintains that *Śāstra* topics have a direct bearing on *śāstrakāvyas;* on the other hand, in poetry proper, they have only an indirect relevance. The fifth *Pariccheda* of *Bhāmaha's Kāvyālaṅkāra* is an attempt to use *Nyāya-vaiśeṣika* terminology to the poetic discourse in an extensive manner. *Bhāmaha* refers to eleven types of *Doṣas* and illustrates ten of them in the fourth *Pariccheda* of *Kāvyālaṅkāra*. The eleventh *Doṣa,* arising from the faulty employment of *Pratijñā, Hetu* and *Dṛṣṭānta* is mainly based on *Nyāyavaiśeṣika* and *Bhāmaha* devotes the entire fifth *Pariccheda* for their consideration. He deals with the definition of concepts like *Pramānas, Pratijñā, Hetu, Dṛṣṭānta* and their varieties mostly from the standpoint of early *Nyāya-vaiśeṣika* and often criticizing the Buddhistic positions.

According to *Bhāmaha,* the Buddhistic stand that perception is entirely devoid of mental constructs *(Kalpaṇāpoḍham)* is untenable as predication is necessary for any type of knowledge *(vṛtti)* and the cognition of individuality. He says :

> *Pratyakṣam kalpanāpoḍham sato'rth āditi kecana*
> *Kalpanām namajātyādiyojanām pratijānate.*
> *samāropaḥ kilaitāvān sadarthālambanam ca tad*
> *jātyādyapohe vṛttiḥ kva kva viśeṣah kutaśca saḥ.*
>
> (Kāvyālaṅkāra – V, 6-7)

Bhāmaha maintains that the theoretical framework of inference accepted in logic is applicable to the poetic discourse also. Accordingly, defective reasoning caused by defects in the components of inferential cognition is applicable to the thought content expressed in poetry also. *Bhāmaha* refers to various types of defective reasoning in logic proper and proceeds to show how they manifest in poetry, of course, with some difference.

In a *Nyāya* syllogism, the first member is called *Pratijñā* or a premise and *Bhāmaha* defines it as the statement of a subject *(pakṣa)* as qualified with the property which is a matter of dispute *(vivādaspadadharmeṇa dharmī kṛtaviśeṣaṇah/pakṣah tasya ca nirdeśah pratijñetyabhidhīyate – Kāvyālaṅkāra,* V.12) He refers to the following defects of the *Pratijñā* :

Defect	Definition	Example
Tadarthavirodhinī	Self-contradiction	I am the son of a *Yati*
Hetuvirodhinī	defective cause	There is soul / *prakṛti*
Siddhāntavirodhinī	contrariness to one's premise	Sound is eternal/ non-eternal
Sarvāgamavirodhinī	contrariness to all *śāstras*	Body is pure, *Pramāṇas* are three/nonexistent
Prasiddhadharma	too well-known property	Sound is grasped through the ear
Pratyakṣabādhinī	contrary to perception	Fire is cold

Bhāmaha further refers to the defects called *hetvābhāsas* also, and maintains that similar defects occur only in *Śāstras*. In poetry proper, the defects related to logic are slightly different, but similar in structure. Here, *pratijñā* seems to signify an oath or a stand taken by an individual and *Pratijñāhāni* its violation. There are four types of this defect, arising out of the violation of *Dharma, Artha, Kāma* and *Kopa.* When *Duryodhana*, after taking an oath to end his life through *prāyopaveśa,* finally coveted royalty, his action furnishes an example of *Dharma virodha.* When *Yudhiṣṭhira* decides to play dice with *Śakuni,* making the declaration that "I will not decline if invited," this furnishes an instance of *Arthavirodhinī Pratijñā. Bhīṣm's* vow to remain celibate for the sake of his father furnishes a case of *Kāmavirodhinī Pratijñā.* When *Paraśurāma* is defeated by *Rāma*, he has to go back from his vow that he will exterminate all *Kṣatriyas* and this is an instance of *Kopavirodhinī Pratijñā.*

Bhāmaha also deals with various types of defects related to *Hetu* and *Dṛṣṭānta* in *kāvya*. But the text being very corrupt here, it is not always easy to understand the allusions made by him here; nor is it possible for us to be convinced that such defects are very relevant in poetry. Probably, *Bhāmaha* means that poetry has a thematic content where logical structure is very important and violation of it is always a grave defect-a position later elaborated by *Mahimabhaṭṭa.*

III

Mahimabhaṭṭ has made use of medieval logic in his devastating criticism of the *Dhvani* theory which he includes in *Anumāna*. This is the theoretical position of later *Naiyāyikas* also. But I have shown elsewhere that he seems to be more influenced by Buddhistic logic as developed by *Dharmakīrti* rather than by classical *Nyāya.*[1] Nevertheless, despite the thin line of *sāhacaryaniyama* separating *Nyāya* concept of logic from that of Bauddhas which is based on *tādātmya* and *tadutpatti*, for all practical purposes, there seems to be no major difference in their perspectives on logic. *Mahimabhaṭṭa* looks upon language as a stimulant triggering off a chain of reasoning in the mind of the reader. According to *Mahimabhaṭṭa,* all the meanings other than the expressed meaning are cognised from language through the process of inference. The expressed meaning here acts as the probans and the cognised meaning is the probandum. Their

1. See my paper, 'Influence of, Buddhist Philosophy on Mahimabhaṭṭa *Oriental Journal* Tirupati, Vol. XLI pp 55-65.

relationship is called *sādhyasādhanabhāva.* All this shows the orientation of *Mahiman* to medieval logic, particularly that developed by *Dharmakīrti*, and some of these principles are seen adopted in later *Nyāya-vaiśeṣika.*

IV

Now we come to the most significant phase of the influence of *Nyāya* philosophy on *Alaṅkāraśāstra.* After the advent of *Navyanyāya,* almost all the systems of philosophy began using its terminology, irrespective of their philosophical predilection. In poetics, it was *Jagannāthapaṇḍita* who performed this mammoth task. *Jagannātha* was not a *Nyāya* philosopher at all; his obvious sympathy was with the *Vedānta* philosophy. But this did not stand in the way of his rewriting the entire *Alaṅkāraśāstra* using *Navyanyāya* terminology. The results were remarkable : *Alaṅkāraśāstra* became more precise and unambiguous; it became a *Śāstra* proper. It is remarkable that through the treatment of Paṇḍita Jagannātha, cven the theories of earlier thinkers become crystal clear. This will be clear to us if we go through his treatment of various theories on *Rasaniṣpatti.* What was only a rough outline in earlier works like *Kāvyaprakāśa* or even *Abhinavabhāratī* now assumed clarity and exhaustiveness. As the entire *Rasagangādhara* is a testimony of the terminological influence of *Navyanyāya,* it is not possible to describe the extent to which *Jagannātha* is influenced by the philosophy in a small paper like this. Instead, we can take the definition of *Kāvya* given by *Jagannātha* as a case in point. At the very outset, *Jagannātha* echoes the *Nyāya* concept of the function of a definition : According to him, a definition of *Kāvya* should fulfill the following requirements.

1. It should be the delimiting adjunct of the qualifiedness of poetry *(viśeṣyatāvacchedaka).*
2. It should be able to delimit poetry from non-poetry. *(taditarabhedabuddhau śādhakam).*

Accordingly, *Jagannātha* defines poetry as *ramaṇīyātārthaprati-pādakah-śabdaḥ* and demonstrates how the definition is free from defects like *ativyāpti* and *avyāpti* as in *Nyāyaśāstra*. He gives more precise definition for each component of the definitions and suggests suitable modifications also. His discussions can be paraphrased as follows :

Poetry is word which describes beautiful meaning. 'Beautiful' means being the subject of a type of knowledge which generates non-worldly pleasure. Non-worldliness is a class attribute belonging to pleasure, also called *camatkāra,* where experience is the only proof. The cause of this pleasure is a type of reflection *(bhāvanā)* characterized by repetition. The qualification is to ward off sentences like 'A son is born to you' and 'I shall give you money' etc. from the purview of poetry. The pleasure given forth by the knowledge arising from the cognition of such sentences is of the worldly type and hence the definition of poetry does not overlap there.

Finally, *Jagannātha* gives three modified definitions for poetry, removing all possible defects:

1. The state of being the word, which describes meaning which is the subject of contemplation giving forth aesthetic pleasure.
2. The state of being that, the meaning described by which is the subject of contemplation whose delimiting adjunct is identical with the generator of aesthetic pleasure.
3. The state of being the possessor of the aesthetic pleasure through the relation of the describer of the meaning delimited by its capacity of being the generator of the former.

The first definition is discarded because in collective mode of knowledge *(samūhālambanajñāna)*, there is always the possibility of poetry being mixed up with some other linguistic discourses and since such collective knowledge will generate aesthetic pleasure, the mixed-up non-poetry will also have claims of poetry. On the other hand, in the second definition, 'poetryness' *(kāvyatva)* is strictly limited to the actual word whose meaning generates aesthetic pleasure. But this definition, being too wordy, is given up for the final one which combines precision and brevity.

Jagannātha displays his logical acumen and profound scholarship in *Nyāya* on innumerable occasions of his treatment, especially when it comes to the criticism of rival theorists like *Appyayadīkṣita*. Some such instances include his criticism of earlier definitions of poetry, the causes of poetry, various divisions of poetry, functions of language like *Abhidhā* and the treatment of individual *Alaṅkāras*. His treatment of *Upamā* is a classical example of his erudition. Starting with an elegant and simple definition of *Upamā* as *sādṛśyam sundaram vākyārthopskārakam upamā,* he demolishes the definitions of the figure given by earlier stalwarts like *Mammaṭa, Vidyānātha,* and *Appayyadīkṣita*. However, the entire range of his scholarship is devoted for his profound *Śābdabodhavicāra* in *Upamā*. He describes, systematically, the verbal cognition in expressions like the following using profuse *Nyāya* terminology :

1. *Aravindasundaram-mukham: aravinda-nirūpita-sādṛśyao-prayojaka saundaryavad – abhinnam mukham.*
2. *Aravindamiva sundaram: aravinda – sādṛsya – prayojaka – saundaryavad-abhinnam mukham.*
3. *Aravindamiva : aravinda-nirūpita-sādṛśyavad.*
4. *Aravindamiva bhāti : aravinda-sādṛśya-prayojaka-dhī-viśeṣyaka.*

V

Another area in *Alaṅkāraśāstra* which has been influenced by *Nyāya-vaiśeṣika* philosophy is the arena of individual *Alañkāras*. The logical structure of several *Alaṅkāras* is based on *Nyāyaśāstra,* especially its categories like cause and effect. The following *Alaṅkāras* can be cited as examples:

1. *Vibhāvanā*. Here the effect comes into existence without cause.
2. *Viśeṣokti*. Here effect does not come into existence even though there is sufficient cause.
3. *Akramātiśayokti*. The simultaneity of cause and effect.
4. *Capalātiśayokti*. The production of the effect at the very mention of the cause.

5. *Atyantātiśayokti.* The reversal of cause and effect.

Many other figures like *Kāvyaliṅga, Arthāntaranyāsa* and *Anumāna* make use of similar logical principles.

To sum up, it can be seen that *Nyāya-vaiśeṣika,* despite its supposed aridness and dreary nature, has exerted significant influence on *Alaṅkāraśāstra.*

Bibliography

Bhāmaha : *Kāvyālamkārasūtra vṛtti*
Gangesó pādhyāya : *Nyāyatattvacintāmaṇi*
Jaganmātha Pandita : *Rasagangādhara*
Kautilya : *Arthaśāstra*
Mahimabhaṭṭa : *Vyaktiviveka*

* * * *

Jain Concept of Mind : A Critique

Dr. B.K. Dalai

In the context of philosophical discussion the concept of mind is very important. Different systems of Indian Philosophy have different opinions on this wonderful concept with reference to its ontological status like what is mind, of what it is made off, where is it located, what is its size etc., with reference to its epistemological status like how to establish mind, its relation with soul, its role in the process of acquiring knowledge and finally with reference to its spiritual status like its role in spiritual development. As is rightly said mind is the cause of everything-bondage and liberation.[1] In the present paper an attempt is made to analyze the problem of mind from the point of view of Jain Philosophy. In Jain Āgama texts we find scattered information regarding mind. We find the discussion of mind particularly in the context of knowledge. Firstly in the context of *matajñāna* which is derived through sense organs and mind. Secondly the knowledge of other's mind – *manaḥparyāya-jñāna*. In first category mind is an instrument of *Ātman* to have the knowledge and in second category viz. *Manaḥ-paryāya-jñāna* in which the *Ātman,* without the help of any other tool, have the direct knowledge of objects residing in other's mind.[2] Here the knowledge is the modification of *Ātman* due to cessation *(kṣayopaśama)* of *jñānāvaraṇīya karma*. The *Ātman* is knower but the object is only mind molecules gathered in other's mind.

---

1. मन एवं मनुष्याणां कर्म (कारणं) बन्ध-मोक्षयोः।
2. SSi. – 1.9.64 परकीयमनोगतोऽर्थो मन इच्युते।

Definition of Mind

Specific definition of mind is rarely available in *Āgama* texts. Whatever is available is in supporting or secondary literature, like *Dravyasaṁgraha bhāṣya, Gommattasāra jivakānda, Yogaśāstra, Manonuśāsanam* etc. In *Dravya-saṁgraha bhāṣya,* the author states it as 'an entanglement of different thoughts'.[3] Other synonyms for mind are *anindriya, noindriya, antahkarana* etc. It is called *anindriya* because of the absence of its external organ or manifestations like other sense organ.[4] In *Tatvārthādhigama Sūtra* author mentions: 'It *(mati-jñāna)* is caused due to *indriya* and *no-indriya'.*[5] Here *no-indriya* indicates mind.

Classification of Mind

Mind is classified into two categories :-[6]

1. Dravyamana
2. Bhāvamana

Dravyamana is the material mind (mentioned above) produced due to fruition of *aṅgopānga-nāma-karman,*[7] whereas *bhāvamana* is the state of *Ātmans* purification caused due to cessation *(kṣayopaśama)* of *vīryāntarāya* and *no-indriyāvaraniya karman.*[8]

Bhāvamana characterized with *'labdhi'* and *'upayoga'* is produced with the support of matter, thus it is also materialistic *(paudgalika).*[9] The matters which conceive the thought process and beneficial to *Ātman,* caused due to *kṣayopaśama* of *jñānāvaraṇīya* and *vīryāntarāya karma* and fruition of *aṅgopāṅga*

---

3. Drav Saṁ Bhā. – 12.30 नाना विकल्पजालं रूपं मनो भण्यते।
4. DhJ. – 444 णो इंदियत्ति सण्णा तस्स हवे सेसइंदियाणं वा
5. TaSū. – 1.14 तदिन्द्रियानिन्द्रियनिमित्तम्।
6. SSi – 2.11.282 मनोद्विविधम्-द्रव्यमनो भावमनश्चेति।
7. SSi – 2.11.282 तत्रपुद्गलविपाकिकर्मोदयपेक्षं द्रव्यमनः।
8. *Ibid* – वीर्यान्तरायनोइन्द्रियावरणक्षयोपशमापेक्षा, आत्मनो विशुद्धिर्भावमनः।
9. SSi. – 5.19.563 भावमनस्ताक्लब्ध्युपयोग लक्षणं। पुद्गलावलम्बनत्वात् पौद्गलिकम्।

nāmakarma can only take the form of mind. Thus they are also *paudgalika.*[10]

On the basis of mind all living beings are divided into two categories.

1. Samanaska or Saṁjñī-living beings with mind.
2. Amanaska or Asaṁjñī-living beings without mind.[11]

Living beings having all five senses may or may not have mind. But rest of the living beings i.e. *jīvas* having one sense organ to *jīva* having four sense organs are all without mind,[12] *jīvas* in hell and heaven are all with mind, but some of the animals with five senses are without mind known as *'asaṁjñī tiryañca pañcendriya.'* Regarding human state *(mānuṣya-gati),* those who are born from all types of excreta of human beings are also human beings without mind known as *'asaṁjñī sammūrcchima manuṣya.'*[13]

Though *asaṃjñī jīva* are without mind viz. without *dravyamana,* still they have Bhāvamana in very subtle form, as *jñāna* and *vīrya* are not completely covered. There is very minute *kṣayopaśama* of these two karmas. The *ātmapradeśas (rucaka-pradeśa)* are never covered by any of the karmas.[14]

This *bhāvamana* of *asaṁjñījīvas* is not powerful enough or rather lacks in *'labdhi'* which inspires to form *dravyamana*, in whose absence the operation of thought process cannot be conducted. Again with that subtle *bhāvamana asaṁjñī jīvas* use their mind while operating their works with other sense organs.[15]

---

10. *Ibid.* – 5.19.563. द्रव्यमनश्च, ज्ञानावरण वीर्यान्तरायक्षयोपशमाङ्गोपाङ्गनामलाभप्रत्या गुणदोष-विचारस्मरणादिप्रणिधानाभिमुखस्यात्मनोऽनुग्राहकाः पुद्गला मनस्त्वेन परिणत्म इति पौद्गलिकम्।
11. TaSū – 2.12 समनस्कामनस्काः।
12. DravSaṁ – 12 समणा अमणा णेया पंचेदिया णिम्मणा परे सब्बे।
13. LokaPra – 7.2.-7.5
14. Nandi. – 71
15. Dhavalā – 1, 99,/281/4 समनस्केषु मनः पूर्वका वचसः प्रवृत्तिः अन्यानुपलम्मात।

Size of Mind

Some are of opinion that mind is Subtle *(anu-parimāṇā)* and others say it is *deha-parimāṇa.* But there is no external manifestation of mind, and again it is produced due to cessation *(kṣayopaśama)* of *jñānāvaraṇīya* and *vīryāntarāya karma. Kśayopaśama* like *karma bandha* and *nirjarā* happens in all *ātmapradeśa* simultaneously. These can never happen in some *Ātman* points only leaving behind other points unaffected, i.e. all *ātma-pradeśa* will be effected simultaneously.[16] So it can never be limited to one place, as other parts of the body cannot conduct the work of mind from those parts. So an *anu-parimāṇa* mind cannot perceive its object from the whole of universe, as mind is a beneficial of matter and matter has its own limitation.

Again it can not be *deha-parimāna,* as there is no external manifestation of this *karana* (mind). It is produced out of very subtle molecules thus making it invisible. It is said that mind is an invisible quality of formless and inactive *Ātman.*[17] *Śvetāmbara ācāryas* agree with the point that mind is *deha-parimāṇa,* having more concentration near heart.[18]

As per our observation from all these discussions, mind is *dehapramāna,* as it is produced with all *ātmapradeśa* simultaneously. Again when we use our mind *(manoyoga)* we feel our internal sensation is more near brain. Thus as per our opinion mind is *dehapramāṇa,* having more concentration near brain.

Shape and Location of Mind

In literatures, written by *Śvetāmbara ācāryas*, they have not mentioned shape or location of mind. They are of opinion that it pervades the whole body. But in *Gomastạsāra Jīvakāṇda* we get the definite shape and location of mind. It narrates 'material

---

16. Bhaga. – 1.3.113 गोयमा! नो देसेणं देसे कडे नो देसेणं सब्बे कडे नो सब्बेणं देसे कडे सब्बेणं सब्बे कडे।
17. SSi. – 5.19.563 अमूर्तस्यात्मानो निष्क्रियस्यादृष्टो गुणः।
18. BrhasṁSu. – pg. 665

mind is verily produced in the heart, from coming together of mind molecules, like full blown lotus with eight petals by the operation of *añgopāñga nāma karma.'*[19]

In this definition one point is to be noted- *'mano-vaggaṇā khandhado'*, this explains about the material by which mind is formed.

There are altogether eight varieties of matter[20] which are taken or received by living being known as *'grahaṇayogya pudgala.'*[21]

Manavargaṇā is one of them which can take the form of the object which has been thought by any *'saṁjñī'* being. It can take the form of subject matter of mind.[22]

The Objects of Mind

Mind can perceive all things, which have form *(rūpī)* or evenformless *(arūpī)*.[23] Mind can inact in few of the modifications of all substances.[24] In short all things, which can be seen, heard or experienced can be the subject matter of mind.[25]

The knowledge acquired in *mati-jñāna* i.e. passing through the stages *avagraha, īha, avāya* by any of the sense organs can be stored in *dhāraṇā* with the help of *dravyamana* and can be remembered long after with the *dravyamana* only. In *Āgama* literature we get so many examples of recollection of past life or of lives *(jāti-smṛti-jñāna)* which is a type of *dhāraṇā* of *mati-*

---

19. GomSā(J.) – 443
    हिदिहोदि हु दव्वमण वियसिय अट्ठच्छदारविदं वा।
    अंगोवंगुदयादो मणवग्गणा खंधदो नियमा॥
20. ĀvNi. – 39
    ओरालविउव्वाहार- तेअभासाणपाण- मणकम्मे।
    अह दव्ववग्गणाणं, कमो विवज्जासओ खित्ते॥
21. BrhSamSu. – pg. 633
22. GomSa.(J.) 443 – मणवग्गणा खंधदो।
23. Pañcā. (Part. 1) – 715 मूर्तामूर्तस्य वेदकं च मनः।
24. TaSū. – 1.27 मतिश्रुतयोर्निबन्धः सर्वद्रव्येष्वसर्वपर्यायेषु।
25. Dhavalā. – 6/1, 1-1, 14/15/11. नोइंदिओ दिट्ठसुदाभूदत्थौ नियमिदा।

jñāna [e.g. In *Uttarādhyayana* 19.7 of *migāputta, namirājarṣi* 9.1, *iṣukāriya* 14.5 etc.]

In *Ācārāṅga* 1.1- इहमेगेसिं नो सण्णा भवइ and 1.2 नो णात भवइ here *samjñā* and *jñtā* these two words are mentioned with similar intention viz. the process for the search for ones own self, which is going to happen with the help of mind.

Contact of Mind with Its Object

For knowledge of any object there should be a contact with that object. But mind like eyes does not need any contact with its objects as it is *aprāpyakari*.[26] It is said that the field of mind where it can perceive is *loka-parimāṇa,* because it does not have to be directly in contact with its object. That is mind does not have *vyañjanāvagraha* in its process of knowledge.[27] It means moving out of the body or without getting in contact, mind can perceive the whole of universe. In other words mind can create a mental screen within the body and can project anything any matter, any place, anybody, any conditions etc., on that screen. Thus it proves that mind can perceive its object without any contact.

Relation of Mind with Sense Organs and Soul

As we have already discussed that a *saṁjñījīva* work with mind in all their activities, thus establishing a relation with sense organs. Again in the same way it has direct connection with soul as it is reduced due to certain modifications of *Ātman* revealed because of *kṣayopaśam* of *jñānāvaraṇīya* and *antarāya* karmas.

Thus though mind has a separate identity, still it works in accordance with all other sensory organs. A *saṁjñījīva*, for functions of sensory organs somewhere or other need the support of mind. That is a *saṁjñī* being while performing any action with sensory organs need the support of mind at the final stage

---

26. S.Si – 1.19.202 चक्षुषा अनिद्रिंयेण च व्यञ्जनावग्रहो न भवति। अप्राप्यकारित्वात्।
27. TaSū – 1.19. न चक्षुरनिन्द्रियाभ्याम्।

of *mati-jñāna* viz. *dhāraṇā*, creating a chain of reactions along with all actions. In other words along with the works of sensory organs mind will start its own function viz. thinking, analyzing etc. which in turn give a way to attachment and aversion leading to bondage of karma *(bandha)*.

Does Mind Move

Mind is an *adṛṣṭa-guṇa* of *amūrta* and *niṣkriya Ātman*, and an *adṛṣṭa* (invisible) object does not have the capacity to move around. Thus mind does not move but *upayoga* towards *manoyoga* gives an impression that mind moves. But actually it is *upayoga* that cannot concentrate with one yoga, and we feel, that mind is unsteady and moves around.[28]

Function of Mind

Three main functions of mind are to think, to remember and to experience. Any one of these can be done at a given time, not all of them.

Process of Functioning of Mind

In working mechanism of mind first requirement is *bhāvamana*- a production of *'labdhi'* which in turn is outcome of *kṣayopaśama* of *jñānāvaraṇīya karman* and *vīryāntarāya karma,* giving way to fruition of *aṅgopāṅganāma-karma* as *dravyamana*. This *kṣayopaśama* also results in fruition of *paryāpti-nāma-karma*.[29]

Pajjatti or *Paryāpti* is the vitality/power in living being by dint of which they take, transform, absorb and assimilate matter. Totally they are six viz. *Āhāra* (food), *śarīra* (body), *śvāsa-osvās* (respiration), *bhāṣā* (word), *mana* (mind). The living beings have these attainments according to their category to posses those attainments. The living being with full six attainments are

---

28. SSi. – 5.19.563 स निष्क्रियः सन्नन्यत्र क्रियारम्भे न समर्थः।
29. KramGr. – 1.49. नियनिय पज्जतिजुया पज्जया लद्दिकारणेहिं।

known as *saṁjñī pañcendrīya paryāpta.* Only this category has the capacity and power to have mind and function it.[30]

Second requirement is *'manobala'* one of the three forces described under the explanations of *prāṇa',* by which a living being is able to live. The *'prāṇa'* are *indriya* (five senses), *bala* (three forces), *manobala, vacanabala* and *kāyabala. Ucchavāsa* (respiration) and *āyu* (life).[31] Thus we regard *jīva* to posses a period of life during which its characteristics are respiration, the employment of five senses and three forces of thought, word and action.

Third requirement is *'manoyoga'. Yoga* is the power of *jīva,* possessing activities of mind, speech and body, by which particles of matter are attracted towards Ātman.[32] Vibrations in *Ātma pradeśa* (soul space) caused due to cessation *(kṣayopaśama)* of *vīryāntarāya karma* and with the support of matter is called *yoga.*[33] *Yoga* is divided into three categories- body force *(kāyabala),* verbal force *(vacanabala)* and mind force *(manobala).*[34] Actual inaction of *manobala* is *manayoga.*

Fourth requirement is mind forming matter *(mano-vaggaṇṇā pudgala)* discussed earlier.

A *saṁjñī pañcendriya paryāpta jīva* or a living being with all five sense organs and complete *manaḥparyāpti*, with the help of *kāyabala* gathers the *manovaggaṇā pudgala* residing in same space point *(ākāśapradeśa)* with *Ātman.* Here with the help of *manobala* and vibrations in the soul space known as *manoyoga,*

---

30. GomSā.(J.); – 119
आहारसरीरिंद्रियपज्जती आणपाणभासामणे।
चत्तारि पंच छुप्पि एइंदियवियलसण्णीणं॥
31. DravSaṁ. – 3 तिक्काले चदुपाणा इंदियबलमाऊ आणपाणो य।
32. GomSā.(J.) – 216
पुग्गलविवाइ-देहोदयेण मणवयणकायजुत्तस्स।
जीवस्स जा हु सत्ती कम्मागमकारणं जोगो॥
33. BrhSam. pg. – 664
34. SSi. – 6.1.610.
अभ्यन्तरवीर्यान्तरायनोइन्द्रियावरणक्षयोपशाभात्मकमनोलब्धिसंनिधाने
बाह्यनिमित्तमनोवर्गणालम्बने च सति मनः परिणामाभिमुखस्यात्मप्रदेशपरिस्पन्दो मनोंयोगः।

shape will be formed from those assimilated matter *(manovagganā pudgala)*.[35] Thus shape or form produced by this matter is nothing else but *dravyamana*. Again immediately that form will be dispersed with the help of *kāyabala*. This process goes on continuously forming one thought at a time or movement *(samaya)* and next moment *(samaya)* they will be dispersed. Thus the matters which have been collected for certain thought process and produced in an appropriate form in *dravyamana*. The thought or psychology *(manovijñāna)* which has been produced with the help of those matters is known as *bhāvamana*.

The process of gathering and dispersing of mind forming matter is very swift and continuous. To retain a thought for a longer period or to have a same thought for a longer time, concentration is required to use *kāyabala* and *manobala* in one manner only, and *upayoga* should be steady in one form of *manoyoga*. Thus clarity of mind or thought depends on the steadiness of *upayoga* with one type of *manoyoga* only.

Knowledge derived through Mind direct or indirect

Ācārya Umāsvāmi in his work *Tatvārtha Sūtra*, narrates that the knowledge which is dependent on others (sense organ and mind) is known as *parokṣa* (indirect).[36] 'But in *Nandi Sūtra* mind is categorised under *indriyapratyakṣa*.[37] But in the same text the detail study of knowledge derived through mind is mentioned under the *parokṣajñāna* (indirect).[38]

Do we need Mind for Knowledge?

Knowledge is an inseparable characteristic of *Ātman*, source of knowledge is *Ātman* itself. *Ātman* in its pure state has infinite knowledge *(anantajñāna)*. But because of the karmic veil or knowledge obscuring karma, *Ātman* cannot perceive the knowledge directly, and has to acquire knowledge through sense organs and mind.

---

35. BrhSam. – Pg. 664
36. TaSū. – 1. 11 आद्येपरोक्षम् ।
37. Nandi. – 2.4
38. Nandi. – 3.42 to 3.46

The living beings without mind have knowledge derived through sensory organs. They do not have logic, sense, intellect, mind, etc., to express or analyse their pain and pleasure. But they feel or experience the pain and pleasure.[39] They have *mati-jñāna* and *śrutajñāna* from their respective sense organs.[40] They can comprehend that much knowledge derived through sense organs. That is without mind *avagraha, ihā* and *avāya* are possible. But in case of *dhāraṇā*, which consists of the lasting impression, which results after the object with its particulars, is definitely ascertained. It is this impression *(saṁskāra)* which enables us to remember the objects afterwards. There is no memory with these *asaṁjñījīvas,* but still with the knowledge of available sense organs and drive of four basic instincts *(saṁjñā)* have desire to live and do activities for there own survival.

This is proved by the 'desire to live' by all living beings and activities towards fulfilling four basic instincts viz. *āhāra-saṁjñā* (food) *bhaya saṁjña* (fear), *maithuna saṁjñās* (sex) and *parigraha saṁjñā* (possession)[41]. These four *saṁjñās* are found in all living beings from *sūkṣma ekendriya* to *paryāpta saṁjñī pañcendriya.*

In *Bhagavai Sutta* while explaining five types of *kriyās* (the activities of *karmabandha*) which *jīvas* undergo, all living beings from *pṛthvīkāya* (earth body) to *asaṁjñī pañcendriya,* living beings with five senses but without mind, have bondage of karma due to all the five *kriyās.*[42] Moreover they do not have logic, intellect, mind or speech to comprehend, what they are experiencing, still they experience the feelings *(vedanā).*[43]

But the *saṁjñījīva* have the mind to interpret all actions of other sense organs. This interpretation due to mind increases the intensity of attachment and aversion. Thus for the *saṁjñījīva*

---

39. Ācāra.-1
40. Nandi.
41. Thāṇa – 4.578 चत्तारि सण्णाओ पण्णत्ता तं जहा - आहारसण्णा, भयसण्णा, मैथुनसण्णा, परिग्रहसण्णा।
42. Bhaga. – 1.3.165
43. Ibid – 1.3.165

only, the sense organs need the association with mind, whereas all other living beings *(asaṁjñī)* can comprehend the knowledge derived from their respective sense organs.

Is Simultaneous Knowledge Possible

Jīva, according to Jaina philosophy, consists of infinite *jñāna*, and *darśana*, but certain karmas viz. *Jñānāvaraṇīya karma* and *darśanāvaraṇīya karma* tend to obscure these. When there is cessation *kṣayopaśama)* of such class the respective *jñāna* or *darśana* are evolved till there is complete destruction of *karma.* The contact between *Ātman* and object is either done partially through *Ātman* directly *(pratyakṣa)* or through sense organs and mind *(parokṣa).* But due to obscuring karma the *Ātman* cannot fully utilise the power of respective knowledge or cognition *(darśana)* at a given time. The medium through which it is derived being materialistic has its own limitations.

Most important action in getting acquainted with the knowledge of any object is *'upayoga'. Upayoga* is the resultant of consciousness or a sort of inclination, which arises from consciousness. In other words, the resultant of consciousness, which is inclined towards any object to accept it, is known as *upayoga.*[44]

Again while explaining *'bhāvendriya'* it says that they *(bhāvendriya)* are due to *'labdhi'* and *'upayoga'.*[45] These terms exactly state the conditions for knowledge. *'Labdhi'* is the cessation *(kṣayopaśama)* of *jñānāvaraṇīya karma* which inspires *Ātman* to create *dravendriya.* This resultant of *Ātman* which is caused due to this creation is known as *'upayoga'.*[46]

Labdhi is the outcome of *kṣayopaśama* which means one can have all *kṣāyopaśamika jñāna* at a time.[47] But one can have only one Upayoga of any one type of *jñāna* or *darśana* at a

44. PañcaSaṁ. Prakrit – 1.178 वत्थुणिमित्तो भावो जादो जिवस्य होदि उवओगो
45. TaSū. – 2.18 लब्ध्युपयोगौ भावेन्द्रियम्।
46. SSi. – 2.18. 296 तन्निमित्त आत्मनः परिणाम उपयोगः।
47. TaSū. – 1.31 एकाकीनि भाज्यानि युपदेकस्मिन्ना चतुर्भ्यः।

time.[48] That is all knowledge derived as a result of karmic veil or knowledge of *kṣāyopaśamika-bhāvas* may exist together, but cannot be used all at a time. Inclination of consciousness cannot be towards all knowledge at a time as *upayoga* is the modification of *Ātman* for a particular knowledge. There cannot be more than one modification at a given time.[49]

There can not be any *upoyoga* in absence of *labdhi* of particular class, but absence of *upoyoga* does not indicate the absence of *labdhi*, e.g. a living being with two sense organs *(beindiyā)* have *kṣayopaśama* of such degree that it has the *labdhi* which can give knowledge from two sense organs only. By any means it cannot perceive the knowledge of remaining three sense organs and mind as the obscuring karma does not allow to have that knowledge. Its *upayoga* will dwell in those two senses only. Whereas a *saṁjñī pañcendriya jīva* whose *labdhi* have full capacity to utilise all five sense organs and mind, but the resultant of *Ātman (upayoga)* can incline toward only one of the knowledge at a given time or moment *(samaya)*. *Samaya* the smallest unit of *kāladravya* is so small that a *chadmastha jīva* can not perceive that single *samaya*. Thus *upayoga* may be changing from one type of knowledge or cognition to another, but because of the subtleness of *samaya* one cannot distinguish the knowledge derived in each *Samaya*. One thinks it is simultaneous knowledge derived from sense organs and mind. But in reality in one *samaya* only one upayoga is possible and thus simultaneous knowledge is not possible. This rule applies to the *kṣāyopaśamik* state of karma, but in *kṣaya* of *jñānāvaraṇīya* and *darśnāvaraṇīya karma* viz. in *keval-jñāna* and *kevala-darśana*, the *upayoga* of these two types occur at the same time *(yugapat)*[50] unlike the *kṣayopaśama* which comes in a sequence.

48. SSi. – 1.30.232 Pg. 97 उपयोग तो एक कालमे एक ही ज्ञान का होता है। अन्य ज्ञान उस समय लब्धि रूप से रहते हैं।
49. KartikeAnu. – 260. एक्के काले एक्कं णाणं जीवस्स होदि उवजुतं। णाणा णाणाणि पुणो लद्धिसहावेण वुच्चंति।
50. SanmPra.

Thus except for the *kevalins* simultaneous knowledge is not possible for all other living beings.

Do Omniscient need Mind?

As in case of an omniscient, who has destroyed four of his *karmas* and with the *kṣaya* of *jñānāvaraṇīya* and *antarāya karma* there is no reason for *bhāvamana* to have any action. If *bhāvamana* is absent there is no scope for *upayoga* in *mati-jñāna* and *acakṣudarśana-* which are the causes of *manoyoga*. But they do have *dravyamana* as the result of *manaḥparyāpti,* and in absence of *upayoga* they use it only to answer the questions to special *jñānis* with the help of *manovaggṇā-pudgala* forming an answer.

Thus we see that mind is a very powerful media for the destruction of karmas. We get good examples of twelve types of contemplation, which help to destroy all existing karmas and stop further bondage. They are better known as *'bhāvanā'* or *anuprekṣā*. This is nothing else but concentration of thoughts which leads to 'reality'.[51]

Further it is said that if one misuses the mind, he will have to take an *asaṁjñī* birth. Thus if we constantly misuse mind our births in *asaṁjñī* state will increase, thus goes on the transmigration. With proper use of mind i.e. having auspicious thoughts one gets the birth of *saṁjñī* state. Maximum period of *saṁjñī* birth can extend till little more than 900 *sāgaropama* period.[52]

In *Ācārāṅga* the word *saṁjñā* appears in the opening *sūtra* as *'Iham Egesi No Saṇṇā Bhavai.*[53] Here this word *saṁjñā* does not mean exactly mind nor the four basic instincts mentioned. It means a special thought process for the search of ones own self. Though *Ātman* is *arūpī* and cannot be objected by sense organs

---

51. Bāras Anu. – 2
 अद्धुवमसरणमेगत्तमण्णसंसार लोगमसुचित्तं।
 आसवसंवरणिज्जरधम्मं बोहिं च चितेज्जो॥
52. Jain ThokaSam.
53. Ācāra. – 1.1.1

and mind, but still the search for this *arūpī* substance will start from the knowledge derived from sense organs and mind, as these are tools for an aspirant to start his campaign.

Again in *Dasaveyāliyam* we have a guideline *'Sampikhae Appagamappaeṇam.*[54] It means 'Look at *Ātman* through *Ātman* only'. Here the first *Ātman* is the object which is pure and the second Atman is the *jñānātman* or a modification of *Ātman* as *jñānaparyāya.* This modification is the outcome of *Mati jñāna* or *śṛta jñāna,* which helps a *sādhaka* to achieve his goal, where mind plays a very important role to perceive *Ātman.*

Observations

From whatever we have discussed in the forgoing pages, the following picture emerges.

1. Amongst the systems of Indian Philosophy, it is only the Jains who have developed a very sophisticate concept and classification of mind. Their division of mind into *dravya* and *bhāva* is an evidence of their advancement towards scientific approach.
2. According to Śvetāmbara tradition, mind is of *deha parimāṇa* (pervading the body)
3. According to Jain philosophy, mind does not move but *upayoga* toward *manayoga* creates an impression of moving.
4. The living beings without mind have knowledge derived through sensory organs.
5. Except *Kevalins* simultaneous knowledge is not possible.

* * * *

---

54. Dasave.

Navya Nyāya – A Brief Profile

Professor Keshab Chandra Dash

Founder & Categories

Navya Nyāya signifies the New school of logic in India. The founder of this school is Gaṅgeśa Upādhyāya (13th C.E.) whose work *Tattvacintāmani* (The Jewel of Thought on Essence) serves as the basic text on which subsequent thoughts and theorics have been developed.

The credit of pioneering the modern school of Logic also goes to Udayana (11th C.E) whose contributions include seven works on Nyāya thoughts. He is supposed to be the last author of Old school and at the same time, the first Original writer of New school. His work *Nyāya Kusumāñjali* is regarded as a celebrated text. Similarly, Śaśadhara (13th C.E) with his work *Nyāya-siddhāntadīpa* stands on a point where new trends of thoughts on *Nyāya* ensue.

This school has two main subschools namely 'Mithila School' represented by Vardhamāna Upādhyāya (14th C.E), Pakṣadhara Mishra (1430-1490 C.E.), Rucidatta (1450-1510 C.E.), and 'Nadiā (Navadvīpa) school' represented by Vāsudeva Sārvabhauma (1430-1540 C.E), Raghunātha Śiromaṇi (1460-1520 C.E), Mathurānātha Tarkavāgīśa (1540-1600 C.E) and Gadādhara Bhaṭṭācārya (1610-1710 C.E).

Basic Assumptions

Navya Nyāya is famous for its methodological rigor and on this line, it has contributed a lot to the Indian *śāstras* so far as the cognitive aspects, linguistic subtlities, stylistic abstruseness and theoretical approximations are concerned. It has nurtured a culture of theoretical science in India.

The principle of theorisation in Navya Nyāya is broadly based on postulation of relations and relational networks. Theorisation itself involves a process of designing a metalanguage which actually gives shape to a theory. A non-technical and non-formal element is put under technical and formalised frame work for its clarity and correctness. It has also evolved a method for extreme thoroughness in interpretation and analysis. The techniques and methodology so moulded have given a separate identity to Navya Nyāya in the sphere of human enquiry.

Epistemology, Ontology, Metaphysics & Ethics

In the spirit of logical enquiry Navya Nyāya has conceived of its own theories in almost all epistemological and ontological topics. According to its scheme, cognition is a particular quality inhering in the soul/self, i.e., the self is the causal substrate of cognition. It is conceptualised in two major levels: (i) the pre-linguistic level in which the cognition appears as undiscriminated whole and (ii) the linguistic level in which the qualificative cognition appears as having its parts clearly distinguished. Language becomes a precondition in this level.

Cognition, in broader sense of the term, exhibits three major aspects : (i) act of knowing (understanding), (ii) instrument of knowledge (intellect) and (iii) result of the act of knowing (cognition). It is also viewed as the non-physical momentary event and an action in point of modification of mind or mental state. Cognition prompts us for both non-linguistic and linguistic behaviours. This prompting is of three kinds, viz : (i) *pravṛtti* (motivation for doing something), (ii) *nivṛtti* (motivation for withdrawing) and (iii) *udāsīnatā* (motivation for remaining neutral). As the material elements are distinguished by their position and magnitude etc., so the cognitive elements are particularised with reference to certain objects. There is a factual basis out of which cognition arises. In other words, cognition is characterised by its content *(viṣaya-nirūpyaṁ-hi-jñānam).* A content structure designated as *viṣaya* is determined by its *dharma* (distinguishing characteristics). This *dharma* may be any of the seven categories of elements like (i) *dravya* (substance), (ii) *guṇa* (quality/attribute), (iii) *karma* (action), (iv) *sāmānya* (universal), (v) *viśeṣa* (particular), (vi) *samavāya* (inherence) and (vii) *abhāva* (absence) or any other inherent abstract property like 'potness' in pot and any acquired property like 'counterpositiveness' in point of its absence. This points to the realistic ontology of the system.

Thus perceptual cognition arises in the soul when it is in contact with *manas* (mind) which at the same time comes in contact with a particular external sense organ and the sense organ with the object.

The micro-form of inferential mechanism in Navya Nyāya is born out of certain causal explanations which takes the forms like *yatra yatra* .... *tatra* (wherever ..... there ..... is). This points to a process of valid inferential knowledge based on *vyāpti* (invariable concomittance) which is realised between *hetu* (probans) and *sādhya* (probandum). The inferential structure may be formalised as :

$$[H. (H \supset S) S]$$

(There is H (*hetu* 'probans'), such that if H then S (*sādhya* 'probandum') and if this is the case then (infer) S.)

This is the central idea on the basis of which *Navya Nyāya* develops the complex structure of inferential mechanism.

Similarly, another means of knowledge based on *similarity* is treated important in *Navya Nyāya*. This knowledge is obtained by comparative description. The process starts with a verbal information and ends with the recognition of the object which was not identified before. More over, this is an inductive procedure mainly based on the knowledge of the relation realised between a name and its bearer *(saṁjñā-saṁjñi-sambandha-jñāna).*

Amongst four sources of knowledge namely (i) *pratyakṣa* (perception), (ii) *anumāna* (Inference), (iii) *upamāna* (Analogy) and *śabda* (speech), the language emerges as the fourth accredited source.

Language in *Navya Nyāya* is viewed as a *pramāṇa* (valid means of knowledge) as well as a *Prameya* (a kind of knowable entity). The *Nyāya* philosophy of language mostly involves the question of logico-epestemic considerations. However, it has not overlooked the functional aspect of language. The focal point is deeply rooted in theoretical account of factual cognition and its representation. It mainly makes an investigation into meaningful discourse including the problem of sentence meaning and the meaning of its different units. The whole process is analysed in viewpoint of addressee.

An important feature of *Navya Nyāya* is introduction of the idea of delimitations through property and relation i.e., delimiting property *(avacchedaka-dharma)* and delimiting relation *(avacchedaka-sambandha)* for specifying cognition and logical communication.

Navya Nyāya does not advance any specific theory of ethics as such. It, however, endorses general devotional and rational attitude for God. This takes its basis from the point that every piece of work is an effect caused by an agent. Similar is the case with the earth and the sprout of a tree etc. The people like us cannot be their creator. Under this circumstance, since the causal relation subsisting between work and its agent is a corroborative argument, God is established as the entity of an agent divinity who is supposed to play a role as the universal instrumental cause *(nimittakāraṇa)* for all productions.

Main Texts and Commentaries

The main original texts of *Navya Nyāya* are :

i. *Nyāya-kusumāñjali* (Udayana - 33th C.E.)
ii. *Nyāya-siddhānta-dīpa* (Śaśadhara-13th C.E.)
iii. *Tattva-cintāmaṇi* (TC) (Gaṅge-śa-13th C.E.)
iv. *Avacchedakatva-nirukti*
v. *Ākhyāta-vāda* (Raghunātha-15th C.E.)
vi. *Nañvāda*
vii. *Śabda-śakti-prakāśikā* (Jagadīśa-16th C.E.)
viii. *Viṣayatāvāda*

ix. *Vyutpattivāda* (Gadādhara-17th C.E.)
x. *Śaktivāda*

Some important commentaries are :

i. *TC Prakāśa* (Vardhamāṇa Upādhyāya-14th C.E.)
ii. *TC Āloka* (Pakṣaḍhara Mishra-15th C.E.)
iii. *TC Prakāśa* (Rucidatta Mishra-15th C.E.
iv. *TC Dīdhitī* (Raghunātha-15th C.E.)
v. *TC Rahasya*
vi. *TC Āloka-Rahasya* (Mathurānāth-16th C.E.)
vii. *Dīdhitī Rahasya*
viii. *TC Dīdhitī Prakāśikā (Jāgadīsī)* (Jagadīśa-16th C.E.)
ix. *TC Dīdhiti Prakāśikā* (Gadādhara-17th C.E.)
x. *TC Āloka-Tīkā (Gādādharī)*

Application

Navya Nyāya has a practical bearing on the representational system in computer applications. This complements the design of practical inference algorithms. The techniques and methodologies of *Navya Nyāya* can be applied to both data based and rule based elements that seem a *conditio sine qua non* for operational process in computer. For instance, the five-membered syllogism popularly known as *pañcāvayava-vākya* (a structure comprising five cognitive substructures) serves as a guideline for knowledge acquisition and validating process in knowledge engineering domain of computer researches. The form of the structure is as follows:

i. *Pratijñā* (Hypothesis/Assertion) : This person has jaundice.
ii. *Hetu* (Reason) : Because he has yellow eyes.
iii. *Udāharaṇa* (Example) : If a person has yellow eyes he has jaundice, as in case of another person who is proven to have jaundice.
iv. *Upanaya* (Application) : This person too has yellow eyes which is invariably connected with jaundice.
v. *Nigamana* (Conclusion) : Therefore, this person too has jaundice.

Spiritual Implications

Standing on the line of a rational Vedic community *Navya Nyāya* holds that the final cessation of sorrow is possible only through discursive realisation of the essence of the world as a whole.

Bibliography

1. Abhyankar V.S. (Ed.) 1978 *Nyāyakośa* (of Bhimācārya), Pune : Bhandarkar Oriental Research Institute.
2. Barlingey S.S. (1976) *A modern Introduction to Indian Logic,* New Delhi, National Publishing House.
3. Bhatt V.P. (1990) *Vyutpattivāda,* Delhi : Eastern Book Linkers.
4. ______ (1994) *Śaktivāda* Delhi, Eastern Book Linkers.
5. Bhattacharya G.M. (1978) *Navya Nyāya* : some Logical Problems in Historical Perspective, Varanasi : Bharatiya Vidya Prakashan
6. Bhattacharya Sibajivan (1990) Gadādhara's theory of objectivity, Delhi, MLBD.
7. Bhattacharya Tarasankar (1970) *The Naṭure of Vyāpti* According to Navya *Nyāya* Calcutta Sanskrit College.
8. Dash K.C. (1991) *Relations in Knowledge Representation,* Delhi, Sri Satguru Publication.
9. _________ (1986) *Reference; A Logico Linguistic Identification,* kendrapadha (Orissa) : Abhaya House of Publication.
10. _________ (1992) *Logic of Knowledge Base,* Delhi Sri Satguru Publication
11. __________(1992) *Lovic of Non-case-Relationship* Delhi : Pratibha Prakashan.
12. Guha D.C. (1979) *Navyā Nyāya system of Logic* Delhi : MLBD.
13. Ingalls Daniel H.H. (1987) *Materials for the study of Navya Nyāya logic.* Delhi, MLBD
14. Jha V.N. (1986) *Studies in Language, Logic and Epistemology,* Delhi: Pratibha Prakashan.
15. _______ (1986) *Logic of Intermediate causal Link,* Delhi, Sri Satguru Publication
16. ________ (1987) *Viṣayatāvāda* (of Harirāma Tarkālaṁkāra) Pune; University of Poona.
17. ________ (1992) *Relations in Indian Philosophy.* (Ed.) Delhi : Sri Satguru Publication
18. Matilal B.K. (1968) *The Navya Nyāya Doctrine of Negation*

Cambridge, Massachusetts;

19. ________ (1985) *Logic, language and Reality,* Delhi, MLBD.
20. ________ (1986) *Perception,* Oxford : Clarendon Press.
21. Mohanty J.N. (1989) *Gangeśa's Theory of Truth,* Delhi : MLBD.
22. Mukhopadhya P.K. (1984) *Indian Realism – A Rgorous Metaphysics,* Calcutta : K.P. Bagchi & Company
23. ______ (1991) *The Nyāya Theory of Linguistic Performance,* Calcutta, K.P. Bagchi & Company
24. Potter K.H. (1977) *Encyclopedia of Indian Philosophies* Vol.II, Delhi : MLBD
25. Vidyabhushan S.C. (1978) *A. History of Indian Logic,* Delhi, MLBD
26. Wada T. (1990) *Invariable Concomitance in Navya Nyāya*, Delhi Sri Satguru Publication.
27. The History and Bibliography of *Nyāya*-Vaisesika Literaturc by Gopinath Kaviraj, Ed. G. N. Shastri, Varanasi, 1982, Sampurnananda Sanskrit University.
28. S. Ramesh 7 M.A. Alwar, 'Knowledge Engineering and Nyāya System' in the proceedings of National Seminar of *Inference mechanism In Śāstras* and *Computer Science,* Melkote, 1994. Academy of Sanskrit Research.

* * * *

Bhagavān Sri Ramaṇa Maharshi – The Restorer of Advaita

Professor Nagaraja Rao

Bhagavān Ramaṇa Maharshi renewed the Advaitic tradition of Śrī Śankara. After a long ascendancy of the *Bhakti* cult he resuscitated the primacy of the Path of Knowledge and the efficacy of *vairāgya* or equal-mindedness. He attached no importance to temporary experiences of vision or ecstasy. He was concerned only with the ultimate realization of the Self.

At a very early age Sri Ramana received the divine call and responded to it unreservedly. He left home for the holy hill of Arunachala at Tiruvannamalai, abiding thenceforth outwardly in Tiruvannamalai, inwardly in the Self.

Existentialist writers describe in terrible words the predicament of man when he encounters death and experiences the impermanence of life and the world. Certainly it is terrible if the foredoomed ego-self is all one can conceive of. Ramana experienced at the early age of sixteen what death really means, and it was rebirth into deathless life. It was about six weeks before he left home for good. There was nothing wrong with his health, but one day a strong presentiment of death suddenly overtook him. As it was the great turning point of his life, his own description of it is given here.

"The shock of the fear of death drove my mind inwards and I said to myself mentally, without actually framing the words: 'Now death has come; what does it mean? What is it that is dying? This body dies.' And I at once dramatised the occurrence of death. I lay with my limbs stretched out stiff as though rigor mortis had set in and imitated a corpse so as to give greater reality to the enquiry. I held my breath and kept my lips tightly closed so that no sound could escape, so that neither the word 'I' nor any other word could be uttered. 'Well then,' I said to myself, 'this body is dead. It will be carried stiff to the burning ground and there burnt and reduced to ashes. But, with the death of this body, am I dead? Is the body 'I'? It is silent and inert, but I feel the full force of my personality and even the voice of the 'I' within me, apart from it. So I am the Spirit transcending the body. The body dies, but the Spirit that transcends it cannot be touched by death. That means I am the deathless Spirit'. All this was not dull thought; it flashed through me vividly as living truth which I perceived directly, almost without the thought-process. The 'I' was something very real, the only real thing about my present state, and all the conscious activity connected with my body was centred on that 'I'. From that moment onwards, the 'I' or Self focused attention on itself by a powerful fascination. Fear of death had vanished once and for all. Absorption in the Self continued unbroken from that time on. Other thoughts might come and go like the various notes of music, but the 'I' continued like the fundamental *ṣruti* note that underlies and blends with all the other notes. Whether the body was engaged in talking, reading or anything else, I was still centred on 'I'. Previous to that crisis, I had no clear perception of my Self and was not consciously attracted to it."[1]

This single act of enquiry brought him to constant, unwavering realization of the Self. He taught from the fullness of his Advaitic experience; he was not a theorist. He remained henceforth established in the core of Reality, perceiving the Self in the world at large and in every being. He realized the unity of existence in the Spirit. The Spirit or Brahman is the sole reality. It is the cause of world-appearance and of the appearent plurality of selves. The empirical egos are many but the transcendental Spirit is one. Ignorance of the unity of the Self is called *Māyā*. It is the power of *Māyā* that is responsible for our feeling of separate, self-subsistent being. The pluralist outlook

---

1 *Ramana Maharshi and the Path of Self-Knowledge,* by Arthur Osborne, pp. 18-19, Rider & Co.

not only hides from us the real nature of the Self but makes us imagine ourselves distinct individuals. As a result of this we do not love our neighbour as ourself but imagine that our good is different from his good. From this arises conflict and antisocial behaviour. Once we believe that we are all separate-individuals with distinct ends we naturally feel that the interests of others are not compatible with our own. Indeed we often feel their ruin to be in our interest.

Bhagavan Ramana enjoined persistent enquiry into the nature of the Self. Spiritual ignorance is the root cause of all bondage and knowledge brings release. Therefore the prescribed primarily *Jñāna mārga*, the Path of Knowledge, with the technique of Self-enquiry. However, by this he did not mean cold, intellectual knowledge. He was full of compassion for all. Through his silent influence even more than by exposition, he taught his followers that Self-knowledge is the culmination of all spiritual discipline. It leads also to true benevolence, since without realization of the fundamental unity of Being one cannot achieve fellowship with other men. Altruistic activity not based on realization of the Self is all too, often mere gratification of the ego and a form of social vanity. Even our virtues, when unenlightened, can mask our egoism.

Sri Ramana did not teach the cultivation of the various virtues, but he embodied them. He taught that if the Self is realized the virtues will flourish spontaneously but if the ego remains it will find an outlet if not in one vice then in another. His words were wisdom and his proximity was a consecration. To talk with him or even to live in his presence was a great force that held at bay the unregenerate thoughts in us. His Grace enabled us to fight the temptations that assailed us. He was the consolation of many who were disturbed by the torments of the age. He had an insight into men's troubles and perceived their spiritual and mental state as soon as he saw them.

The Maharshi spent about twenty-four years in caves on Arunachala, speaking little and rather resisting than welcoming fame. After that He lived for about twenty-eight years as a world-famous figure in the Ashram that grew up around him at the foot of the hill. Throughout this long period there was absolutely no change in him or his teaching. This was because he was not expressing ideas but voicing realized truth. His Realization permeated all he did and said. He had no flaw of flesh, no error of mind. He was a perfect *Jīvanmukta.* His love went out to the animals in the Ashram as well as the people. His living voice and vibrant silence inundated us with Grace which awakened us from our unreflective state into the need for realizing our true Reality. Unostentatiously he performed all the functions ascribed to a *Guru* in the *Upaniṣads.* There was nothing of the narrow cult in his teaching. Not only did he not ask us to believe blindly, he also did not expect us to surrender to any outside person as *guru.* He only asked us to surrender ego to Self, ignorance to Knowledge.

However, simple though it may appear, Self-enquiry is really very difficult. Only his Grace makes it possible for us. Man's love of ego prevents him from seeking what lies behind it. To trace the mind back to its source is no easy task. It is hard to break all accustomed props and cherished illusions and see the naked truth. We have to pierce the veil of many colours to perceive the white radiance of eternity. The Maharshi often used to say: "Man is not the body or senses or states of consciousness or intellect but that which uses all of them. He is Spirit, one, indivisible and infinite." To realize this we have first of all to put our mind in order and cleanse it of error-producing impurities. If the window panes are dirty how can we see inside?

The Maharshi had a rare technique when he expressed his teaching in words: he clothed wisdom in humor. But it always was pure, uncompromising wisdom. He always reminded us that the goal is realization of pure non-dual consciousness.

He revived in his teaching and exemplified in his life the truth of *Advaita.* Three traditional phrases summarise this for us: *nāhaṁ deham,* 'I am not the body'; *koham,'* 'Who am I?' and *'Soham,'* 'I am He'. The nature of Reality and of spiritual experience is summarised in the *Taittiriya Upaniṣhad* (1.6) :

"The Reality realized through spiritual experience is the soul of Truth, the delight of life, the bliss of the mind and the fullness of Peace and Eternity."

* * * *

(This scholarly article is reproduced from the January 1966 issue of 'The Mountain Path' with the permission of Sri Ramanāsramam, Tiruvannamalai. – Eds.)

Three Characteristics : *Anicca, Dukkha* and *Anatta*

Dr. O.P. Pathak

Describing the three characteristics of the world, *anicca, dukkha,* and *anatta,* Lord Buddha teaches us that whether a perfect one appears in the world or not, it still remains an ineluctable condition, an immutable fact and fixed law that all *saṅkhāras* or formations are impermanent *(anicca)*, subject to suffering *(dukkha);* and that everything is without a permanent entity, essence, or soul *(anatta).* In his own words :

> *"Sabbe saṅkhārā*[1] *aniccāti, yadā paññāya passati;*
> *Atha nibbindati dukkhe*[2]*, esa maggo visuddhiyā."*[3]
>
> "Transient are all conditioned things, when this with wisdom one discerns, then is one disgusted with ill; this is the path to purity."
>
> *"Sabbe saṅkhārā dukkhāti, yadā paññāya passati;*
> *Atha nibbindati dukkhe, esa maggo visuddhiyā."*[4]
>
> "Sorrowful are all conditioned things, when this with wisdom one discerns, then is one disgusted with ill; this is the path to purity."

---

1. *Saṅkhāra* is a multivalent term. Here it is used in the sense of things conditioned by causes. Supramundane Nibbāna is not included in *saṅkhāra* as it is not conditioned by any cause. It is causeless and timeless.
2. Suffering caused by attending to the five aggregates i.e. *rūpa, vedanā, saññā, saṅkhāra* and *viññāṇa.*
3. Dhammapada, verse 277.
4. Dhammapada, verse 278.

"Sabbe dhammā anattāti, yadā paññāya passati;
Atha nibbindati dukkhe, esa maggo visuddhiyā."[5]

"All dhammas are without a soul, when this with wisdom one discerns, then is one disgusted with ill; this is the path to purity."

Thus we see that the Buddha teaches that the three characteristics of *saṃsāra*, the world, are *anicca* or impermanence, *dukkha* or suffering, and *anatta* or insubstantiality. They are the most salient features of sentient existence. In the Buddha Dhamma, they are called *'Tilakkhaṇa.'*

Everything in the world we see undergoes change; it is impermanent and unstable. Just like the oscillation of waves over the surface of the ocean, phenomena arise and pass away in succession. The transitory nature of life is recognized in all religions and philosophies. Take the example of our own bodies. They constantly change from the time of birth to death, passing through all the stages of childhood, youth, family, and then finally old age and decay. Consequently we see that impermanence, as an easily recognizable characteristic of the world, is listed as its first characteristic. The Buddha says that what is not stable, is not worthy of our attachment. Ultimately, no true happiness can be derived from that which is so ephemeral. It is also this same transiency which eliminates the possibility of an essence or substratum that underlies phenomena. When *anicca* and *dukkha* are understood properly, an awareness of the insubstantiality of all things, or *anatta* is sure to follow. The Buddha's doctrine is one which leads to non-attachment and dissatisfaction with the fleeting vicissitudes of life. Naibbāna is not a heaven up in the sky with the unspeakable boredom of eternal life and eternal happiness *(sukha);* it is instead a state of serenity that comes with the eradication of greed, ill-will, and ignorance, i.e., *lobha, dosa,* and *moha*. The person grounded in virtue *(sīla)* who treads the Noble Eight Fold Path can go beyond the impermanence and the unsatisfactory nature of life and attain

5. Dhammapada, verse 279.

the eternal bliss of *Nibbāna.*

Anicca must be experienced and understood through practice. Intellectual or scriptoral knowledge of the Buddha's Dhamma is not enough for the release of *Nibbāna*; only through continual phenomenological awareness, and the experiential insights that proceed it, will this be achieved. Solely via such experiential understanding of the nature of *anicca* within oneself can one come to understand impermanence in the way the Buddha wanted one to understand it. To fully comprehend *anicca,* one must follow the Noble Eight Fold Path, which is divided into the three groups of *sīla* or morality, *samādhi* or concentration, and *paññā* which is wisdom. *Sīla* is the basis for *samādhi.* It is only when *samādhi* is good that one can develop *Paññā*. Therefore, *sīla* and *samādhi* are the prerequisites for *paññā*. By *pañña* or wisdom is meant the understanding of *anicca* or impermanence, *dukkha* or suffering, and *anatta* or nosoul through the practice of Vipassana Meditation.

Vipassana is one of India's most ancient meditation techniques. It was rediscovered 2500 years ago by Gotama, the Buddha, and is the essence of what he practiced and taught during his forty-five year ministry. During the Buddha's time, large numbers of people in northern India were freed from the bonds of suffering by practicing Vipassana, allowing them to attain high levels of prosperity in all spheres of life. Over time, the technique spread to the neighboring countries of Burma, Sri Lanka, Thailand and others, where it had the same ennobling effect.

Five centuries after the Buddha, the noble heritage of Vipassana had disappeared from India. The purity of the teaching was lost elsewhere as well. In the country of Burma, however, it was preserved by a chain of devoted teachers. From generation to generation, over two thousand years, this dedicated lineage transmitted the technique in its pristine purity.

In our time, Vipassana has been reintroduced to India, as well as to citizens from more than eighty other countries, by Shri S.N. Goenka. Goenkaji was authorized to teach Vipassana by the renowned Burmese Vipassana teacher, Sayagyi U Ba Khin. Before he died in 1971, Sayagyi was ablc to see one of his most cherished dreams realized. He had the strong wish that Vipassana should return to India, its land of origin, to help ameliorate its manifold problems. From India, he felt sure it would then spread throughout the world for the benefit of all mankind.

Goenkaji began conducting Vipassana courses in India in 1969. After ten years, he began to teach in foreign countries as well. In the twenty-seven years since he started teaching, Goenkaji has conducted over 600 ten-day Vipassana courses, and trained over 750 assistant teachers who have conducted more than 3000 courses worldwide. In addition, eighty-five centers for the exclusive practice of Vipassana have been established : fifty-three in India, the remainder in thirty-two other countries. The invaluable gem of Vipassana, long preserved in the small country of Burma, can now be practised in many places throughout the world. Today ever-increasing numbers of people have the opportunity to learn this art of living, which brings lasting peace and happiness.

In the past, India had the distinction of being regarded as a World Teacher. In our time, the Ganges of Truth is once again flowing out from India to a thirsty world.

To learn Vipassana it is necessary to take a ten-day residential course under the guidance of a qualified teacher. For the duration of the retreat, students remain within the course site, having no contact with the outside world. They refrain from reading and writing, and suspend any religious practices or other disciplines. They follow a demanding daily schedule which includes about ten hours of sitting meditation. They also observe silence, not communicating with fellow students; however, they are free to discuss meditation questions with the teacher and material problems with the management.

There are three steps to the training. First, students practice abstaining from actions which cause harm. They undertake five moral percepts, practising abstention from killing, stealing, lying, sexual misconduct, and the use of intoxicants. The observation of these percepts allows the mind to calm down sufficiently to proceed with the task at hand. Second, for the first three-and-a half days, students practise Anapana meditation, focusing attention on the breath. This practice helps to develop control over the unruly mind.

These first two steps of living a wholesome life developing control of the mind are necessary and beneficial, but are incomplete unless the third step is taken: purifying the mind of underlying negativities. The third step, undertaken for the last six-and-a-half days, is the practice of Vipassana: one penetrates one's entire physical and mental structure with the clarity of insight.

Students receive systematic meditation instructions several times a day, and each day's progress is explained during a taped evening discourse by Shri Goenka. Complete silence is observed for the first nine days. On the tenth day students resume speaking, making the transition back to a more extroverted way of life. The course concludes on the morning of the eleventh day. The retreat closes with the practice of metta-bhāvanā (loving-kindness or good will towards all) in which the purity developed during the course is shared with all beings.

Vipassana meditation is the personal purification of the mind. It is the highest form of awareness, the total perception of phenomena in their true nature here and now. It is a refuge in the real, the choiceless observation of things as they are. Vipassana is the meditation the Buddha developed after trying all other forms of bodily mortification and mind control and finding them inadequate to free him from the seemingly endless round of birth and death, pain and sorrow.

Vipassana meditation has nothing to do with the development of supernormal, mystical or special powers, even though they may be awakened. Nothing magical happens. The process of purification that occurs is simply an elimination of negativities, complexes, knots and habit energies that have clouded pure consciousness and blocked the flow of mankind's highest qualities: *mettā* (pure love), *karuṇā* (compassion), *muditā* (sympathetic joy), and *upekkhā* (equanimity). There is no mysticism involved in Vipassana. It is a science of the mind that goes beyond psychology in that it is not only an understanding, but also purifying, of the mental processes.

After understanding the first characteristic of life or *saṃsāra*, i.e., *anicca* or *anityatā,* instability, we pass on to the *dukkha* or suffering which is the second characteristic of life, and as stated above, is closely linked with the first. It is this instability that makes *dukkha,* the unsatisfactory nature of life, a predominant aspect of the universe. Etymologically *'du'* means difficult or unpleasant, *'kha'* means to bear. Thus the word *dukkha* connotes difficult and unpleasant to bear. It includes all of life's difficulties and sorrow's from slightest irritation, boredom, and frustration, to actual mental and physical pain. In order to comprehend *'dukkha'* fully, one must be able to take into consideration the entire process of perpetual wandering in *samsāra,* the long chain of re-births.

The problem of suffering is universally recognized. It is the corner stone that the Buddha founded his doctrine upon. "One thing do I teach," declared the Buddha, "and that is suffering and how to get rid of it." Elsewhere the Buddha has said that just as there is one flavor in all the ocean, that of salt, there is one flavor in his doctrine and that is how to be free from suffering, understanding the Four Noble Truths through Vipassana. The Buddha's first sermon gave recognition to the universality of suffering. In it, the Buddha exhorts us to follow the Noble Eight Fold Path and make an end of suffering in *saṃsāra*. The delusion called attachment to existence has to be abandoned by understanding the true nature of life in the light of knowledge of the first noble truth of suffering. This understanding is conducive to progress on the Eight Fold Path through Vipassana.

The third feature of all forms of existence is *Anatta* or *anātma*, absence of soul. This is the most difficult of the Buddha's teachings to comprehend, as almost all of the other religion and philosophical systems, including the six systems of Hindu Philosophy, teach that there is something enduring permanently in man, which they often call soul. Lord Buddha rejected all the theories regarding the immortality of the soul and said that the mind of man undergoes change even more rapidly than the body and that there is therefore no place for a soul in either the mind or the body. The mind flux that persists during one's life, and manifests itself again in a new life after death, is not to be mistaken for an unchanging, eternal soul. According to the Buddha, the illusion that this mind flux is an eternal soul, immutable and changeless is the greatest of all delusions. This fallacy is the cause of all unrest in the world. Just like the term 'chariot' is used to refer to a combination of wheels, shaft, axle etc.,[7] we similarly use the term 'man' to a combination of psycho-physical forces.

In this way, if a person attains high levels of knowledge, his power to understand the three characteristics of *anicca, dukkha,* and *anatta* will increase and he will accordingly come nearer and nearer to the goal of the *ariya* or noble saint, which every householder should keep in view. This is the age of science. The man of today has trouble relating to notions of utopia. He will not accept anything unless the results are good, concrete, vivid, personal, and here-and-now. Such rigorous parameters of experimentation are perfectly concordant with the technique of Vipassana Meditation. In order to progress in Vipassana meditation, a person must keep aware of *anicca* as continuously as possible. The Buddha's advice to meditators is that they should try to maintain the awareness of *anicca*, *dukkha,* and *anatta* in all possible postures. Continuous awareness of *anicca,* and so of *dukkha* and *anatta*, is the secret of success in all realms of life.

* * * *

---

6. *Mahāsamuddo ekaraso loṇaraso,* Aṅguttaranikāyapāḷi, 3.8.40, (VRI edition)
7. *Yathā hi aṅgasambhārā hoti saddo ratho iti;*
   Evaṃ khandhesu santesu hoti satto'ti sammuti.
   Milindapañho (Lakkhaṇapañho), page 25, Bombay Edition, 1972.

Sanskrit and the Cultures of the World

Dr. Lokesh Chandra

The nineteenth century saw Sanskrit emerge from the silence and anarchy of centuries, as the living ground of an emerging European consciousness. Thinkers and poets, historians and grammarians, philosophers and men of natural sciences were taken up by passionate intensity for the deep wisdom of Sanskrit to elevate the mind of man. It became a propulsive force and profound movement in the onward march of ideas and institutions. As monarchial rule was overthrown in the United States and France, the people discovered an emotional identification with the forms and images of the ancient republics. Greece and Rome became the living birth-place of freedom and democracy. The passion for Hellenism brought Europe ever closer to Sanskrit. The Greeks had admired India as the source of philosophy. Lucian says that the goddess of philosophy first descended upon the Indians, the mightiest nation upon earth.

The European quest for the origin of languages is recorded as early as Herodotus. He noted that since the days of Psammetichus of Egypt men searched for the origin of language and the reason for their similarities and diversities. The Greek Euhemerus in the third century BC; the Roman scholar, orator and statesman Cicero in the first century BC, and several others were unable to find the roots of their languages. In Mediaeval Ages, Hebrew was taken as the starting point for the evolution of Greek and Latin, for instance in Richardson's "A Dissertation on Language", published in 1777. The Hebraic hypothesis led to blind alleys.

Boxhorn was the first to postulate a theory of common origin of Indo-European languages. He did not publish any work. His ideas became known through his friend George Horn in the latter half of the 17th century. He postulated some sort of a common language he called Scythian, as the mother of Greek, Latin, German and Persian.

The great philosopher Leibniz added his authority to this theory of the 'Scythian' origin of the peoples and the languages of Europe. In the first volume of the Memoirs of the Berlin Academy, Leibniz attacked the old Hebraic hypothesis. He put forward a theory which was very similar to that of Boxhorn and he clearly distinguished the Indo-European from the Semitic and the Finno-Ugrian groups. Now linguistics had rightly bid goodbye to the Hebraic thesis. The term 'Scythian' was due to the fact that ancient Greeks were overwhelmed by Persian might. William Jones wrote a letter to Prince Czartoryski dated 19 Feb 1779: "Procopius, I think, mentions the great intercourse both in war and peace between the Persians and the nations in the north of Europe and Asia whom the ancients knew by the general name of Scythians. Many learned investigators of antiquity are fully persuaded that a very old and almost primeval language was in use among these northern nations from which not only the Celtic dialects but even the Greek and Latin are derived."

In 1786, William Jones sparked off the discovery of comparative and historical philology: "The Sanskrit language, whatever be its antiquity, is of a wonderful structure; more perfect than Greek, more copious than the Latin, and more exquisitely refined than either, yet bearing to both of them a stronger affinity, both in the roots of verbs and in the forms of grammar, than could possibly have been produced by accident; so strong indeed, that no philologer could examine them all three without believing them to have sprung from some common source, which, perhaps no longer exists". The discovery of Sanskrit was a self-discovery for Europe, to interpret the several strands that wove the magnificent fabric of their classical culture. The word 'Europe' itself has born out of the myth of the young princess Europa who was carried away by Zeus disguised. Zeus was the mythical deep of European time. Europe had to wait for 2300 years to know the origins of Zeus, when the nexus with Sanskrit was discovered in the 18th century.

The European mind had been moving away from the Age of Reason, to a movement that is known in general as Romanticism. The idea that the Europeans migrated from a distant and unknown land soon fired the imagination of the romantic mind. The English translation of the Śakuntalā of Kālidāsa was done into German in 1791 by George Foster, and it awakened the highest enthusiasm of literary men like Herder and Goethe. The European writers were surprised that India too had excellent dramas. Dramas were no more the monopoly of the Greeks. The Romantic Movement idealized the Classical world of Greece and Rome. To the classical Graeco-Roman world was added the more ancient and pristine Classical world of India. For the Romantic School, headed by the brothers Schlegel, Indian literature had a special attraction. Friedrich Schlegel, the father figure of the Romantic Movement, expected from India nothing less than "the unfolding of the history of the primeval world which up till now is shrouded in darkness."

Franz Bopp published in 1816 the results of his researches on the conjugation system of the Sanskrit language in comparison with those of Greek, Latin, Persian and German. He established the term "indo-europaisch". Europe had found a new identity with Sanskrit. To cite Pablo Neruda: "deracination of human beings leads to frustration in one way or another obstructing the light of the soul". Winternitz says: "if we wish to learn to understand the beginnings of our own culture, if we wish to understand the oldest Indo-European culture, we must go to India, where the oldest literature of an Indo-European people is preserved".

From Historical Development to 'Evolution' in Biology

Sanskrit led to two many principles in the methodology of research: (i) comparative study, and (ii) historic development. The newly evolved comparative-historical method was applied to the study of language and it resulted in the publication of the biggest Sanskrit – German Dictionary in seven large volumes by Böhtlingk and Roth in 1852. It created a new intellectual climate in which evolution of language was established as a part of human march onwards. This milieu influenced the natural sciences. Seven years after the appearance of the dictionary came out Darwin's monumental work "Origin of species" in 1859, who soundly established the theory of organic evolution, that became a milestone in the development of natural sciences.

Sanskrit culture and civilization evolved on the banks of rivers, in contradistinction to the Judaic paradigms, which arose in desert environs. Water of the river flows, while the sand of the desert is static. Standing water stagnates. Flowing water gave rise to the centrality of flow, movement and progress in thought. Without the banks, the water will cease to flow. Banks of rivers with water ever flowing became the inspiration for the spontaneity of regulation from within, the basis of value-systems of Saṁskāra. The mind of man enshrined in Sanskrit was a perennial flow, an eternity imbued with movement, constant change, and progress. No idea was constrained. Horizons replaced frozen frontiers.

Abstraction of Thought

The role of Sanskrit as a medium of the abstraction of thought has been fundamental to the last five millennia. Sometimes in the fourth millenium BC or even earlier, we moved along the banks of unknown rivers towards the West. It was the *Drang nach Westen*. The names of European rivers bear testimony to this route. Prof. Hans Krahe has pointed out that old European names of rivers, like the Don, Donets, Dnieper, Dniester are derived from the Ṛigvedic word *dānu* for 'river'. The River Danube is *Danu-vius* where the first element *dānu* is transparently clear. Skomal and Polome point out that the names of rivers in the Baltic region, like Indura, Indus, Indra, are from the Sanskrit *indu* 'drop'. The languages spoken in Europe were saturated with Sanskrit from the most common words like mother, father, son and daughter (from *mātri, pitṛi, sūnu,* and *duhitṛi)*, upto the abstractions of *poiema* for a poem, 'a structured expression', from poie 'to arrange, order' and the suffix *ma* like the suffix *ma* in *dhar-ma, kar-ma.* The speech of daily physical needs developed into the sophisticated language of academics by the formation of new words from roots and suffixes. The prefixes (like pro-, pre-, ad-, etc.) provided a whole new order of subtlety of expression: in-spect, su-spect, a-spect, re-spect, con-spectus: all from spect-, specere 'to see, to look at'. The use of prefixes in the development of vocabulary is unique to Sanskrit, and its transplantation into the languages of Europe made them instruments of the highest abstraction. It was to flower several centuries later, from the Renaissance on to our times. Language had become an effective medium, with inner dynamics of the formative potential of Sanskrit. Words were created, through them ideas, thoughts, categories, and they in turn have brought into existence solid objects, machines, and so on. Language is a living organism. It gives man an ever-renewing life. Language has led to science. Language is the epic of creativity. Sixty percent of English vocabulary is based on prefixes and suffixes.

Sanskrit led to the Rise of Modern European Languages

As Sanskrit broke upon the scene, European languages found a new *raison detre* for their efflorescence. European languages were trying to assert themselves for at least five centuries. For instance, Martin Luther (1483-1546) translated the Bible into German. His remarkable handling of the German language influenced and shaped the development of modern German. English prose owes in abundant measure to King James' Authorized Version of 1611.

With the study of Sanskrit, dictionaries of European languages were taken up on historical principles. These lexicographical monuments revealed their deep roots, their evolution over centuries, and their rich semantic spectra. The European languages gained a new self-confidence. Moreover, Greek and Latin were no longer the original or prime languages. Sanskrit was more ancient than both of them, more transparent, more logical, and could explain the formation of these classical languages themselves. Now modern European languages could stand by the side of Greek and Latin, which like them, stood in the same relation to primordial Sanskrit.

German. Dictionaries of European languages on historical principles were undertaken on the model of the Sanskrit-German Wörterbuch. In 1854 was published the first volume of Grimm's German dictionary, whose completion took a century. Jacob Grimm and Wilhelm Grimm were the most distinguished brother – scholars of the German Romantic Period, renowned as the collectors and editors of "Grimm's Fairy Tales" (1812-15). They worked assiduously at the great dictionary of the German language, a task so large that it was impossible for the brothers to finish it themselves. Its last volume appeared in 1960.

English. "Ever since the Normans conquered England in 1066, the every-day tongue of the British Isles had suffered a long eclipse. Even in its native land, English was a second-class citizen, owning neither the status of Latin and Greek nor the aristocratic patina of French. Those who studied the origins of the language of Chaucer and Shakespeare were essentially amateurs, as there was little prestige to be gained by such work". In 1857 James Murray commenced "A New English Dictionary on Historical Principles" to show the extensive heritage of the English language. Its first section was printed in January 1884 by the Oxford University. It gave the historical development of every English Word. It opened up a new wonder. Its editor, James Murray, was knighted. It embodies and interprets to this day the culture of the English language from its earliest documentation to the present times. English now had a rich heritage and was as respectable as any of the classical languages, or elegant French or intellectual German. The Oxford Dictionary took the etymologies of English words far back to Sanskrit, e.g. the word thousand has the base teu: Sanskrit *tavas* 'strong, energetic' (from the root *tu*) and hundred. It can be seen in Old Norse *thus-hund*, Old Frankish *thūs-chunde*, as the 'great hundred'. Thousand was power, strength. Time, Latin tempus was Sanskrit *tapas* (with a nasal *m* inserted) which means 'heat'. Day is the hot part of the cycle of 24 hours. Continuous development arising out of historical-comparative studies afforded a new esteem to European languages.

Czech. The National Revival (about 1775-1850) of Czechoslovakia was a great social movement characterized above all by a national consciousness on the part of the people, and a drive for economic and cultural independence. Thanks to one of the reforms of Joseph II, the German language became the only official language of the country. At the same time he abolished feudalism in 1781. As a result former serfs could now move to the towns and their children could study. The Czech language started to gain momentum. Dobrovsky (1753-1829) wrote a definitive grammar of Czeck. The existence of linguistic connection between Czech and the ancient and perfect Sanskrit was a great encouragement to the oppressed nation in its efforts to improve its language. Many others shared Dobrovsky's interest in India. The advocates of Czech pointed out that their language was closer to Sanskrit than German, hence was more ancient, and deserved a place for honour. They cited the example: *stara matra dati medu* = Sanskrit – *sthavirā mātā dadāti madhu* स्थविरा माता ददाति मधु 'the old mother offers honey' (to the guest).

The **Bulgarians** struggled hard in the 9th century against the three Language Doctrine. According to this dogma church services could be held only in Hebrew, Greek and Latin. Brothers Cyril and Methodius created the Cyrillic alphabet to replace them by Old Bulgarian, so that in every Bulgarian church the people would hear their own tongue. Cyril defended the right of the Slavs to have their own language. "How is it that you are not ashamed of recognising only three languages, and of decreeing that all other nations and tribes should be deaf and blind? A people are naked without books." Once again in the 19th century, during the struggle of National Revival language became important. Leaders were proud that their language Bulgarian was closer to Sanskrit and hence older than any current non-Slavic European language. Old Bulgarian has *synu* for

Sanskrit *sūnu* "son", and *dini* for Sanskrit *dina* "day". This fired the Bulgarians with a new enthusiasm for their language.

Lithuanian. The Germanization of Lithuania started from the 12th century as a result of the proclamation of a crusade against them by the Pope. The Lithuanians lost on the battle field, lost their ancient faith and as a result their language declined. Czarist regime in the 19th century forbade the use of Lithuanian. The intimate relationship of Lithuanian with Sanskrit gave them a new enthusiasm for their language. A professor at the Vilnius University writes on the black-board:

Lithuanian	Sanskrit	Meaning
kas to esi	*kas twam asi*	Who are you?
kas tavo sunus	*kas tava sūnuḥ*	Who is your son?

The Theory of Causation

Cause-and-effect was intrinsic to the understanding of the relation of life to nature in the Sanskrit tradition. *Ṛita* (cosmic order) gave rise to *Satya* (existence or life). Their interdependence was inevitable, and it was reflected in the theory of karma. The concept of causation became the foundation of philosophic thought as well as of natural sciences which were the classical *Ṛita* in practical application. To Pythagoras, Plato and other thinkers of Greece, India was an "idealized country".

As is well-known, zero as a concept and as a symbol, is India's contribution to the world. Likewise, the formation of atomism goes back to the *Vaiśeṣika* system. When Rutherford smashed the atom at the Cavendish Laboratory of the Cambridge University, Prof. A.B. Keith wrote the book "Indian Atomism" which was published by the University of Oxford. He pointed out that the earliest conceptualization of atomish is in the *Vaiśeṣika-sūtras* of around 1000 BC. The founders of Modern physics, like Schrodinger, Niels Bohr, and Heisenberg were influenced by Indian thought. Oppenheimer paid tribute to Indian's theory of atomism by reciting a stanza from the *Gītā* as he conducted the very first nuclear explosion.

Sanskrit opened up new universes of thought in the dynamics of vocabulary creativity in the Classical Greco-Roman world. The Classical heritage has shed minds and horizons into the miracles of modern science. Modern sciences are the aroma of Sanskrit's legacy of abstraction through language, the concept of development and progress from the riverine flow of the Vedic sages, primacy and nobility of thought paradigms in perennial evolution as contrasted to faith in revelation frozen in historic time, the theory of causation, the beyond flowering in the mathematical zero, and atomism leading humans into the very heart of energy into and beyond the atom.

China. Chang Chien the envoy of the Chinese Emperor Wu-ti, took back Mahātukhāra melodies of Sanskrit to China in 138 BC. The son-in-law of the Emperor wrote 28 tunes based on this melody which were played as military music. Thus began the might of the Han Empire. Sanskrit sūtras, cotton cultivation, wooden drums for martial music, horses for war were part of Chinese strategy. To them Sanskrit was 'power and Virtue': the first monastery in China was the 'White Horse Monastery': a white horse in the mount of a cakravartin monarch.

Sugar is terme *shi-mi* 'stone honey' in the Sui Annals, which renders the Sanskrit *śarkara,* from sarkara 'granules, śtonelets'. In AD 647 Emperor Tai-tsung sent a mission to Magadha to study the secrets of boiling sugar. The official history of the Sui dynasty, completed in AD 610, contains a catalogue of Sanskrit works on astronomy, mathematics, calendrical methods and pharmaceutics under the generic caption of P'o-lo-men or Brahmin books. The earliest specimen of printing from China is a printed sheet with the figure of the Six-armed goddess Pratisarā in the centre, with Sanskrit mantras in the ornamental Rañjanā script, written concentrically around the figure. It is dated AD 757. The world's oldest printed book dated 11 May 868 is a work on transcendental wisdom entitled *Vajracchedikā,* now in the British Museum. Printing began an integral part of the ritual requirements of large number of mantras for lakṣa pūjā. Over 3000 Sanskrit works are found in Chinese translations, most of which are lost in their Sanskrit originals.

Korea. A princess of Ayodhya went from India to Korea in AD 48 aboard a ship. She became the queen of the founder of the first Korean State of Karac. In gratitude to the Sea-god who allowed safe passage to the queen to his shores, the king built the Haeun-sa "Temple of Sea Grace" that stands to this day atop Punsong Mountain. In 384 monk Mallananda brought Sanskrit Buddhism to Paekche, together with scholars,sculptors, painters and architects. In 1251, 80,000 wood blocks of the Dharma Treasure were carved to avoid national disaster. These blocks are still preserved at the Haein-sa monastry and are a national treasure of Korea. The famed celadon wares of Koryo were intimately connected with Dhyana Buddhism. In the beautiful deep of blue porcelain were reflected the ideal planes of Dhyana. In 1443 the Hangeul script was developed in Korea on the pattern of the Sanskrit alphabet.

Japan. In the sixth century, Japan received her Dharma as recorded in the Nihon-shoki Annals in the years 463, 544, 588. Japan emerged from the limbo of her prehistory under Prince Shotoku (574-621) who drew up her first constitution in Seventeen Articles wherein the Triratna (Buddha, Dharma and Sangha) were a fundamental factor. The new order was consecrated by the Uṣṇīṣavijyā-dhāraṇī, whose Sanskrit manuscript is preserved at the Horyu-ji monastery.

In 806 Kobo Daisi returned to Japan with the new way of Mantra-yana, wherein every individual was a potential Buddha. This led to the universalisation of education. The personal contacts of Kobo Daisi with the great Kashmirian Prajñātāra during his sojourn in China, produced a profound effect on the cultural evolution of Japan. After his return, Kobo Daisi started spreading education to the children of all classes. To democratise and advance literacy, Kobo Daishi invented the syllabary of Fifty Sounds *(goju-on)*, stating *a i u e o, ka ki ku ke ko,* etc. its basis was the Sanskrit alphabet.

Tibet. Sanskrit Buddhism has conditioned to the minutest detail the life and thought of Tibet inspite of its forbiddingly high mountains, untamed rivers, deep gorges, immense waterless deserts and icy howling winds. The Tibetan script, grammar, vocabulary, literary style, paintings, medicine, astronomy, folksongs – all bear the deep impress of Sanskrit culture. Entire Tibetan literature is translated from Sanskrit, and the flame of intellectual life kindled by its inspiration an indigenous literature arose and evolved. For all knowledge is centred in the nan-rig or exploration of the Inner Deeps. The warm reality of Tibetan life pulsates in the vibrant levels of her Sanskrit culture.

Mongolia. Sanskrit reached Mongolia in the sixth century, when two Buddhist teacher Śākyavaṁśa and Narendrayaśas went and worked there. Ever since, Buddhism has been their heart and soul. It replaced nomadic life by a sedentary civilization. It brought peace to the Mongols and a high degree of civilization which was the envy of Russian deportees in the 17th and 18th centuries. The Mongolian Professor Rinchen used to relate with pride: "if you happen to stop in any yurt, the first one falling on your way in the vast steppes, where the night may overtake you, before the fire of a hearth you will hear from the mouth of an old shepherd the philosophical poem *Bodhicaryāvatāra* composed by the famous Indian poet and thinker, Śantideva, translated into the Mongolian language already in the thirteenth century. You will not be surprised if the old shepherd sitting thoughtfully on the hillock near the grazing herds, having come to know you to be a philologist will enter into animated conversation with you regarding the Sanskrit grammar of Pāṇini which was translated into the Mongolian language already in the seventeenth century the level of which was achieved by Euròpean linguists only during the last century".

Ganoes merchants secured Mongol slaves from traders whole sailing in the Black sea ports. Thousands of these "Tartar" slaves worked in every major Italian City, which reached its climax in the middle of the 15th century. These Buddhist slaves used hot air turbines for turning their prayer-cylinders. This gave rise to screw propeller of ships, and steam-jet blowers in the shape of birds dateable to 1579.

The national flag of Mongolia is Soyombo or Svayambhū topped by the *candra, bindu* and *nāda* of *praṇava.* Let us not forget that Goraksh was the first Mongolian cosmonaut to go into sansar. Space is sansar in modern Mongolian. Buddhism is the invariable presence in the long time and lonely sublime of Mongolia.

Indonesia. The most magnificent cultural presence of Indonesia is the historic cosmogram of Borobudur, the grey silence of endless stone reliefs, enshrining the vision of a king in an ecstasy of form. Conceived and concretised by a poet, thinker and architect, named Gunadharma, it holds the heart in rapture in transcreating adoration along the path of endless time. The Indonesian word for independence is *merdeka,* derived from the Sanskrit *maharddika.* The constitution of Indonesia is called *Pancasila.* The national motto *bhinneka tungal ika* 'unity in diversity' is derived from the Sutasoma kāvya in the Classical Kawi language.

Cambodia. In the light and languid clime of Cambodia, into the specious majesty of Angkor monument follows on monument, ruins edge upon ruins, the walls of vegetation screen and hide and curtain, masonry masses mingle into the fantastic flowering of the jungle. By moonlight these buildings take on an appearance of solid majesty which is awe-inspiring. In the twilight gloom of these jungles a naga slithers over the sensuous limbs of an apsara petrified in a seductive pose of her dance in honor of a cakravartin crowned with the rājasūya rites of the Ṛigveda, by a *hotṛ.*

Arabic. Sanskrit acted as a source of inspiration to Arabic in literature and mathematics. An Indian introduced a treatise on astronomy in 773 which was translated into Arabic by the order of the Caliph. Al-Khwarizmi syncretised the Sanskrit and Greek systems of astronomy. The decimal system was brought by Indians to Baghdad, whence it entered Europe. Ibn-al-Muquaffa translated the *Pañcatantra* from pahlavi into Arabic in the eighth century, under the title Kalila wa Dimna, from the names of the two jackals Karataka and Damanaka. Thanks to this work,

Muqaffa is called the creator of Arabic prose.

Sanskrit has been the fountain-head of thought and belle letters, of visual and performing arts, of life and ritual, of power and virtue in Central Asia, in East Asian lands and SE Asia through Buddhism. The first Sanskrit texts were introduced to China by the yueh-chih, Sanskrit sutras were translated into Chinese by East Iranians of Partiah like An Shih kao. Amoghavajra of Samarkand transmitted the *homae* rites to China which travelled thence to Japan and are performed there to this day. Sanskrit became the classical language of Cambodia and Thailand while their sutras are in Pali. The great Pali grammar Saddaniti was written by a Burmese Bhikku on the basis of the *Mahābhaṣya.* The Buddhist dynasty of the Śailendras of Indonesia patterned Kawi language, metres and ideas on Sanskrit. To our own day, the highest number of students of Sanskrit, after India, are in Buddhist Japan. Sanskrit has been a dynamized centre, treasured in the distant corridors of etymology of Indo European languages, and alive in the cathedrals of the hearts of China, Korea, Japan and Vietnam; Bhutan, Tibet, Mongolia and Buryatia; Srilanka, Burma, Cambodia, Laos and Thailand, and in the rich linguistic textures of Indonesia, Malaysia and neighbouring isles. In the last two years, ten thousand folios and fragments of Sanskrit texts written on palm leaf, birch bark and vellum, from the first to the ninth century, have been dug from the earth in Afganistan, and are now in Norway, U.K. and Japan.

When European and hence modern life is threatened by unnatural developments, like the mad cow disease, humankind will have to find its rhymes in the deeper universes of being. Sanskrit enshrines saṁskāras or values that can illumine the tonality of the future, beyond cloning, computers and other manifestations of the technosphere.

* * * *

Nīti Kāvya in Samskṛt

Dr. A.D. Mathur

Samskṛt poets and rhetoricians have been fully conscious of the power of the pen. One of the fundamental tenets of Samskritik rhetorics is that poetry must serve the social purpose of educating people in right and wrong. A culturally and philosophically rich society that India has been for centuries, the rights and the wrongs for different individuals and social groups as well as the mechanism for their further evolution are fairly well defined. 'Dharma' i.e. the science of right and wrong forms the basic core of all Indian literature.

From the earliest available literature i.e. the Ṛgveda to the Rāmāyaṇa, the Mahābhārata, the Purāṇas and even pure fiction there is an overwhelming emphasis on 'dharma'. The Rāmāyaṇa, the Mahābhārata and the Purāṇas are source books of dharma. There has also emerged a special class of literature in the form of *dharma sūtras, smṛtis,* commentaries and digests (*nibandhas*) dealing exclusively with *'dharma.'*

Fiction or kāvya literature in Sanskrit is greatly influenced by dharmic literature. It extensively borrows plots, characters, themes, treatment from the Rāmāyaṇa, the Mahābhārata and the Purāṇas. Mahākāvyas, dramas and other kinds of literary works abound in wise sayings, quite often taken for the *smṛti-itihāsa-purāṇa,* corpus, which give a deep insight into different aspects of life. Many a time such statements are deliberately added to enhance the value of a literary work but in all fairness to our poets, their words are very profound and can have a deep impact upon a reader's mind.

There is also a special genre of literary works called nīti literature whose declared objective is to guide and educate people.

The word nīti may variously mean path, rule, method, conduct, strategy or policy. Nīti literature has a wide spectrum. While some texts lay down higher and therefore, universal principles, others are addressed to smaller audiences. Some are purely theoretical or idealistic in their approach, the others are very pragmatic and seek to expose the true face of the world.

Nīti texts deal with one's conduct in day to day life and talk about social relationships and the conduct of members of various varṇas and of people placed in different relations vis-a-vis other individuals or about general principles like truth, generosity, charity, self discipline etc. which impinge upon man's life in a very big way. The subject matter of the texts of this kind is *'loka nīti'* i.e. conduct of the people. *Nīti kāvyas* are both poetry and instruction simultaneously. They are rich in imagery, literary embellishments of sound and sense and very profound in thoughts.

Rājanīti is an important sub class of nīti. It deals with *arthaśāstra* or *rāja dharma* i.e. the science of administration and governance. However *rājanīti* texts do not qualify to be literary works and hence do not form a part of the discussion here.

Yet another species of nīti literature is spirituo-philosophical. These texts deal with themes like life and death, rebirth and karma, God, devotion, enlightenment and finally *mokṣa*. However, there is no absolute compartmentalisation of subject matter and social or moral teachings co-occur with spirituo-religious exhortations.

Most nīti works are in verse, mostly *anuśtup,* to facilitate quick recall. Several texts carry the word nīti in their titles while some have expressions like *upadeśa* (instruction or message). These texts are essentially anthologies of independent verses. In some the numbers of verses is close to one hundred and hence they are called *śatakas* i.e. anthologies of one hundred verses.

***Nīti Dviṣaṣṭikā* of Ācārya Sunder Panday (5th C.?)** seems to be the earliest known work of nīti. As the name suggests it had 62 verses but is not available now. Some of its verses are cited in other works. The following verse shows the author's versatility in imagery and his dexterity in the use of words: bad persons never come close even while living together like a lotus flower and water but there is mutual affection between good people even if they are far away from each other like *kumudas* and the moon.

Cāṇakya Nīti is one of the most popular texts on Nīti. It is available in several recensions in several languages spread far and wide from the middle-East to South-East Asia and the far east. In all about two thousand verses are floating in various combinations under the name of Cāṇakya. Centuries ago many of these verses were translated into local languages in Mongolia, Nepal, Srilanka, Burma, Cambodia, Laos and cven China. These verses pertain more to life's general experiences than to pure politics as Cāṇakya's name might suggest. The following verses show the difference between a good and a bad son : The entire family is destroyed due to one bad son just as one buruing tree in a forest can reduce the entire forest to ashes and the whole family benefits from one good son just as one flowering tree can fill the whole forest with sweet fragrance.

Bhartṛhari (7th C. ?) Three Śatakas are ascribed to Bhartṛhari Nīti Śatakam, Śṛngāra Śatakam and Vairāgya Śatakam. His *Nīti Śatakam* contains more than one hundred verses on diverse subjects viz. the conduct of a fool, the conduct of a wise person, charity, patience, self discipline and the like. One finds an interesting debate on human endeavour versus fate. Many verses establish self respect as the highest virtue. Bhartṛhari is highly critical of those who barter their self respect for a morsel. He compares such a man with a greedy dog. He advises people to be wise and shed ignorance; give up arrogance, cultivate humility and respect scholars.

In the *Śringāra Śataka* Bhartṛhari condemns women for obstructing man's journey towards final emancipation. He advises men to save themselves from getting shot by Kāma's arrows though he is aware that it is not an easy task. Some of the verses are too bold in the description of man's obsession with physical love. It has a brief version of the *Ritu Saṁhāram* in verses describing the state of lovers in different seasons. After describing the joys of love the poet compares women with sweet poison or snakes and thence seeks to lead men to the path of renunciation.

The *Vairāgya Śatakam* condemns desire, human body, objects of pleasure and eulogises the renouncer who is content with begging in the streets of Vārāṇasī. This is also a very male centric work and shows how man is doomed due to his fatal attraction for women. The ultimate purpose is to impress upon man that he must seek fulfilment in renunciation and not in fulfilment of his worldly desires. A recluse sleeps with joy in the company of his beloved called detachment, on bare earth; his arm becomes his pillow, the sky the tent, breeze is his fan and autumnal moon the lamp. His extremely derogatory and sweeping generalizations against women should be seen in the light of his male centric philosophy of renunciation.

Kṣemendra (Kashmir - 13th C.) is one of the greatest satirists in Sanskrit literature. His expertise is in short metrical works which expose, ridicule and seek to humiliate in public eye all those who appear to be great upholders of virtue but in fact are great imposters. Declaring his motive he says in the Deśopadeśa that a person humiliated with satire dares not to indulge in misdeeds and hence he was undertaking to write a work like the Deśopadeśa.

In his *Kalā vilās* he shows how doctors, hermits, lawyers, ascetics, singers, merchants and people belonging to other professions cheat the gullible. There are con doctors who kill several patients, astrologers who predict others' future but know not what their own wives do when they are away. Kṣemendra is particularly harsh on government officials. In a verse royal wealth, swindled by bureaucrats by fudging records, is personified and shown shedding tears smeared with black collyrium in the shape of black ink flowing from their pens.

Narma Mālā seeks to expose the corrupt ways of bureaucrats. *In Deśopadeśa* the author describes the conduct of rascals, misers, prostitutes, procureresses and of different professionals. The *Chaturvarga Samgraha* deals with the four puruṣārthas.

Bhallaṭa Śatakam by Bhallaṭa (Kashmir - 9th C.) Bhallaṭa's 103 verses are in *anyokti* style where a verse is addressed to some other thing or person but indirectly applies to another. The author passes strict strictures against the so-called 'big people' of his times.

That a person who renders selfless service to others is maltreated is indicated in the following verse addressed to a tree "O tree! why did you grow at the crossing? Why did you bear fruit? Why did you give dense shade? Why did you bend so low? Now suffer the consequences of your misdeeds. People will pull, shake, bend and break your branches." "It is ironical indeed that gold is tested on a piece of stone," says he, rejecting peoples' criterion of judging merit. "O scare crow! you were installed here to scare away birds and animals but due to your indifference those very birds and animals are eating the crop in your very presence." What a scathing attack on ineffective rulers!

Mugdhopadeśa by Jalhaṇa (Kashmir - 12th C.) This is very brief work with a mere 66 verses whose purpose is to prevent the youth from being infatuated with prostitutes. He warns them that a person must first make collyrium white, stones soft, neem sweet and bows straight, then alone can he make a prostitute love him genuinely.

Śānti Śatakam by Silhaṇa or Śilhaṇa (Kashmir – 13th C.?) Philosophical in import, this work containing 101 verses is divided into four parts; i) cessation of pain, ii) birth of discriminatory knowledge, iii) teachings regarding one's duties and iv) realization of Brahman. Silhana praises non-attachment and holds ones actions to be superior to the Creator for He is bound by our actions. He is disappointed that instead of being devoted to God people become slaves to petty village chieftains.

Anyokti Muktālatā by Śambhu (Kashmir – 14th C.) is an anthology of 108 verses dealing with miscellaneous matters. In one of the verses the author criticizes men of riches who do not spend for a good cause. He is also critical of masters who do not give due recognition to achievers but promote hangers-on. Śambhu's verses are addressed to trees, plants and other animate and inanimate objects and only indirectly convey the true intent of the author. He says to a camel, "Let your heart be eager to eat thorns, it does me no harm if you munch neem leaves but how can I withstand your criticism of sweet pieces of sugarcane?" The suggestion is that an ignorant person is free to enjoy his trivialities but it becomes very painful when he speaks low of the meritorious.

Kalividambana – Nilakantha Dikṣit (17th C.) A work with 102 *anuṣtup* verses is a comment on the conduct of both scholars and laymen in the age of Kali. The author's deep understanding of the ways of the world is reflected in each verse. Some scholars try to win debates by raising their voices while others seek to browbeat judges by accusing them of being biased, he says in a verse.

Apart from these dozens of other nīti works are known. Variously named as *Nīti Mālā, Nīti Mañjarī, Nīti Sāra, Nīti Ratna* or *Nīti Kalpalatā* many of these texts are still in the manuscript form.

Sanskrit has a rich tradition of devotional poetry which is also didactic in parts. Many of the stotras are beautiful pieces of poetry which propound the ephemerality of the world and inspire people to take to the path of Truth or God. They also .contain lessons in general social morality. Stotras ascribed to *Śankarācārya* are particularly very lyrical, rich in poetic embellishments and delineation of rasas.

Fable literatures is very rich in nīti. The story mode infact shows the practical form of nīti rules. Nīti statements are always summarised in verses to enable people to memorise them. However, nīti verses in fables are directly didactic and hence cannot be categorised as poetry as such.

The *Pañcatantra* is most important text in the class of works preaching nīti. Essentially designed to teach the principles of politics to errant princes it contains many stories on general worldy wisdom as well. In the Pañcatantra animals replace men in a beautiful world of fantasy to put across difficult lessons in politics. The *Hitopadeśa* of Narayan Pandit is a later version of the Pañcatantra which has several redactions within and outside India.

Vetāla Pañca Vimśatikā has twenty five stories which raise significant legal or philosophical questions and the wise king Vikrama answers them all. These stories highlight the then prevailing social and cultural values. One story for instance suggests that manhood consists in protecting women while the other declares that a person is what his thoughts are.

Dvātrimśat-Puttalikā-Simhāsanam has stories of the great king Vikram's extraordinary generosity. He gives away most fantastic of his possessions obtained after extreme hardships and even severed his own head to help another. The stories are also interspersed with pithy words of common wisdom viz, importance of dharma, immanence of worldly pleasures, definition of a good friend etc. Some of these verses have been patched on the stories they don't really fit into.

These Nīti works have had a profound influence on Indian life through the ages. Many of their 'sayings' have continued to be a part of peoples' daily conversation so much so that appropriate verses or phrases therefrom are often cited as testimony to press a point. Many of these ideas have travelled down to the vernaculars and have thus become immortalised.

* * * *

Life and Death in the Works of *Kālidāsa* with Special Reference to *Raghuvaṁśa* and *Kumārasambhava*

Dr. T.V. Vasudeva

"Human birth itself is the result of virtuous deeds one had done during the previous births" – says *Śrī Śaṅkarācārya* in his *Vivekacūḍāmaṇi* (verse-1). Among the connotations of the term 'life' the one which means 'existence' will be appropriate. It is synonymous to the Sanskrit word *'Sat'*. The *'Sat'* is the supreme soul, the Brahman. It (the word *Sat*) forms part of the definition of Brahman conveying its essential nature. The definition runs as *sat cit ānanda* (Existence, Consciousness, Bliss) and also *'Satyam jñānamanantam brahma'* (Reality, Knowledge, Infinitude).

'Life' in its general sense also means the duration between birth and death. An attempt is made in this article to bring out some of the ideas connected with 'life' and 'death' as dealt by *Kālidāsa* in his two *mahākāvyas* namely *Raghuvaṁśa* (RV) and *Kumārasambhava* (KS). Of these two, the former has more references to the subject than the latter. *Kālidāsa* while describing the kings of the Solar race *(Sūryavaṁśa)* does not fail to mention their adherence to severe austerities stipulated in the *dharmaśāstra.* Though their aim was to discharge their duties whether political or religious they were not attached to them.

Coming on to the next term, 'death' literally means 'the end of life'. It is the individual soul's departure from the body. In other words the individual soul 'ceases to be' in the body and proceeds towards another one after experiencing the result of its deeds, virtue or vice. *Bhagavad Gītā* (II.22) says – 'It is like removing the worn out clothes and taking up new ones- the soul also leaves the present body to take up a new one'. The body that is the combination of the five elements *(pañca mahābhūta)* namely Earth *(pṛthivī),* Water *(āp),* Fire *(tejas)* Air *(Vāyu)* and Ether *(ākāśa)* is impermanent and the soul that is beyond these elements is permanent. It goes from one body to the other according to its *Karma* (action). It is the ignorance of people which identifies the body with the soul. *Śri Śaṅkara* condemns this ignorance in his *Aparokṣānubhūti* (verses 17-21).

Kālidāsa

Without going into the biographical details of *Kālidāsa,* it will be ideal to analyse his poetic genius. He shows his mastery in all branches of learning. His description of the kings in *RV* and the penance of Lord *Śiva* and *Pārvati* in *KS* are a few samples worthy to be mentioned. According to some scholars (R.C. Dwivedi, *Kalidāsa Granthāvali,* Banaras Hindu University, Banaras. 1976. p.99) only eight cantos in *KS* are said to have been written by him. Comparatively *RV* has not only more number of cantos but also, as already stated, more information with regard to 'life' and 'death'.

Raghuvaṁśa (RV)

In the very first canto while describing the qualities of the kings of the solar dynasty from king *Vaivasvata, Kālidāsa* brings in the advaita concept of the four essential means namely – *Sādhana Catuṣṭaya.* The life led by those kings was according to the injunctions of *dharmaśāstra* and *Nītiśāstra.* Dilīpa, the second king to be described after *Vaivasvata* experienced pleasure without attachment, sought wealth without greed.

Dilīpa's acquisition of the knowledge of statecraft from the previous birth through the latent impressions *(Saṁskāra)* is described by *Kālidāsa* (I.20) :

तस्य संवृतमन्त्रस्य गूढाकारेङ्गितस्य च।
फलानुमेयाः प्रारंभाः संस्काराः प्राक्तना इव॥

This idea is similar to the one mentioned by *Śrī Śaṅkara* in his *Vivekacūdāmani (VC),* verse 188.

अनादिकालोऽयमहंस्वभावो जीवः समस्तव्यवहारवोढा।
करोति कर्माण्यपि पूर्ववासनः पुण्यान्यपुण्यानि च तत्फलानि॥

As long as liberation or realisation is not achieved, the individual soul undergoes many births and deaths. This idea is repeatedly mentioned in many of the advaita works. Liberation also is possible only through the removal of ignorance and not by reading the texts and following them blindly or by worshipping gods. *Śrī Śaṅkara* in *VC* confirms this :

पठन्तु शास्त्राणि यजन्तु देवान् कुर्वन्तु कर्माणि भजन्तु देवताः।
आत्मैक्यबोधेन विना विमुक्तिः न सिध्यति ब्रह्माशतान्तरेऽपि॥

In the second canto *Kālidāsa* describes *Dilīpa* as having the second aspect *śama* etc. of the *Sādhana catuṣṭaya.* This is evident through the dialogue between *Dilīpa* and the lion (verses 44-59). *śama* etc are defined in the *Tattvabodha* as –

शमः मनो निग्रहः। दमः चक्षुषादि ब्राह्येन्द्रियनिग्रहः। उपरमः स्वधर्मानुष्ठानम्। तितिक्षा शीतोष्णसुखदःखादिसहिष्णुत्वम्। श्रद्धा नाम गुरुवेदान्तवाक्यादिषु विश्वासः। समाधानं चित्तैकाग्रता।

Towards the close of the second canto *Dilīpa* after crowning his son *Raghu* as the successor enters into the third stage *(āśrama)* of life namely the forest life *(vānaprastha)* according to the custom adopted by his ancestors.

In the fifth canto the birth of *Aja* is described. *Kālidāsa* says that *Aja* did not differ from his father like the light that does not differ from the flame. This idea is mentioned by *Śrī Śankara* in his *Sarvavedāntasiddhāntasārasaṅgrahaḥ* (verse 525).

दीपाद्दीपो यथा तद्वत् पितुः पुत्रः प्रजायते।
पितुर्गुणानां तनये बीजाङ्कुरवदीक्षणात्॥

Kālidāsa describes the 'death' through *Aja.* In the eighth canto *Aja* is described as one who is ignorant of Reality. *Aja* laments over the death of his wife *Indumatī* and is prepared to follow her in death. By then the preceptor of the solar race, Sage *Vasiṣṭha* appears and consoles him. *Mallinātha* in his commentary on the verse no. 83 states that "those which are born are bound to die".

उत्पत्तिमतां जन्मवतां विपत् विपत्तिः उपस्थिता सिद्धा।

Yāskācārya in his *Nirukta* (I.2) enumerates the six stages of a thing that is produced or born.

अस्ति जायते वर्धते विपरिणमते अपक्षीयते नश्यति।

Sage *Vasiṣṭha* in his consolatory words (VIII. 85 b) tells *Aja* that even if he *(Aja)* desires to follow his wife in death he cannot do so towards the other regions.

परलोकजुषां स्वकर्मभिर्गतयो भिन्नपथा हि देहिनां।

Mallinatha's commentary on this is noteworthy.

परलोकजुषां लोकतन्त्रभाजां देहिनां गमयन्त इति गतयः
गम्यस्थानानि स्वकर्मभिः पुण्यपापैः भिन्नपथा पृथक्कृतमार्गा
हि परत्रापि स्वस्वकर्मानुरूपफलभोग्य भिन्नभिन्नदेशगमनान्......

The significance of the concept of life and death is clearly stated by *Kālidāsa* in VIII. 87.

मरणं प्रकृतिः शरीरिणां विकृतिः जीवितमुच्यते बुधैः।
क्षणमप्यवतिष्ठते वसन्यदि जन्तुरनु लाभवानसौ॥

Death is natural so those who are born and the opposite of that (Death) is life. *Viṣṇupurāna* (I. 17. 58) also confirms this.

मृतस्य च पुनर्जन्म विद्यते तच्च नान्यथा।
आगमोऽयं तथा तच्च नोपादानं विनोद्भवः॥

The sorrow that is caused by death of dear ones is again due to lack of discrimination between eternal and non-eternal things *(nityānityavastu viveka)*. Wise men are those who do not get affected or afflicted by this because of their non-attachment. This idea is repeated by *Kālidāsa* when he defines wise men (I.59) –

विकारहेतौ सति विक्रियन्ते येषां न चेतांसि त एव धीराः।

In canto XVII, *Kālidāsa* extols *Atithi* the son born of *Kumudavatī* and *Kuśa. Atithi* wiped away the sins of men by his presence, removed their ignorance by telling them the factual meaning, like the rising sun who removes the darkness (verse 74). The second quarter of this verse can be interpreted according to Advaita. The individual soul unaware of its supremacy undergoes all sorts of miseries due to ignorance *(avidyā)*. This ignorance is removed only through hearing *(śravaṇa)* of the *mahā vākya (Tat Tvam Asi)* from the Guru (an able preceptor) and repeating the same *(manana)* and contemplating *(nididhyāsana)* on that. The sun that is given as the simile can be taken to mean knowledge which removes ignorance. This removal of ignorance *(avidyā nivṛtti)* itself is the liberation in Advaita Vedānta.

In the beginning of the eighteenth canto *Atithi's* ascendance to Heaven through Karma is mentioned. The *svargaphala* is not superior to realisation of one's own self. While the stay in Heaven or enjoying the pleasures of Heaven will last until the result of the virtue is exhausted (and the soul has to take birth after that) the realisation of one's own self *(ātma Sākṣātkāra)* is eternal. That is why the upaniṣads also proclaim thus (*Chāndyogyopaniṣad* VIII. 1.6.)

तद्यथेह कर्मजितो लोकः क्षीयते, एवमेवामुत्र पुण्यजितो लोकः क्षीयते।

In this connection *Nala's* (the son of *Atithi*) approach differs from his father with regard to the fourth stage of life mentioned in the first canto (verse 8 : *yogenānte tanutyajām*). Nala departed to the forest to do penance to avoid rebirth as said by *Kālidāsa* (verse 7).

मृगैरजर्यं जरसोपदिष्टमदेहबन्धाय पुनर्बबन्ध।

Here *Kālidāsa* continues the description of the kings of *Raghu* race who realised Brahman and got liberated. King *Viśvasaha's* liberation is described in verse 28.

यशोभिराब्रह्मसभं प्रकाशः स ब्रह्मभूयं गतिमाजगाम।

ब्रह्मिष्ठमाधाय निजेऽधिकारे ब्रह्मिष्ठमेव स्वतनुप्रसूतम्॥

In the same manner *Puṣya* son of *Putra* being afraid of the worldly life, *Samsāra,* approaches sage *Jaimini,* offers himself to get taught about the ways and means to avoid birth (verse 33). On this *Mallinātha's* commentary is very interesting.

मनीषिणे ब्रह्मविद्याविदुषे जैमिनये मुनये अर्पितात्मा। शिष्यभूतस्सन्नित्यर्थः। सयोगाद्योगिनः तस्माज्जैमिनेर्योगं योगविद्यामधिगम्य जन्मने जन्मनिवृत्तये मोक्षायाकल्पत समपद्यत।

In the canto XIX, *Kālidāsa* describes the last king of the *Raghuvamśa* namely *Agnivarṇa. Agnivarṇa* also did penance without attaching himself to the result or in other words uninterested in the result *svarga* (verse 2). Later this king is depicted as the one who is drawn towards sensual pleasures, *Kāma. Kāma* though one among the four *puruṣārthas*, was equally treated on par with the other three by the ancestors of *Agnivarṇa.* This *kāma* when experienced with attachment, grows more and more like the fire when the *ghee* is poured. *Śrī Śaṅkara's* advice in *Sarvavedāntasiddhāntasāra Saṅgrahaḥ* (verse 53 & 55) is highly proper.

काम एव यमः साक्षात् कान्ता वैतरणी नदी।
विवेकीनां मुमुक्षूणां निलयस्तु यमालयः॥

and

यमस्य कामस्य च तारतम्यं विचार्यमाणे महदस्ति लोके।
हितं करोत्यस्य यमोऽप्रियस्सन् कामस्त्वनर्थं कुरुते प्रियः सन्॥

Kālidāsa further proceeds to describe how the king *Agnivarṇa* met his end due to this influence of *Kāma* and concludes the work on *Raghuvamśa.*

Kumārasambhava (KS)

Following the edition of Prof. R.C. Dwivedi in his *Kālidāsa Granthāvali,* the present article concentrates only on the first eight cantos. The story as well-known deals with the birth of *Kumāra* to Lord *Śiva* and *Pārvati.*

In the first canto *Kālidāsa* describes the penance of Lord *Śiva* in his penance posture and the concentration or control over the mind.

विकारहेतौ सति विक्रियन्ते येषां न चेतांसि त एव धीराः।

Again in canto III (verse 40) *Kālidāsa* says – that *Śiva* was not affected by the disturbances caused through the songs of the nymphs. Those who have mastered their senses *(indriya nigraha)* do not have obstacles in their path.

आत्मेश्वराणां न हि जातु विघ्नाः समाधिभेदप्रभवो भवन्ति।

In canto V *Pārvati's* penance is described. When her hopes to attach Lord *Śiva* by her beauty failed to procure the desired result she rebuked her beauty and then resolved to achieve Him through penance. *Nārāyaṇa Paṇḍita's* commentary on verse 2 regarding this deserves close attention.

अत्यन्त दुरवापेऽर्थे तपसामेव साधनत्वमुक्तं मनुना -

"यद् दुष्करं यद्दुरापं यद् दुर्गं यच्च दुस्तरम्।

तत्सर्वं तपसा प्राप्यं तपो हि दुरतिक्रमम्॥"

इति। अत्र आत्मशब्दस्यार्थप्रकरणाभ्यां सिद्धत्वेऽपि

आत्मनो नित्यत्वात् तपोभिः शरीरं परित्यज्य जन्मान्तरेषु

स्वमनीषितं साधशिष्याम्येवेति स्थिरनिश्चयत्वं प्रतिपादयितुमुपादानम्॥

During *Pārvati's* penance, *Kālidāsa* describes her tender body and says that she did not care about the difficulties in observing the penance with the only aim fixed in achieving the desired object. *Nārāyaṇa Paṇḍita's* commentary on verse 18 is also important.

स्वस्य शरीरस्य यन्मार्दवं शिरीषकुसुमादप्यधिकं सौकुमार्यं तदपि अनपेक्ष्य अविचार्य तपः चरितुं कर्तुं प्रचक्रमे। शरीरमार्दवानपेक्षणे हेतुमाह .... । सर्वत्र शीतोष्णप्रियादिषु द्वन्द्वेषु समा तुल्यबुद्धिः।

And this is the forebearance *(titikṣā)*. The definitions given in the texts for the word *titikṣā* is

सहनं सर्वदुःखानां तितिक्षा सा निगद्यते।

In canto VI the nature of wise men is mentioned as –

स्त्रीपुमानित्यनास्थैषा वृत्तं हि महितं सताम्। (12)

Those who realise the Brahman as all-pervasive, one and non-dual see themselves in every being without any difference as male or female. The attributes of the body are not connected with the soul. This has been explained in the introduction of the *bhāṣya* on the *Brahmasūtras* by *Śrī Śaṅkarācārya.* In the next canto (VII) *Kālidāsa* mentions the non-dual Brahman which though appears as *Viṣṇu, Śiva* and *Brahma* (verse 44).

एकैव मूर्तिर्बिभिदे त्रिधा सा सामान्यमेषां प्रथमावरत्वम्।

विष्णोर्हरस्तस्य हरिः कदाचित् वेधास्तयोस्तावपि धातुराद्यौ॥

In the last canto VIII *Kalidāsa* mentions that the effect caused by time etc., cannot bother those with the pure mind without any attachment. He says (verse 65).

विक्रिया न खलु कालदोषजा निर्मलप्रकृतिषु स्थिरोदया॥

Commenting on this Nārāyaṇa Paṇḍita also says –

कालदोषाज्जाता विक्रिया निर्मलप्रकृतिषु निर्मलस्वभावेषु स्थिरो निश्चलः उदयः आविर्भावः यस्याः तथाविद्या न खलु। खलुशब्दः प्रसिद्धौ। अत्र रक्तशब्देन विषयेषु अत्यन्तशक्ति मण्डलशब्देन स्वराष्ट्रं, प्रकृतिशब्देनामात्यादयश्च ध्वन्यन्ते।

The king's attachment to sensual pleasures in the youth was later removed by the old ministers and thus the king became pure through non-attachment.

Besides these ideas shown above, there are many other aspects related to the concept of life and death in the works of Kālidāsa. The present paper is only an attempt in that direction to bring out some such references related to the concept of life and death and to view them from the standpoint of advaita philosophy. References to the advaita view are selected mostly from the *prakaraṇa* works of Śrī Śaṅkarācārya who is the founder of the advaita system of philosophy. Glimpses of advaitic concepts can be traced from Ṛgveda and from then in all the works in Sanskrit literature.

* * * *

Arthāntaranyāsa in Kumārasaṃbhava

Professor S.K. Jadhab

Introduction

Innumerable researches have been done on the works of Kālidāsa and it is not even possible to attempt a brief survey of those. A critical survey of the entire researches on Kālidāsa reveals that no attempt has been made to study the *alaṅkāras* or a particular *alaṅkāra* from the point of view of the art of application except a few on *Upamā alaṅkāra.* For example Pillai K.C. Chellappan has studied the *'upamās'* in his work 'Similes of Kālidāsa'. There are some articles in the same line like 'Kālidāsa's similies' by Balakrishnan Parasu published in Triveni (June : 1944): 'Upamā Kālidāsasya' by V.S. Musalgaonkar published in Vina (1959). However no systematic research has been conducted on the Kālidāsian art of employment of *Arthāntaranyāsa* or any other *alaṅkāra* except one article titled *'Arthāntaranyāsa:* Theory and practice and its usages in the Meghadūta' presented by Prof. R.C. Dvivedi (in the A.I.O.C. Gauhati 1965). If one goes through the writings of Kālidāsa he will be convinced that though Kālidāsa is known and is acclaimed for his excellent usage of *upamā* still he has employed *Arthāntaranyāsa* in a very apt, skilled and appropriate manner. And in appreciation of his charming application of *Arthāntaranyāsa* as against the apt quoted saying *upamā kālidāsasya* – some unknown poet writes:

Upamā kālidasasya notkrsteti matir mama ।
arthāntarasya vinyāse kālidāsa viśiṣyate. ॥

In the present paper an attempt is made to study the employment of *Arthāntaranyāsa* in one of his important work, Kumārasambhava.

Cases of *Arthāntaranyāsa* where *Kālidāsa* has employed this figure are meticulously and minutely collected from Kumārasambhava. Each case of occurrence is individually analyzed quoting the context as per their occurrence. The complete verse is quoted followed by an explanation of the context along with a critical analysis and an observation wherever possible. In most of the cases reference is made to the available commentary, literature and their view and comment are recorded as far as possible. The paper is arranged in two parts. In the first part a general introduction on various aspects of this *alaṅkāra* is added, which serves as the background and facilitates further studies. Main references in the text are from the critical edition by R.C. Dvivedi.

Definition of *Arthāntaranyāsa*

Bhāmaha defines Arthāntaranyāsa thus :

upanyasanamanyasyayadarthasyoditādṛte ।
jneyo'rthāntaranyāsaḥ pūrvārthanugato yathā ॥ 2/71 ॥

According to him when there is (*upanyasana*) mentioning of the statement related with the expression mentioned first and different from it, it is a case of *arthāntaranyāsa.* The definition of Daṇḍin states that it is *arthāntaranyāsa* when a statement is mentioned first and another statement capable of establishing it follows. He writes :

Jñeyah so'rthāntaranyāso vastu prastutya kiñcana ।
tat sādhana samarthasya nyāso yo'nyasya vastunaḥ ॥ 2 ॥

Coming to Udbhata, he has not given the definition of *arthāntaranyāsa,* but has given four different illustrations based on the corroboration of *'viśeṣa'* by *'sāmānya'*. From this it cannot be concluded that he did not intend the corroboration of *'sāmānya'* by *'viśeṣa'*. Vāmana has defined *arthāntaranyāsa* as follows:

Uktasiddhaye vastuno'rthāntarasyevanyasam
arthāntaranyāsaḥ.

His definition resembles the definition as given by Bhāmaha, Daṇḍin and Rudraṭṭa. For example, Rudraṭṭa has defined

Arthāntaranyāsa as a corroboration of *'sāmānya'* by *'viśeṣa'* and vice versa, both based on *sādharmya* and *vaidharmya.*

In later period his definition has influenced to a large extent the definitions of *Arthāntaranyāsa.* Jinaseṇāchārya for the first time introduced *'Kārya-kāraṇa bhāva'* in the definition of *Arthāntaranyāsa,* where as the credit of introducing *'sāmānya-viśeṣa bhāva'* and systematizing it goes to Rudraṭṭa.

The commentator Jayaratha on Alaṅkāra Sarvasva of Ruyyaka do not accept *Arthāntaranyāsa* based on *'Kārya kāraṇa bhāva saṁbandha'* and proposes it to be included in Kāvya-liṅga Alaṅkāra. The definition given by Visvesvara, Kavichandra is based on the definition of Daṇḍin and Bhoja. We noticed the impact and influence of Panditarāja Jagannātha on Pandit Prabhakarashastri Gadgil and of Appaya Diksita on Achyutarāya Modak.

After discussing the definition of *Arthāntaranyāsa* the varieties of *Arthāntaranyāsa* are given here. Bhāmaha, the founder of Alaṅkāra śāstra has not clearly mentioned the varieties of this alaṅkāra. But from his presentation it can be concluded that he proposed two types of *Arthāntaranyāsa.*

1. *Arthāntaranyāsa* with the expression *'hi'* (*hi sabda sahita*).
2. *Arthāntaranyāsa* without the expression *'hi.'* (*hi sabda rahita.*). After Bhāmaha, Daṇḍin has enumerated eight varieties of this Alaṅkāra as recorded in the following verse.
   Visvavyāpi viśeṣastha ślesavidho virodhavān ı
   ayuktakari yuktama yuktayukto viparyayaḥ ıı 5 ıı

He has explained all these varieties with suitable examples. It may be observed that the types of *Arthāntaranyāsa* enumerated by Daṇḍin are but the varieties of corroboration than basic conceptual distinctions.

The commentator Ratnasrijñāna has added two more varieties namely, 1, *Aviruddha* and 2, *Aviruddhā-viruddha* to Daṇḍī's list of eight. Regarding further varieties, Daṇḍin mentions that the other varieties can be understood from the word *'adi'*. *(Ityevam ādayoḥ-bhedah, prayogesvasya laksita)* Udbhaṭa has enumerated four varieties, which are as follows.

samarthakasya pūrvam yat vaco'nysya ca pṛṣṭataḥ ı
Viparyayena vā sas syāt viśeṣoktyat anyathāpiva ıı
sa ca samarthakasya prāgupādānena samarthasya,
veti dvibhedaḥ pratibhedas ca hi śabdena yogviyogo veti,
caturvidhaḥ.

It seems, this supposition has not been followed in the later period. Rudrata has enumerated four varieties of *Arthāntaranyāsa* which are as follows :

1. Corroboration of *'viśeṣa'* by *'sāmānya'* in *'sādharmya'*
2. Corroboration of *'viśeṣa'* by *'sāmānya'* in *'vaidharmya'*
3. Corroboration of *'sāmānya'* by *'viśeṣa'* in *'sādharmya'*
4. Corroboration of *'sāmānya'* by *'viśeṣa'* in *'vaidharmya'*

In later period the influence of his definition and classification is noticed on most of the rhetoricians like Mammata, Srivatsalanchana, Bhattacharya Visvanātha Deva Kavikarnapura, Panditarāja Jagannātha, Sri Vidyabhusana Pt. Visvalabdhavara Pandey, Krsnasudhi, Srikrsna brahmatantra Parakala Svami, Pt. Prabhakara Sastri Gadgil, Govinda Pandit, Bhanudutta Sivadutta Visvanatha Sahrdaya Siromani and Narendra Prabha Suri. Jinasenacarya has accepted three varieties namely, the corroboration of *'sāmānya'* by *'viśeṣa',* corroboration of *'viśeṣa',* by *'sāmānya'* and corroboration of *'kāraṇa'* by *kārya.* Where there is the corroboration of *kārya* by *kāraṇa* he has accepted *kāvyaliṅga* instead of *arthāntaranyāsa.* Rudraṭṭa has accepted *arthāntaranyāsa 'ubhayanyāsa* 'and *pratyanikanyāsa'* as three distinct figures, where as Bhoja has included *ubhayanyāsa* in *arthāntaranyāsa.* In later period Visvanatha Haridasa Siddhantavagisa and Dr. Sankaradeva Avatare have accepted the classification of Ruyyaka.

Kumārasambhava is most probably the first Makhākāvya of Kālidāsa. There is controversy regarding the extent of this kāvya, namely, whether it contains eight or seventeen cantos. However, we have taken the entire seventeen cantos of Kumārasambhava into consideration and examined some one thousand and ninety-six verses.

(60+64+76+46+86+95+95+91+52+60+50+60

+51+51+53+51+55 = 1096).

In some sixty-nine cases we have identified *arthāntaranyāsa* out of which forty instances are from the first eight cantos only, and twenty-four from the rest of the cantos. It is observed that Kālidāsa in most cases has used only one category of *arthāntaranyāsa* namely, the corroboration of *'viśeṣa'* by *'sāmānya'*. Out of sixty-nine cases, in sixty-four occasions his *arthāntaranyāsa* is of this type. We quote here some beautiful cases of *arthāntaranyāsa* from Kumārasambhava:

1. *Anataratna prabhavasya yasya,*
himaṁ na saubhāgya vilopi jātam ।
ekohi doṣo guṇa sannipāte,
nimajjatendukiranesvev ānkah ॥ *(Kumāra. I. 3).*
2. *Divākarāt rakṣati yo guhāsu,*
līnam divā bhīta ivāndhakāram ।
kṣudro'pi nūnaṁ saranaṁ prapanne,
Mamatvam uccaiḥ sirasām satīva ॥ *(Kumāra. I. 12).*
3. *Ayi samprati dehi darśanam,*
smaraparyutsuka eṣa mādhavah ।
dayitāsvanavasthitam nṛṇām,
na khaluprema calam suhṛj jane ॥ (*Kumāra. IV. 28*).
4. *śaśinā saha yāti kaumudī,*
sahameghena tadit pralīyate ।
pramadāḥ pativartmagā iti,
pratipannam hi vicetanair api ॥ *(Ibid. IV. 33).*
5. *nivāryatāmāli kimapy ayam vatuḥ,*
punar vivakṣuḥ sphuritottarādharaḥ ।
na kevalaṁ yo mahato, pyabhāṣate,
śṛṇoti yasmād apisa pāpabhāg ॥ *(Ibid. V. 83).*

As already stated, we will not explain all these verses but only a few as sample from which one can get an idea of the employment of *arthāntaranyāsa*.

In the first verse the poet describes the beauty and the greatness of Himalaya. Since it is the source of innumerable ratnas the presence of snow does not affect its greatness and beauty. This is the statement of *'viśeṣa'* which is corroborated by *'sāmānya ukti'* namely a single blemish or fault in the plethora of virtues merges in it, as in the case of the black spot on the moon.

Observation

In employing this *arthāntaranyāsa* Kālidāsa has resorted to a charming *subhāśita* based on a universal truth that a minor fault in the case of a virtuous person is always neglected. Commenting on this verse Mallinatha writes :

atra upamā anuprānito 'arthāntaranyāsalankāra ।
tallakṣaṇaṁ tu jñeyaḥ so'arthāntaranyāsovastuprastutya kiñcana ।
Tat sādhana samarthasya nyāso yonyasya vastunaḥ iti dandī
(Sanji. p. 4.11.20.22).

Narayana Pandit and Arunagirinatha have also identified *arthāntaranyāsa* in this verse. (Vivarana. p. 11.11.10-11; Prakāśikā. p. 9.1.16).

In the next verse Kumāra. I.12. Kālidāsa while describing the greatness of Himalaya, narrates that he protects darkness by giving shelter in its caves. This statement of *'viśeṣa'* is supported by the expression of in the form of generalization namely, even towards insignificance coming for shelter are protected by great or noble persons. In this verse commentators like Mallinatha, Arunagirinatha and Narayanapandita have identified *arthāntaranyāsa*. In our analysis we have made use of the views of commentators like Katayavema, Sankarnarahari, Nilakantha, Raghavabhatta, Ghanasyama, Abhirama, Sahrdyatilaka, Rama Pisaroti, Ramasankar Pandey, Ramchandra Mishra, Sriranga Verma, Appasastri Rasivadekar, Surendranath Sastri, Navakishore Shastri, Shiva Prasad Dvivedi, and Gaurinath Pathak.

Conclusion

Taking very selected examples we have studied the employment of *arthāntaranyāsa* in Kumārasaṁbhava. Now we may present our conclusion of the present study in the form of observation. On the definition of *arthāntaranyāsa* it has been maintained that corroboration of *'viśeṣa'* by *'sāmānya'* and vice versa is the basis of this *alaṇkāra.* According to Rudraṭṭa the expression of corroboration should follow the expression to be corroborated. But no such order is prescribed by any other *ālaṅkārikas.* The definition of Rudraṭṭa as the corroboration of *'viśeṣa'* by *'sāmānya'* and vice versa in *'sādharmya'* and *'vaidharmya'* is accepted by most of the later *ālaṅkārikas.* For the first time he included the term *'sāṁanya-viśeṣa'* in the definition of *arthāntaranyāsa.* Jinasenacarya has introduced *kārya-kāraṇa bhāva* in the definition, which is accepted by Ruyyaka. However his commentator doesn't accept *arthāntaranyāsa* on the basis of *kārya-kāraṇa-bhāva* and in that case accepts *Kāvyaliṅga.*

On the classification of *arthāntaranyāsa* there are many varieties. Daṇdin has suggested eight kinds of *arthāntaranyāsa.* Bhāmaha, Vāmana, Jayadeva, Viśvesvara, Ciranjiva, Trimalabhatta, Bhavadevasuri, Mankhaka, Appaya Diksita, Kuntaka, Agni Purana, Visnu Dharmottara Purana, Silameghasena Sudhindratirtha Prasad have not given any classification. Rudraṭṭa has proposed four main varieties namely, corroboration of *viśeṣa* by *sāmānya* and vice versa in *sādharmya* and *'vaidharmya'* which is mostly accepted by the later rhetoricians. Ruyyaka has rejected the classification based on the presence of *'hi'* and without it, due to lack of charm.

On the varieties of *arthāntaranyāsa* employed by Kālidāsa, he has mostly used the first two varieties, namely corroboration of *'viśeṣa'* by *'sāmanya'* in *'sādharmya'* and *'vaidharmya'*. The examples of corroboration of *'sāmānya'* by *'viśeṣa'* are of rare occurrences. For example, we have the employment of the corroboration of *'viśeṣa'* by *'sāmānya'* in sixty-four cases in Kumāra, where as in only ten cases the *'sāmānya'* is supported by *'viśeṣa'*.

We think that there is no need to include the corroboration based on *'kārya-kārana bhava'* in *arthāntaranyāsa.* If there is some charm they may be treated as *hetu* or *Kāvyaliṅgālaṅkāra.*

On the question, namely whether *arthāntaranyāsa* is *'sādṛsya mūlaka'* or *'tarka mūlaka'* we maintain that *arthāntaranyāsa* is rooted on the notion of corroboration. The link of either *'tarka'* or *'sādṛsya'* cannot be avoided altogether.

Regarding the commentaries and commentators it may be recorded that we have made use of seven commentaries on Kumāra. It is observed that the commentators are mostly indifferent towards the identification of this *alaṅkāra.* Mallinatha, Arunagirinatha, Raghavabhatta, and Sthiradeva have identified this *alaṅkāra* here and there.

Some times the commentator raises doubt about the presence of more than one figure and gives his own view. Nārāyana Pandit in Kumara. I.IV. discusses in greater detail the presence of *arthāntaranyāsa* or *dṛṣṭānta* and concludes it to be *arthāntaranyāsa. 'atra svabhāvastu kumāram- drṣṭāntam upanyasyati....atra eko hi doṣa ityatra viśeṣasya-sāmanyena samarthanāt arthāntaranyāsaḥ'.* (Vivarana. p. 11, LL. 2-11.)

In most cases of Kumārasaṁbhava (I-VIII) the commentators have identified this figure where as in the rest, particularly in Kumāra (VIII-XVII) they are not so particular.

References

1. Bhāmaha : Kavyālaṅkāra, Delhi, 1965.
2. Hemachandra : Kāvyānuśāsana, Bombai, 1938.
3. Jinasena : Alaṅkāra Cintamani, Darabhanga, 1957
4. Kālidāsa : Kumārasambhava, Kalidasa Granhavali, Varanasi
5. Mamatta : Kāvya Prakāsha, BORI, Poona, 1968.
6. Rajasekhara : Kāvyamīmāmsā, Baroda, 1934.
7. Ruyyaka : Alaṅkārasarvasva, Delhi, 1965
8. Vāmana : Kāvyālaṅkāra Sūtravṛtti, NSP., BOMBAY, 1989.
9. Vāgbhata : Vāgbhatālaṅkara, Jaipur, 1957.
10. Viśhwanāth : Sāhityadarpana, NSP, Bombay, 1933.

* * * *

Section-C

Bhakti, Yoga and Poetics

Bhakti, Yoga and Poetics

In this section, we are presenting seven articles – two on Bhakti, four on Yoga and one on Hermeneutics and Poetics. True, all these articles do not fully represent the three themes of this part. They do, however, highlight certain aspects of these subjects.

Dr. V. Kameswari has briefly surveyed Bopadeva's works which primarily deal with the sentiment of Bhakti. Bopadeva belonged to the latter part of the 13th century A.D. and although Bhakti had emerged quite early in human evolution, Bopadeva gave it a status of *Rasa,* in the Indian Poetics. He was at the earlier end of the Bhakti Movement. Dr. Kameswari points out that Bopadeva's works spread towards the East, crossing all the language barriers and perhaps, served as a cue to the Bhakti movement of Bengal during the 15th century.

The second article is '*Bhakti in Bhagvadgītā*' by Dr. Ujjwala Panse. Here, Dr. Panse has corelated the definition of Bhakti as in *Naradīya Bhakti Sūtra* with wordings in the *Gītā.* She says that, apart from Chapter 12 in the *Gītā,* which squarely deals with *Bhakti yoga,* there are a number of couplets in the *Gītā* which describe the way of *Bhakti* as a means of salvation. Dr. Panse has also presented both, the traditional and the modern interpretation of *Bhakti*. Among the modern interpreters, she refers to the contributions of Bankim Chandra, Sw. Vivekananda, Tilak, Aurobindo, Gandhi, Vinoba, Radhakrishnan, and Sw. Bhaktivedanta. She also points out the significance of Bhakti in removing the tensions in the modern world.

There are four articles on *Yoga*. The first one is by Dr. K.S. Balasubramanian – '*The Construction* of *Maṭha according to Yogic Texts'*. The writer has culled the information from important texts on *Haṭha-yoga* viz. *Yoga Yājñyavalkya, Haṭha Yoga Pradīpikā, Haṭharatnāvali, Śiva Saṁhitā, Haṭhasanketacandrikā,* and *Gheraṇḍa Saṁhitā.* He has also referred to some *Purāṇaṣ*. The writer believes that environment is a prime factor in *Yoga sādhanā.*

In an article titled *Nārāyaṇatīrtha's Contribution to the Yoga Philosophy,* Dr. Penna Madhusudan has taken pains to interpret the commentaries by Nārāyaṇatīrtha on *Yogasūtras.* It is somewhat strange that a single commentator should write three commentaries on a single text. It, however indicates that the commentator values this text greatly and wants it to be thoroughly understood by the inquisitive readers. The writer tells us that the longest commentary by Nārāyaṇatīrtha on the *Yogasūtras* is *Yogasiddhāntacandrikā* (also mentioned in the colophone as *Gūdhārthadyotikā*) and that it takes note of a variety of concepts in relation to Yoga, as expounded by Vācaspati Miṣrā and Vijñānabhikṣu.

Dr. Vinod Verma in her article on *Aṣṭāṅgayoga* draws our attention to the eternal energy that functions within an individual and outside. The means of harnessing this energy are narrated. Yoga serves as a ladder to reach a state of Samadhi.

Dr. Anuradha Oka, deals with the concept of *Pratyāhāra* as expounded by Patañjali and by other seers in *Yoga upaniṣads.* She has presented various definitions of *Pratyāhāra* in various *Yoga-upaniṣads.* This is an interesting study indicating the widening of the concept of *Pratyāhāra* to the extent of *Advaita Jñāna.*

The last article in this part is '*Hermeneutics and Indian Poetics*' by Dr. T. Devarajan. He has taken a stock of wide range of literature and has pointed out how, in India, the goal of all intellectual and literary activity was the exposition of the Vedas. He refers to Abhinavagupta and enumerates the eleven objectives of a literary work. He has surveyed the contributions of eminent authors on poetics such as, Bhatta Lollata, Śaṅkuka, Bhatta Nāyaka. The essay also deals with *Dhvani, Rasa and Pratyabhijñā.* He also points out, how in India, the aesthetic theories took a transitional course to spiritualism and self knowledge.

All the topics dealt in this part were very dear to Prof. JNK and in his writings he has touched them on a number of occasions. We are happy that we could extend this fare to all the admirers of Prof. Kaul.

– Editors

Bopadeva and His Contribution to Bhakti Cult

Dr. V. Kameswari

> "A warmth within the breast would melt
> the freezing Reason's colder part,
> and like a man in wrath the heart
> stood up and answered 'I Have felt'"
> – Tennyson

Bhakti, like philosophy, begins in wonder arising out of the feelings of awe in perceiving God's beauteous creation. The feelings of awe and wonder in turn develop into emotions of admiration, gratitude and reverence. The single word *'bhakti'* denotes, all these at the same time.

The term *bhakti* is derived from the root *'bhaj'* which in one of its uses, means 'to adore'. It is adoration of the God-head, the universal Supreme Being, One and the only One, addressed in different ways by followers of different religions.

Nārada, Śāṇḍilya, Prahlāda and Uddhava have expounded in detail, the various modes of Bhakti. They unanimously describe Bhakti as the spiritual love which is directed towards the Supreme Being. When a person loves the Supreme Being he loves all the creations of the God and hates none. The true devotee sees God in all and everything as the manifestation of God. Nārada terms Bhakti as *parama prema* and Śāṇḍilya declares that God is *paranuraktīśvare.*

According to historical studies, the influence of Bhakti cult spread from South to North. The Bhakti cult has come down to us as a distinct tradition receiving inspiration from the practical life of Bhaktas like Prahlāda, Janaka and others. During the Muslim period of Indian history, it received new impetus from the Sufi saints which led to the two distinct types of Bhakti movement as *Nirguṇa* and *Saguṇa*. And also there arose two classes of founders of Bhakti literature (i) those who wrote in Sanskrit and (ii) those who wrote in vernacular.

Amidst the writers of the Bhakti school who contributed a lot to Sanskrit Literature, Bopadeva secures the foremost place for himself. Dr. V. Raghavan, in his book on *Rāmāyaṇa, Mahābhārata and Bhāgavata Writers*[1] deals in details about the date and the works of Bopadeva. According to him, Bopadeva belonged to the latter half of the 13th century.

Bopadeva was a pioneer in analysing the *Bhāgavata Purāṇa* in a topical manner. He was also the first person to consider the emotion of *bhagavad bhakti* as a *rasa*. An historical analysis of the Bhāgavaṭa cult, shows that Bhakti Rase theory travelled from Bopadeva and his followers to Bengal. Caitanya and his followers nourished it.

Bopadeva claims in his commentaries on his own works *Harilīā* and *Bhāgavata Muktāphala* that he has written "10 excellent works on grammar, 9 famous works on medicine, 1 wonderful work on *Tithinirṇaya* (Dharma-Jyotiṣa), 3 on poetry and 3 expounding the *real meaning of the Bhāgavata*". Dr. Raghavan adds to these twenty-six works, the commentary on the *Śivamahimnāstava* of Puṣpadanta.

In all, Bopadeva's contribution to Bhakti literature can be numbered as four: (1) *Hariliālā* with the commentary *Hariharapriyā;* (2) *Bhāgavatamuktāphala* with the commentary *Kaivalyadīpikā,* (3) *Paramahamsapriya,* a commentary on *Bhāgavata* and (4) commentary on *Śivamahimnāstava.*

Dr. V. Raghavan in his book *Number of Rasas*[2] and later in his article on Bopadeva referred to above, discusses the authorship of all these works. While in the *Number of Rasas,* he ascribes the authorship of the commentaries on *Harilīlā* and *Muktāphala* to Hemādri, Minister of Yādavas in the latter work

1. Cultural Leaders of India Series, Publication Division, Ministry of Information and Broadcasting, Govt. of India, Delhi, 1978.
2. Adyar Library and Research Centre, Madras, 1940.

he proves that both the commentaries are by Bopadeva himself. He also disproves the arguments that the commentaries on *Bhāgavata* and *Śivamahimnāstava* are by Madhusūdana Sarasvatī. He asserts with logical argumentation that they are also by Bopadeva.

A brief note on each of the works of Bopadeva is given below:

1. The commentary on *Śivamahimnāstava* follows the *Advaita-cum-bhakti* tradition "whose seeds can be traced to Śaṅkara himself". On the same lines, Bopadeva contends that Advaitins believing in *Nirguṇa Brahman* can have Bhakti towards the *Saguṇa Brahman,* the personal God.
2. The same concept is reflected in his *Harilīlā* and the commentary on it. In *Harilīlā* XII. 1 and the commentary on it, he states that there is no difference between the impersonal and the personal; the personal form may be one or the other, Śiva or Hari. To show that Hari and Hara are one and the same, Bopadeva claims that he wrote this commentary called *Hari-Hara-Pakṣīya* interpreting each verse first as relevant to Śiva and then to Hari.
3. The commentary on *Bhāgavata* called *Paramahamsapriya,* a fragment of which alone is available, covers the first three verses of the *Bhāgavata.* While commenting on the 3rd verse, Bopadeva waxes eloquent on the *rasa – kṛṣṇa bhakti,* while explaining the term *"rasikāḥ"*. He also calls it '*Bhakti-rasa.*'
4. The *Muktāphala* on the *Bhāgavata* is the most important work of Bopadeva. It is arranged in four sections providing the verses selected from the *Bhāgavata* with linking passages in prose. The four chapters are;
   (i) *Viṣṇu-prakaraṇa* – dealing with the nature of Viṣṇu, His manifestations, His glory etc.
   (ii) *Viṣṇu bhakti* – its forms and greatness.
   (iii) *Bhaktīaṅgas* – chiefly *śravaṇa, manana, kīrtana* and *smaraṇa.*
   (iv) *Bhaktas* – their characteristics, different kinds of attitudes and sentiments through which they view the Lord or seek Him.

This chapter is the longest section of the text and here Bopadeva expounds the aesthetics of Bhakti-rasa. He begins his analysis of the Bhaktas into nine kinds from the angle of the nine *rasas*. by Abhinavagupta and others. To Bopadeva, Bhakti is the Supreme *rasa* and all the nine *rasas* are subservient to it. In dealing with this aspect, the commentary runs as a short treatise on *rasas,* as dealt with by Bharata and other Ālaṁkārikas upto Bhoja who is amply quoted.

According to Bopadeva, the 'delectation' produced through *śravaṇa, manana* etc. of the story of the Bhaktas which embody the nine *rasas* is Bhakti-rasa: He then illustrates devotion through each of these nine *rasas* by bringing the relevant verses of the *Bhāgavata* under each one of them:

Hāsya : Gopīs and boy Kṛṣṇa's pranks with them.

Śṛṅgāra : *Sambhoga* - Love of the Gopīs towards Kṛṣṇa. *Vipralambha* - Gopīs in separation.

Karuṇa : Arjuna's lamentation before Kṛṣṇa, Sunīti's words, verses uttered by Prahlāda, Aditi, Nārada etc.

Raudra : Episodes of Hiraṇyakaśipu and Śiśupāla - their violent personalities subserve the purpose of the constant thought of the Lord.

Bhaya : Similar obsession of the thoughts of Kṛṣṇa through fear - Kamsa, Durvāśas, and the expression of fear by devotees.

Bībhatsa : Expressed through disgust towards the body and mundane pre-occupations.

Śānta : This is intimately connected with Bhakti. The commentary answers at length the objections of Ālaṅkārikas against *Śānta rasa* – e.g. Kapila, Akrūra, Mucukunda.

Adbhuta : Sudāma episode. Also the wonderful spiritual experiences of Śuka, Uddhava, Prahlāda, Akrūra.

Vīra : Of Bali, Pṛthu, Parīkṣit, Rudra and others. Both *dānavīra* and *dharmavīra* varieties are illustrated.

Thus, aesthetics of *Bhakti Rasa* given in the *Muktāphala*

and its commentary is the most important contribution of Bopadeva. This also has great influence on the Beṅgal Bhakti cult of Caitanya school as shown below:

1. Rūpagosvāmin, the most-prominent Caitanya rhetorician expresses his indebtedness to Bopadeva and *Muktāphala* in his *Ujjvalanīlamaṇi.*
2. Sanatāna Gosvāmin refers to Bopadeva and *Muktāphala* in his commentary *Vaiṣṇavatoṣiṇī* on *Bhāgavata.*
3. Jīvagosvāmin and Gopāla Bhaṭṭa also record their indebtedness to Bopadeva.
4. The Bengali *Bhaktamālā* includes the life of Bopadeva.

From the above enumeration, it could be easily perceived that Bopadeva has greatly contributed to Bhakti literature and the cult. A forerunner in establishing the *Bhaktirasa* and maintaining that all the other nine *rasas* are subservient to it, Bopadeva's greatness lies in his character as a true Bhakta. As Dr. Raghavan aptly puts it: "The Bhāgavata is his Bible and Kṛṣṇa Bhakti is the anchor of his heart".

* * * *

Bhakti in Bhagavadgītā

Dr. Ujjwala Panse Jha

Introduction

The topic of my paper is quite popular in both, the intelligentia and the community of common people. Many scholars have written on this subject quite at length and from many angles. Remembering them with due acknowledgement, let us deal with this subject in the following manner:

(1) What is Bhakti? How to attain it?

(2) Bhakti is Bhagavadgītā (BG) i.e. as found in the verses of BG.

(3) Interpretation 1: Traditional

(4) Interpretation 2: Modern

(5) Observations.

1. What is Bhakti? How to attain it?

Nārada, in his *Bhaktisūtra* (NBS) after proposing: *Athāto bhaktim vyākhyāsyāmaḥ,* has defined *Bhakti* as: *Sā tvasmin paramapremarūpā.* Which means 'devotion is the greatest love in Him' and adds: *amṛtasvarūpā ca.* Its nature is like that of *amṛta* or nectar. While stating the result of *bhakti* just in the following *sūtra* Nārada says, *yal labdhvā pumān siddho bhavaty amṛto bhavati tṛpto bhavati.*

When a man attains devotion he becomes a *yogin* (it is also translated as he becomes successful which may not be befitting in the context.) he becomes *amṛta* or immortal and satisfied. To explain this further, Nārada says, after attaining devotion there remains no desire, no pain, no aversion, no amusement and no over-enthusiasm (it has been also translated as he does not become zealous - which may lead to mean he becomes lazy but that is not the sense intended.) (Vide the tr. of Nandalal Sinha)

To explain the same in a positive manner i.e. to state how the perfect *bhakta* looks like, Nārada says: *yaj jñātvā matto bhavati stabdho bhavati ātmārāmo bhavati.*

By knowing devotion he becomes overjoyed, quiet and self-satisfied.

It is not something which is achieved by desire. If we proceed to see how *bhakti* is achieved and what exactly is the nature of the love in God which is said to be devotion, then Nārada explains that the nature of *bhakti* is of the form of *nirodha*. *Nirodha* is *loka-vedavyāpārasya nyāsaḥ* i.e. to get rid of or to deposit the performances carried on in the day-to-day life or those prescribed by the Veda. Once this is done then the devotee should achieve *tasminnananyatā* and *tadvirodhiṣūdāsīnatā* i.e. the state of whole-heartedness towards Him and indifference towards everything that is antagonistic to Him.

Thus, according to Nārada, one who is desirous of leading the path of devotion shoud observe the above-mentioned states of mind strictly and should not perform any ordinary or Vedic activities. This of course does not mean that the *bhakta* needs to stop all his studies as Nārada sanctions: *Bhavatū niścayadārḍhyād ūrdhvam śāstrarakṣaṇam.* To translate is, he allows the devotee to continue with his studies of the *śāstras* after deepening his faith in God. There is also a solid reason for which he prescribes *śāstrarakṣaṇa* for a devotee and that is,: he otherwise would be considered as a *nāstika,* a skeptic. To quote Nārada, *anyathā pātityaśaṅkayā.* 13. (This has been translated by Sinha as, ... 'lest, otherwise, there may be a fall', which though literal seems to be incorrect. Here, in my opinion *pātitya* stands for *nāstikya* because, if one does not perform any scriptural rites he will be taken to be antagonistic towards the scriptures and even though he strives hard in attaining devotion of God he will be labeled as a *nāstika* or a skeptic, who does not believe in the authenticity of the Vedas.) While stating the manifestation or main marks of devotion, Nārada says: *Nāradastu tadarpitākhilācāratā, tadvismaraṇe paramavyākulatā iti (NBS* 19). And gives the example of the *gopis* of Vraja (*yathā vrajagopikānām NBS* 21).

What is the status of devotion according to Nārada? Nārada opines *sā tu karma jñānayogebhyo'pyadhikatarā*. NBS 25). He has placed devotion on the higher plane than the trio of *jñāna; karman* and *yoga* and has given the reason for doing so in the following two *sūtras* namely: *phalarūpatvāt NBS* 26; and *Īśvarasyāpyabhimānidveṣitvād dainyapriyatvācca.*

The reason to place *bhakti* higher is two-fold. First is that devotion in itself is an achievement, it itself is the result for which the devotee longs and secondly, God also likes those persons more who are solely dependent upon Him i.e. who are not carried away by their own identities – who do not have any pride in their achievements or knowledge or wisdom for that matter.

From all the above discussion and also from the definition of *bhakti* given by *Śāṇḍilya, Sā parānuraktirīśvare,* that we may say it is the supreme attachment or love towards God, it becomes clear that a devotee is that person who is closely and permanently attached to God. Nārada states that it is in itself its own result. In other words, the devotee attains his desired goal, if and when, he attains the perfect state of devotion.

It is this nature of devotion which takes it to the higher plane than that of *jñāna* knowledge, *karman* action or *yoga* i.e. *samādhi* or concentration. All of these are the means of the final goal but *bhakti* in itsef is the final destination says Nārada. Now on this background, let us see how *bhakti* is described in the BG.

2. Bhakti in the BG.

It is well known that the twelfth chapter of the BG is known as the *bhaktiyoga* or the chapter on devotion to the Lord Kṛṣṇa. But in fact, the pearls of devotion are woven in the string of the philosophical thought of the Gītā, right from the second chapter, where Arjuna requested Kṛṣṇa to preach him at the difficult hour of his life.

Śiṣyas te'ham śādhi mām tvām prapannam. BG. 2. 7. It is

true that the role of Arjuna here is that of a disciple and thus he makes the Lord his teacher or preacher but by his meekness he suggests that the Lord is almighty and omniscient, whereas he is just his ignorant pupil to whom He should advise. Lord Kṛṣṇa also has assured him that He will free him from all evils and he need not feel sorry or worry.

ahaṁ tvā sarvapāpebhyo mokṣayiṣyāmi mā śucaḥ.
(BG. 18.66)

Not only this but the Lord declares in 8.16 that there are birth cycles which go on repeating themselves, but once a person attains me, he does not have any rebirth.

ā brahmabhuvanāl lokāḥ punarāvartino'rjuna.
mām upetya tu kaunteya punarjanma na vidyate. (BG. 8.16)

The Lord Himself says further:

avyakto'kṣara ity uktas tam āhuḥ paramāṁ gatim.
yaṁ prāpya na nivartante tad dhāma paramaṁ mama.
(BG. 8.21)

puruṣaḥ sa paraḥ pārtha bhaktyā labhyas tv ananyayā.
yasyā 'ntaḥsthāni bhūtāni yena sarvam idaṁ tatam.
(BG. 8.22)

i.e. that last resort can be obtained through wholehearted devotion. While commenting on this, *Śaṅkarācārya* interprets:

Tallabdherupāya Ucyate - Puruṣa iti. Puruṣaḥ puri śayanātpūrṇatvātvā, sa paraḥ partha! Paro niratiśayo yasmātpuruṣānna param kincit. Sa bhaktyā labhyastu jñānalakṣaṇayā' ananyayā "ātmaviṣayayā."

The Lord has said that

Ananyacetāḥ satataṁ yo māṁ smarati nityaśaḥ.
tasyā 'haṁ sulabhaḥ pārtha nityayuktasya yoginaḥ.
(BG. 8.14)

I am easily obtainable for such a *yogin* who remembers me wholeheartedly for ever and further assures, once he reaches me, there is no rebirth for him which is the source of all evils.

mām upetya punarjanma duḥkhālayam aśāśvatam.
nāpnuvanti mahātmānaḥ saṁsiddhiṁ paramāṁ gatāḥ.
(*Ibid* - 8.15)

Thus, two points become clear from these utterances of the Lord. (1) He is obtainable through devotion which is His permanent remembrance – whole-hearted attachment to Him and (2) once He is obtained by the devotee, there is no rebirth for him. Another verse also may be referred to, in this context:

abhyāsayogayuktena cetasā nā'nyagāminā.
paramaṁ puruṣaṁ divyaṁ yāti pārthā 'nucintayan. (BG. 8.8)

After perceiving the all-pervading form of the Lord when Arjuna came to his senses again,

dṛṣṭve 'daṁ mānuṣaṁ rūpaṁ tava saumyaṁ janārdana.
idānīm asmi saṁvṛttaḥ sacetāḥ prakṛtiṁ gataḥ. (*Ibid* - 11.51)

The Lord told him that the form, the omnipresent manifestation of the Lord was seen by Arjuna not because of any other reason than his whole-hearted devotion towards the Lord.

nā 'haṃ vedair na tapasā na dānena na ce'jyayā.
śakya evaṁvidho draṣṭuṁ dṛṣṭavān asi māṁ yathā.
bhaktyā tv ananyayā śakya aham evaṁvidho 'rjuna.
jñātuṁ draṣṭuṁ ca tattvena praveṣṭuṁ ca paraṁtapa.
(BG. 11.53, 54)

Here again we understand that the status of *bhakti* is quite uncomparable so far as the question of obtaining the Lord is concerned. The Lord Himself refutes all other means to obtain Him in favour of the whole-hearted devotion to Him. And it follows from this that Arjuna is his great devotee who could perceive the divine omnipresent form of the Lord which is a desireratum, even of all the deities. It is in this context that Arjuna asked the Lord that there are people who worship you whole-heartedly and there are persons who pursue the abstract Brahman – who between these two groups really know the *yoga*?

And the Lord answers, those who worship me always placing their heart unto me and by full faith in me are the ones who are the real *yogins*. Lord Kṛṣṇa further says that even those who worship the abstract Brahman ultimately come to me only and I bring them out of the ocean of the cycles of deaths i.e. of births very soon.

ye tu sarvāṇi karmāṇi mayi saṁnyasya matparāḥ.
ananyenai 'va yogena māṁ dhyāyanta upāsate.
teṣām ahaṁ samuddhartā mṛtyu saṁsāra sāgarāt.
bhavāmi nacirāt pārtha mayy āveśita cetasām.
(BG. 12. 6,7)

3. Interpretation 1: Traditional

Thus, After looking into the general concept of *bhakti* as given by Nārada's *bhaktisūtra* and also the same in the *B.G.* Let us now look into the traditional interpretation of the concept of *bhakti* and its status in achieving the final goal of life. The final aim of human life is to free the soul from all bondage which will give him the freedom from all pain and will help him be in his own form.

Now, how to achieve this? The whole cycle of pain and bondage has its root in ignorance. Because of this ignorance only the soul is in the state of *saṃsāra.* To remove the ignorance one must, therefore, have the correct cognition of the knowables. Thus, *tattvajñāna* is the *sādhana* for the ultimate goal of the soul – *Tattvajñāna* or correct cognition is possible only when the mind is pure and not polluted. Hence the means of *tattvajñāna* is the pure, unpolluted mind. To make mind pure like the clean mirror it must be detached from the worldly things thus *nivṛtti* is the means to achieve the purity of mind. To achieve *nivṛtti* the means is *karmayoga* or the doing away with the *kāmyakarman* or the desire for the result. For achieving this, one should try to do all activities as they are done for the Lord," *Īśvarārpaṇabuddhikṛtakarman.* This is nothing but devotion.

Thus, *bhakti* becomes the means of salvation through various processes that help *tattvajñāna* arise.

But there is another way also. *Bhakti* directly helps the devotee become free from the *saṃsāra.* This is what th Lord himself has assured.

Now, if a question is raised here how is it possible, then the answer would be through God's grace as there is no other answer which may sound more logical or more convincing. As Nārada in his *sūtra* 51 states: *anirvacanīyam premasvarūpam; mūkāsvādanavat* (52) and further adds *prakāśyate kvāpi pātre* (53). The nature of God's love or devotion towards Lord is inexplicable just like the taste of a dumb person. It manifests itself in a proper or deserving or fit person. So it is only God's grace that his devotee attains salvation. Nārada says; *anyasmāt Saulabhyam bhaktau.* 58 *pramāṇāntarānapekṣatvāt svayampramāṇatvāt.* 59 *Śāntirūpāt paramānandarūpācca.* 60 The very state of devotion is peace and supreme joy. It does not need any other proof as it itself is the destination of the devotee and this is the reason why *bhakti* is the easier means to attain salvation.

Only the *bhakta* has to love God earnestly, having abandoned the pride and hypocricy (*abhimāna-dambhādikam tyājyam* – 64). Without involving in disputes (*vādo nāvalambyaḥ* – 74) and in listening to the talks about women, wealth and the behaviour of the unbelievers (*strīdhananāstikacaritram na śravaṇīyam* – 63) and observing *ahimsā* harmlessness, *satya* truthfulness, *śauch* cleanliness, *dayā* kindness and *āstikya* faith in God (vide *sūtra* – 78). So in short,

Sarvadā sarvabhāvena niścintaiḥ bhagvāneva bhajnīyaḥ. (*Ibid* – 70) and then *Sa kīrtyamānaḥ śīgramevāvirbhavati anubhāvayati bhaktān.* (*Ibid* – 80)

Thus Nārada, the very name of whom reminds us of the foremost devotee of the Lord, say that He manifests Himself very soon to a real devotee and the Lord has also assured that :

teṣām ahaṁ samuddhartā mṛtyu saṁsāra sāgarāt.
bhavāmi nacirāt pārtha mayy āveśith cetasām. (*BG.* 12.7)

Thus, by God's grace alone *bhakti* would directly lead to the attainment of the goal of human life-nay, it itself is the goal.

4. Bhakti in Bhagavadgītā Interpretation 2: Modern

So far as the modern interpretation of *BG* is concerned, many names flash before our mind like those of Bankim Candra Chatterji, Bal Gangadhar Tilak, Shri Aurobindo, Mahatama Gandhi, Vinoba Bhave, Svami Vivekananda and S.

Radhakrishnan, Svami Bhaktivedāntā so on and so forth.

Remembering them with gratitude let us try here to look at *bhakti* in the *BG* in the context of our modern times i.e. on the threshold of the 21st century.

In my opinion, the concept of *bhakti* in BG is very essential to be practised in our modern lives – where science and technology are regarded as religion.

Anxiety, stress, uncertainly, insecurity are the by-products of the new ultra-modern culture. At this juncture, if we talk about salvation to be attained through *bhakti,* it may not seem very relevant, though it is essential to understand the original meaning of the text. But once we have understood it, we may try to give new meanings to these terms and accordingly interpret them in the modern context to suit the modern times as it is done by the above-mentioned modern interpreters of the Gītā to suit their times, their purposes and their relevant contexts.

Let us look at *bhakti* in this way: One should perform it, observe it as one's own duty. It may be accepted to lead to the purification of mind, if not salvation. *Bhakti* will help one get freedom from stress, by performing his own duty as God's service. If one can achieve this *Īśvarārpaṇabuddhikṛtakarman* then he should also place the responsibility of his deeds on God and that will take all his burden or stress off. This may be desired by him for material prosperity but gradually becoming free from the stress, the mind will be pure and capable of higher thinking, which ultimately will make a man humane more and more so.

This humanity may be depicted as the limited goal of human life in the modern context. Once, man achieve this, he is sure to lead to the spiritual path and then realise the ultimate reality. Now if we look into BG we find that God has taken care of all the problems that a fickle human being may face on the path of devotion.

He Says:

mayy eva mana ādhatsva mayi buddhiṁ niveśaya.
nivasiṣyasi mayy eva ata ūrdhvaṁ na saṁśayaḥ. (*BG.* 12.8)

O Arjuna, you place your mind and intelligence unto me and by that devotion you will come to me and live in me.

But then the Lord says, if it is not possible for you, then try it over and again, if that also is not possible for you, then you try to perform activities related to me, if that also is not possible for you, then at least give up the desire for fruits of actions.

Thus, if one gives up the desire of fruit, then this will lead him towards God slowly and steadily.

The Lord has assured that

ananyāś cintayanto māṁ ye janāḥ paryupāsate.
teṣām nityābiyuktānāṁ yogakṣemaṁ vahāmyaham. (*BG*. 9.22)

So even material prosperity which is today's foremost concern of a human being is guaranteed by God for his devotees.

Not only this, but the Lord has shown very simple way of devotion which is very helpful for a person to take his burden of responsibilities off his shoulders and put it on someone else.

yat karoṣi yad aśnāsi yaj juhoṣi dadāsi yat.
yat tapasyasi kaunteya tat kuruṣva mad arpaṇam.
śubhāśubhaphalair evaṁ mokṣyase karmabandhanaiḥ.
saṁnyāsa yaga yuktātmā vimukto mām upaiṣyasi.
(*BG*. 9.27, 28)

Not only this, but the God has assured even a very sinful person that if he worships me wholeheartedly he has to be known as a good person.

api cet sudurācāro bhajate mām ananyabhāk.
sādhur eva sa mantavyaḥ samyag vyavasito hi saḥ.
(*Ibid* – 9.30)

And he will never be
na me bhaktaḥ praṇaśyati. (*Ibid* – 9.31)

Thus, if today's modern man begins his journey, he is sure to reach the goal of self-realisation, sooner or later.

5. Observations

To sum up one may say: That concept of *bhakti*, the seeds of which are to be found in the Vedas, may be understood clearly from the *bhakti-sūtras* as well as from the *BG* which is the heart of our tradition and philosophy.

It directly or indirectly helps achieve the goal of human life, namely, salvation. In modern times the goal of human life may be slightly modified in the beginning, to convince those who are most confused and have lost their track of our age-old tradition and *bhakti* may be placed as means to achieve that goal by changing even the meaning of *bhakti* slightly to suit our purpose and context. This will sure enhance the level of humanity, which, in turn, will help lead the path of higher plane in spiritual kingdom. Once this is achieved, there is no way back but only attainment of bliss.

Bibliography

1. *Śrīmadbhagavadgītā* with *Śāṅkarabhāṣya,* Works of Śaṅkaracharya in original Sanskrit, Vol. II, Motilal Banarsidass, Delhi, 1988.
2. *Bhakti Sūtras of Nārada,* Tr. Nandlala Sinha, Oriental Publishers, New Delhi.
3. *The Gītā: A Theory of Human Action* S.S. More, Indian Books Centre, Delhi, 1990.
4. Gītā Sandesh: Message of the Gītā Swami Ramdas, Bharatiya Vidya Bhavan, Bombay, 1966.
5. Modern Indian Interpreters of the Bhagavad gītā Ed. Robert Minor, Indian Books Centre, Delhi, 1991.

* * * *

The Construction of Maṭha According to Yogic Texts

Dr. K.S. Balasubramanian

From time immemorial the homosapiens have been seekig three basic necessities to sustain their livelihood-food, shelter and clothing. Over these centuries of human existence, they have endeavoured to construct different types of buildings for dwelling according to their requirements, status, taste and also to exhibit their aesthetic sense of mind. The huts, houses, mansions, forts, palaces, temples, monasteries and other forms of buildings – many of which exist even today, bear testimony for their skill in architecture and also serve as important monuments for us to understand the social, cultural, economic and religious conditions of our ancestors. The vast literature available on this subject also support this view. In the Kriyāpāda of *Śaiva Āgamas,* details of temple construction are given. Similarly we have other literature which deals exclusively on construction of various types of buildings.

The ancient Ṛṣis and Yogis who wanted to lead a life in secluded place chose to live in hermitages or monasteries. Many texts on Haṭhayoga like *Yoga-yājñavalkya, Haṭhayogapradīpikā (HYP),* of Svātmārāma, *Haṭharatnāvali (HR)* of Śrīnivāsa Yogīndra, *Śivasaṁhitā (SS) Haṭhasaṅketacandrikā (HSC)* of Sundaradeva, *Gheraṇḍasamhitā (GHS)* and also some Purāṇas emphasise that a true *Sādhaka* of Yogic practices should avoid the company of people. For example, *HYP* (I.15) enumerates six obstacles in achieving success in Yoga:

अत्याहारः प्रयासश्च प्रजल्पो नियमग्रहः।
जनसङ्गश्च लौल्यं च षड्भिर्योगो विनश्यति॥

(Yoga fails by the six causes-over-eating, over-exertion, excessive talk, the observance of unsuitable disciplines, promiscuous company and unsteadiness.) Lord Kṛṣṇa says in the *Bhagavadgītā (Bg. G)* (VI.10)

योगी युञ्जीत सततमात्मानं रहसि स्थितः।
एकाकी यतचित्तात्मा निराशीरपरिग्रहः॥

(A Yogi should always try to concentrate his mind living alone in solitude having subdued his mind and body and got rid of desires and possessions.) Hence the need for choosing a proper place for practising Yogic exercises is emphasised in Yogic texts, for the selection of the right place gives the *Sādhaka* psychological as well as physiological benefits.

Place

Before constructing the *maṭha* (monastery), one shold pay attention to the place where he wants to practise Yoga. The *Śvetāśvatara Upaniṣad* (II.10) gives some hints on this subject.

समे शुचौ शर्करावह्निवालुका विवर्जिते शब्दजलाश्रयादिभिः।
मनोनुकूले न तु चक्षुपीडने गुहानिवाताश्रयणे प्रयोजयेत्॥

(One should perform one's exercises in concentration resorting to caves and such other places helpful to its practice – places where the ground is level without pebbles and the scenery pleasing to the eyes; where there is no wind, dust, fire, dampness and disturbing noises.)[1]

The *Vasiṣṭha samhitā* (II.57-58) says that the hermitage should be surrounded by trees with abundant fruits, root and water, the place should be beautiful and clean, at the bank of a river or the temple and the building should be well protected.

तपोवनं ततो गत्वा फलमूलोदकान्वितम्।
तत्र रम्ये शुचौ देशे नद्यां देवालयेऽपि च॥
सुशोभनं मठं कृत्वा सर्वरक्षासमन्वितम्।

1. Dust, dampness, fire and smoke that accompany the fire, make the air impure and thus render Prāṇāyāma dangerous. A pleasing scenery helps one to compose the mind, while noise and strong wind disturb the mind practising meditation.

The *Yogayājñavalkya* (V.7-11) while agreeing with above views, adds that the *maṭha* can be constructed in a village or a city. It also adds that some people opine that the place should be uninhabited, beautiful and also bereft of heat and cold.

देवालये वा नद्यां वा ग्रामे वा नगरेऽथ वा।
सुशोभनं मठं कृत्वा सर्वरक्षासमन्वितम्॥
केचिद्वदन्ति मुनयः तपःस्वाध्यायसंयुताः।
निर्जने निलये रम्ये वातातपविवर्जिते।

However it is only the later texts on Haṭha yoga which give descriptions on the external and internal features of a *maṭha*. *HYP* is the prominent text on Haṭha yoga and hence we can start from this text. *HYP* (I.12) says:

सुराज्ये धार्मिकेदेशे सुभिक्षे निरुपद्रवे।
धनुःप्रमाणपर्यन्तं[2] शिलाग्नि जलवर्जिते॥
एकान्ते मठिकामध्ये[3] स्थातव्यं हठयोगिना।

(He who practises Haṭha yoga should live alone in a small *maṭha* situated in a place free from rocks, water and fire to the extent of a bow's length and in a virtuous, well-ruled kingdom, which is prosperous and free of disturbances.)

The *HSC* of Sundaradeva[4] deals on this topic elaborately. According to this text (p.7. V.2-3)[5] the monastery may be constructed in the following places: caves, places of worship, castle, uninhabited place, slopes of mountain, beautiful place, place bereft of sin; or else the *maṭha* can be constructed at a place where alms are available, in a good country ruled by a righteous king, clean location, wealthy place.

---

2. धनुः प्रणामं-चतुर्हस्तमात्रम्, says *Jyotsnā*, com. on *HYP*. See also *HSC* p.8.
3. अल्पो मठः-मठिका
4. Unpublished text, Ms. No. R. 3239, GOML, Chennai. The present author has made a critical study of this text under the guidance of Dr. S.S. Janaki, at the K.S.R. Institute, Chennai and was awarded the *Vidyāvāridhi* degree by the Rashtriya Sanskrit Sansthan, N. Delhi.
5. All the references of this text pertain to the ms. available at GOML, Chennai.

गह्वरायतनतीर्थे सुदुर्गे निर्जनेऽथ धरणीधरवप्रे।
शोभनेऽस्तकलुषे विषये वाऽभ्यासधीः शुभमठं विदधीत॥
अथवा
सुभिक्षे शुभधार्मिकैकभूपते बहुसुभिक्षतवति तत्तये शुचौ।
सुकृतशालिनि मालिनि वैभवै मनसि योगविधौ मतिमाश्रयेत्॥

HSC adds that the *maṭha* should not be constructed at the following places:– Well hidden place, full of mosquitoes; place with snow or heat, fertile land or saline land, (or desert), where there are thorns, dry leaves, place of worship, burial ground, place near ant-hills and cross-way etc.

अतिनिगूढपदं मशकोज्झितं तुहिनतापविवर्जितमन्तरम्।
उर्वरकण्टकशुष्कदलोज्झितं पितृगृहानवगोष्वमृतेमलम्॥
वल्मीकसञ्चयचतुष्टय वर्जं ....
.... योगार्थमेवमवलोक्य मठो विधेयः॥

Further, one should not practise Yoga in the following places: In the road, the joining place of sea and river, old building and sacrificial shed.

रथ्यान्तरे सिन्धुसरिन्नदान्तरे चिरन्तने वेश्मनि चैत्यदेशे।
योगं विदध्यान्न कदापि साधकः खेदो मनस्यादि भवेत् कृतेऽत्र॥

(*HSC* p.9 V.15)

The *Mārkaṇḍeyapurāṇa (MP)* (XXXIX. 48-50) also deals on this topic. It says, "A learned man should avoid practising Yoga in a place where their is noise, or fire, or water, or where study is going on, in a decayed cow-shed, at a place where four roads meet, amidst the collection of dry leaves, in a river, in a burning-ground, in a place infested with snakes, in a place of fear, or on the edge of a well, where there are funeral piles or ant-hills. If the appearance of the place is not good, he should avoid it."

सशब्दाग्नि जलाभ्यासे जीर्णगोष्टे चतुष्पथे॥
शुष्कपर्णचये नद्यां श्मशाने ससरीसृपे।
सभये कूपतीरे वा चैत्यवल्मीकसञ्चये॥

दशेष्वेतेषु तत्त्वज्ञो योगाभ्यासं विवर्जयेत्।
सत्वस्यानुपपत्तौ च देशकालं विवर्जयेत्

The *GHS* (V.3) also gives a brief note on this subject, where it says that one should not construct hut for the practice of Yoga in a place which is far off, or in a forest or very near the capital or metropolitan city.

दूरदेशे तथारण्ये राजधान्यां तथान्तिके।
योगारम्भं न कुर्वीत .. .. ..

It does not give any new information on this subject.

What is the need for selecting the right place for construction of the *maṭha*? From time immemorial, people have been conscious of choosing the right place for their residence or for the practice of Yogic exercises. While the references given above from some of the texts dealing with Yoga stress the importance of choosing the right place, *HSC* (p.7 V.1) goes further to caution the practitioners that if the right place is not chosen they may acquire the following six psychological and physiological disorders: Loss of memory, dumbness, dullness, fever, sluggishness and deafness.

अनादृत्य देशञ्चकालं विमूढो भजेद्यस्तु योगं नरस्तस्य दोषाः।
स्मृतिभ्रंशमूक्त्वमान्द्यं ज्वरश्च जडत्वञ्च बाधिर्यमेतेऽत्र षट्स्युः॥

MP (XXXIX. 52-53) adds blindness also to the list of physical disorders to that person who does not choose the right place.

बाधिर्यजडतालोपःस्मृतेर्मूकत्वमन्धता।
ज्वरश्च जायते सद्यः तत्तदज्ञानयोगिनः॥

Hence the need for selecting the appropriate place for constructing *maṭha* for practising yogic exercises, is emphasised in ancient texts.

Maṭha (Monastery)

The word *maṭha* is derived from the root मठ–मदनिवासयोः. It is residential place for the students, says *Amarakośa (A.K)* (II.2.8.) "मठश्छात्रादि निलयः". Mallinātha, commenting on this passage says, "अन्तेवासस्याश्रयो मठःस्यात्". However, *Mayamata*

(IX. 40d) defines *maṭha* as a place where ascetics dwell. "मठमिति पठितं यत् तापसानां निवासम्". The word *āśrama* is also commonly used to denote a place where ascetics live, the other names being, *parṇaśālā* and *uṭaja*.[6] *Mayamata* (XXIII. 97) says tht the monastery of the Master (*guru*) should be in the South or East but opens to the South.

"यमदिशि गुरुमठमुदितं पूर्वस्मिन् वाऽप्यवाग्वदनम्"

The External Features of Maṭha

The *HYP* (I.13) says that the *maṭha* should have a small door and should be without windows; it should be level, without any holes; it should be neither too high nor too low, not too long. It should be very clean, being well smeared with cow-dung and free from all insects. Outside, it should be attractive with a small hall (*maṇḍapa*), a raised seat and a well, and surrounded by a wall. These are the characteristics of a Yoga-maṭha as laid down by the Siddhas who have practised Hatha Yoga.

अल्पद्वारमरन्ध्रगर्तविवरं नात्युच्चनीचचायतं
सम्यग्गोमयसान्द्रलिप्तममलं निःशेषजन्तूज्झितम्।
बाह्ये मण्डपवेदिकूप रुचिरं प्राकारसंवेष्टितं
प्रोक्तंयोगमठस्य लक्षणमिदं सिद्धैर्हठाभ्यासिभिः ॥[7]

The *HR* and *HSC* also repeat the same.

The *Jyotsnā* by Brahmānanda, while commenting on this verse quotes *Nandikeśvarapurāṇa* and says that the monastery should be surrounded by flower gardens and groves so that the eye of the Yogin resting upon them might become calm.

Internal Arrangements

HSC deals on the internal arrangements of the *maṭha* giving importance to both the psychological and physiological aspects. It says (p.8 V.6-8) that the Yogi should draw the pictures of

6. See also Mallinātha's com. on *A.K.* (II.2.6).
7. cf. *Gheraṇḍasamhitā,* V.6-7.

gods on the wall, so that whenever he looks at them, he would get encouragement in his practice. Also he should draw the pictures of burial ground and other terrible forms by looking at which his mind would turn against the worldly file which is full of sorrow, misery, diseases, death etc.

योगिराट् हठमठालयमध्ये संलिखेन्भगवन्मण्डलमुच्चैः।
वीक्ष्य चित्रगतशान्तसमूर्तिरुद्यमं कलयते मतिरस्य॥
तत्र घोरनरकन्लिखेत्सतान्सायुधैर्यमभटैर्भयदास्यैः।
ताननुक्षणमुदीक्ष्य भीषणाङ्गाकृतीनथ भवद्गतसारम्॥
दुःखशोकमृतिरोगगृहीतान्नरकान् पितृवनानि च पश्यन्।
जन्तुसङ्घमतिविह्वलदीनम् अभ्यसेदपतृडस्तविकारः॥

Regarding the physiological aspect, *HSC* (p.24 V.8) suggests that one should use only the lamp with ghee and not oil. If the oil-lamp is used, it produces smoke which would also get inhaled during the practice of *Prāṇāyāma*. Hence when *kumbhaka* is practised, the impure air is retained and it affects the purified blood which is circulated in the body. This, in turn, would cause many diseases. Hence the lamp with ghee should be used.

अभ्यासिना भूमिगृहे मठे वा न तैलदीपः प्रविधेय ईक्षणे।
अस्मिन् ज्वलत्येति सुकुम्भितो द्राक् प्राणो विमार्गं व्रजतीत्यमुं त्यजेत्॥
अतः योगमठे घृतदीप एव उपयुज्यते।

However, in modern times, we can make use of electrical bulbs etc.

The *Kapālakuranṭakayoga,*[8] an unpublished manuscript gives an interesting description of the monastery (hut) with regard to different practices like vasti, vajrolī etc.

"मठिकालक्षणं चतुर्हस्तप्रमाणमूर्ध्वं तिर्यक्।
भस्ममठिका मुद्राभ्यासार्थम्।
आरक्त मृत्तिकामठिका आसनाभ्यासार्थम्।
सुधामठिका वस्त्यभ्यासार्थम्। ....."

---

8. q. by Sri M. Venkata Reddy, in *HR,* p.121. The Kaivalyadhama, Lonavla, possesses a copy of this ms. as known from their Note in their edn. of the text *Satkarmasamuccaya,*1970.

Practice in one's House

Some Yogic texts say that one can also practise Yoga by remaining in the house itself and doing the duties of a householder. According to *yogayājñavalkya (YY)* one should adhere to one's duty and practise Yoga. For example, *YY* says, "स्वाश्रमं धर्ममाचरन्" (I.18)

चतुर्णामाश्रमस्थानामहन्यहनि नित्यशः।
विध्युक्तकर्म कर्तव्यं .. ..॥ (I.38)
स्वाश्रमस्थः सदाचारः .. ..। (V.5)

This implies that one can practise Yoga by remaining in one's house itself. *HSC* (p.77 V.4) also supports this view when it says, "विध्युक्तवर्गाश्रमकर्मनिष्ठः". The *Śivasaṁhitā* is very clear on this subject. It says (V. 254-55) :

गृहस्थानां भवेत् सिद्धिः ईश्वराणां जपेन वै।
गेहे स्थित्वा पुत्रदारादिपूर्णः सङ्गंत्यक्त्वा चान्तरे योगमार्गे।
सिद्धे चिह्नं वीक्ष्य पश्चात् गृहस्थः क्रीडेत् संवै सम्मतं साधयित्वा॥

It can be deduced from this that one can lead a house-holder's life and still practise Yogic exercises. Swami Vivekananda, the great saint of modern India also has expressed his opinion on this. He says, "Those of you who can afford it will do better to have a room for this practice alone. Do not sleep in that room, it must be kept holy. You must not enter the room until you have bathed and are perfectly clean in body and mind. Place flowers in that room always; they are the best surroundings for a Yogi; also pictures that are pleasing. Burn incense morning and evening. Have no quarrelling, nor anger, nor unholy thought in that room. Only allow those persons to enter it who are of the same thought as you. Then gradually there will be an atmosphere of holiness in the room, so that when you are miserable, sorrowful, doubtful, or your mind is disturbed, the very fact of entering that room will make you calm."[9]

9. p.34, *Rājayoga,* Swami Vivekananda, Advaita Ashrama, Calcutta, 1962.

Utility of the Maṭha

It is not enough if one constructs a *maṭha* according to one's choice, taste or as suggested by the yogic texts. It is equally important to make the best use of the facilities available in the *maṭha* for one's spiritual evolution. Otherwise it would be waste of money, time, effort and the human labour involved in constructing such a *maṭha*. A temple is a place for worship; a school for education; and a monastery or an Ashram for spiritual *sādhanā* alone. If the monastery is used only as a place of retreat from routine work, tourist centre or eating place it would be a disgrace to the noble ideals set forth by our great saints who sacrificed everything for the well-being of the humanity.

Perhaps it would not be out of context here to refer to Udayana's sharp wit against the Buddhists who lived in monasteries (Vihāras). In his *Nyāyakusumāñjali* he chides the Buddhists as hypocrites, who seek monasteries because early meal is available there; some lazy people go there because there is no routine of daily ordained duties and so on.

"सम्भवन्ति हि हेतवो बौद्धाद्यागमपरिग्रहे। तथा हि भूयः तत्र कर्मलाघवमिति अलसाः, पतितानामप्यनुप्रवेश इत्यनन्यगतिकाः, भक्ष्याद्यनियम इति रागिणः..........."[10]

Jayanta Bhaṭṭa also excels in criticising Buddhists. In his *Nyāyamañjarī,* he exclaims– "There is no soul, yet you have Caityas, you worship and go to heaven; all our experience is momentary, but let us build *permanent Vihāras* for ourselves; everything is void, but give us donations – Oh, what greater hypocrisy can there be than this?"

नास्त्यात्माफलभोगमात्रमथ च स्वर्गाय चैत्यार्चनं
संस्काराः क्षणिका युगस्थितिभृतश्चैते विहाराः कृताः।
सर्वं शून्यमिदं वसूनि गुरवे देहीति चादिश्यते
बौद्धनां चरितं किम्मन्यदियती दम्भस्य भूतिःपरा॥[11]

10. q. by Dr. V. Raghavan in his "*Comic Element in Sanskrit Literature*", The Samskrita Ranga, Madras, 1989. p.50.
11. *ibid.* p.51

This was the sarcastic criticism against the Buddhists by the well-known Naiyāyikas. However, there are many positive aspects about the utility of an Ashram. My Master, Shri P. Rajagopalachariji, President, Shri Ram Chandra Mission, says, "Ashram is a place where we go for Śreyas. An Ashram is essentially a place where one goes to be with his Master and to grow spiritually."[12] He also adds, "Ashrams in Sahaj Marg[13] are dedicated to meditation only, all other activities are normally not allowed in the Ashram. An Ashram is usually charged by the Master who creates a special atmosphere of spirituality in which we meditate."[14]

I would like to conclude that such an Ashram exists at Manapakkam, Ramavaram (off Guindy-Porur National Highway) and I invite you all whole-heartedly to visit this holy place and be blessed.

Bibliography

1. *Amarakos'a* (Vol. I&II) with unpublished South Indian Coms., ed. Prof. A.A. Ramanathan, The Adyar Library and Research Centre, Madras, 1971, 1978.
2. *Complete Works of Ramchandra* (Vol. I), Shri Ram Chandra Mission, Shahjahanpur (U.P.), 1989.
3. *Gheraṇḍa Samhitā,* with Hindi transl. by Chamanlal Gautam, Samskriti Samsthan, Bareli-234001, 1974.
4. *Haṭharatnāvali* of Śrīnivāsa Yogīndra, ed. M. Venkata Reddy, Vemana Yoga Research Institute, Secunderabad, 1982.
5. *Haṭhasaṅketacandrikā* of Sundaradeva, unpublished ms. Ṛ 3239, GOML, Chennai.
6. *Haṭhayogapradipikā* of Svātmārāma with Com. *Jyotsanā* of Brahmānanda and Eng. transl., The Adyar Library and Research Centre, Madras, 1975.
7. *Mārkaṇḍeya Purāṇa,* Gurumandal Series No. 23, Calcutta, 1962.
8. -do- Eng. transl. by Pargiter F. Eden, Indological Book House, Delhi, 1969.

---

12. p. 81, *Principles of Sahaj Marg,* Vol.VI.
13. A modified system of Rājayoga being advocated by Shri Ram Chandra Mission, a world-wide spiritual organisation.
14. p. 378, *Complete Works of Ramchandra,* Vol.I.

9. *Mayamata* (Vol. I&II) critical edn. with Eng. trans. by Bruno Dagens, IGNCA, New Delhi, 1994.
10. *Nyāyamañjarī* of Udayana with Coms., Srimad Annayarya Mahadesika Vidvat Sabha, Tamil Nadu, 1979
11. *Nyāyamañjarī* of Jayanta Bhaṭṭa, Vizianagaram Sanskrit Series No. 10, Benareṣ, 1895.
12. *Principles of Sahaj Marg* (Vol. IV), Shri P. Rajagopalachari, Shri Ram Chandra Mission, Shahjahanpur (U.P.), 1988.
13. *Raja Yoga,* Swami Vivekananda, Advaita Ashrama, Calcutta, 1962.
14. *Śiva Samhitā* with Hindi trans. by Camanlal Gautam, Samskriti Samsthan, Bareli, 243 001, 1975.
15. *Śrīmad Bhagavadgītā,* Tapovanam Publishing House, Tirupparaitturai, 1965.
16. *Śvetāśvatara Upaniṣad,* Ramakrishna Mutt, Madras, 1979.
17. *Vasiṣṭha Samhitā* (Yoga Kanda), Ed. Swami Digambarji *et. all,* Kaivalyadhama S.M.Y.M. Samiti, Lonaval, 1984.
18. *Yogayājñavalkya,* ed. P.C. Divanji, Bombay, 1954.

* * * *

Nārāyaṇatīrtha's Contribution to the Yoga Philosophy

Dr. Penna Madhusudan

A strong desire to know one's own self has been as old as man himself. The *Bṛhadāraṇyaka Upaniṣad* (4-5-6) states that the self should be realized through *Śravaṇa* (Knowing about the self from the Upaniṣadic statements), *Manana* (Knowing and ascertaining the nature of the self by reasoning) and *Nididhyāsana* (Realizing the self through Yoga). Among these means of self-realization, the Yoga occupies the highest place because it alone is capable of enabling the aspirant to realize the self. The upaniṣadic ideology was taken and pondered over by the later seers and their reflections are recorded in the sūtra form. In the Yoga-philosophy, the *Yoga-Sūtra* of *Patañjali* has a unique place as it presents a very systematic analysis of Yoga, its varieties and its summum-bonum '*Kaivalyaṃ*'. The *Yoga-Sūtras* of Patañjali have been then commented upon by *Vyāsa* to elucidate the abstruse theories of Yoga such as the nature of mind, distinct characteristics of the Yoga-varieties and so on.

The *Yoga-Sūtras* and *Vyāsa bhāṣya* have been over the centuries explained by great commentators like Vācaspati Miśra, Vijñāna bhikṣu, Bhoja, Nārāyaṇatirtha and others. Compared to the others, Nārāyaṇatirtha's (NT) commentaries are exhaustive. The fact that NT composed three commentaries on the same *Yoga-sūtra* signifies his keen interest in the Yoga system in general and in the *Yoga-sūtra,* in particular.

In this paper, an attempt is made to throw some light on the three commentaries of NT on the *Yoga-sūtra* which seem to have drawn less attention from researchers, salient features of those commentaries have also been highlighted

Narāyaṇatīrtha : In the seventeenth and the eighteenth centuries, there flourished many scholars and saints with the same appellation Nārāyaṇatīrtha. This caused some confusion regarding the identity of NT of Yoga-commentaries. Scholars like K. Natarajan, Mr. Ko Endo (University of Nagoya, Japan) made extensive research and produced some valuable evidence.

NT commented on the *Bhāṣāpariccheda* of *Viśvanātha*. This commentary is known as '*Nyāya chandrikā*' (Chowkhamba Publications, Varanasi, 1981). From the closing verses of the *Nyāyasūtravṛtti* of *Viśvanātha* it is evident that Viśvanātha flourished around AD 1634. If *Bhāṣāpariccheda* is also accepted to have been written around the same period i.e. AD 1634, NT's period should be after 1634 AD as he commented on it. This is the upper limit of NT's flourishing period.

For the lower limit of his period, the dates of his disciples can be conclusive. Among the wellknown Advaita-scholars, Gauḍa Brahmānanda Saraswati is known as a disciple of NT. He commented on the *Siddhāntabindu* of Madhusūdana Sarasvati and the commentary '*Nyāyaratnāvalī*' is said to have been transcribed in A.D. 1687. Considering these factors, Ko Endo concluded that the flourishing period of NT is AD 1600-1690.

The commentaries of NT bear the name '*Rāmagovinda Tīrtha*' as the teacher of NT. And, according to the New Catalogus Catalogorum (Vol. X. 75-76) NT's father's name is Nīlakanṭhasūri of Vāraṇasī. NT was known as Govindaśāstri. He had three *gurus*. Śivarāmatirtha initiated him into *Sannyāsa*, Rāmagovinda tīrtha and Vāsudevatīrtha taught him the *śāstras*. Among the disciple's of NT, most popular are Gouḍabrahmānanda Sarasvatī, Maheśvaratīrtha (*Rāmāyaṇa* commentator) and the author of *Jyotsnā* commentary on the *Haṭhayogapradīpikā*.

NT's Three Commentaries on the *Yogasūtra*

NT is know to have composed three commentaries on the same text i.e. the *Yogasūtras* of *Patañjali*. Among these, the *Yogasiddhāntacandrikā* or *Gūḍhārthadyotikā* is the longest.

i *Yogasiddhāntacandrikā* :– This, as stated earlier, is the longest commentary among the three. Another title is also known from the colophon and introductory verse 3. This title '*Gūḍhārthadyotikā*' reflects the nature of this commentary. This was edited by Paṇḍita Ratna Gopāla Bhatta and published under the Chowkhamba Sanskrit series in 1910, 1911. But, this edition has the text till the third *sūtra* of the fourth *Pāda* i.e. *Kaivalyapāda*. Scholars therefore believe that the text of '*Yogasiddhāntachandrikā*' is incomplete. In 1990, Ko Endo mentioned in his research dissertation that the complete text of *Yogasidhāntacandrikā* is available in Telugu script.[1]

ii. *Yogasūtravṛtti* : This commentary is existing in manuscript form in the Central library (Oriental Institute) Baroda. This Ms. bears the accession no. 7565 and is of sambal age 1810 (saṃvat). This corresponds to AD 1754. In the colophons, another title '*Yogacandrikā*' is also found. (vide p.32 of the Ms.). There are few references to the *Yogasiddhāntacandrikā* in the text. In the beginnig verses it is mentioned that the Yoga-doctrine is difficult to understand in spite of the learned commentaries of Vyāsa, Vāchaspatimiśra and Vijñānabhikṣu. NT explains the sūtra word by word and deliberately avoids discussions. When it is very important to explain any sūtra elaborately, he refers to his *Yogasiddhāntacandrikā* (p. 23).

iii. *Yogasūtravṛtti* : This commentary does not agree with the *Yogacandrikā*. This is found in the Oriental Institute, Baroda in Ms. form. It's accession no. is 12574 and age is 1718 (śaka) corresponding to AD 1796. In both the Mss. no (ii) and (iii), the author's name is mentioned as Nārāyaṇatirtha, disciple of Govindatīrtha. And, at the end it is mentioned that the commentary was made by Nārāyaṇatirtha at Prayāg. From the introductory verse it can be understood that this commentary has another title '*Sūtrārthabodhinī*'and is composed to give the essence of the *Yogasūtra* in nutshell

1. However, the writer of the present article prepared an edition of this text ready for publication.

without entering into discussions or arguments.

NT's Contribution to the Yoga-Philosophy

As remarked by Prof. Shrinivasa Shastry in his introduction to the '*Kusumānjalikārikā vyākhyā* of Nārāyaṇatīrtha (Kurukshetra University Sanskrit series – No-2, AD 1974), NT is known as '*Sarvatantrasvatantra*' like the great Vāchaspati Miśra. (p.xix). NT was, no doubt, a great scholar and saint of his age. He commented on the important texts of almost all the systems of Indian Philosophy. None the less, he maintained his position as an Advaitin following the footsteps of great Madhusūdana Sarasvati.

NT's *Yogasiddhāntacandrikā* is composed with a special purpose of distinguishing Yoga system from the other systems and of exposing the stand-point of the system in issues like the *Nidrā, Smṛti, Avidyā* etc. NT does have the other important commentaries on the *Yogasūtra* before him while discussing any matter. Thus, he refers to Vāchaspatimiśra, Vijñānabhikṣu very often and tries to reinterpret their views for a better understanding of the Yoga philosophy. He may be the only commentator on the *Yogasūtra* who dealt with the topics like concept of *Avatāra, Puruṣa, Bhakti in Yoga* and various types of Yogas.

NT's significant contribution to the Yoga-philosophy is his synthesis of Yoga in the *Yogasiddhāntacandrikā.* NT opines that all the varieties of Yoga like *Bhaktiyoga, Haṭha Yoga, Vāsanāyoga* etc. are mutually complementary. *Patañjali* himself must have this in his mind while writing the sūtras. NT dexterously handles the tough task of authenticating the fifteen varieties of Yoga by showing them in the *Yogasūtras* itself. Thus, for example, the *sūtra* (1-33) suggests the *caryāyoga,* the *sūtra* (1-34) suggests the *Haṭhayoga* and the *sūtra* (1-37) gives the *Vāsanāyoga* and so on.

This kind of a synthesis is indeed a great achievement on the part of the commentator as this helps the aspirant of Yoga achieve mental equanimity discarding all feelings of hatred, jealousy etc. towards the other Yoga-varieties.

In the opinion of NT, the *asṃprajñāta Yoga* also is a *chitta-*

vṛtti. Of course, he is well aware of the statement of Vyāsa in the *bhaṣya* that *asamprajñāta samādhi* is absence of *all* kinds of *Vṛttis*. Still he tries to interpret *Vyāsabhāṣya* so as to mean 'the absence of *all opposite chitta vṛttis.* To NT, *asaṃprajñāta samādhi* is an indeterminate thought-wave which is uninterrupted by any other thought-wave and which has the self as its object. In this kind of interpretation of the *asaṃprajñātasamādhi*, NT is undoubtedly influenced by the *Paiñgala-Upaniṣad* (3-1) and by the ideaology of Vidyāraṇya as found in the Pañcadaśī (1-56). NT seems to believe in the theory that the *asṃprajñāta* is also a thought-wave, because this view appears not only in the *Yogasiddhāntacañdrikā* (1-1) but also in *Yogacandrikā* (p. 6), in *Bhakticañdrikā* (commentary of NT on the *Śāṇḍilya Bhakisūtras*), in Sāṃkhya Candrikā (NT commentary on the Sāṃkhya kārikā p. 75) and in the *Nyāyacandrikā* (NT's commentary on the *Bhāṣāpriccheda* of *Viśvanātha,* p.63*).*

By giving this kind of interpretation, NT seems to differ even from Vijñānabhikṣu (author of *Yoga Vārtika* on the *Yogasūtra*) who maintains that the indeterminate thought-wave is present only in the *saṃprajñātasamādhi* (*Yogasūtra* 1-3, p.16). He openly refutes the doctrine of neo-advaitins who hold the opinion that the *asaṃprajñātasamādhi* is indeterminate-thought-wave. NT finds this view of Advaitins as tenable and holds on to it firmly.

To NT, the *khyātivāda* held in the Yoga system is *Sad-asat khyāti* and not *anyathākhyāti* as maintained by Vijñānabhikṣu in the *vārtika* (1-8, p.37). NT explains this view in detail elsewhere also (2-5). In the instance of 'rope and snake' illusion, the snake is non-existent (*Asat*) at the time of illusion but is existent (*sat*) elsewhere. Therefore, the illusion is *Sad-asat-khyāti* as propunded by the *Sāṁkhya* system. While explaining the concept '*avidyā*' in the Yoga system, Vijñānabhikṣu says that 'understanding the presence of pleasure etc. in the self through the relation of inherence (*Samavāya*) is *Avidyā*' (1-24). NT corrects this by saying that the *samavāya* is not accepted in the Yoga system and *Tādātmya* must be taken in lieu of *Samavāya*.

Apart from these, NT throws more light on pertinent topics

like *Avidyā, Avatara, Ahimsā, Āsana, Prāṇāyāma* etc. in his commentary '*Yogasiddhāntacandrikā*'. As remarked by Ko Endo in his dessertation (p.57), the emphasis on *Bhakti-Yoga* ma' ·s the *Yogasidhāntacandrikā* a unique text in the Yoga literature. By a sincere study of this text and other texts of NT on systems like *Nyāya, Advaita* etc. one tends to conclude that NT is by all means a '*Sarvatantra-svatantra*'.

Bibliography

1. *Yogasidhānta Candrikā of Nārāyaṇatīrtha* ed. Ratnagopāla Bhatta Chowkhamba Sanskrit Series, Varanasi, 1910-11.
2. *Yogasutras* with *Vyāsabhāṣya* and *Vārtika* ed. Nārāyana Mishra.
3. *Haṭhayoga pradipikā* with *Jyotsnā Vyākhyā* Adayar Publications, Mylapor, Chennai.
4. *Śrīkṛṣṇalīlātaranginī* ed. B. Natarajan, Chennai,1988.
5. The works & flourishing period of *Nārāyaṇatirtha* by Ko Endo Department of Indian Philosophy University of Nagoya JAPAN,1993.
6. *Bhaktichandrikā* of *Nārāyaṇatīrtha* ed. Baldev Upādhyay Varnasi,1967.
7. *Kusumānjatikārikā vyākhyā* of *Nārāyaṇatīrtha* ed. Srinivasa shastry, Kurukshetra University, 1974.
8. *Nyāyacandrikā* of *Nārāyaṇatīrtha* ed. Dhundhiraja Shastry, Chowkhamba Sansthan, Varanasi, 1981.
9. *Sāmkhyacāndrikā* of *Nārāyaṇatirtha* ed. Dhundhiraja Shastry, Chowkhamba Sanskrit Series, 1977.
10. *Pañcadaśī* of *Vidyāraṇya,* Chowkhamba Sanskrit pratishthan, 1987, Delhi.
11. Alphabetical Index of Sanskrit Manuscripts in the Adyar Library, Adyar, Chennai.
12. A Triennial Catalogue of Mss. vol. II Govt. Mss. Library, Chennai,1917.
13. *Sūtrārthabodhini* of *Nārāyaṇatīrtha*(Manuscript) Oriental Institute, Baroda.
14. *Yogacañdrikā* of *Nārāyaṇatīrtha* (Manuscript) Oriental Institute, Baroda.
15. *Yogasidhānṭacandrikā* of *Nārāyaṇatīrtha* (Manuscript) Oriental Manuscripts Library, Triplicane, Chennai.

* * * *

Aṣṭāṅga Yoga and Its Timeless Wisdom

Dr. Vinod Verma

The Essence of the Yogasūtras

We human beings are extremely involved with our pains and pleasures. Our physical existence or life span is only for a limited period but somehow, we love the idea of its being permanent. This idea enhances our pain further as in this world all is temporary and transitory. We think that our reality is our physical self and we consider that as our identity. There is something more to our existence than our physical self; that is an invisible energy in us, which makes the physical body alive. This energy is indestructible and immortal and it is our real self. This real self or soul is in fact our continuity in the cosmos. When one physical body expires, this energy becomes the cause of life in another body and thus our real self continues to exist. The inability to distinguish the immortal real self from the ephemeral physical self is unwise and leads to suffering. We learn, we earn, we accumulate different means of comfort and pleasure for us. We indulge into various sensuous pleassures and gradually, we have to give up all these due to old age and finally death. However, an individual's continuity is soul, which leaves the body at the time of death and acquires a new body in due course of time. The quality of the next life (health, wealth, education, and type of family etc.) depends upon the results of the previous *karma.* The sum total of the remains of previous *karma* in the form of *saṁskāra* also determines our personality. The cycle of life and death goes on forever.

The stock of the previous *karma* is the base of afflictions and at birth the afflictions may be visible or hidden. That means the accumulated *karma* from previous life or lives may unfold themselves at birth or later as the occasions come. The *Karma* unfold themselves at an appropriate occasion as they are related to other people and places. At a right time, space and opportunity, our give and take or other kinds of exchange with others take place. This, however, does not mean that everything is determined before hand. The present *karma* intervenes and thus the joys and sorrows we go through in life are the combination of the result of previous and the present *karma*. In other words, we have to go through the results of our previous *karma,* but how we handle the existing circumstances with our present *karma* can make a tremendous difference. For example, if we are rich due to or past *karma,* how we manage with the wealth will decide about many of the future events. If we do good deeds like donation, helping the poor and the needy and other acts in this direction, we further accumulate good *karma* and due to that, we may gain more wealth. In the similar case, we may not do good deeds but invest the wealth intelligently and also gain more wealth in this case. But it is quite possible that the stock of our good *karma* may get exhausted one day and we may suffer not necessarily the financial loss but may suffer from an ailment, emotional disturbances and so on. We ourselves are responsible for doing good or bad *karma,* and that we choose with our ability to discriminate, the *buddhi. Buddhi* is the *sattva* state of mind. With yogic practices, we can reach a level of mental lucidity and at that state our actions and decisions are driven by *buddhi,* and not by heart or by mind. Thus, attaining a lucid state of mind is essential and benefical not only for a yogi but also for a normal worldly person for attaining emotional and spiritual strength and for the well being of present and future.

Aṣṭāṅga Yoga or the Eight-fold Yogic Practice

It is important to destroy afflictions or *kleśa* to obtain *viveka* or the discriminative knowledge and that is done through various yogic practices. There are eight yogic practices described by Patañjali and these are known as Patañjali's *Aṣṭāṅga* Yoga (the eight-fold yogic practice). We will discuss below each of these steps in detail.

The eight different parts of the yogic practices are like the steps of a ladder. Each is independent and makes a base for the next step. Each accomplished step takes us a degree higher towards the aim.

The first of the eight practices is called *yama* or forbearance. There are five *yamas.* The first is not to kill or cause pain to others. It is called *ahiṁsā.* Directly or indirectly harming others or causing pain or motivating others for such acts come in this category. *Ahiṁsa* was preached intensively by many saints in India when Yogasūtras were written and the most prominent amongst them are the Gautama Buddha and Lord Mahāvīra. The followers of these saints founded later on the two major religions, the Buddhism and Jainism. They, particularly Jains follow the tradition of *ahiṁsa* very strictly. Earlier, India was largely meat eating country, and the Buddha and Mahāvīra have influenced greatly the way of life and that is why India remains until today largerly a vegetatiran country.

The second *yama* is to always speak the truth and never to distort it or tell lies. The third *yama* is not to steal or take away things from others. The fourth *yama* is continence, which means to exercise restraint from yielding to impulse or desire or any of the bodily activities. Not to covet is the fifth *yama,* which means not to desire onself the means of enjoyment.

'These *yamas,* irrespective of caste, place, period, time, are the great universal duties' (Sutra 31). Patañjali is very categorical here about *ahiṁsa* and the other *yamas,* and affirms that one cannot say that someone is a butcher by profession or caste and therefore, is exempt from killing or another person is a medical student or researcher and may be liberated from this duty. Or under certain circumstances or at certain places or at certain age, one can eat meat or tell lies or steal and so on.

The second of the eight fold yogic practices is self-discipline, which consists of 1) purification, 2) contentment, 3) austerity, 4) silent repetition of a mantra or a sound or a symbol and 5) a profound devotion to *Īśvara.* Purification is physical as well as mental. The physical purification is done by cleaning the body externally as well as internally. For internal purification, there are several methods in yoga like cleaning the nasal passage, cleaning by drinking water and vomiting out and cleaning intestines by drinking excessive water. Mental purification means to get rid of afflictions. The third, fourth and fifth practices have been already described above.

When the adept of yoga has developed an attitude of complete harmlessness towards the creatures around him/her, even the dangerous and aggressive animals do not attack and are in harmony with him/her.

The adept who practises the complete veracity gets the fruits of good deeds even without performing those deeds.

The abstinence from theft gives rise to an expression of complete trustworthiness and the adept gets many precious offerings.

When continence is complete, strength and vigour are gained.

Covetousness is not merely the means of enjoyment but it is also soul's coveting of the body.

Purification gives rise to censoring one's own body and in that case, no desire is left for another person's body. In addition to that, purification leads to subjugation of senses and intensity of mind.

The second part of the self-discipline is contentment or *santoṣa.* This gives rise to inner joy. The third part of the self-discipline or *niyama* is austerity, which gradually leads to the removal of afflictions, and senses attain a higher discerning power.

Japa or the silent repetition of a *mantra* leads to the vision of one's favourite deity or of whatever the *mantra* is aimed at. The perfection in meditation comes from profound devotion to *Īśvara.* However, if *japa* is done by *mantra* OM and with devotion, it leads to perfection. We have already discussed above that Patañjali refers to *Puruṣa* or the Absolute by the word *Īśvara.*

The third of the eight yogic practices is *āsana* or a yogic posture. Patañjali defines it as that 'which is steady and pleasant'. That means that when one is in a particular yogic posture, it should be as comfortable as normal sitting posture and then only we can say that *āsana* has achieved perfection. There should be no wavering or trembling and one should not feel unpleasant or uncomfortable while in an *āsana.* This is achieved by gradual practice and concentration. The extent of effort one has to make depends upon an individual's body flexibility and health conditions. *Āsana* is to enhance the steadiness of the body and that leads to the steadiness of the mind. After having achieved mastery on *āsana*, one is not affected by extreme conditions like cold, heat, hunger, thirst and so on.

The fourth of the eight yogic practices is *prāṇāyāma,* which should be practised after the *āsana.* It is a regulated inhalation and exhalation with intervals. The three aspects of *prāṇāyāma* are long or short and are directed by place, time and number. The outer, (*bāhya*) refers to exhalation, the inner (*abhyantara*) refers to inhalation and the steady (*stambha*) refers to when one is holding the breath inside or holding the lungs without air. These three terms originally used by Patañjali are later referred to as *recaka, pūraka* and *kumbhaka* respectively. These three are more popular in modern day yoga terminology.

The outer, the inner and the steady are directed by place, time and number and then termed as long or short. The place refers to the part of the body to which vital air is guided. The time is the duration of performance and the number refers to the number of repetitions of the process of inhalation, exhalation and the steady state.

The fourth aspect of *prāṇāyāma* assumes 'both the outer and the inner spheres' (Sūtra 51). After practising *prāṇāyāma* for a long period, the inhalation and exhalation are reduced to sucha degree that the restraint of breath is spontaneously achieved. The transfer from motion to steady state is no longer sudden.

The soul is the pure form of wisdom. It is that light or energy which puts life into the material body. However, we are unable to use this Inner Light as it is covered with the darkness of *avidyā* or ignorance. The ignorance is to mistake our physical self as our real self. *Avidyā* forms a thick and dark blanket, which obstructs the light emerging from our inner source, soul. Practice of *prāṇāyāma* weakens this obstruction of the Inner Light. That means, it destroys *avidyā.*

With the removal of *avidyā,* the mind becomes capable of attention or *dhārana,* which is the sixth of the eight yogic practices.

The fifth of the eight yogic practices is restraint or *pratyāhāra.* It is the indifference of the senses to their objects and their uniformity with the nature of the mind. Object of sight is form and colour, object of hearing is sound and so on. When senses abandon their objects and abide in their own nature, then the mind acquires complete control over the senses and becomes capable of controlling them. In other words, we withdraw the senses temporarily from their capabilities and contol their functions with our will. This is called the subjugation of senses.

The last three of the eight yogic practices are *dhārana, dhyāna* and *samādhi. Dhārana* may be translated as attention or concentration. It is defined as 'Fixing the thinking principle on the internal space' (Sūtra 1). The internal space means the energy points of the body like areas around the navel, around the plexus, between the eyes, tip of the tongue etc. Later, in the history of yoga, different energy points acquired very sophisticated nomenclature and were called the seven *cakras* or the concentric energy points of the subtle body. A continuum of *dhāranā* is *dhayāna. Dhāranā* can be compared to continuous drops of falling water whereas *dhyāna* is like the flow of a liquid of thick consistency like oil.

Samādhi is the last of the eight yogic practices and is defined as when *dhyāna* reaches a state where only awareness of its meaning remains and even the personal identity is lost. That means when *dhyāna* reaches a state when only the consciousness of its aim remains and other consciousness is lost, it is termed as *samādhi* or meditation. This is a state where consciousness of the fact that 'I am meditation' is also lost.

Conclusion

The yogic wisdom is not only meant for the adept of yoga but it is also very beneficial for human health, well-being and happiness. Ancient Ayurvedic texts advise to use the principles of yoga. According to Caraka, most of our ailments come due to a mental state of dissatisfaction or *asnatoṣa.* Similarly Caraka has written about all the ailments one can get due to excessive use of senses and due to a lack of control over the activities of one's mind. Thus, the message for the ancient gurus as well as the present day gurus to practice yoga will lead the humanity to hearth and lasting happiness.

* * * *

Pratyāhāra in Yogopaniṣad

Dr. Anuradha Oak

Introduction

It is proposed to discuss the concept of *Pratyāhāra* on the basis of the *Yoga Upaniṣads* in this paper. The term *Pratyāhāra* ordinarily means – to withdraw, to retreat, to hold back. But, *Pāṇinī* in his *Aṣṭādhyāyī* used this term in a technical sense i.e. '*Samkṣepa*'[1]. In *Yoga Sūtra* of *Patañjali, Pratyāhāra* is used in the sense of withdrawal of the sense organs etc., from their respective objects, which form one of the most important part of Yoga Philosophy.

In later *Upaniṣads* of *Yoga* this term is discussed in detail. I have taken some selected *Yoga Upaniṣads* for analysis edited by Pandit A. Mahadeva Sastri[2].

The present analysis is organised as follows in following headings:

1. The definition and meaning of the term *Pratyāhāra.*
2. The condition favourable for attaining *Pratyāhāra.*
3. The importance of *Pratyāhāra* in *Yoga Philosophy.*
4. *Pratyāhāra* in relation to other *Aṅgās* of Yoga.
5. Observations.

I. Patañjali's definition of *Pratyāhāra*

Lord Patañjali in his *Yoga Sūtra* in *Sādhanā Pāda* and *Vibhuti Pāda* describes *Aṣṭānga Yoga,* the eight stages of *yoga* namely *Yama, Niyama, Āsana, Prāṇāyāma, Pratyāhāra, Dhāraṇā, Dhyāna, Samādhi.*[3] The first five angas are included in *Bahiraṅga*

1. 1.1.71 Pāṇini's Aṣṭādhyāi Sūtra
2. The Adyar Library Publication Madras, 1920
3. Y.S. II.26

Sādhanā and the rest of the three in *Antaraṅga Sādhanā* *Pratyāhāra* is fifth among them which form a bridge between these two *Sādhanās*.

Why *Pratyāhāra* is the fifth stage of Yoga? Because upto that stage Patañjali in *Sādhanā Pāda* describes only about the physical body and its activities in which breathing is one of the activities which cannot be controlled by brain otherwise, but can be controlled by practicing *Prāṇāyāma,* where the last stage called *Keval Kumbhaka* is achieved. In that the *Yogī* neither inhales nor exhales. And after that he says: धारणासु च मनसा योग्यता ।[4] now onwards he starts discussing about mind.

Patañjali defined *Prātyāhāra* as follows :

स्वविषय असंप्रयोगे चित्तस्य स्वरूपानुकार इव इन्द्रियाणां प्रत्याहरः ।[5]

It means - withdrawing the senses, mind and consciousness from contact with the external objects and then drawing them inwards towards the seer, is *Pratyāhāra.*

Now the mind is able to concentrate and the sense no longer importune the mind for their gratification. They lose interest in the tests and favours of their respective objects and are drawn back from the external world in order to help the mind in its inner quest. This is *Pratyāhāra.*

The *Yoga Suītra* is called as the manual of Indian Psychology. So naturally it is related to the mind and its functions. Patañjali definitely knows that without controlling external limbs *Yogī* cannot go deeper inside the body because the mind is most complicated thing. So, for that, *yogī* should have absolute control over his physical body, then only he will be able to control his mind. After achieving last stage of *Prāṇāyāma* – that is *Keval Kumbhaka.*

The Yogī becomes very steady, calm and *sthitiprajñya.* He perceives everything but does not respond. Here arises the question, where this activity of withdrawing of the sense etc. is forcefully made or is it a spontaneous and natural happening?

4. Y.S. II.53
5. Y.S. II.54

Because in *Darśana and Śāṇḍil'ya Upaniṣad* the definition of *Pratyāhāra* is given as :

विषयेषु विचरतां इन्द्रियाणां बलादाहरणं प्रत्याहारः ।[6]

Here it is significant to observe that the interpretation of the expression in the sense of withdrawing the sense organs forcefully as is done by many scholars like T.R. *Srinivasa Ayyanger* etc., is not very sound.[7] Here I feel that this should be interpreted as *not forcefully* but *firmly* because when the state of *Keval Kumbhaka* is achieved by the yogī he can stay without breathing. This is the supermost part of control: one cannot be alive without breathing. So his inner power becomes so potent that he can control his mind easily. It would not make difference even in the functional state of the sense organs. So withdrawing sense organs from the objects and making the mind turn inwards becomes very easy task for the *yogī*. Thus the state of *Pratyāhāra* according to Patañjali naturally occurs after *Keval Kumbhaka* which is very spontaneous and natural.

In the forgoing pages I have presented the concept of *Pratyāhāra* on the basis of *Yoga Sūtra*. Now, one may proceed to see in detail how *Yoga Upaniṣads* explain or interpret this concept. I have already pointed out elsewhere that the treatment of *Pratyāhāra* in the *Yoga Upaniṣads* is more detailed, elaborated and clear. Possibly the explanation as given in those *Yoga Upaniṣads* will serve as an aid to better understand the concept.

There are many definitions in *Yoga Upaniṣads* : cited below, *Amṛtnāda, Darśana, Yoga cūḍāmanī, Yogatattva* and *Śāṇḍilya.*[8] In some sense these definitions are similar, still there are some essential differences which are explinative. I reproduce here some of the selected definitions of *Pratyāhāra* from these *Upaniṣads.* Before doing so, it may be recorded that the definitions or rather the elaborations of this concept in different *Yoga Upaniṣads* though vary in terminology, convey similar ideas.

---

6. Śāṇ Up. Chap. I.8.1
7. The Yoga Upaniṣads English Translation by - T.R. Srinivas Ayyangar p.143
8. The Yoga Upaniṣads edited by Pandit A. Mahadeva Sastri

Darśanopaniṣad in this regard is more clear and descriptive. I quote a few definitions from that *Upaniaṣad.*

1) इन्द्रियाणां विचरतां विषयेषु स्वभावतः।
   बलादाहरणं तेषां प्रत्याहारः स उच्यते॥
2) यत् पश्यति तु तत् सर्वं ब्रह्म पश्यन् समाहितः।
   प्रत्याहरो भवेदेष ब्रह्मविद्भिः पुरोदितः॥
3) यदयच्छुद्धमशुद्धं वा करोत्यामरणान्तिकम्।
   तत् सर्वं ब्रह्मणे कुर्यात् प्रत्याहारः स उच्यते॥
4) अथवा नित्यकर्मणि ब्रह्माराधान बुद्धितः।
   काम्यानि च तथा कुर्यात् प्रत्याहारः स उच्यते॥
5) अथवा वायुमाकृष्य स्थानात् स्थानं निरोधयेत्।
   दन्तमूलात् तथाकण्ठे कण्ठादुरसि मारुतम्॥[9]

As one can notice, in *Yoga Upaniṣads,* meaning of *Pratyāhāra* is not limited only to withdrawal of sense organs but to Ātman e.g. in *Amṛtnāda, Śāṇdilya, Yogatattva* and *Darsāna* the seer says : "यधत् पश्यतिचक्षुर्भ्यां तत्तदात्मेति भावयेत्"[10]. And it is same and true in case of other sense organs as well. What actually it means is that, what one perceives through ones sense organs, that knowledge is only Ātman. In normal human behaviour, if some one perceives something external he perceives it as his self. In other words, he is indifferent towards the objective reality of the entity he perceives. This is the state of indifferenceness with regard to the nature of the object of the sense organs and that state of self is *pratyāhāra.*

Let me cite an example for clarification. If someone is reading a book and simultaniously listening to music, then, it is possible that either one is reading the book without paying attention to the music, or one is listening the music without following what one is reading. Now this depends where one is concentrating. Suppose the book is very interesting and one is fully engrossed in the book, it will so happen that one will not listen to music

9. Dar. Up. Chap. VII. vss.1.8
10. Y.T. Up. vs.69

even if it is there. How does this happen? Because of concentrating on a particular work. Similarly the *Rishi* says, 'a *Yogi* who is practising *Aṣṭāṅga Yoga* should become involved in his work to such an extent that he feel everything as *Ātman'*. What he hears is *Ātman* though he is hearing respective object. This indeed is difficult to achieve, but for the spiritual development it is very necessary to detach oneself from every worldly affair. Then only, he will achieve upper stages like *Dhyāna, Samādhi* and *Pratyāhāra,* the borderline of these *Antaraṅgas* which are more difficult to achieve. Therefore, yogi has to achieve *Pratyāhāra* which is the foundation of *Antaraṅgas.*

This concept of *Pratyāhāra* in *Yoga Upaniṣad* is similar to Advait Philosophy : "ब्रह्म सत्यं जगन् मिथ्या" *Yoga Upaniṣads* says that one perceives through the sense organs only *Ātman.* So ultimately it means everything seen in this world is falsehood, the ultimate truth is *Brahman. Yoga Upaniṣads* say that *Yogī* cannot stop his activities, so his sense organs have to work. That means, mind which is meditator of the objects and the organs involves in the result and then it again wants to do the same activity, if it gives pleasure. Therefore, involvement in the worldly matters remains the same. So how can one be able to withdraw the sense from their respective objects. For that, the seer gives a tip that the *Yogī* should not think about the result - pain, pleasure, but he should think that all these things which he comes across are only the different forms of Ātman.

The *Yoga Upaniṣads* give various ways to attain *Pratyāhāra* e.g. in *Śāṇḍilya* or in *Darśana* the seer describes that in every stage of *Yoga* namely *Yama, Niyama, Āsana, Prāṇāyāma* there is *Pratyāhāra.* Because *Pratyāhāra* also means to hold back. Relating to that meaning *Pratyāhāra,* in other stages means holding or controlling the mind. When the *Yogī* reaches the stage of *Pratyāhāra,* it is not that he has given up *Yama, Niyama* etc. But now onwards he has to follow them differently. The work he is doing, practising *Āsana* and *Prāṇāyāma* is not only for his progress but for the betterment of the society. When *Yogī* reaches from physical level upto spiritual level then only he will be able to practice further. That clearly means following up *pratyāhāra* is not a physical work but a psychological process. *Yoga Cūḍāmaṇi* defines *Pratyāhāra* as :

विकारं मानसं योगी प्रत्याहारेण मुञ्चति ॥[11]

The *yogin* gives up mental transformations by withdrawing the mind. But mind is not something which can be seen but it is the energy-force in the body through which body activities happen. If *Pratyāhāra* only means as said earlier then a psychic person becomes *Yogī,* because what even he does he does not bother about the result but he does it unknowingly, and his mind, and his sense organs and the intellect don't work together. But in case of *Pratyāhāra* body, they do.

In *Śāṇdilya Upaniṣad* the *Rishi* says, *Yogī* should control eighteen *marmasthānas* with the breathing which is physical as well as intellectual activity; अष्टादशसु मर्मस्थानेषु क्रमात् धारणं प्रत्याहारः ।[12] So one should remember that according to *Yoga Upaniṣad, Pratyāhāra* is also the part of practice. *Yoga Upaniṣads* are mainly based on *Haṭha Yoga* which emphasices practice than theory. So though *Upaniṣads* are main part of philosophy, *Yoga Upaniṣads* are more practical but simultaneously they also preach ultimate simple philosophy. See for example the definition of *Pratyāhāra* in *Śāṇdilyopaniṣad,* "सर्वविषयपराङ्मुखत्वं प्रत्याहारः ॥"[13] i.e. turning one's face away from all sensual pleasures is *Pratyāhāra.* Here one can see how it is applicable in everyday life.

Conclusion

According to *Upaniṣads Pratyāhāra* means not only the control of mind which can be achieved often in *keval Kumbhaka* but it is continuous process which has to be followed at every step of life i.e. in one's work one has to control ones feelings; emotions, one has to detach from wordly affairs without cutting

11. Y. Cū. Up. vs.109
12. Śāṇ Up. Chap. I.6.1
13. Ibid. Chap. I.8.1

off completely from *Saṃsāra*. That means it is not the state of Sanyāsa. One should do all activities but should not expect fruits therefore then only one will be able to progress further and concentrate one's mind on *Kaivalya*. And for that, *Pratyāhāra* is the beginning. Therefore, one has to achieve this stage of *Aṣṭāṅga Yoga*. *Yoga Upaniṣads* elaborate very simple and easy ways of attaining it which can be followed in day to day life.

A comparison between the concept of *Pratyāhāra* is given in sequence here. The definition in *Yoga Sūtra* is precise and leaves many questions unanswered. Thus it becomes difficult to understand and to follow as well for a common seeker to grasp and attain it. It says *Pratyāhāra* is the state of being within oneself which is not a simple goal to achieve. And here lies the importance and significance of *Yoga Upaniṣads* which suggest the means along with the goal. One has to perform one's duty without any attachment to it, without expecting any reward for it i.e. 'निष्कामकर्मनित्यविहितकर्मफलत्यागः प्रत्याहारः ।'[14] and of course having or rather maintaining absolute control over ones sense organs. Thus in conclusions it would be apt to observe that one can understand properly and easily the *Yoga Sūtra* with the help of *Yoga Upaniṣads*.

* * * *

14. Ibid.

Hermeneutics and Indian Poetics

Dr. T. Devarajan

Hermeneutics is the science of interpretative principles to discover truth and values of religious texts. It has originally been studiously cultivated as a theological discipline. The factors of divine revelation and inspiration impose their appropriate hermeneutical principles. But exegesis is the critical interpretation of sacred book to bring out its meaning. Vedic exegesis is done on a religious, social and philosophical perspective. The language of the Veda which is treated as sacred bear a greater weight to theological and religious significance. In the situations of religious or theological exigencies, polemical or apological situations anticipate the truths or values to be discovered and thus the type of exegesis or hermeneutics is used. As an instance of Hermeneutics, the context in which Ahalya is relieved from the curse by the touch of Rama's foot, anticipates explanations to *Rāmāvatāra,* and also the concept of chastity and moral value from the ancient lores.

The principles of hermeneutics were rampant in India from the very early period, particularly in the schools of religion. Such principles were adopted to keep the validity of the Veda sustained. In worldly circumstances, virtue or vice of the earlier births is inferred in a context where no justifiable explanations could be given. It is done so to eliminate the flaws found in the cause (of an effect) fixed ont he rigid validity of the Veda. If such principles of inference are not supplemented, the pre-supposed valid cause will err to make the whole of Vedic knowledge invalid,

loke hi balavatā pramāṇena āgamādinā sati kāraṇatā nirṇaye paścādupasthitasya vyabhicārasya vāraṇāya janmāntarīyam

anyathānupapatyā kāraṇam dharmādharmādi kalpyate /
anyathā tu vyabhicāropasthityā pūrvavṛttakāraṇatānirṇaye bharmatva pratipattirevajāyate /[1]

Hermeneutics or the science of interpretative principle and exegesis or critical interpretation go hand in hand with each other in Indian literary criticism. The science of interpretation is a much developed branch of learning in India. Originated in the different schools of the Vedas, it was later applied to the grammatical and philosophical studies for simplifying the content of the text under consideration. In the field of grammar, the *Vārtikas* of Kātyāyana and the *Bhāsya* of Patañjali are worth mentioning. The validity of these interpretations were summed up in the saying – *uttarottaram munīnām prāmāṇyam* – the views of the succeeding sage is more valid than the preceeding one. Philosophers, particularly the Vedantins have also adopted different principles of interpretations to establish their views by expounding the *Prasthānatraya*, viz. Upaniṣads, Brahmasūtras and Bhagavadgītā. Among the expositions of *Prasthānatraya,* Adi Śankara's profound one is considered as the first and foremost because of its high standard and scientific method. The principle of interpretation was later adopted to the branch of poetics from the schools of grammar and philosophy.

Commentaries on literary works and poetics form a genre of independant literature that interpret, evaluate and simplify original works so at to express the aesthetic nuances. They are of several types such as *vṛtti, ṭīkā, ṭippaṇī, vivṛti, vivaraṇa, vyākhyā* and *vyākhyānā*. Each one of them bears a specific definition also. A commentary may generally contian five things separation of words, furnishing their meaning, dissolution of compounds, arrangement of words in accordance with the sense, objections raised (ākṣepa) and justification of the arguments in the light of evidence.

padacchedaḥ padārthoktir vigraham vākya yojanā /
Ākṣepo'tha samādhānam vyākhyānam pañcalakṣaṇam //[2]

---

1. Panditaraja Jagannatha, *Rasagangādhara,* Chowkhamba Sanskrit series, Varanasi, p.31.
2. Quoted from *Nyāyabhāṣya*

The interpretors of *Alaṅkaraśāstra* have adopted the principles for explaining theoretical works. The search for a soul as the essence of poetry by critics has given a philosophical outlook to the expositions of poetics. As the interpretor sees into the life of things, the pro-verb – "*kavitārasa cāturyam vyākhyātā vetti na kaviḥ* – the aesthetic nuances of poctry is enjoyed more by the critic than by the poet" became current in the field of commentary.

Abhinavabhārati, a polemic exposition on Nātyaśāstra by Abhinavagupta can be taken as a paradigm for analysing the principles of a standard commentary. Abhinavabhārati – the ever-new views (words) of Abhinavagupta on poetics is acclaimed as an exposition of unique, unbiased and authentic observations on Indian poetics.

At the outset of his commentary, Abhinavagupta enumerates the purposes served by his scholium and the methods adopted by him as a commentator –

1. to discover a valid conclusion – *tattvārthasiddhiḥ./*
2. to expose the idea under discussion in brief – *saṇkṣiptavṛtti vidhiḥ./*
3. to highlight the noteworthy idea under discussion – *upādeyasya sampāṭhaḥ./*
4. to limit the untenable idea by mentioning only its constituents – *tadanyasya pratīkanam./*
5. to make the idea intelligible and perfect – *sphuṭavyākhyā/*
6. to justify the objections – *virodhinām parihāraḥ/*
7. to support the ideas with valid knowledge – *supūrṇatā/*
8. to stick always to the topic under discussion – *lakṣyānusaraṇam/*
9. to make the unintelligible ideas intelligible with supporting evidences – *kliṣṭa vaktavyāmśa viviecanam/*
10. to justify the suitability of repetitions if any – *paunaruktyānām saṅgatiḥ/*
11. to reconcile the views with supporting statements form other sources – *samādhānasamākulam saṅgrahaḥ/*[3]

3. Bharata, *Nātyaśāstra* with *Abhinavabhārati,* Banaras Hindu University, Varanasi, 1971, pp.6-7.

These main objectives, eleven in number, adopted in Abhinavabhārati by the sage aesthetician have standardized hermeneutics in Indian poetics. These methods could easily be applied for the exposition of all branches of learning as they seem to be the only available standard scale for interpretation.

The five characteristics demanded in a usual commentary cannot be considered as a standard one compared to that of Abhinavagupta. They are insufficient to explain the depth and breadth of a text.

Yogabhāṣya points out the general drawbacks of the commentators (1) the unintelligible portion is left out with the remark-it is quite clear-*spaṣṭārtham* (2) the easily intelligible portion is detailed unnecessarily (3) confuse the reader by beating about the bush and (4) diverge from the topic under discussion.

durbodham yadatīva taddhi jahāti spaṣṭārthamityuktibhiḥ
spaṣṭārtheṣvativistṛtim vidadhati vyarthaiḥ samāsādikaiḥ /
asthāne'nupayogibhiśca bahubhir jalpairbhraman tanvate
śrotṛṇāmiti vastuviplavakṛtaḥ sarve'pi ṭīkākṛtaḥ //[4]

Abhinavagupta makes it explicit that the interpretation may be done on three view points – viz., from the view point of the author (poet), actor (stage performer) and the audience (critic or reader). This triangular interpretation is adopted by Abhinavagupta while explaining the introductory sentence to the *rasasūtra* of Bharata.[5] Keeping in mind the above methods of Abhinavagupta and the drawbacks of a commentator one can uphold the measurements for a standard commentary.

Hermeneutics and exegesis are seen mixed up in the several interpretations of the *rasasūtra* has got several interpretations because Bharata, the exponent of *Rasa* theory left two words of his aphorism, viz, *samyoga* and *niṣpatti;* unexplained. The ambiguity in meaning of the above words has brought varying interpretations by different scholars.

---

4. Quoted from *Yogabhāṣya*
5. Bharata, *Nātyaśāstra,* op.cit., p.620

Of the eleven available interpretations of *rasasūtra,* four are authentic and famous.[6] They are the *Utpattivāda* of Bhattalollata, the *Anumitivāda* of Sri Sankuka, the *Bhuktivāda* of Bhattanayaka and the *Abhivyaktivāda* of Abhinavagupta. The former two followed a materialistic approach while the latter two, the spiritualistic. The semantic change of '*Samyoga*' and '*Niṣpatti*' was caused by the philosophic views of the interpretors of the *rasasūtra.*

Bhattalollata (800-840 A.D.) a native of Kashmir,[7] strongly maintained his attachment to the *Apūrvavāda* theory of the *Pūrvamīmāṃsā* in his explanation to the *rasasūtra.* According to *Apūrvavāda,* if a ritual is performed following the rules of the Veda, a new thing called the *Apūrva* or *Adṛṣṭa* originated. In the same way when a drama is performed following the directions of the Natyaveda, there evolved a new thing, called the sentiment by the combination of the excitants, etc. This manifestation of a new thing, called the sentiment, is superimposed on the actor and relished by the aesthete. Lollata explained the words *samyoga* and *niṣpatti* as 'union' and 'manifestation' respectively.[8]

Sri Sankuka (9th century A.D.), another scholar from Kashmir, interpreted the *rasasutra* on the philosophic vew of Nyāya. He argued that sentiment is inferred from a poetic composition. The excitants, ensuants and variants would act as invariable concomitants (*liṅgas*) for the inference of the latent emotion. So the relation between sentiment and excitants, etc., is that of inferred object and agents promoting inference (*liṅgi liṅga jñāna*). *Niṣpatti* means inference. The inference in poetry has a peculiar charm of its own, different from other inferences of the world. The sentiment is imagined, though non-existing, subsisting mainly in the reproducting actor and is relished by the spectators through their pre-disposed tendencies. *Rasa* is called inferred emotion (*anumita sthāyi*) because the delight of

6. Panditaraja Jagannatha, op.cit. pp.87-127.
7. Bharata, *Nāṭyaśāstra,* op.cit., p.p.621-23.
8. Panditaraja Jagannatha, op.cit., p.129.

the aesthete is by inference. It is also called imitated emotion (*anukṛta sthāyi*) because the actor imitates the latent emotion originally present in the hero.[9] By the 9th century, the word *Samyoga* meant the relation between the object inferred and the agents promoting inference – *liṅgi liṅga jñāna. Niṣpatti* meant inference.

Bhattanāyaka (9th century A. D.) a third critic from Kashmir, commented on the *Rasasūtra* in the light of Śaivādvaita. He raised his theory of universalisation (*sādhāraṇīkaraṇa*) in poetry which has become one of the most important contributions of India to the world of aesthetics. He was the first to prove that poetic delight is primarily centred in the aesthete, rather than in the hero and the actors. He postulated two more functions to poetic words in addition to the expressive (*abhidhā*) and indicative (*lakṣaṇa*) powers. The aesthetic contemplation (*bhāvanā*) and relish (*bhukti*) were the two functions supplemented by him for postulating the theory of universalisation and aesthetic relish respectively.[10]

Bhāvanā, a peculiar presentative potency, endowed with the words of poetry and drama, tends to universalise both the aesthete and the excitants, ensuants, etc. The aesthetic contemplation (*bhāvanā*) tends the aesthete to identify completely with the experience of the hero. In fact, *bhāvanā* causes a similar mental condition in which the *sattvaguṇa* is revealed through a particular latent emotion by suppressing the mental layers of passion (*rajas*) and ignorance (*tamas*). By universalisation all the spectators become like minded with the *sattva* glowing through a particular latent emotion. This generalised latent emotion, i.e., *bhāvitasthāyī,* is called sentiment by Bhattanāyaka. The *bhāvanā* generalises the excitants, ensuants, etc., also, thus creating a favourable condition by dispelling the hostile ones of relish. So *sādhāraṇīkaraṇa* signifies the preparation of the spectators to a state of smilar psychic mood to respond and merge with the

9. Bharata, *Nātyaśāstra,* op. cit., p.627.
10. The theory of Bhattanayaka is summarised in a verse. vide, Bharata, *Nātyaśāstra,* op.cit., p.647.

actors on the stage. The actors are also universalised by which they lose their identity and appear to the audience like mere men and women possessing emotions generally relishable to everyone. The theory of Bhattanāyaka is called *bhuktivāda* because the universalised emotion called sentiment is relished by *bhukti,* the second function of poetic words conceived by the author. Here the permanent emotion is relished with the *Sattva. Sattva* being a concentrate of bliss and light, all sentiments are felt joyous. The word '*samyoga*', according to Bhattanāyaka, meant the relation between the revealed and the act of revelation – *bhāvya bhāvaka sambandhāt. Niṣpatti* meant relish or *bhukti.*[11]

Abhinavagupta (11th century A.D.), a preceptor of Śaiva monism and a great critic on literature from Kashmir, was the fourth commentator on *rasasūtra.* He perfected spiritualism in Indian aesthetics. The philosophic part of Śivādvaita is called *Pratyabhijñā.* The *Pratyabhijñā* was greatly influenced by the Vedānta doctrine of Śankara. While Advaita preached the oneness of the individual and Supreme Soul, *Pratyabhijñā* taught the identity of the individual self (ātman) with the Supreme Being (*Maheśvara*) or the awareness of the supreme inheritance of the individual self.

Abhinavagupta maintained that the mind of every spectator of poetic sensibility is laid with latent emotions as predispositions.[12] These latent emotions become suggested with the blissful consciousness by such agents like excitants, ensuants and variants. They are recognised in their most generalised form and they operate as agents of suggestion (*vyañjakas*). These agents serve to realise the latent disposition with the consciousness by their suggestive power. The suggested latent emotion (*abhivyakta sthāyī*) is sentiment (*rasa*). It is the revelation of the Self, the blissful consciousness accompanied by the roused latent emotion. The essence of sentiment lies in its being relished and it lasts as long as agents of suggestion continue to exist. Such pleasure being devoid of obstacles, enter

11. Ibid., p;646.
12. Ibid. p.665

directly into the heart of the aesthete. The pleasure thus suggested makes one feel the rapturous bliss of Brahman.

In his theory, Abhinavagupta has incorporated the ideas of *Dhvani, Rasa* and the *Pratyabhijñā*. The term *Pratyabhijñā* implies knowing or recognising self as the Supreme Being or the Ultimate Reality, which is Brahman in Vedānta and Maheśvara in Śaivādvaita. *Pratyabhijñā* (recognition) means recognising or knowing the self. It has a two-fold function, first perceiving some of the aspect of a thing that serves as a sign, second remembering all of its aspects in their totality as cognised before. Somānanda used the term, for the first time, in a philosophic sense of realising Śiva, the Supreme Reality, as immanent in the world by the direct experience (perception) of one of his aspects. So experience of direct perception (dṛṣṭa) and rememberance (*smaraṇa*) are unified in the experience of recognition – *dṛṣṭa smaraṇayoraikye sthite tadupapadyate.*[13]

The recognition of a thing requires the previous cognition (*anubhūtapūrva*) of all of its characteristics in their totality and their effect in the ever-existent transcendental self. They remain partly hidden by the veiling power of the Self and become manifest again in their totality by partly perceiving some of its characteristics.

13, Śaivadarśana is known as *Trika* since it deals with the triple principle – Śiva, Śaktī and *Aṇu*; or *Pati, Pāśa* and *Paśu*, or *Nara, Śaktī* and *Śiva*; or *Parā*, *Aparā* and *Parāpara*. It is also called *Trikā* for the reason that its cheif authority is the triad consisting of the three chief *Āgamas – Siddha, Namaka* and *Malini* (Tantraloka, 1,36) or for the reason that it includes all the three systems – *behda, abheda* and *bhedābheda*. It can also be called *Trika* for the reason that it teaches the three-fold method of Agamic realisation, viz., *Sambhavopāya, Śāktopāya* and *Āṇavopāya*. The philosophic import of *Trika* lies in its .true sense in the *Pratyabhijñādarśana*. *Trika*, of several branches, represent the whole system of religious cult originated from *Tantric* and *Āgamic* dogmatism. The philosophic content of the *Trika* is invariably called *Pratyabhijñā*. Abhinavagupta, the great expounder and innovator of the system named it, first as *svātantryavāda*. But it was Madhavācarya (14th century A.D.) who called the system *Pratyabhijñā* on the basis of *Īśvarapratyabhijñā*, the main treatise of the system by Utpaladeva. After Mādhavācārya the system came to be known as *Pratyabhijñā*.

smaraṇānubhavārūḍhā samānādhikaraṇyā dhīḥ /
saṃskārendriya janyā ca pratyabhijñā prakīrtitā //[14]

Pratyabhijñā is the mere removal of the veil of obscuration. In *abhivyaktivāda,* too, there is the shedding of the veil of obscuration of the self by suggestion (*vyañjana*). It is the recognition of a latent emotion (already existing in the aesthete) by the direct experience (perception) of the *vibhāva, anubhāva.* etc. As in *Pratyabhijñā*, aesthetic delight is associated with the experience of the direct perception (*dṛṣṭa*) of the *vibhāva.* etc., and thereby the rememberance (*smaraṇa*) in totality of the self-reflected through the latent emotion. In philosophy there is the recognition of the Ultimate truth, and in aesthetics there is the delight of the Self when one is absorbed in it through the latent emotion, or the beauty of the self is relished when reflected through the latent emotion. In both cases, relish or bliss is the same. The *Dhavani* and the *Pratyabhijñā* have some common factors. The elements of direct perception of *Pratyabhijñā* are substituted by vyañjakas like *vibhāva, anubhāva,* etc., in the *Dhvani* theory. The rememberance in totality of the *Pratyabhijñā* is equalled by suggestion and suggested sense or sentiment in poetry.

It is to be noted that through the interpretation of *rasasūtra,* the aesthetic theories were taking a transitional course from materialism to spiritualism following the philosophic system in which the interpretors were proficient. Prominent literary theories like *sādhāraṇīkaraṇa* was evolved by applying the principles of hermeneutics to Indian poetics.

The Kāvyaprakāśa (KP) of Mammatabhaṭṭa is a trend setter in the matter of numberless commentaries. It equals *Bhagavadgītā* and *Paribhāṣenduśekhara* in respect of a number of commentaries. More than 105 major and minor commentaries are listed on the KP. The popularity of KP as a standard and authoritative manual on poetics urged scholars to comment on

14. Sri Somanandanatha, the *Sivadṛṣṭi,* with the *Vṛtti* of Utpaladeva, Madhusudan Kaul (ed.) Kashmir Series of Texts and Studies, Srinagar, 1934, IV, 120

the work. The work also remained as a touchstone to reveal one's scholarship, and commenting on it confirmed one's versatality in poetics. Certain portions of KP are seen incomprehensible both to students and to scholars. This also necessitated more and more commentaries to make the ideas of the author legible. Maheśvāraṇyayālaṅkara points out while commenting on KP that the text of KP remained unintelligible even though *Ṭikas* were written on it at every home:

kāvyaprakāśasya kṛtā gṛhe gṛhe/
ṭīkā tathāpyeṣa tathaiva durgamaḥ//[15]

Bhattavāmana observes in his introduction to the *Bālabodhinī,* a simplified exposition for the KP that he had evaluated 46 earlier commentaries and his own consists of the essence of the earlier ones. There may occur some belemishes, yet it may not be neglected by the scholars. Is not the *ketaka* flower is adorned by the heavy hipped ones even if it consists of many thorns.

prayatnena ca saṅgṛhya samālocya ca tattvataḥ
sāram tābhyaḥ samuddhṛtya ṭikeyam kriyate mayā /
na ketakīm kim bahukaṇḍakāpi
sandhāryate mūrdhni nitambinyaḥ //

Bhaskaramisra, another expositor requests to his readers to give up curiosity to follow other *Ṭikas,* instead to consider his own in which he has included the observations of his predecessors.

It is interesting to note that scholars from different faculties have commented upon KP. Famous logicians like Gadadhara Cakravarti, Jagadisa Tarka Pancanana, Narasimhatakkura and Govinda Takkura, Nagoji Bhatta, the great grammarian; Kamalākarabhaṭṭa, a famous Mimamsaka and Gokulanatha, a Tantrika are some of them. Famous authors on poetics like Ruyyaka, Candidasa, Visvanatha and Nṛsimhasuri are commentators on KP. Their commentaries put forward varying views and diffeent observations on one and the same text.

15. Vamanacharya Jhalakikar, *Bālabodhini* (com.) on KP, Bhandarkar Oriental Research Institue, Poona, 1950, p.30.

Also it is interesting to note the commentators and the names of their commentaries. The minister of Mithileswara has commented on KP. His commentary was further commented upon by his son Ratnapani. Bhattacarya's Kāvyadarpana was further commented upon by his son Ravi, in the *Madhumatī*.

Saṅketa, Dīpikā, Pradīpa, Prabhā, Darpaṇa, Ādarśa, Nidarsana, Udyota, Kaumudī, Bhāvārtha etc, are some of the known commentaries on KP.

Abhinavagupta's *Locana,* the famous commentary on Dhvanyāloka has got several commentaries from Kerala. It is to be noted that only the southern scholars were competent to elucidate the profound exposition of Abhinavagupta. *Kaumudi* by Udayottunga, *Añjana* by Dāśarathi Namputiri, *Bālapriyā* by Ramapiṣāraṭi, *Ujjīvanī* by Nilakanthasastri are simplified commentaries on *Locana* from Kerala. *Upalocana* by Kuppuswami Sastri is another simplified version of *Locana.*

Conclusion

Hermeneutics was originated and developed in India as a specific literature in the schools of religion It was adopted to philosophy and literary criticism on a later period. Specific methods and standard rules were laid down to interpret and evaluate profound works. The succedding interpretations always evaluated critically the views contained in the preceeding ones and such evaluations have helped to bring out accurate conclusions on a subject under discussion. Some of the valuable observations contained in earlier but lost works are being kept preserved in the later expositions. Suitable verses quoted as illustrations from lost works and the names of anonymous authors are also being preserved. They have not only preserved many works from extinction but also have shed light on true history, customs, practices, social, religious, philosophic, literary and linguistic tradition of the period. A veritable treasure of glossary having new meaning and definition, interdisciplinary studies, idiomatic expressions, scholastic as well as simple prose for the use of scholars and bigginners, etc. are some of the noteworthy contributions of hermeneutics to the branch of poetics. Misinterpretation has brought blunders round about a meaning imparting misunderstanding which is a drawback of the interpretor.

* * * *

PART-III

SPIRITUALITY AND DIVINE PATH

Spirituality and Divine Path

In this part, we are presenting five articles, which may not be research articles but all the same, they spell out our cultural values. These values are an integral part of our culture and form our national ethos. Prof. Jankinath Kaul in his long educational career emphasized value education.

Dr. Sarada Natarajan traces briefly the life and teachings of the saint of Arunacala. The young Venkataraman "was gripped by a fear that he was going to die ....." The fear was so intense and there was no escape from it. It made him search within and ultimately enlightenment had happened. His subsequent life is an open book for the aspirants to read. The writer has presented here the glimpse of his simple living at the ashram and how he enjoyed the universal consciousness throughout his life.

In his article titled 'Some thoughts on Vedanta', Dr. Karan Singh has drawn our attention to the perennial philosophy of India as condensed in the Upaniṣads. He says, " Fanning the spark of divinity within us into the blazing fire of spiritual realization is the true goal of human existence". Towards this goal one has to formulate one's way either through Bhakti, Karma, Jñāna or Rāja yoga. All these yogas have their sources in the Gītā. Dr. Karan Singh has synthesised the Vedāntic thought of the Upaniṣads with the mystical experience of the Sufis and of some Western poets. Further he draws our attention to the concepts of *Bahujana Sukhāya, Bahujana Hitāya ca,* and the concept of service to *Daridra Nārāyaṇa.* He also draws our attention to the need of worshipping the mother, *Bhavānī Vasundharā,* the goddess who nourishes us. Any neglect of *Vasundharā* is bound to bring a catastrophic end to life on this planet.

Prof. Sujata Miri has drawn our attention to the rich variety of tribal religions prevalent in Arunachala Pradesh. These religions are simple and sublime. They indicate the robust wisdom of the people in this area. They have the highest regard for ethical values. The entire group is well knit in basic moral principles. One of their sayings – *"Dola Dola Daiya Hakin, Dagla Dagla Hope Pakiu"* meaning when we sit together, walk together, our unity is strengthened. This is just an echo of the Vedic saying *"Sangacchadhwam Samvadaddhwam sam no manāṅsi jānatām"*. Thus we get the feel that the simplicity of tribal mind was on a par with the spirituality of the Vedic *ṛisis.*

Lt. Col. R.K. Langar has briefly elaborated the Integral Yoga of Sri Aurobindo. The philosophy of Sri Aurobindo rests fully on the Vedas and the Upaniṣads and yet the structure rises sky high and elevates one to that height. The Integral Yoga also emphasis the way of Bhakti, work and knowledge, for raising one's own self to the self same *Ātman.* Sri Aurobindo believed that India will rise again and will remould the life of the world and would restore peace and harmony.

The last article describes the need of value education in the scheme of our educational programme.

All these five essays spell out the spiritual culture of India. Pandit Jankinath Kaul throughout his life pursued the ideals enshrined in Indian Culture and these articles are a fitting tribute to him.

– Editors

A Glimpse into the Life and Teachings of Bhagvan Sri Ramana Maharshi

Dr. Sarada Natarajan

A new visitor was wandering around a hermitage, an āsrama. Suddenly from the kitchen garden, he heard a childilike voice saying *'Chee, Asatte* (stupid fellow)!' He looked in the direction of the voice. Mostly hidden by the leafy bushes, there was an enchanting old man wearing only a loincloth sitting on his haunches. He was golden in complexion. He had a short white beard and white hair. He had a lovely face and the most beautiful, bright eyes. His legs were folded up to his breast. A small goat rested between his knees. A little monkey sat close by. The monkey rested its head on his right knee. A squirrel perched on his left knee. He had a paper packet in his left palm. He picked groundnuts from this packet one by one and fed the goat, monkey, squirrel and himself by turns. The scolding had come because the monkey was about to snatch the squirrel's share. The monkey looked suitably ashamed and the four companies continued to enjoy their little party. They kept close to each other and looked at each other with great love. They seemed to have forgotten their different species and were just four good friends. The nuts were over, he threw the packet away and said *'Pongoda* (go for boys)', just like a grandfather talking to his children. The goat, the monkey and the squirrel left. He got slowly and walked to the hall.

One Consciousness

Who was this man in whose presence every creature felt perfectly at home? He was the one, the new visitor had come to see in the āsrama. He was Bhagavan Sri Ramana Maharshi.

How was it that he seemed to be a squirrel to the squirrel, a goat to the goat, a monkey to the little monkey? How was it that with him they had forgotten all their differences and were filled with love and sharing? It was because he had no distinctions between himself and others. He had realized that there is one consciousness alone that shines in everyone, as everyone. This he called the 'Self'. Once a devotee asked him whether there was no difference between Bhagavan and herself, her servant and a man standing nearby. 'Are all the same?' she asked. 'All are the same, including those monkeys', he answered showing some monkeys outside the hall. She was shocked and said that the monkeys were not people. Surely they must be different. But he answered firmly, 'They are exactly the same as people. All are the same in one consciousness'.

What is this? 'One consciousness?' It is a thought? It is some idea in the head of Ramana Maharshi? Or is it something that he had read about and believed in? No. It is something which he had experienced for himself even as a boy of sixteen. And he expereinced it without ever being told anything about it or reading about it. How did this happen?

Enlightenment

It was the 17th of July 1896. In Madurai, there was a young schoolboy Venkataraman. He was alone in his favourite upstairs room of his uncle's house, 11, Chokkappa Naikan Street. He was just 16 years old and it would be difficult to find anyone healthier than he was then. Suddenly, just out of the blue he was gripped by a fear that he was going to die. There was no reason for this fear and he did not try to give any reason or explanation either. The fear was very intence and immediate. It was so immediate that he had to do something about it at once. There was no escaping it. He did not try to run away from the fear either. He did not rush to a doctor, to any elders or friends. His great courage was equal to his fear so he decided to turn around and face the fear. How does one face fear? By doing what, one fears? If one is afraid to speaking in public, one keeps on speaking in public until the fear is no more. If one is afraid of lizards, one takes a lizard on one's palm. When one is afraid of death, how should one face it? Venkataraman had seen his father dead. So he decided to make his body similar by acting as if he was dead. It is best to describe the experience in his words.

"The shock of the fear of death drove my mind inward....... Instinctively I held my breath and began to enquire into my own nature. I stretched myself like a corpse, and it seemed to me that my body had actually become rigid .... but though the body was dead and rigid 'I' was not dead. 'I' was, on the other hand conscious of bring alive, in existence. So the question arose in me, 'What is this 'I'?' I felt that it was a force or current working despite the rigidity or activity of the body, though existing in connection with it. It was that current or force or centre that ...... kept me acting, moving etc. The fear of death dropped off. 'I' being a subtle current had no death to fear ...... The awakening gave me a continuous idea or feeling of my personality being a current, force or *Āveśam,* on which I was perpetually absorbed whatever I did, read and when I walked, spoke or rested." Venkataraman was no more. Enlightenment had happened. The sage of undying wisdom was born.

What he experienced was not mere imagination or thought but the truth. In any case, he had no idea at all about the subject before the experience. So how could he have thought about it or imagined it? Other than Periyapuranam and Bible class texts taught in school he had read no religious or spiritual books. He had not attended any classes or lectures or heard any spiritual topics discussed. So his awareness was based totally on his experience. The current, the force that is consciousness, makes the body act and remains even when the body is not acting or is dead. This awareness came to him naturally. That which is natural belongs to everyone, it is universal. It is not dependent on any external condition. The beauty of Ramana's enlightenment is that it establishes the universal, spontaneous, natural state. Therefore, his life and teachings are natural, simple and direct.

There was no change in his state from that moment. There

was nothing further for him to achieve. Yet, from that moment many events began to unfold. These events fulfilled the purpose of Ramana's life as a pathfinder for all mankind. From that moment all preferences dropped off. He ate whatever food was given to him. He did not bother about his friends teasing him and went through his studies mechanically. Immersed in the extraordinary joy of the current of 'I' – 'I', he became indifferent to everything else. Six weeks later, he left his home and reached Arunachala (Tiruvannamalai) on September 1, 1896.

All the Time

Ramana sang in his 'Necklet of Nine Gems on Arunachala', 'I was born in Tiruchuzhi to Azhagu and Sundaram'. Then he adds, 'To rescue me from this barren worldly life, Arunachala Śiva in the form of a Hill famous throughout the universe, gave me His own state of bliss.' Why did he do this? For what purpose? So that His heart may rejoice. But not only that. So that His own glory may flourish. What is the glory of Arunachala? What is Arunachala? Ramana has said repeatedly that it is the Self-embodied. It is the 'Knowledge-Hill.' Hence Ramana came and stayed to reveal the glory of Self-knowledge through his life and to lead to that knowledge through the path of self-enquiry. Such an instance would find no parallel in history. Where else can we find a person who, for nearly fifty-four years, was available to anyone and everyone all through the day and night. And, except for the first few months, when he stayed in the Arunachaleswara temple and in the underground Pātāla Lingam, there was always someone with him. His every movement, his every word could be noted and recorded. And much of it has been too. We have answers by him for nearly thirty thousand questions of earnest seekers. And we have a life of perfection. For not a moment did he swerve from the state of steady Self-awareness. Not a moment did he move away from absolute equality and supreme love. Where can we find a life so utterly transparent and at the same time so flawless?

Natural Happiness

Paul Brunton was a journalist from England, in search of the spiritual secrets of India. He visited many sages but did not find satisfactory answers to his many queries. When he came to Ramana's presence he still had his long list of questions with him. But in the overpowering silence all his questions dissolved. Though he was reminded that he needed to get some clarifications, Brunton preferred to remain silent. It was only later that Brunton gave expression to his most important doubt, the essence of his seeking. Brunton asked Ramana, 'I wish to have the experience of enlightenment. Can you assist me to experience enlightenment?' Ramana replied, 'You say 'I'. 'I' want to know. Tell me, who is that 'I'? Know first that 'I' and then you shall know the truth. There is only one thing to be done. Look into your own self. Do this in the right way and you shall find the answer to all your problems.' Ramana also explained to Brunton that this self-enquiry could be pursued as well in a London flat as in a jungle hermitage. If one does self-enquiry rightly for a few minutes in the morning, the current would continue through the day. Ramana would emphasise that it is the mind which is important in everything. If one does work with total attention it would be joyous. At the same time we would not be wasting our energies on worrying about the results. All worries and anxieties actually spring only from our wrong notion about happiness and about ourselves.

Ramana pointed out that everyone, in fact every being is constantly in search of happiness. Nobody wants to be unhappy ever. Why is this so? Because happiness is natural just as health is natural, says Ramana. That is why the moment we are ill we do all that we can to become healthy again. Similarly we try our level best to be happy always. We only make one small mistake in all this. We think happiness lies in objects or situations that give us pleasure. But this is not the case. Then where does happiness lie? In our selves. It is our nature. If happiness was in an object, should not that object make everyone happy at all times? Does not fire burn anyone and everyone always? Will not water always make wet? Why? Such is the natural property of water and fire. Then, can we name an object or experience that has the property called happiness? Chocolates are liked by many but not by all. Even those who like chocolates may not like them at all times, especially not if they have a painful tooth! There is no object which can give happiness to everyone or even to one person at all times. So it is clear happiness does not lie in the object but in the subject, the individual who experiences it.

Who am I?

But then, if happiness is our nature why don't we experience it all the time? Because we don't really know ourselves in the first place, says Ramana. This may shock us, yet it is true.

A conversation which Ramana had with a devotee makes this point clear.

Ramana: You say 'I wish to see God'. First tell me who you are.

Devotee: My name is Devadatta Sharma.

Ramana: That is your name but who are you?

Devotee: I have already told you I am Sharma, I am a Brahmin.

Ramana: That is an indication of your caste but who are you?

Devotee: I am a lecturer in a college.

Ramana: That is your profession but who are you?

Devotee: I am a human being.

Ramana: That is your birth womb but who are you?

Devotee: I am a man.

Ramana; That is your gender. I would like to know who it is that desires to meet God.

Devotee: It looks as if I do not know myself.

Ramana's questions may seem strange to us when we first hear them. But if we think a little we realize the truth in them. Surely we cannot be our name or caste or profession or status, can we? All these can change but the 'I' would still be 'I'.

Would it not? Science has now provided a possibility for changing one's gender and may even make it a reality to change species! But whatever 'I' becomes it is only "I" who becomes 'this' or 'that'. Now what is that 'I'?

We take ourselves to be a certain name and form based on our waking experiences. In dream, however, we may take on totally different names and identities. A king may become a pauper or a teacher, a student while dreaming. Still the sense of 'I' is continuous, is it not? On waking we may laugh and even say, 'Can you imagine I had become a lion in my dream? But I was a sweet lion, I didn't frighten anybody or bite anybody. I was a vegetarian lion too!' If 'I' can become a lion in a dream, if 'I' can be a brother and a father or a daughter and a friend all at once and at different times while waking, what is that 'I'? If I feel just like 'I' even though my body never remains the same from five to fifty five, what is that 'I'?

When one begins to look at one's own true nature, one discovers at first that the mind is central to our feeling of 'I'. In fact, it is because of the mind that we know the entire world and even our own bodily experiences. Great physical pain may not be registered if the mind is engaged in something else. The most marvellous physical experiences may also hold no meaning if the mind is depressed. It is only the mind which creates the whole world in dreams, putting the 'I' also in that very world! So it is evident, that the mind is the 'I'. The next question is one's search for the 'I' would therefore, be, 'What is the mind?' Ramana says that when one enquires what the mind is one will find, there is no such thing as mind. What does this mean? One will find that mind is not one 'thing'. It is only a stream of thoughts. Each thought comes and goes, sometimes slowly, but mostly so rapidly, that we seem to be having many thoughts at a time. If that is the case then which thought is the mind? To all the thoughts, there is one that is central, like the fulcrum of the wheel to which all the spokes are connected. This is the 'I' -thought or the feeling of individuality, the feeling 'I am so-and-so'. It is only when 'I' pay attention that other thoughts can come in the mind. The moment the attention of the 'I' goes to something else, the earlier thought must fade. So, for purposes of understanding, Ramana says simply that the 'I' – thought is the mind.

And what happens to this sense of 'I' in deep sleep? Where does it disppear? Find out where this 'I' sets and from where this 'I' arises on waking. Find this by first focusing attention on the 'I' and keeping attention on it till it subsides in its source. Then you have the answer to everything, says Ramana. This search for the self is called self-enquiry. It is the essential teaching of Ramana. For this search he has given two tools, two questions, one 'Who am I?' and the other 'Whence am I?' or 'Wherefrom in me does the feeling of 'I' arise?'

There is an interesting story about the tenth man given by Ramana in this context. Long, long back, ten friends were travelling from one place to another. At nightfall they found that they had to cross a river to reach their destination. Being good swimmers, they swam across. After reaching the other bank, they decided to take a head count just to ensure that all were safe. The first one counted and found only nine. Worried, he asked another to count. The second friend also counted only nine. Each of them counted and came to the same conclusion. They then started weeping for their lost tenth friend. A passerby noticed the situation. He offered to do the counting, made them stand in a row and tapped each one on the hand. He asked them to call out successive numbers as they were tapped. So they called out 'one' 'two' 'three' and so on until the last one called out 'ten'! They were all overjoyed. Where had the tenth man gone all the while? Nowhere. Each of the ten had forgotten to count himself while doing the counting. Even so, Ramana points out that the one essential truth, the Self, is ever present. We simply forget it. It is the fullness of happiness but we do not pay attention to it. Hence, thinking we have lost happiness we hunt for it, high and low. We weep that we cannot find it. Yet it is all the time our own, our very self. We are so busy counting all the other things in life that we never take out true nature into account. Ramana gives another example, of gold and ornaments made from it. Gold is the essence of all golden ornaments but we see only the names and forms and forget the essence. So we face all kinds of problems in life.

Search or Surrender

This esence is the Self. This is also the Divine. Therefore, Ramana would say that if we do not have faith in the Supreme Power then we should find out the fullness of our own strength. If we believe in the Divine Power, then we simply have to surrender to it. When we travel in a train do we not keep our luggage in the place for it? Do we carry it on our heads or on our laps? Similarly, in life. Why should we carry our burdens on our heads? Cannot God who is in charge of everything take care of us also? Ramana explained what is the true meaning of surrender. He narrated how a man had the practice of eating his food only after worshipping Gaṇeśa. One day he was traveling and could not reach home in time for food. He decided to eat a piece of jaggery that he was carrying in order to satisfy his hunger. Before eating he remembered that he had not performed his daily worship. So he made an image of Gaṇeśa from the jaggery he had and offered worship to it. Then he came to the part where he must offer food to God. But he had no eatables apart from the jaggery. So he pinched a bit of it and offered it to Gaṇeśa. What is it that really belongs to us to give to God? Everything that we have is only a gift from God to us. To give the same things back is like pinching a little bit of jaggery from a jaggery image of Gaṇeśa and offering it to Him, says Ramana. Then what are we to surrender? We must surrender our ego, our sense of individuality. What is this? This is the feeling 'I know' 'I have the power to do as I please'. We must recoginze that all the power we have comes from God. But this very power is in every one of us as our Self. So, if we discover our own true nature we would have got reconnected to the divine current. We would become aware of our nature as the fullness of happiness, peace and love. Ramana lived in this awareness continuously, but it is not special to Ramana, it is universal.

What is Enlightenment?

In fact it is only to establish that the truth belongs to all that Ramaṇa stayed in the body for nearly fifty-four years after his enlightenment. Otherwise, what was there for him to achieve? No matter what the circumstances, Ramana was blissful and everyone in his presence could experience this joy too. He had no possessions yet there cannot be anyone happier than him. He had no family yet he loved every being in the universe and every one loved him. He had no power, position or status. Yet even kings came to his presence for peace and joy. And of course he was utterly indifferent to his body. Its condition made no difference to his natural state of surging joy.

In early February 1949, Ramana developed sarcoma. At that time a small growth was removed surgically from Ramana's left elbow. No one guessed that this minor operation was to be the beginning of the end of Ramana's sacred body. From then till April 1950, four major operations had to be performed. The pain was excruciating. Doctors who came to attend on Ramana were shocked by the peace radiating from him. Anyone else in such a physical condition should have been screaming with pain.

Mahāsamādhi – Preparing the Devotees

In spite of this great pain Ramana's compassion and love were unwavering. The management decided to limit the hours when people could see him. They decided to close the doors for a couple of hours in the afternoon. But Ramana had them opened immediately saying that no one should be inconvenienced. A day after his third operation, against the doctor's advice for rest Ramana left the dispensary and went to the hall for darsan. When he became too weak to go to the hall he was shifted to a room now called the *nirvāna* room. His couch used to be put in the verandah outside the room. Devotees would go past in a row both morning and evening. Throughout these months Ramana prepared the devotees for his departure. He revealed to them everyday that the body did not matter. He was not limited to the body. The truth about everyone is the unlimited, infinite Self that has no death, that it is bliss itself.

On April 14, 1950 Ramana thanked his attendants. In the evening, at about 5 o'clock, he asked to be helped to sit up. Just then devotees started chanting 'Arunācala Śiva'. Ramana's face became radiant with joy. Tears were flowing from his eyes for a long while. Then his breathing gradually became slower. At 8.47 p.m. it subsided quietly. Just at that time, suddenly a bright luminous body arose from the southern horizon. It slowly went up and descended in the north behind Arunachala. It was larger than a meteor and its movement was slow. It was so bright that when it was at the zenith the light shed by its trail stretched till the horizon. It was like an arc in the sky. It was seen in Chennai and all over South India. A devotee saw it even at Mumbai. Even to this day many recall their having seen this light.

The Light is Here

As a body of sixteen Ramana had 'seen' that truth and never wavered from it. Hence he was untouched by death. Whenever devotees cried that he was going away, he asked 'Where can I go? I am here'. 'I am here' not 'I will be here'. 'Am' is present, present continuous, always present. And here? Here is every place, is it not? Wherever one may be, it is 'here'; it has to be 'here'. Ramana's presence is felt everywhere, wherever anyone turns to him, his presence and guidance are availble there.

* * * *

Some Thoughts on Vedānta

Dr. Karan Singh

Hinduism has a vast corpus of wisdom, coming down from the very dawn of our civilisation, from the Vedas, thousands of years ago. The Vedas can be likened to the great Himalayas. Kalidāsa in the first sloka of the *Kumārasambhava* has a beautiful description of the Himalayas, standing like a great measuring rod by which alone the depth and the grandeur of human history and civilisation can be measured. The Vedas are like the Himalayas because in the same way the life-giving streams come down from the Himalayas to irrigate the land below, so also our great scriptures have flown down to the present day. And if the Vedas are like the Himalyayas, then the Upaniṣads are like those great peaks bathed in the eternal sunshine of wisdom that you see if you are flying parallel to the Himalayas. The Upaniṣads therefore represent, in some ways, the high watermark of our cultural and spiritual tradition. They are dialogues very much structurally like the Socratic dialogues.

The Upaniṣads are not monolithic commands issued by some invisible deity. They are dialogues between the *guru* and the *śiśhya,* the sage and his disciples. And the dialogues deal with the great questions of human existence, of why we are here, what is our goal in life, what is the meaning of everything around us, what is the power that energises all of us, our minds, our hearts, our bodies and which permeates the entire universe.

I begin with the five cardinal principles and I suggest that the teachings of the Upaniṣads are becoming increasingly relevant as we move into global society. A scripture is only really valuable to the extent that it helps us where we are today; otherwise, it becomes merely an archival text for research scholars and Ph.D.

thesis. The immediacy of a scripture, the power and inspiration of a scripture depends upon its relevance to our contemporary condition. I would submit that the teachings of the Vedānta are in fact becoming more relevant and important in the present world.

There are five concepts that I would place before you. The first concept is the concept of the all-pervasive Brahman: the power, the light that pervades this entire universe; not only this tiny speck of dust that we call the planet earth, but the billions upon billions of galaxies in the endless universe around us, *anantakoti brahmāṇda.*

The second is the concept of the Ātman, the Self: the realisation not of God but of the self. This is not about the false self, not the ego that accompanies us everyday with self importance, but the deepest self which is in the inner recesses of our being, of our consciousness-that is known as the Ātman. It is this Ātman which is present in every creature and every being. As we move up the ladder of evolution to come to the human race, the Ātman there becomes self-consciousness. As Shri Aurobindo points out, for the first time with the advent of the human race we have a creature capable of self-consciousness and self-realisation. The Upaniṣads have a marvellous term for the human race, *amṛtasya putraḥ:* the children of immortality'.

It is fanning this spark of divinity within us into the blazing fire of spiritual realisation that is the true goal of human existence; the joining of the Ātman and the Brahman. The word yoga means to join, and comes from the same root as the English word to yoke, to join. Yoga is that which joins the Ātman with the Brahman. It is time to say a few words here about yoga, because yoga is very often trivialised and looked upon simply as a series of physical exercises. Yoga is a profound concept, for it is nothing less than joining God imminent within us with God transcendent, the Ātman with the Brahman. There are four main paths of yoga found in our scriptures and in the Upaniṣads, and also later. The first is the Jñānayoga, the way of wisdom, that is the way of intellectual discrimination between what is real and what is unreal, *satya-asatya viveka.*[1] This could be likened to the way of Plato, the contemplation on the great truths, the archetypes that lie behind manifested existence. And therefore the Jñānayoga is par excellence the way of the mind, of the discriminative mind. That is one of the powerful ways for achieving the union between the Ātman and the Brahman.

Then there is Bhaktiyoga, the way of the heart, the way of devotion to a personalised form of the Divine. With Jñānayoga you can contemplate upon the Supreme, you can contemplate upon a flame; but for the heart to open in ecstasy in devotion, in surrender, you need a focus which necessarily has to be a divine figure. Bhaktiyoga is the opening of the heart in love and surrender and tenderness. In theWest, it would be the way for example of St. Francis of Assisi, St. John of the Cross, or St. Teresa of Avila. In India you have the great South Indian mystics, the Nyanmars and the Alvars, the Vaiṣṇava saints and the Śaiva saints. You have the bhakti singers, Mirabai, Tulsidas, Surdas, Kabir, Guru Nanakdev, Shri Chaitanya, Shankaradeva.

The third is Karmayoga, the way of arms, of hands, of work. What we do in our daily lives, our activities are not something different from our spiritual quest. One of the basic insights of the Vedānta and of the Hindu tradition is that religion is not seen as separate from life. If is not something that you keep for your half-an-hour puja every morning, or for your visit to a church every Sunday or to a mosque every Friday. It has to permeate our entire being and our entire lives The Bhagavad Gītā is par excellence, a text of Karma yoga. Karmayoga is the distilled essence of our activity which we place at the feet of the Divine, says Ādi Śankarācarya. Therefore, any offering full of selfishness, desire, hatred or negativity cannot be looked upon as Karmayoga.

We then have Rāja Yoga, the royal path, the way of psychospiritual practice. We have learnt in our texts that within the human body itself are hidden the secrets of enlightenment. It is not something ultimately which will come to us from outside.

1. Also *nitya-anitya viveka.*

It is something which is within us, in the deepest recesses of our consciousness. Through the Rāja yoga, through *prāṇāyāma,* various practices of breathing and meditation; there is a possibility of a transmutation of consciousness. Rāja yoga involves what is known as the awakening of the *kuṇdalinī śakti:* the serpent power, three and a half times coiled, and believed to be seated at the base of the spine. This is a highly technical matter which would require an entirely different type of presentation.

So you have these four methodologies, four broad paths, with hundreds and hundreds of methodologies within these paths. I speak of the all-pervasive Brahman, the Ātman within us, and these paths of yoga to join these two. These are essential messages because Vedānta is not simply an intellectual inquiry, not academic gymnastics. It is a way of liberation; therefore, it covers all these various aspects of the human psyche.

We come then to the third major element in Vedānta, which is the concept of *vasudhaiva kutumbakam.* If the Divine inhabits all human beings, the human race is looked upon as an extended family. That 'this is mine, that is yours', is a small divisive way of looking at reality. For those of the greater consciousness the world itself is a family. Now this concept of the world as a family is remarkable because it cuts across all barriers of race and religion, caste and creed, language and nationality, sects and social status.

Let us go one step further. Vedānta speaks about the essential unity of all spiritual paths: *ekam sad viprāḥ bahudhā vadanti,* 'the Truth is one, the wise call it by many names'. At the time of the Upaniṣads none of the other religions were there; but nonetheless within Hinduism itself there were many paths to the one goal. Hinduism has never been a monolithic religion; you could worship a *Nirākāra Brahman,* a God without form like many other religions do; or a *Sākāra Brahman,* a God with form.

Much of the tension that has gone into human history has come from this claim of a monopoly of wisdom. Religion has played a very noble part in human history. Much that is great in human history, in human civilisation, art and architecture, music and dancing and literature and moral codes and spiritual practices came to us from the great religions of the world. Humanity would be much poorer had it not been for them. On the other hand, more people have been massacred, tortured, killed, burnt and persecuted in the name of religion than for any other cause. As citizens of the 21st century we must realise that no longer can monopolistic claims be entertained. We have to respect all the different religions. India par excellence is a land of religion: four of the world's great religions were born in India, Hinduism, Jainism, Buddhism and Sikhism. Four religions came to us from West Asia: the religion of Zarathustra-Prophet of Iran, Judaism, Christianity and Islam and now the Bahai faith. 'Let noble thoughts come to us from every side' is a Vedic dictum and provides the basis for this acceptance. The Upaniṣads clearly assert that there are many paths to the Divine, and that there is an essential unity of all religions.

The mystical tradition is like the golden thread that binds the peoples of the world together – whether it is Maulana Jalauddin Rumi with his magnificent Masnavi which is one of the great religious texts of the world; or Francis Thompson, when he says,

Not where the wheeling systems darken
And our benumbed conceiving soars,
The drift of pinions, would we harken,
Beats at our clay-shuttered doors.
The angels keep their ancient places,
Turn but a stone and start a wing,
'tis ye', your strange faces that missed the many-splendoured things.

The many splendoured light of the Divine, 'the light that lighteth every man that cometh into the world', as the Bible says, is the '*Noor e-Ilahi* of the Sufis, and again the *Ek Onkar* of the Sikh gurus, and is also the light of a thousand suns of the Upaniṣads. "I have seen that great Being shining like a thousand suns beyond the darkness, that is the light which we must seek within ourselves". Alama Iqbal talks of *khudi ki bulundi,* enhancing the inner self. That is what yoga is all about, that is what religion is all about-not the fundamentalism, the hatred, the atrocities, the abominations that are found in the name of religion. And therefore, when we go back to Vedānta we have this clear stream coming out from the very source of our civiliation; and that stream, that light shines till today.

I have sopken of the four major concepts of the Vedānta: the all pervasive Brahman; the Ātman residing in all beings and their joining through yoga; the concept of the human race as an extended family; the idea that all religions are different ways to the same goal. Finally, the Vedānta talks about the welfare of all beings, *bahujana sukhāya, bahujana hitāya ca.* It is not a selfish creed that you simply sit in your cave and meditate upon your navel and forget the rest of the world. It is something which exhorts us to come into the battlefield of life, to try and see how we can help. There are two goals of human existence: we work for the liberation of our souls, but we also work for the welfare of society. Unfortunately in India we have been obsessed with *Ātmano mokhṣhārtham;* and we can have neglected *jagat hitāya ca.* That is why every social reformer within Hinduism has started off with saying go back to the poor, go back to the *daridranārāyaṇa.* Vivekananda went to the extent of saying that to preach religion to someone who is starving is an insult, first of all fill his belly and then give him your philosophy.

This concept of *bahujana sukhāya, bahujana hitāya ca* is a very important concept; and it is not only the welfare of human beings but the welfare of all life on this planet. That is why the Vedic prayers are for peace on the earth, in the heaven, in the sky, in the forests, in the mountains, in the oceans among vegetation, among animal life. Our ancient seers realised that human beings were an essential part of the natural environment. Billions of years ago, we have come up from the slime of the ocean through the process of evolution, to where we are today. If we neglect the environment or destroy the environment, as we have done and are doing, ultimately the human race itself will be destroyed. And therefore the concept of the welfare of all beings is the basis of our environmental awareness. It is much deeper than simply the question of technology, it is a question of whether we are going to honour and sustain Mother Earth, Bhawānī Vasundharā, Gaia in the Greek tradition, the Mother that has been nurtured for billions of years; or whether we are going to destroy her and in the process destroy ourselves.

These universal concepts of the Vedānta have no room for sectarianism or narrow thinking or communalism in the sense in which they are used. Taken together, these concepts provide a holistic paradigm and a global philosophy which can sustain us in this period of intense transition. This philosophy stresses convergence in place of conflict, cooperation in place of competition, and holism in place of hedonism. This concept encourages interfaith dialogue, that encourages environmental values, and encourages gender equality because there is no gender discrimination as far as the Vedānta is concerned. The Ātman, whether it is within a man or woman or boy or girl, the light of the Ātman is there.

All the desirable goals that we seek to follow in this century can find inspiration in the Upaniṣads. I agree it is not an easy task. There are no soft options left now, either for individuals or for collective salvation. But the Upaniṣads, the Vedānta can provide us with inspiration, power and guidance. These texts are so luminous, that if you go to the texts there are beautiful translations of the Upaniṣads. If you go to the texts themselves, even in translation you will find them full of power and inspiration. I will therefore, end this peace presentation with two famous verses from the *Mundaka Upaniṣad,* one of my favourites, which says.

Taking as a bow the mighty weapon of the Upaniṣads, fix in it the arrow sharpened by constant meditation, drawing it with a mind wholly dedicated to the Divine penetrate, O good looking youth, that imperishable target. (2.2.4)

The aum is the bow, the arrow is the self, Brahman is said

to be the target. With an unfaltering aim it is to be penetrated – to become one with it – as the arrow becomes one with its target.

If the bow is not drawn fully, if the mind of the drawer is vascillating and disturbed, if the arrow has not been sharpened by meditation, you will not hit the target. The Upaniṣads thus present us not only with a philosophy but also with a methodology to achieve liberation.

* * * *

The Spiritual Life with Special Reference to Arunachal Pradesh

Professor Sujata Miri

The concept of religion brings together a variety of phenomena under it. Rituals and beliefs are radically different from one religion to another religion and there are so many religions. In Arunachal Pradesh for example beside the major religions of the world, namely, Hinduism, Buddhism, Islam and Christianity you have a fantastic variety of tribal religions.

There is a long debate in western culture about the theme of precedence of the particular and the individual over the abstract and the noumenal in matters of spirituality. While some equate spirituality totally with transcendence from this world, distancing it from the everyday and the mundane, others find the spiritual vision authentically available in everyday palpable human life.

The Oxford Dictionary defines spirituality as signifying a craving for the spirit and the supernatural in opposition to the longing for material things. Influenced by such an understanding of spirituality a peculiar image of spiritual people has come to capture the public imagination. The moment one hears of a spiritual person one prepares oneself to be initiated by him into the mysteries of creation and renunciation, futility of being and essential unity with the transcendent (whatever way we define it). If, for instance, one is wedded to nature and earthly pursuits, one is labelled as devoid of spirituality. This has led to the viewing of the religious man as other worldly, as one who regards the phenomenal world as either illusory or as not the "true" world.

If spirituality is identified with the pursuit of eternal interests at the cost of the temporal, then the spiritual man would be expected to shun off any participation in the political life of his community.

For the political implies an interest in the matters of the state/ government and public affairs in general. Now doing and action are supposed to be of interest to the wordly man and not to the man who wishes to raise himself above the world away from "the maternal depths of Nature". (Carl Jung)

No spiritual person sees life and the world as lacking in ethical content. Whatever the identity of the religion, spirituality is expected to entail a high degree of concern for the welfare of mankind. Take the following prayer of the *Nishings,* a neighbouring tribe of the Adis, which asks for the well being of the world as well as for the preservation of moral values.

"Donyi Bo Kapa Do, Si Bo Tapa Do".

(Mother Donyi always watches over our activities, so we should do good and be good).

If the politics also aims at the good life then the spirituality and the politics cannot be isolated in separate realms. The Nishing urge all people in the lap of mother earth to stay together in harmony. The same prayer is articulated in the proverb *"Dola Dola Daiya Hakin, Dagla Dagla Hopo Pakiu"* meaning, when we sit together, walk together our unity is strenghthened.

Indeed the most prominent tradition of spirituality in Arunachal Pradesh, namely, Donyi Poloism, accepts the Sun and the Moon as the symbols of truth, peace, perfection and greatness. Oshong Ering has listed some of the fundamental teaching of Donyi Polo:

1. Follow the truthful path.
2. Cultivate wisdom and justice
3. Enjoy the warmth of equality.
4. Cultivate selflessness.
5. Follow the path of continuity and straightforwardness.
6. Cultivate kindness and mercy.
7. Take shelter in peace and tranquility.

The sun and the moon are the medium or symbol of the aspirations of the Adis. For men cannot see the supreme reality (Sedimelo) but they can perceive the supreme power through the medium of the rays of the sun and the light of the moon. Hence the sun and the moon are the teachers or guides for mankind. The sun is the principle guide to truth while the moon stands for sympathy, love and kindness.

Some traditions of spirituality have equated spirituality with the ascetic ideal of renunciation of this world and of being absorbed into the absolute (Zehner). But I find it hard to accept the suggestion that there can be a spiritual/religious tradition which sees the world and life in it as devoid of ethical content. The tribal religions have also been alleged as lacking in spirituality and the vision of the good life. Let me say a word about the latter first. The *duo* of sun and moon, *Donyi-polo* is regarded as above the rest of creation, because they are endowed with light and they *illuminate the world* and lift the cover of darkness. They can favoured with a position high up in the sky so that they can look after humanity from there. They are the force behind nature, the animal world and the earth, invoked invariably in the beginning of all Kebangs (village councils of the Adis) to help reveal the truth and catch law-breakers.

Asceticism also is pursued not at the cost of the good life but as a stepping stone to self-mastery and self-realization. Unfortunately, it is the phenomenon of religious communalism which has strenghtened the hands of modern secular ideologies. Not accepting what they call the "falsehood" of religions they yet use the various factions for purposes far removed from the goals of the spiritual.

Inter-community voilance and rivalry that is growing , is a phenomenon of recent times. Earlier there were fueds and war between groups, but these were for different reasons. In the present political system the communities in the old sense, where they derived their strength from within themselves. Inter community hatred is a direct consequence of the kind of politics that we have today which is used in the pursuit of power by a few. Although we are a democracy, democratic practices have never filtered down to the lives of communities. And communities now have become mere constructs used as pawns by the politicians to pursue their own ends and thus the communities have lost their own moral and spiritual coherence.

* * * *

Sri Aurobindo's Integral Yoga

Lt. Col. R.K. Langar

Sri Aurobindo was a mystical philosopher. He was a great yogi and a visionary. Sri Aurobindo related man to God. To him God is the foundation and man's existence which includes man's nature and activity. He integrated the religious, social and moral dimensions of man in his evolutionary vision. Aurobindo in his writing presented man as a socio-religious being. He says that man who is the highest of consciousness of life on earth is a transitional being. Man is too imperfect to be the last specie on earth. From stone to plant, plant to animal, animal to man- so the man is yet to proceed to a still higher level of existence. According to Aurobindo it is the spiritual evolution of man on earth which matters and this new consciousness is to be attained through divine fulfilment of life. In the words of Sri Aurobindo, this change of man from an ordinary level of consciousness to the supermental level is to be attained through the practice of Integral yoga. While presenting the Integral Yoga Aurobindo agrees with the teachings of Upaniṣads that Brahman is supreme and pure existence and it is within the power of Brahman to manifest itself in the world of finite objects and selves. Sri Aurobindo says, that in the process of evolution all existents constantly return to Brahman which is the very source of their being. Sri Aurobindo asserts that every existence animate or inanimate is spiritual at core and those who do not recognise soul or spirit are atheist. According to him there is in a man a spiritual urge to overcome ignorance by knowledge and attain the highest spiritual goal wherein there is unity, harmony, wisdom, peace and joy. It is within the power of man to evolve into the highest spiritual being to realise the Upniṣadic truth, thou art that. This state is described by Sri Aurobindo as truth consciousness which enables a man to establish world order in which peace, freedom and justice prevail. The way to reach this state is by practising Integral Yoga.

What is Integral Yoga as preached by Sri Aurobindo? In his own words, Integral yoga is the way of complete God realisation, a complete self-realisation, a complete fulfilment of our being and a complete transformation of our nature. All this implies a complete perfection of life on earth and not a return to an eternal perfection elsewhere. The change from a human into a divine consciousness and nature is the character of Aurobindo's Integral Yoga. Aurobindo emphasizes that divine realization through Integral yoga is not for the sake of the individual but something to be gained for earth conciousness. Sri Aurobindo rejects the world as Māyā. According to him life is real and has meaning. All life, according to Aurobindo is a school and perfection of life to be obtained on earth. The Integral Yoga does not aim at a departure from world and live in Heaven or attain Nirvana, but it teaches that individual achievement of divine realisation is to be gained by complete tranformation of earthly life. Aim of Integral Yoga is not world shunning but realising and manifesting Divine in the world. It is not departure from world but a change of life on earth. Integral Yoga is not for personal salvation but its aim is to bring about radical change on earth. To achieve this human mind, will, heart, life, body, outer and in most existence, conscious and subconcious part must all become means and a field for divine realisation. The novelty of Aurobindo's Integral Yoga is that the world is neither a creation of Māyā or Divine play or *Līlā* but it is a field of manifestation in which there is a progressive evolution of the soul from matter through life and mind. Aurobindo explains that in the Integral Yoga the individual with the help of yogic – sādhanā is able to transcend the mental level and enter into supramental state. In this yoga, there is first the ascent of human consciousness by rejection of the movements of lower nature and then there is a descent of new consciousness. The Integral Yoga is not a Yoga of *Bhakti* alone but there must be knowledge and work also. In addition Integral yoga includes a total change of human nature to seek perfection so that the nature also may become one with the nature of the Divine. Aurobindo explains that it is not only the heart that has to turn to the Divine but the mind also for which knowledge is necessary. Also the human will has to turn towards Divine for which works are necessary. The three yogas of Bhagwad Gītā, Love, Work and knowledge are to be practised together in the Integral Yoga. It emphasizes on the rejection of the movements of lower nature like desires, demands, craving, lust, greed and doubts, to deliver the self involved, in the lower nature, so that it can rise to the higher nature. To achieve this a strong aspiration is needed for attaining the higher consciousness. It is only after the rejection of lower nature that one can surrender to Divine in every plane of consciousness. The Integral Yoga of Aurobindo ignores no part of human being and takes into account all facets of it which are harminiously integrated so that the lower acts under the direction of higher till it is completely transformed. This would enable the man to live in peace and joy according to the law of spirit within. This according to Aurobindo is divine life on earth which can only come about by a spiritual change of our being.

Sri Aurobindo's Integral yoga can also be described as a movement of humanity from *Falsehood to Truth,* from *Weakness to Force,* from *Pain to Bliss,* from *Death to Immortality,* from *Self division to Unity* from *Imperfection to Perfection* from *Duality to Unity* and from *Egoism to Divine Consciousness.* In practising this Yoga no daily rituals are required to be observed, no vigorous austerity needs be undertaken and no formal initiation from a Guru is required. In the Integral yoga the Divine Himself become one's Guru. The personal effort required, in Sri Aurobindo's words, is "A triple labour of Aspiration, Rejection and Surrunder". A strong aspiration is necessary for raising oneself to a higher state which would enable one to reject the movements of lower nature in order to surrender to Divine. the stronger the aspiration, more inclined the individual will be towards rejecting his lower nature and surrendering to Divine.

Sri Aurobindo conceived the idea of Integral Yoga when there was not so much of decline in the moral values, as we find today. Today a man besides himself being under the captivity of his own lower nature is also surrounded by evil all around. A much greater and sincere effort is required by man to break through the resistance within and around to seek perfection. If all of us decide to elevate ourselves as per the theme of Sri Aurobindo's Integral yoga, the earth will automatically become a better place to live in. Those who can perceive the shortcomings of the society must see that such shortcomings are first removed from within themselves. People should not wait for the arrival of some perfect person to change them but should themselves become good for reforming the society.

Sri Aurobindo was a great Yogi who had realized the greatness of India in contributing towards uplifting the world order. He said that India is the Guru of the nations and the physician of the human soul in its profounder maladies. She is destined once more to re-mould the life of the world and restore the peace of human spirit. In the present era of globalization, Sri Aurobindo's words assume great significance. India's ability as a world reformer, as conceived by Sri Aurbindo, has to put to an action plan by the right thinking people of our country.

* * * *

Value Education for the New Millennium

Dr. N.B. Patil

Our beautiful earth has long past. It was born out of a bang and since then she is revolving around herself and around the sun along with other globules in the cosmos. It took long for her to cool and develop her own atmosphere. She cooled and it was water everywhere. The solid matter consolidated itself and peeped out of the waters. It became harder and harder and due to earth's revolutions around herself it formed itself into various stretches of land. Over the millennia, the land produced vegetation and life sprawled on this earth. Life evolved and the simple amoeba in the course of millenia evolved itself into the most complex human machine and here we are, the homosapien- the human beings facing the second millenium.

When we look back to the millenium that is almost over we feel proud of our achievements. We have developed machines and tools to reach the Moon and other planets and have been scratching them. We may inhabit them in future, if we survive. At the same time, we are forgetting certain human values and that endangers our future. Almost all the nations on the earth are worried about their security. Every nation is spending large amount on defense and external security. Our neighbours are forgetting to have good and amicable relations with us. Large amounts spent on military defence burdens the exchequer and less money is available for education and human resource development. The proverty spread out throughout the nation becomes more accentuated. Plans for development get stalled. We, the human beings have encompassed the Moon but have estranged ourselves from our earthly brothers. Fraternity ceases to spring up in our hearts. This should cause concern for the future of mankind. Along with the global frontiers, let there be expansion of fraternal feelings and of human kindness. This won't happen unless men turn their attention within.

There was a point in human history, when four millennia ago, man in India turned inwards and explored his soul and revealed unto himself its immense capacities. These included the capacity to identify his own reality. This was the fabulous reseach in human mind. New Vistas opened before him not in the outside locale but within him and he could grapple with his own conciousness. Those who experimented in this area could with great difficulty, record some of the glimpses and till this day these records are said to be the most precious heritage of mankind. In the Vedas and the Upaniṣads, we find an in-depth study of man. This literature sustained the culture in this part of the world over the millennia.

It was this literature which was at the core of the educational system in India till the recent centuries. Over a century and a half of the British regime in India, the indigenous system of education was solely replaced by a British one and the first casualty was the self respect of the people. Macauley desired a perpetual supply of clerical staff for the Raj and to a large extent he succeeded in his design. The earlier Gurukul system ceased to exist. In this system students used to be under the direct tutelage of the teacher. The system is no more in vogue except in a modernised form in certain public schools. The content of education at the school and college levels shifted to Western literature and science during the early twentieth century and it did create a change for the better. That type of education, particularly at the university level, did produce poets, patriots and philosophers and we had a sustained leadership for over a century. But at the same time it resulted in a large scale Westernisation that alienated most of the subsequent generations. It was for this reason that Mahatma Gandhi and some of his ardent followers devised *Buniyadi Talim,* – a system of basic education. This was an attempt to make the budding generations sensitive to the needs of this land. Unfortunately there was no popular response to this scheme and it did not survive.

There has been a number of reports, which evaluated our educational system after independence. They reviewed the system from time to time and suggested certain reforms. With all these efforts we could not, as yet, devise a system that would be worthy of the citizens of the next millenium.

Whatever the system we would devise needs to be value-based. What is a value? In the human context,value is that which fulfills the needs of a man. These needs might be physical, psychological and spiritual. The things, which nourish the body, have food value. The things, which cure ailments and diseases, have medicinal value. There are certain modes of social behaviour, which are meant for moral growth. They are said to have moral and social behaviour, which are meant for moral growth. They are said to have moral and social values.

With the social evolution, certain basic values have also come up. These are Truth, Honesty, Dharma or Righteousness, Democracy, Scientific Temper etc. The socicty, which adores these values, has evolved a pattern of social life. This in its turn evolved a rich culture.

The ancient India has evolved a unique value system for her citizens, individually and collectively. The purpose of human life was set as the perfection of the four valucs viz. *Dharma, Artha, Kāma* and *Mokṣa.*

Dharma is a moral base for any human action. Human life is nothing but a series of action. It commences with birth and ends with death. Action should be righteous. It should not kill or hurt anyone. It should be truthful (*Ahiṁsa* and *Satya*). There should be no stealing (*Asteya*). There should be pursuit purity and dedication to the Lord (*Brahmacaryam*). There should be non-acceptance of favours (*Aparigraha*). Actions in conformity with all these are based on *Dharma.*

Then there is another value that is *Artha. Artha* means earning and also meaning. Pursuit of this value saves you from penury. This means reasonable satisfaction of wants. Pursuits of this value adds meaning to your life. Our earnings should arise out of the righteous way of living.

Kāma is the third value and it means desire. Satisfaction of desires in a righteous way leads to fulfillment. Sri Kṛṣṇa states in the *Gītā,* "*Kāma* is my manifestation so far as it sustains life" (*dharmāviruddho bhuteṣu kāmosmi, Bharatśabha* – Gītā 7.II). This concept of *Kāma* in consonance with *Dharma* sets the Indian Culture far above the sensate western culture.

The fourth is *Mokṣa* ie. liberation. All the above three values when pursued sincerly culminate in *Mokṣa,* the summum bonum- the end of human pursuits in this world.

Apart from these traditional four values in the ancient Indian culture, we have accepted in our constitution certain other values viz. Liberty, Equality and Fraternity as also democratic spirit and scientific temper.

It is not enough to have an idealistic view of values. Their inculcation through educational system is of utmost importance. The colonial education system deliberately neglected the inculcation of the traditional Indian values. We may now omit the word traditional, if we want, but what is important is the look back at our own history to ascertain the roots of our culture. For, if the roots were intact and taken care of, the tree would suck the water of life and would continue to flower and fructify.

It is well known that a child as a member of a group imbibes the attitudes and values of the group and moulds itself according to the group norms. This adjustment with the surroundings constitutes its value orientation. Value education is a process of aiding the child in such orientation. It also develops its feelings and emotions. Value education thus includes both, thinking morally and behaving morally.

Although morality and religion are closely connected, value education programme in a pluralistic society may lead to religious, cultural, social and political prejudices. So in a country with a secular education system, a scheme will have to be devised to obviate such prejudices and integrate harmoniously the religious and moral teachings of all major religions. The common teachings of all religions can be used to reinforce moral values to be inculcated by the younger generation. This aspect of value education is extrmely important and demands close attention of those who are at the helm of affairs.

Swami Vivekananda defined education as the manifestation of the potential divinity within the child. According to him education was life building, man making and character building assimilation of ideas. This being the goal of education, we have to devise a system whereby a child would achieve this, through healthy physical growth, concentration, by observing chastity, by developing love for truth and love for fellow beings. Pursuit of all these values would inculcate *Śraddhā* i.e. self-confidence among the youth. *Śraddhā* is nothing but faith in one self as well as in the unfailing Cosmic power, which is at the back of one's individual self. With *Śraddhā,* one can face all the challenges that confront one. Also, one can face the failures with a smile. A person with *Śraddhā* is ever resourceful.

With the cultivation of values individual's knowledge will turn into wisdom and a man of wisdom will be valued in a society. The society which has men of wisdom will not only save the humanity from destruction but would lead it towards brighter horizons of knowledge and bliss.

* * * *

Contributors

1. **Acarya Dinanath Yaksha :** Retired as Head-Pandit, J&K Research Department, Srinagar, Kashmir. Has deciphered a number of Sanskrit manuscripts, most of which have been published. Has guided many scholars from India and abroad in their research assignments who have fully acknowledged his contribution.
2. **Dr. Shashidhar Sharma :** Mahāmahopādhyāya, Mahākavi, Yoga-Tantrasamrāt, Viśvaratna. A great Sanskrit scholar and an indologist of repute. Has made a number of worthy contributions of critical and creative nature and has embellished almost each and every branch of Sanskrit literature from Vedas upto the Tantras.
3. **Sri D.M. Sapatnekar :** Retd. Judge of Maharashtra State. Retired Professor of Law in Symbiosis Law College, Pune. A spiritually elevated soul. Translated Tagore's *Gitanjali, Gardner* and *Post Office* into Marathi. Chief interest in scriptural readings of Advaita Vedānta.
4. **Prof. S. Bhatt :** Held various responsible positions in the Govt. of India. Hon. Professor of International Law, JNU (1993-1998). Currently Hon. Professor, Centre for Federal Studies, Hamdard University, New Delhi. Published fourteen books.
5. **Sri M.N. Trakru :** Served the Govt. of India in various capacities in New Delhi, Pakistan, Britain and elsewhere. Was engaged in reporting and broadcasting news and commentaries over AIR. Now functioning as a Freelance Journalist and also writes in some magazines.
6. **Dr. A.N. Dhar :** Formerly Professor and Head, Department of English, University of Kashmir. Was UGC Emeritus Fellow, Universsity of Jammu. Senior Fellow (Literature),

Ministry of HRD, Govt. of India. Presently Editor, *Suddhavidya,* a cultural bi-annual.

7. **Prof. K.L. Bhalla :** Retired Professor of English is deeply interested in social work and has founded an NGO "Save Education Committee" to stem the rot in the present day system of education.
8. **Sri B.L. Khar :** Retired Director (codes) Financial Department, J&K Govt., Jammu. Venturing, with all humility to have a peep into the ancient Indian philosophy. This pursuit brought him under the superbly striking tutelage of the Revd. Pt. Jankinathji Kaul.
9. **Sri Upinder Bhatt :** A seeker of truth, Chartered Accountant, has a great interest in cultural and spiritual development with particular reference to Kashmir. Associated with Sri Ramakrishana Ashrama, Kashmir.
10. **Srimat Swami Lakshman Joo :** (d. 1991) A great saint – scholar of Kashmir and a born Yogi. Practised and taught the teachings of Kashmir Śaivism with deep penetration among national and international scholars and devotees.
11. **Sri M.P. Pandit :** (d. 1993) was chairman of the World Union International. Served as editor for many Socio-political, Philosophical and Spiritual journals. He was an authentic exponent of the Yoga and Philosophy of Sri Aurobindo and the Mother. His interpretations of the Vedas, Upanisads, Tantras, form a bridge between the ancient and the modern thought.
12. **Prof. Raffaele Torella:** Professor of Sanskrit at the University of Roma "La Sapienza." Ordinary member of IsMEO (non ISIAO); responsible for the Indological section in the Rivista degli Studi Orientali; member of Editorial Committee of École Francaise d'Extrême Orient – Départment d'Indologie, Pondichéri; member of the staff of the *Tāntrikābhidhānakośa* (Vienna).
13. **Dr. S.S. Janki :** (d. 1999) Formerly Diretor, the Kuppuswami Sastri Research Institute, Chennai. Served as Part-time tutor, Oriental Institute, Oxford; Boden Fellow, Oxford University.

Lecturer-cum-Research Asstt. Madras University.

14. **Dr. Kapila Vatsyayan :** President, India International Centre, New Delhi. A learned scholar and celebrated authority on Indian Art and Culture.
15. **Dr. E.G. Kahrs :** Teaches Sanskrit and Indian studies in the Faculty of Oriental studies, University of Cambridge. He is a fellow of Queens' College, Cambridge.
16. **Dr. Navajivan Rastogi :** Formerly Professor and Head, Department of Sanskrit and Hony. Director, Abhinavagupta Institute of Aesthetics and Śaiva Philosophy, Lucknow University. Inheriting his insight into Abhinava thought and Kashmir Śaivism from his teacher K.C. Pandey, he has many publications to his credit. Specialized in *Krama* branch of Śaivism, he is presently engaged in editing Encyclopaedia of India's Philosophies' Volume on Kashmir Śaivism with Karl H. Potter.
17. **Dr. Bettina Bäumer :** Professor at the Institute for the study of Religions, Universiity of Vienna. President of the "Abhishiktananda Society". Consultant, Alice Boner Foundation for Research on Fundamental Principles in Indian Art, Varanasi and Zürich. Visiting Professor, University of Vienna. Hon. consultant IGNCA, Varanasi.
18. **Dr. Kaushalya Walli :** Retired Professor of Sanskrit, University of Jammu. Currently working on a project of Kashmir Śaivism.
19. **Dr. N. Gangadharan :** (d. 2002) Retired Professor of Sanskrit, University of Madras. Ex. Director, Anantacarya Indological Research Institute, Mumbai. Ex. Jt. Director, Sree Sarada Education Society Research Centre, Chennai. Specialised in Pauranic studies, was a keen student of Indology.
20. **Dr. Godabarisha Mishra :** Presently Reader, The Dr. Radhakrishnan Institute for Advanced Study in Philosophy, Madras University. Specialised in Advaita Vedanta and other schools of Indian thought, Buddhism and Hermeneutics.
21. **Prof. V.N. Jha :** Currently Chairperson and Professor of

Sanskrit, Centre for Sanskrit Studies, JNU, New Delhi. Formerly Director, Centre for Advanced Study in Sanskrit, University of Pune. Scholar of international repute with mastery over Nyāya-Vaiśeṣika School of thought.

22. **Dr. C. Rajendran :** Professor and Head, Department of Sanskrit in the University of Calicut. His 'Transcultural Approach to Sanskrit Poetics' was acclaimed as a notable contribution to comparative literature.
23. **Dr. B.K. Dalai :** Director, Centre for Advanced Study in Sanskrit, University of Pune. Specialisation in Indian Logic, Prakrit, Jainism, Linguistics, his special fields of interest are Indian Philosophy and Indian Poetics.
24. **Dr. K.C. Dash :** Currently Professor of Nyāya Darśana in Sri Jagganath Sanskrit University, Puri. As a poet, Novelist and writer of profound depth, he is famous for exploring a new dimension of Sanskrit writings. He has established a tradition of excellence both as an outstanding scholar and celebrated creative writer in Sanskrit.
25. **Prof. Nagaraja Rao :** He was a reputed writer and an outstanding scholar with special inclination towards Advaita Vedānta as expounded by Ādi Śankara.
26. **Prof. O.P. Pathak :** Director, Vipassana Research Institute, Nasik. Contributed research papers to various National and International journals. Published five books and two are in the press.
27. **Dr. Lokesh Chandra :** Buddhist world, Social work, Culture, Education and World Affairs (culture and classical Heritage) are his fields of activity. Multilinguist, Social worker, Political thinker, Educationist and Writer. Has 365 books and 195 articles and research papers related to International understanding to his credit. Member of various literary, social and educational organisations.
28. **Dr. A.D. Mathur :** Presently Reader and Head, Department of Sanskrit, St. Stephen's College, Delhi. He has specialisation in Dharmaśāstra and has some original literary Sanskrit texts to his credit.

29. **Dr. T.V. Vasudeva :** Lecturer-cum-Research Assistant, The Kuppuswami Sastri Research Institute, Chennai. Specialisation in Advaita, Dharmaśāstra, Technical and Philosophical literature, Sanskrit language and literature.
30. **Dr. S.K. Jadhab :** Professor and Head, Department of Sanskrit, Shivaji University, Satara. Specialisation in Vedānta and Sāhityaśāstra.
31. **Dr. V. Kameswari :** Lecture-cum-editor, The Kuppuswami Sastri Research Institute, Chennai. Specialisation in Sanskrit language and literature, Alaṅkara Śāstra, Scientific and technical literature, Art, Architecture and Aesthetics.
32. **Dr. Ujjwala Panse :** Reader, Centre for Advanced Study in Sanskrit, University of Pune. Specialisation in Purvamīmāṁsā. Nyāya, Mimāṁsā, Dharmaśāstra and Vedas are her special fields of interest.
33. **Dr. S.K. Balasubramanian :** Lecturer-cum-Research Assistant, The Kuppuswami Sastri Research Institute, Chennai. Specialisation in Yoga, Mysticism, Technical and Philosophical Literature. Hon. Jt. Director, Sahejaraj Research and Training Institute.
34. **Dr. Penna Madhusudan :** Asstt. Professor of Sanskrit, Kalidasa Sanskrit Universsity, Nagpur. Specialized in Nyāya, Yoga, Vedānta and Vyākraṇa.
35. **Dr. Vinod Verma :** Founded NOW in 1986 to spread the message of holistic living, preventive methods of health care and to promote the use of mild medicine and other self-help therapentic measures. Published seven books on Yoga and Ayurveda in various European languages and is doing several research projects on medicinal plants and their combinations in the form of remedies.
36. **Dr. Anuradha Oak :** Lecturer at Navalmal Firodiya Yoga Vaidyaka Adhyasana Kabir Bang Math Sanstha, Pune. Besides having specialisation in Yoga philosophy she is an expert in practical Yoga.
37. **Dr. T. Devarajan :** Professor and Head, Department of Sanskrit, University of Kerala. Specialized in Sanskrit

literature, Drama, Dramaturgy and Aesthetics. He is a member of many national and international organisations.

38. **Dr. Sarada Natarajan :** A creative artist and has developed special music blending best of different streams of music and dance. Has specialised training in Bharatnatyam. Hony. Editor, The Ramana Way, a monthly of the Ramana Maharishi Centre for Learning, Bangalore.
39. **Dr. Karan Singh :** With his deep insight into the Indian Cultural tradition as well as his wide exposure to Western Literature and Civilization, he is recognised as an outstanding thinker and leader in India and abroad. He is an author of distinction, having written a number of books on political science, religion, philosophical essays and poems in English.
40. **Prof. Sujata Miri :** Professor of Philosophy, North-Eastern Hill University, Shillong. Specialisation in Indian philosophy, Philosophy of Religion, Philosophical Anthropology and philosophy of culture. A vast teaching and research experience. Also a fiction writer and a Novelist.
41. **Lt. Col. R.K. Langar :** Retired Army officer, a keen student of Indology, a practising writer and Socio-cultural critic and analyst.

* * * *